GERTRUDE STEIN
and ALICE B. TOKLAS

a reference guide

A
Reference
Guide
to
Literature

Ronald Gottesman
Editor

GERTRUDE STEIN and ALICE B. TOKLAS

a reference guide

RAY LEWIS WHITE

G.K.HALL&CO.

70 LINCOLN STREET, BOSTON, MASS.

Library of Congress Cataloging in Publication Data

White, Ray Lewis.
  Gertrude Stein and Alice B. Toklas.

  Includes index.
  1. Stein, Gertrude, 1874-1946—Bibliography.
2. Toklas, Alice B.—Bibliography. I. Title.
Z8838.9.W48 1984   016.818′5209   83-12896
[PS3537.T323]
ISBN 0-8161-8057-1

This publication is printed on permanent/durable acid-free paper
MANUFACTURED IN THE UNITED STATES OF AMERICA

Contents

The Author

Ray Lewis White, professor of English at Illinois State University, is a graduate of Emory & Henry College and the University of Arkansas. He has published extensively on the American author Sherwood Anderson; among his books are editions of Anderson's three memoirs and the writer's correspondence with Gertrude Stein. Professor White's other books and articles concern Heinrich Böll, Günter Grass, Gore Vidal, Pär Lagerkvist, Ernest Hemingway, Willard Motley, H.L. Mencken, R.K. Narayan, Nathanael West, Ben Hecht, John Steinbeck, Kawabata Yasunari, Eldridge Cleaver, Raja Rao, Evan S. Connell, Jr., and Wallace Stevens. In 1977 G.K. Hall published Professor White's Sherwood Anderson: A Reference Guide.

Preface

The history of Gertrude Stein-Alice B. Toklas bibliography is
short to write. In the 1940s appeared two useful checklists of works
written by Gertrude Stein. Julian Sawyer's <u>Gertrude Stein: A Bibli-
ography</u> began the attempt to identify and classify this author's publications, and Robert B. Haas and Donald Gallup's <u>A Catalogue of the
Published and Unpublished Writings of Gertrude Stein</u> enumerated Yale
University's vast collection of Stein materials. In the 1940s also
appeared in the <u>Bulletin of Bibliography</u> a series of checklists by
Julian Sawyer that attempted to document the already extensive writings about Gertrude Stein's work, life, and personality. Thereafter
no useful bibliographies were published until the Stein-Toklas revival
in the 1970s, when Robert A. Wilson published an admirable primary
study in <u>Gertrude Stein: A Bibliography</u>; and when Maureen R. Liston
published <u>Gertrude Stein: An Annotated Critical Bibliography</u>.
Liston's compilation of writings about Gertrude Stein is regrettably
not exhaustive enough or reliable enough for dependable use by the
serious student of Stein, Toklas, and their milieu. Thus the present
volume is the most complete secondary bibliography for Stein and
Toklas to date.

<u>Gertrude Stein and Alice B. Toklas: A Reference Guide</u> contains
1920 entries--not only items to be found listed in previous bibliographies about Stein and Toklas but also many, many items new to
Stein-Toklas bibliographies: the literary, artistic, and personal
friendships; the movements in literary and artistic history in which
the women took part; the criticism of their published and unpublished
writings--all are given detailed coverage herein. Because Gertrude
Stein and Alice B. Toklas lived together, worked together, and wrote
about each other, the bibliographer should logically and practically
provide one master secondary bibliography for study of these two
famous paired women; such an organization governs the present volume,
which gives to Toklas for the first time the literary recognition
that she deserved but did not court until after Stein's death and
late in her own life. Now Alice B. Toklas may be studied as she
lived and as she is buried--side by side with Gertrude Stein.

Gertrude Stein and Alice B. Toklas: A Reference Guide is arranged chronologically, the 1920 entries being listed under each year from 1909 through 1981. Within each yearly listing, entries are arranged alphabetically by authors' names or--for entries of undetermined authorship--by titles of books or articles. The few items not located but shown to exist in previous checklists are included but marked with asterisks and cited with the sources of original information. Theses and dissertations are cited and annotated from Dissertation Abstracts International so that authors may be allowed to summarize their own findings. In fact, all of the annotations in this bibliography are based on the principle that when writers themselves provide kernel or core statements in their discussions of Stein and Toklas, such statements--if well-phrased and succinct-- are the best of all possible summaries of the writers' intentions and conclusions.

Entries are identified by year of publication and by numerical order of presentation; cross-references guide the researcher to serializations and to reprintings, in whole or in part. These entry numbers are used instead of page numbers in the index, which is comprehensive in references to authors, individuals, Stein and Toklas publications, and artistic and creative works by associated writers and artists. The index otherwise contains two useful headings-- Biography and Bibliography.

Because Gertrude Stein and Alice B. Toklas were devoted to the career of Gertrude Stein and to collecting apparently every printed mention of Stein that ever came to their studio, the massive collection of Stein-Toklas material at Yale University is one of the most formidable archives to be encountered by the scholar of American literature. Yet for reasons of importance, inclusiveness, and intrinsic interest, this trove must attract the devoted researcher. The present bibliography makes accessible for the first time the invaluable mass-periodical, obscure-periodical, and small-press discussions of Stein and Toklas that the women privately collected from 1909 through 1967 and that no routine checklist or limited bibliographical study could indicate. Entries for these materials from the Stein-Toklas archive at Yale are necessarily often bibliographically incomplete, given the form of the documents as collected by the two women; yet with these non-standard entries a reader may for the first time see clearly in both detail and in depth the development of the Stein-Toklas legend from the earliest days to the deaths of both women.

My indebtedness to librarians for materials and information is so great that I must reluctantly thank here only Donald Gallup and David Schoonover of the Beinecke Rare Book and Manuscript Library of Yale University and Joe Kraus and Helga Whitcomb of Milner Library of Illinois State University. At various times I have been aided in this work by graduate assistants--Hilary Gow, Barry

Brown, Claire Lamonica, and John Reynolds. For encouragement of various kinds I thank Charles Harris, William Woodson, and C.A. White of Illinois State University.

I publish this book in memory of Maude N. White (1903–1981), devoted mother, and in memory of H. Blair Rouse (1912–1981), mentor nonpareil.

Introduction

It was Sherwood Anderson who in 1921 described best the general idea of Gertrude Stein: "Years ago when her work first fell under my eyes and I was startled and profoundly stirred by its significance I made inquiry concerning her. Strange stories came out of Paris. She was a fat woman, very languid, lying on a couch, people came into the room and she stared at them with strange cold eyes. There was a power in her. . . ." Instead of the exotic creature that Anderson had expected to meet in Paris in 1921, he found in Gertrude Stein a woman who was "the very symbol of health and strength. She laughs, she smokes cigarettes. She tells stories with an American shrewdness in getting the tang and the kick into the telling." Stein was, Anderson confirmed, a serious and charming person.

This fortuitous meeting of Sherwood Anderson and Gertrude Stein was to result in his writing an introduction to her Geography and Plays--the book of non-traditional works which launched Stein into the 1920s as a literary phenomenon. Before publication of Geography and Plays, the small audience aware at all of Gertrude Stein could have wondered whether she would become a literary exotic or a minor mainstream author. Geography and Plays sealed her future as a nonconforming writer.

Stein's first book, Three Lives, received in 1909-10 merely polite acceptance. Because these Flaubertian, Jamesian life-studies of three poor women seemed orthodox if halting in style, one might have predicted for the author a secondary career in writing biographical fiction. Instead of providing the expected sequel to Three Lives, Stein in 1914 gave jollity to the nations and delight to the literati with Tender Buttons, the very title of which elicited hearty guffaws or delicate adoration. Who would dare describe "A Piece of Coffee," "A Little Called Pauline," or "Peeled Pencil, Choke"? Only a genius or an idiot would attempt Stein's non-objective descriptions of objects, food, and rooms--and the popular press seized happily upon Tender Buttons as the latest degenerate, giddy export of a depraved Europe. A few quotations from Tender Buttons and the columnist's day was made. Charges of lunacy, feeble-mindedness, and charlatanism would after this book become part of the connotation

of "Gertrude Stein." Surely no author would dare repeat such an
obvious faux pas as Stein had perpetrated with Tender Buttons.

And for several years Gertrude Stein did seem to disappear from
newspapers and magazines, which were soon after 1914 caught up in
war talk and then in war reporting. Only a few friends would have
known that Gertrude Stein had not after 1914 returned to colloquial,
traditional style as in Three Lives. Instead Stein had pushed non-
objective, nonbiographical prose beyond that in Tender Buttons. The
new pieces of experimentation remained unpublished. But Sherwood
Anderson, who cared about Stein's writing and who came to Paris to
tell her of his care, introduced Geography and Plays to an age ready
for the bizarre, the outré, the avant-garde. To read Gertrude Stein
in the 1920s was to be among those enlightened souls who said that
they understood Ulysses, The Waste Land, and vers libre. The lost
generation--so christened by Gertrude Stein--flocked to Paris to
approach the siren and to be charmed into the spider's web. The
young in art, dance, music, and literature sought welcome at Queen
Gertrude's court. The reality of 27 rue de Fleurus was--however enchanting the salon--never equal to the reputation that everybody who
was anybody eventually came to call. And yet Gertrude Stein's name
in the 1920s evoked wonderment far more than did her actual writings.
Sure then of acceptance guaranteed by fame, Stein in 1925 published
her self-described, long-ago-completed masterwork--The Making of
Americans. Epic, exhaustive, profound the author found her story
of an American family; but the public for such a monument was minus-
cule and Stein again realized the discrepancy between mere fame and
knowledgeable appreciation. Unable to interest conventional publishers in her work, Stein in 1930 undertook official self-publication,
for she had the necessary self-confidence of the true egotist. The
resulting volumes of her "Plain Edition"--now highly prized collect-
ibles--created no stir of demand for Stein's books . . . and, then,
suddenly, Gertrude Stein became a best-selling author.

Realizing that the Stein legend was firmly embedded in popular
culture, Stein tried to capitalize on her fabulous years among the
now very famous, of whom William James, Picasso, Picabia, Gris,
Matisse, Anderson, Hemingway, Fitzgerald, Pound, Eliot, and Whitehead
were merely the first-rank. Being historical pleased Stein, who in
The Autobiography of Alice B. Toklas (1933) recreated (some said
created) a central role for herself in twentieth-century art and
literature. At the height of the Great Depression in America many
thousands of troubled people found in Stein's simply-narrated and
cleverly-conceived autobiography the thrilling, feverish escape to
Paris and life among the surrealists and the liberated that America
itself did not provide. From rare exotic to mass-market celebrity
delighted Stein, who after The Autobiography of Alice B. Toklas,
beginning at sixty, knew exactly how to maintain her new popularity.

The year 1934 was the peak in fame in the life of Gertrude Stein.
Buoyed by the success of The Autobiography of Alice B. Toklas, Stein

early in that year learned that her opera <u>Four Saints in Three Acts</u>
was the scandalous hit of the theatre in America. Having in the
<u>Autobiography</u> written clearly and entertainingly for the masses,
Stein in <u>Four Saints</u> wrote obscurely and entertainingly for whoever
would come to hear her weird libretto and Virgil Thomson's ultra-
modern music. The public came indeed, usually to laugh but always
to be amazed at the audacity of Gertrude Stein. And later in 1934
Stein herself appeared, back in America for the first time since
1904. The darling of newspaper and magazine reporters, Stein talked
cleverly and clearly at interviews and press-conferences; and the
foil-like presence of Alice B. Toklas confirmed that the secretary-
companion, first publicized in <u>The Autobiography</u>, did indeed exist
and must be dealt with.

Until Gertrude Stein and Alice B. Toklas actually arrived in
America, many people doubted the existence of the latter, in spite
of Stein's perfect recreation of Toklas's acidic personality and
anecdotes in <u>The Autobiography of Alice B. Toklas</u>. Visitors to 27
rue de Fleurus since 1909 could have affirmed the very formidable
existence of Alice B. Toklas, who determined definitely who did and
who did not gain and maintain acquaintance or friendship with Gertrude
Stein. In public self-effacing, in the salon assigned to talk with
the wives of callers, Toklas in private ruled Stein through a very
tough loving. Ever the Victorian lady, Toklas had wept for days at
Stein's proposal of marriage-understanding in 1908; thereafter she
lived only to keep Stein happy, faithful, enthralled, productive, and--
if ever possible--famous as a writer. Willing for Stein to write often
but always hermetically of her love for Alice and even of their actual
lovemaking, Toklas nevertheless permitted no public discussion whatever of their lesbianism and remained in public always the mousy, dark,
unattractive "secretary" who walked just behind Gertrude Stein but who
somehow managed to place herself firmly between her loved one and any
possible inconvenience or discomfort.

Not only did the 1934 tour of America dispel doubts of Toklas's
existence; but Stein's tour of lecture halls, college campuses, and
society teas conquered most doubters of her sanity and her serious-
ness . . . and assured a ready market thereafter for whatever she
might write in her clear style--and notice, at least, for whatever
she might thereafter perpetrate in her opaque style. Stein through
the late 1930s wrote in both of her modes--clearly in <u>Everybody's</u>
<u>Autobiography</u> (1937) and <u>Picasso</u> (1939); obscurely in <u>The Geograph-</u>
<u>ical History of America</u> (1936) and <u>The World Is Round</u> (1939).

Stein opened the new decade with <u>Paris France</u> (1940), her love-
letter to her home since 1904 and an inadvertent elegy to a city fac-
ing foreign occupation in World War II. Jewish, Stein and Toklas
took refuge from Nazis in rural France, where Stein continued to
write, where the French protected them, and where American soldiers
and journalists sought to find and liberate the two women. Free
again to live in Paris, Stein wrote (clearly, again) of her recent

experiences in Wars I Have Seen (1945) and Brewsie and Willie (1946).
Dead of cancer in 1946, Stein was buried in Paris; and Alice B. Toklas,
now alone after almost forty years with Gertrude Stein, faced her
chosen task of guarding Stein's reputation and publishing the remain-
ing unpublished works.

In eight volumes, the Yale Edition of the Unpublished Writings of
Gertrude Stein appeared from 1951 through 1958. These scholarly editions were scarcely noticed by the public, which remembered Stein for
her life and for Three Lives and The Autobiography of Alice B. Toklas;
and the scholarly audience would wait two decades to make great use
of the Yale volumes. At the same time as she was publishing Gertrude
Stein's works, Alice Toklas was becoming an author and an individual
in her own right. In two well-selling cookbooks and in an autobiography, What Is Remembered (1963), Toklas popularized gourmet cooking
and eulogized her years with Stein. Dead in 1967, Toklas had perfectly completed her role in life and found burial beside Stein in
Paris.

Because Gertrude Stein has always been more popular than Gertrude
Stein's books, would-be biographers of Gertrude Stein should have come
forward in numbers to chronicle this famous life soon after its close
in 1946. Yet the first ambitious and extensive studies of Stein's
life appeared in the late 1950s; and Alice B. Toklas must have much
blame for the unfortunate delay. Adamant in protecting Stein's memory as a noble genius, Toklas fought bitterly against the people with
real interest in the private life of Gertrude Stein or the real public life of Gertrude Stein. Toklas's concern was perhaps admirable
and understandable, for she was the heir and the widow and the cus-
todian; but her chilling presence turned away objective study and
even cautious inquiry. Even the two very admiring biographies of
Stein that did appear while Toklas lived--Sprigge's in 1957 and
Brinnan's in 1959--displeased the acrid old woman living on alone in
Paris: to Alice B. Toklas, only the literary works of Gertrude Stein
were proper subjects for study. There should, therefore, be no surprise that only after Toklas's death in 1967 did biographers arrive
to chronicle and display the richness and the reality of Gertrude
Stein . . . and, finally, of Toklas herself. At least a half-dozen
studies of Stein's life appeared in the 1970s--biographies ranging in
scope and quality from the juvenile and childish (Burnett, 1972;
Wilson, 1973; Rogers, 1973; Greenfeld, 1973), to the adulatory
(Hobhouse, 1975), to the truly impressive (Mellow, 1974). Certainly
Charmed Circle by James Mellow is the outstanding biography of
Gertrude Stein, for this author had the requisite knowledge of
writing, reading, and thinking to synthesize the facts about Gertrude
Stein; and he brought to his work the abilities of a good art critic
and historian and an enthusiasm for the twentieth-century esthetic
experimentation that Stein embraced and practiced. And in 1977 there
appeared the book that Toklas would most have vilified and tried to
suppress--Linda Simon's Biography of Alice B. Toklas, finally an open,
honest, and admiring biography of the power that ruled over and beside Gertrude Stein.

Introduction

Although biographical study of Gertrude Stein suffered until the 1970s because of Alice B. Toklas, critical study of Gertrude Stein should have flourished while Toklas lived to encourage it. The problem is that, despite Toklas's devotion to Stein's literary creations, few critics who studied or wrote in the 1940s and the 1950s cared for Stein's obscurantist and hermetic writings. At a time when even William Faulkner and James Joyce were not being given critical due, surely Gertrude Stein would be generally ignored as a writer. True, Miller's Gertrude Stein: Form and Intelligibility (1949) would introduce Stein as worth close textual study and Sutherland's Gertrude Stein: A Biography of Her Work (1951) would pioneer that study; but it took a candidly negative study of Stein's writings in 1958—Reid's Art by Subtraction—to stimulate really valuable assessments of the literary achievement. Arguing that Stein tried to take from narrative all traces of plot and character and theme, Reid found the literary residue sadly unrewarding. Correct or not, Reid's analysis of Stein's failure has brought forth at least nine full-length studies of the literary corpus of Gertrude Stein. A few of these books are general surveys of Stein's career as a writer, from Frederick J. Hoffman's pamphlet Gertrude Stein in 1961 to Michael J. Hoffman's informed and complete Gertrude Stein in 1976. Several scholars have chosen to study certain aspects of Stein's writings—for example, her abstraction (M. Hoffman, 1975), her use of language (Weinstein, 1970), her psychology (Stewart, 1967), her sense of time (Copeland, 1975), and her autobiography (Neuman, 1979). Yet only one book of criticism published since Reid's in 1958 can be considered a major scholarly study—Richard Bridgman's Gertrude Stein in Pieces (1970). Realizing that a writer as complex as Gertrude Stein would not allow development of a unified field-theory of critical approach, Bridgman wisely divided the Stein canon into manageable pieces and then brilliantly dissected the pieces, all the while integrating for the first time the biography and the bibliography so essential to understanding just what the phrase "Gertrude Stein" should mean to the world's culture . . . and why.

The biographical success of Mellow in Charmed Circle and the critical success of Bridgman in Gertrude Stein in Pieces would not have been possible without some earlier serious and important works on Stein that usually never appeared as published studies—the dissertations that allow apprentice scholars to demonstrate mastery of their disciplines. Yet, attractive as Gertrude Stein and her exciting milieu should have been to doctoral-degree students in search of research topics, such students did not, unfortunately, rush to Stein until she became an already respectable area for investigation or until dissertation writers and directors caught up with the general public interest in Gertrude Stein. In the 1950s only three dissertations dealt with just Gertrude Stein—studies of her dramas and her literary salon. It was likewise in the 1960s, when three dissertations discussed Stein as a cubistic writer or studied her earliest manuscripts. But popular-culture trends in the 1970s—Gay Liberation, Women's Studies, artistic radicalism—made Gertrude Stein

belatedly the object of doctoral study; and the thirty-four dissertations completed on Stein by 1981 claim attention for their scope and
for their academic modernity. There have been doctoral studies of
Stein as autobiographer, as pioneering post-modernist, as liberated
feminist, as consummate linguistic experimenter, and as rhetorical
genius. Stein has become at last not only historical but also most
happily current. So prolific, indeed, are writings by now about
Gertrude Stein and Alice B. Toklas that a master chronicle, a comprehensive catalogue of writings about these two intriguing women,
is desperately needed . . . and here provided.

Writings by Gertrude Stein and Alice B. Toklas

Writings by Gertrude Stein and Alice B. Toklas

Narration, 1935

The Geographical History of America, 1936

Everybody's Autobiography, 1937

Picasso, 1939

The World Is Round, 1939

Paris France, 1940

What Are Masterpieces, 1940

Ida, 1941

Wars I Have Seen, 1945

Brewsie and Willie, 1946

Selected Writings, 1946

In Savoy, or Yes Is for a Very Young Man, 1946

Four in America, 1947

The Mother of Us All, 1947

Blood on the Dining Room Floor, 1948

Last Operas and Plays, 1949

Things As They Are, 1950

Two, 1951

Mrs. Reynolds, 1952

Bee Time Vine, 1953

As Fine As Melanctha, 1954

Painted Lace, 1955

Stanzas in Meditation, 1956

Alphabets & Birthdays, 1957

A Novel of Thank You, 1958

Writings and Lectures, 1911-1945, 1967

Selected Operas and Plays, 1970

Gertrude Stein on Picasso, 1970

Fernhurst, Q.E.D., and Other Early Writings, 1971

A Primer for the Gradual Understanding of Gertrude Stein, 1971

Sherwood Anderson/Gertrude Stein, 1972

Reflections on the Atomic Bomb, 1973

How Writing is Written, 1974

The Yale Gertrude Stein, 1980

WRITINGS BY ALICE B. TOKLAS

The Alice B. Toklas Cookbook, 1954

Aromas and Flavors of Past and Present, 1958

What Is Remembered, 1963

Staying on Alone: Letters, 1973

Writings about Gertrude Stein
and Alice B. Toklas

1   "FICTION, BUT NOT NOVELS." Kansas City Star, 18 December,
     p. 5.
          With publication of Three Lives by Gertrude Stein, "Here is
     a literary artist of such originality that it is not easy to con-
     jecture what special influences have gone into the making of her.
     But the indwelling spirit of it all is a sweet enlightened sym-
     pathy, an unsleeping sense of humor and an exquisite carefulness
     in detail."

2   "NOTABLE PIECE OF REALISM." Boston Globe, 18 December.
          In Three Lives, "the author, Gertrude Stein, has given ex-
     pression to her own temperament, to her own way of seeing the
     world. The style is somewhat unusual; at times it is a little
     difficult to follow, and sometimes it becomes prosy. It is only
     when one has read the book slowly--not as a story, but as a seri-
     ous picture of life--that one grasps the author's conception of
     her humble characters, their thoughts and their tragedies."

3   REVIEW OF THREE LIVES. New York Sun, 25 December.
          "The realism consists in dwelling persistently on the sor-
     did side of the women's lives and in ascribing to their minds the
     vacancy and monotony which impress their employers. . . . It is
     obvious that the same stories could have been made bright and
     cheerful with equal truth, if the author had preferred to tell
     about other realities."

4   REVIEW OF THREE LIVES. Rochester (N.Y.) Post-Express,
     24 December.
          "Gertrude Stein's book may be 'realistic,' but it seems to
     us that the pages devoted to a description of the habits of dogs
     and maid-servants are both tedious and distasteful."

5   "THREE LIVES." Washington (D.C.) Herald, 12 December.
          The problem with Three Lives is that Stein's repetitive,
     monotonous exploration of lower-class minds is dull: "If she

should attempt the same things with minds of a higher caliber, the result might be more interesting."

1910

1   "CURIOUS FICTION STUDY." Chicago Record-Herald, 22 January.
     Three Lives best compares with aspects of Henry James's fiction: "Now, Miss Stein has no such tense, active, intellectual world to show us as James. She presents obscure, humble, vague, flowing, undefined life; but she presents it by an analogous method. She gives us no mosaic of life bits, but the living mass as it flows. Her murmuring people are as truly shown as are Henry James' people, who not only talk but live while they talk."

2   "AN EXTRAORDINARY BOOK." Springfield (Mass.) Union, 14 August.
     Three Lives is remarkable "in the line of realistic fiction. The style is peculiar and, if intentional, it is certainly a work of art, as the author has succeeded in reproducing commonplace thought and talks. . . . It is not a book that will command general or popular reading. It is a literary curiosity and whether the tergiversations of thought and language embodied in the stories are sui generis to the author or accurately reproduced studies of actual persons is what puzzles the reader."

3   "FICTIONIST'S ART." Philadelphia North American, 8 January.
     With Three Lives, "At first the author's style repels, like some vulgar mannerism. But soon it appears that there is assured purpose and masterly skill back of what at the outset seems like a barrage of words, all repetition and reminiscence, with broken imagery, sudden catches, and abrupt stops. There is the picture of real life, drawn rudely, yet with unsparing and vigorous touches."

4   "A FUTURIST NOVEL." Philadelphia Public Ledger, 10 April.
     With Three Lives, "we cannot read these lives without thinking and sensitive minds. We must study the lines, the colors, the directions and, above all else, the spirit of the author. The mind must be keen and alert. For the blur which this futurist in writing at first creates cannot be cleared until we are willing to bring the thought and intelligence to its interpretation which we needed when examining The Nude Descending the Stairs. Let us welcome the new art, if it brings such wealth of simplicity and effectiveness as Miss Stein has shown in these sketches."

5   HALE, PHILIP. "Unconventional Tales." Boston Herald, 8 January.
     Three Lives "should attract notice, for a volume penetrated with such amazing vitality does not come before our eyes in many

a long day. It is worth reading with careful patience. Here is
something really new."

6   REVIEW OF THREE LIVES. Brooklyn Eagle, 2 March.
        "An unusually strong and original book--an extraordinary
piece of realism. It is singularly put, but it carries. The
author sees things and forces differently from other writers and
writes as she sees and feels. You would like to correct her, but
you can't. She has the right of way and uses it and brings
things to pass."

7   REVIEW OF THREE LIVES. Cleveland Plain Dealer, 29 February.
        "Three Lives is told crudely, with naive disregard of lit-
erary and rhetorical conventions. It is about colored people,
and very realistic."

8   REVIEW OF THREE LIVES. New York Post, 22 January.
        The stories in Three Lives "have a quite extraordinary
vitality conveyed in a most eccentric and difficult form. The
half-articulated phrase follows unrelentingly the blind mental
and temperamental gropings of three humble souls wittingly or
unwittingly at odds with life. Whoever can adjust himself to
the repetitions, false starts, and general circularity of the
manner will find himself very near real people."

9   REVIEW OF THREE LIVES. Philadelphia Booknews, 1 February.
        "These three pictures are unique and original, to such an
extent that the reader continues in wonderment."

10   REVIEW OF THREE LIVES. Pittsburgh Post, 17 January.
        "The literary style, if it may be dignified by that phrase,
is suggestive of the speech of the German immigrant after he has
acquired a partial knowledge of the English language. The thought
is exceedingly rudimentary, and therein it may be regarded as
typical of the brain processes of the characters. . . . But
the iteration, the repetition, the peculiarities of construction
and grammar and the lack of proper punctuation render the trilogy
decidedly difficult to read."

11   REVIEW OF THREE LIVES. Springfield (Mass.) Republican,
     16 October.
        "The phraseology of the book is unusual, and the trick of
repetition and reiteration make[s] the style rather wearisome.
It, however, has a peculiar vividness. . . ."

12   "THREE LIVES." Boston Transcript, 29 January.
        "The characterization in these stories is unique; the psy-
chology is interesting because of its quaintness, and the themes
touch the lives of some commonplace colored people. Miss Stein
lays bare their subjective selves in a strong, realistic way."

13   "THREE LIVES." Nation 90 (20 January):65.
      In Three Lives, Stein's stories "utterly lack construction
and focus, but give that sense of urgent life which one gets more
commonly in Russian literature than elsewhere. . . . From Miss
Stein, if she can consent to clarify her method, much may be expected. As it is, she writes as a Browning escaped from the bonds
of verse might wallow in fiction, only without his antiseptic
whimsicality."

14   "A ZOLAESQUE AMERICAN." New York Press, 13 February.
      Stein has become known to Paris for "strong personality,
independence of thought and an utter disdain of conventionalities,
and by her brilliant qualities and lovable traits she charms all
who come in contact with her."

                              1913

1   DODGE, MABEL. "Speculations, Or Post-Impressionism in Prose."
      Arts and Decoration 3 (March):173-74.
      "In a large studio in Paris, hung with paintings by Renoir,
Matisse and Picasso, Gertrude Stein is doing with words what
Picasso is doing with paint. She is impelling language to in-
duce new states of consciousness, and in doing so language be-
comes with her a creative art rather than a mirror of history."
Reprinted: 1913.2.

2   _____. "Speculations." Camera Work, June 1913, pp. 6-9.
      Reprint of 1913.1.

3   KING, GEORGIANA GODDARD. "A Review of Two Worlds: Gertrude
      Stein." International 7 (June):157-58.
      "Truth to one's own new and insistent sense of things will
work out in fresh forms its inevitable expression. In what line
that expression will find itself may well be indicated to us, who
falter and draw back on the threshold, by the certainty and seri-
ousness, among others, of Gertrude Stein."

4   PRESTON, WILSON. "Grande Fête Américaine." Saturday Evening
      Post, 22 March.
      In a Paris café a "tall, pale, serious young man" read
aloud Gertrude Stein's Portrait of Mabel Dodge at the Villa
Curonia, which he called "the greatest work of the century."

                              1914

1   "THE AMAZING GERTRUDE STEIN." St. Paul Pioneer Press, 5 July.
      In Tender Buttons Gertrude Stein "is using words to convey
sensations, not ideas. The cubist artists justify themselves by
the claim that they do not paint what you see but the emotions
which you experience in the art of seeing."

                                4

2   "AND SHE TRIUMPHED IN THE TRAGIC TURNIP FIELD." Cleveland
Leader, 21 June.
     "In her latest book, Tender Buttons, she goes even farther
than she did before. Words are used with a freedom that is anar-
chistic, and [Stein's] friends assert that they are charged with
greater pregnancy. The last shackle is struck from content and
collocation and each unit, each word of the sentence, stands out
independently and has no relation to its fellows."

3   ASHLEIGH, CHARLES. Review of Tender Buttons. Chicago Evening Post, 7 August.
     With Tender Buttons, "Yes, I admit that I am beaten! I am
left behind. I resign myself sadly to sink into the murky depths
of outworn and senile Philistinism. I may only hope that, some-
time, understanding may be vouchsafed to me, even if it be at the
last."

4   BURTON, RICHARD. "Posing." Minneapolis Bellman, 17 October.
     "The case in point is Gertrude Stein, 'cubist' of litera-
ture, futurist of words, and self-advertiser of pseudo-intellectual
antics. She has written a book or so of inconceivably idiotic
drivel, compared with which the babble of a three-year-old child
is Hegelian. Her specialty seems to be the throwing together of
language absolutely meaningless and insulting alike to one's sense
of taste and decency. . . . It will not do to say that nobody
takes her seriously; newspapers do, or they would not give up so
much space to her. And the crack-brained enthusiasts of art do,
for how can they defend cubism without defending her?"

5   "CUBIST LITERATURE." San Antonio Light, 14 January.
     With Tender Buttons, "the high priestess of 'cubism' has
broken into words. She has perpetrated the 'cubist' literature,
and it is great reading."

6   "CUBIST POETRY." Chicago Advance, 18 June.
     "At last the world knows what literature would be if daubed
on with the big brush after the manner of the cubist. Gertrude
Stein has issued a book called Tender Buttons. . . . We could
comment on the foregoing but we forbear. We leave the matter to
the tender judgment of our readers."

7   D., N.P. New York Commercial Advertiser, 6 June.
     "The way to make a word-salad is to sit in a dark room,
preferably between the silent and mystic hours of midnight and
dawn, and let the moving fingers write whatever comes. The idea
is not to think. Thinking would be ruinous. So this is how Miss
Stein works, and we have some results in Tender Buttons."

8   "EXAMINING THE MUSE." Chicago Tribune, 6 June, p. 6.
     Perhaps Miss Stein "was inspired to the title of her volume
[Tender Buttons] by viewing the cubist picture of A Suspender
Button Defending Its Young."

9   "FLAT PROSE." Atlantic Monthly 114 (September):430-32.
     In Portrait of Mabel Dodge at the Villa Curonia, "Miss
Stein has indubitably written nonsense, but she began with sense.
For words have their sound-values as well as their sense-values,
and prose rhythms do convey to the mind emotions that mere denota-
tion cannot give. . . . There will be reaction, explosion, revolution. The public will get its flat prose, and--in addition--
not one, but a hundred Gertrude Steins."

10   "FOR THOUGHTS LIKE THESE." New York World, 13 June.
     "It is said that Miss Stein writes her Futurist-Cubist
prose--poetry, too--in a dark room surrounded by the most awesome
works by Picasso and Duchamp. We find this easy to believe. We
also should see things in such case and, possibly, put words to
them."

11   "FUTURIST ESSAYS." Los Angeles Times, 9 August.
     "We do not purpose to be mean and bitter in discussing Ten-
der Buttons. It lends itself to invective and satire; it is an
excellent butt for ridicule, and offers a rare opportunity for
all sort of sarcasm and funniness. But we restrain ourselves,
having little sympathy with those who mock and tease the foolish."

12   GABIROL, IBN. "My Friend the Incurable." Little Review 1
     (1914):43-44.
     Stein learned the use of verbal repetition in Tender Buttons
from the examples of Kandinski.

13   "GERTRUDE STEIN AS LITERARY CUBIST." Philadelphia North
     American, 13 June.
     In the new style of Tender Buttons, "words are not employed
logically and syntactically to convey ideas; but are synthesized,
helter-skelter, to produce certain impressions."

14   "GERTRUDE STEIN, PLAGIARY." New York Sun, 13 June.
     Mining quotations from early works with lines from Tender
Buttons may illustrate "the way in which linguistic conceptions
smother the content of thought in certain forms of insanity or
how mere sound association sometimes overcomes the orderly association of ideas."

15   "HAVE THE STEINS DESERTED MATISSE?" New York Press, 21 June.
     From Paris comes the report that the Steins have "sold all
the weird paintings by 'friend Henri' [Matisse] that once adorned
the walls of their Paris studios and are now industriously buying
Renoirs."

16   J., F. "Futurist Language And Ancient Verse." Empire and
     Mail (Toronto), 11 July.
     With Tender Buttons, Stein has advanced beyond old literary
masters: "Away with all niceties of meaning in words. They may

be strung together in a chaotic and impressionistic jumble. With
no rules of language to guide you to the thought which they aim
to convey, you can find nothing you like in them."

17 K., A.S. "The Same Book from Another Standpoint." Little
    Review 4 (July):63.
         Tender Buttons consists of "pretty pieces Picasso, Picabia
    plus Plato, Hegel, Cézanne, Kandinsky, more plenty more. . . ."
    [Parody]

18 MARQUIS, DON. "Gertrude Is Stein, Stein Gertrude." New York
    Sun, 15 October.
         "Let us search not, seek not, ask not, / why the blessing
    has been sent-- / Little Groups, we have our Gertrude: / worship
    her, and be content!" [Parody of Tender Buttons]

19 _____. "Gertrude's Hints for the Table." New York Sun,
    28 August.
         Stein's ideas on food in Tender Buttons are profound but
    commonplace in sequence.

20 _____. "Gertrude Stein on the War." New York Sun, 2 October.
         "I asked of Gertrude Stein: 'Explain / Why they are fight-
    ing on the Aisne.' / She mused a space and then exclaimed:/ 'What
    seal brown bobble can be blamed?'" [Parody of Tender Buttons]

21 _____. "The Sun Dial." New York Sun, 3 October.
         "Oh, much-appealed-to Muses Nine!/ Where shall the Super-
    Fake be found / To put the thoughts of Gertrude Stein / Into the
    Verse of Ezra Pound?" [Parody of Tender Buttons]

22 _____. "Thoughts of Hermione, a Modern Young Woman." New
    York Sun, 13 October.
         "We've taken up Gertrude Stein--our little group of serious
    thinkers, you know--and she's wonderful: simply wonderful. She
    Suggests the Inexpressible, you know."

23 M[ENCKEN], H.L. "A Cubist Treatise." Baltimore Sun, 6 June,
    p. 4.
         As one reads Tender Buttons, "the beauty of these super-
    sentences begins to caress the refined mind, and in the end the
    effect is almost electrical. Not, however, upon the bonehead.
    The common earthworm will gag at such filaments of fancy. They
    demand a special education. They presuppose a cubist and resil-
    ient cerebrum."

24 _____. "A Review of Reviewers." Smart Set 44 (October):
    158-59.
         "It is the great achievement of Miss Stein that she has
    made English easier to write and harder to read."

25   "NEW BOOKS BY GERTRUDE STEIN." New York Press, 7 June.
         Perhaps Henry James's The Sacred Fount "is a first primer
for clarity when compared to this style of Gerty's [in Tender
Buttons]. But then, of course, it may not be proper to use style
in connection with this way of throwing words together. Style is
old-fashioned. We look forward eagerly to a translation of this
precious work."

26   "OFFICER, SHE'S WRITING AGAIN." Detroit News, 6 June.
         "After reading excerpts from [Tender Buttons] a person
feels like going out and pulling the Dime Bank building over onto
himself. For the benefit of those who are planning to go crazy
the following extract from the volume is offered. . . ."

27   "OUR OWN POLO GUIDE: THE GAME EXPLAINED À LA GERTRUDE STEIN."
      New York Sun, 13 June.
         "For the benefit of this vast and enfranchised autocracy of
toil and the movies, we now present our own guide to polo, explaining the technicalities of the game so that he who pays may
know what it's all about and who's who in sport and the charity
ball. We have adopted the phraseology of Gertrude Stein for the
purpose because it harmonizes so well with our clear understanding of the game and all its ramifications, hot or cold."

28   "PUBLIC GETS PEEP AT EXTREME CUBIST LITERATURE IN GERTRUDE
      STEIN'S 'TENDER BUTTONS.'" Chicago Tribune, 5 June, p. 15.
         Stein is "the literary Cubist," "an affluent American
resident in Paris," "high priestess of the new artists, the
Cubists and Futurists, and her home is an amazing museum of
their baffling output."

29   REVIEW OF TENDER BUTTONS. Chicago Herald, 29 June.
         "Am I insane, O sister, or has the printer gone insane
before me? Be comforted, brother, the lost wits belong neither
to you nor the printer. These are but questions from the Tender
Buttons of Gertrude Stein, the 'literary cubist. . . .' For a
nervously organized reader to fall into the Stein whirlpool un-
warned is to run grave dangers of going stark, staring, raving
crazy--mad. Mad. MAD!"

30   REVIEW OF TENDER BUTTONS. Detroit Free Press, 28 June.
         "The author, it is said, has studied at Radcliffe and
Columbia and the obvious inference is that much learning hath
made her mad. Certainly the attempt to make sense out of such
nonsense is calculated to put her readers into insane asylums."

31   REVIEW OF TENDER BUTTONS. Pittsburgh Dispatch, 6 June.
         "Gertrude Stein is to literature what the Cubists and
Futurists are to art, maybe everything and nothing, all mumbled
in a scramble of meaningless words. . . . She casts away every
vestige of intelligibility in her madness. She is the most

talked-about creature in the intellectual world today, and is
either a genius or--or something else."

32   ROGERS, ROBERT EMONS. "New Outbreaks of Futurism." Boston
      Transcript, 11 July, p. 12.
          With Tender Buttons, "a page read aloud, quite apart from
      its sense or nonsense, is really rhythmical, a pure pattern of
      sound, as Picasso's canvases are pure patterns of color. Some
      feel a curious hypnotic effect in her sentences read aloud. By
      complicated repetition and by careful combinations does she get
      the effects she wishes for. And to some listeners there comes a
      perception of some meaning quite other than the content of the
      phrases."

33   "TENDER BUTTONS." Boston Advertiser, 22 June.
          "To one who can extract any meaning from this a Cubist por-
      trait would be as plain as a worsted dog in Grandmother's tidy."

34   "TENDER BUTTONS." Louisville Courier-Journal, 6 July.
          "The words in the volume entitled Tender Buttons are
      English words, but the sentences are not English sentences
      according to the grammatical definition. The sentences indicated
      by punctuation do not make complete sense, partial sense, nor any
      other sense, but nonsense. Miss Stein is probably a shrewd ob-
      server of a certain side of human nature."

35   "TENDER BUTTONS." Pittsburgh Post, 4 July.
          "Cubism in literature would seem to transcend all the
      bounds of possibility. Yet the work of Gertrude Stein reveals
      with almost stunning obviousness that the forward movement is
      not confined to painting."

36   "TENDER BUTTONS." Pittsburgh Sun, 17 July.
          "Miss Stein should learn to make her art valid; in the new
      criteria of art, she must avoid the shocking commonplaces of her
      style"--such as English words and agreement of subjects and verbs.

37   "TIME TO SHOW A MESSAGE." Omaha World, 7 June.
          In Tender Buttons, Stein "has indicated a means readily at
      hand thanks to which all may become literary artists. She has
      discharged us of the burden of grammar and rhetoric and logic
      and form, of the need for academy and college, and shown us how
      the humblest among us may hope to express his inner soul as flu-
      ently and truly as did Keats himself."

38   VAN VECHTEN, CARL. "How to Read Gertrude Stein." Trend 7
      (August):553-57.
          Stein has added the quality of vagueness to English and
      should be considered nonrepresentational in her art. Tender But-
      tons has a majestic authority in prose innovation.

1915

1   "ART NEWS AND COMMENT." New York Sun, 21 March.
Inclusion of Gertrude Stein in Rogue will surely tide the periodical over the difficult early issues in publication.

2   KREYMBORG, ALFRED. "Gertrude Stein: Hoax and Hoaxtress."
New York Telegraph, 7 March.
". . . serious or hoaxtress, Gertrude Stein has provided the world with a new kind of entertainment for some time past. Whether you wrinkle your brow and curl your tongue for a long, ponderous defence of her work, or whether you scowl and short your tongue for a venomous attack, or whether you merely lean back in your velvet easy chair and open your mouth for a good roaring laugh, Miss Stein will have benefited you."

3   MARQUIS, DON. "The Sun Dial." New York Sun, 18 January.
A performance of Tender Buttons for piano could be arranged by placing candy on various keys and letting the family dog eat freely.

4   _____. "The Sun Dial." New York Sun, 13 March.
"We--our little group of serious thinkers, you know--have been giving an entire week to her, and the more we study her the more esoteric she seems and the more fascinating. A great many people, you know, pretend they are understanding her when they really aren't. The way to tell is to give them a test sentence, and then watch them as they say it over and over."

5   _____. "The Sun Dial." New York Sun, 26 March.
"'Peppercorns and purple sleet / Enwrap me round from head to feet, / Wrap me around and make me thine,' / Said Amy Lowell to Gertrude Stein. / 'Buzz-saws, buzzards, curds and glue / Show my affinity for you. / You are my golden sister-soul,' / Said Gertrude Stein to Amy Lowell." [Parody of Tender Buttons]

6   REVIEW OF THREE LIVES. Judge, 13 March.
Three Lives is not the inscrutable Gertrude Stein of late; hence these old stories are "characterized by a crudity common to all."

1916

1   "DR. LOWES FINDS TENDER BUTTONS POETIC ASPARAGUS." St. Louis
Post-Dispatch, 29 March.
Professor John L. Lowes disparaged so-called poetry in Tender Buttons and praised Amy Lowell, Fiona Macleod, and Maurice Hewlett.

<u>1920</u>

1 MANSFIELD, KATHERINE. "So me New Thing." <u>Atheneum</u>,
   15 October.
       In <u>Three Lives</u>, "Miss Gertrude Stein had discovered a new
   way of writing stories. It is just to keep right on writing
   them. Don't mind how often you go back to the beginning, don't
   hesitate to say the same thing over and over again--people are
   always repeating themselves--don't be put off if the words sound
   funny at times: just keep right on, and by the time you've done
   writing you'll have produced your effect." Reprinted: 1930.6.

2 REVIEW OF <u>THREE LIVES</u>. <u>Times</u> (London), 30 September.
       "It is a curious and sombre book that is made by these
   three pictures side by side of patient, lonely women. They gain
   their quality from the tender brushwork with which the common figures are limned in the common surroundings; from the pathetic significance given to these sad little lives working themselves out
   from year to year until the close; with no passion, no romance,
   no fight against fate. And the effect is perhaps heightened by
   the baldness of the narrative style--so simple that it drops sometimes into the manner of a primitive folktale."

<u>1922</u>

1 ANDERSON, SHERWOOD. "Four American Impressions: Gertrude
   Stein." <u>New Republic</u> 32 (11 October):171.
       Stein "is making new, strange and to my ears sweet combina-
   tions of words. As an American writer I admire her because she
   in her person, represents something sweet and healthy in our
   American life, and because I have a kind of undying faith that
   what she is up to in her word kitchen in Paris is of more importance to writers of English than the work of many of our more
   easily understood and more widely accepted word artists." Reprinted: 1926.1.

2 _____. "The Work of Gertrude Stein." <u>Little Review</u> 8
   (Spring):29-32.
       Stein is at work in Paris revolutionizing the concept of
   words: "For me the work of Gertrude Stein consists in a rebuild-
   ing, an entire new recasting of life, in the city of words."
   Reprinted: 1933.6.

3 BUSS, KATE. "The Writing of Gertrude Stein and <u>Geography and
   Plays</u>." <u>Voices</u> 2 (Summer):133-36.
       Stein has a literary method and is sincere: ". . . she is
   a student of people, an intellectual therefore not a dilettante
   to be amused to play a lifelong joke upon herself."

4 "WE NOMINATE FOR THE HALL OF FAME: GERTRUDE STEIN." <u>Vanity
   Fair</u>, August, p. 72.

"Because she is entitled to write both L.L. D. and M.D.
after her name; because she was instrumental in promoting the
early fame of Matisse and Cézanne; because her Parisian salon is
one of the most serious and interesting the city of famous colors;
and finally, because her experiments in style have already had an
influence on the younger French writers."

1923

1   BATCHELOR, E.A. "Here Every Word Gets a Chance to Live Its
     Own Life Its Own Way." Detroit Saturday Night, 26 May,
     pp. 2-3.
         Geography and Plays is "better reading than the telephone
directory to the non-intellectual because the type is larger.
It is not so good as the Century and New Standard dictionaries
because there are no pictures in it. Yet it has a distinct ad-
vantage over any other printed volume we have ever seen because
you can pick it up at any time, start to read on any page in any
direction, left to right, or right to left, up or down the page,
and it makes equally good sense."

2   BURKE, KENNETH. "Engineering with Words." Dial 74 (April):
     408-12.
         Geography and Plays demonstrates that Stein's is an art of
subtraction, and she sacrifices much by under-emphasizing the
selection of subject matter: "And her method leaves us with
too little to feed on."

3   CARMICHAEL, P.A. "Gertrude, Gertrude." Roanoke (Va.) World
     News, 10 July.
         Geography and Plays "would subvert all forms of orderliness
in the mind and make it out as illogical and unscientific as an
oyster. Her book reads like a stenographer's transcript of what
an idiotic child said in its sleep."

4   COLUM, MARY. Review of Geography and Plays. Freeman 8
     (17 October):140.
         If Geography and Plays "gives Miss Stein pleasure, it gives
too little pleasure and has too little meaning for other people
to warrant Miss Stein in doing so to any great extent."

5   CRAWFORD, JOHN W. "Incitement to Riot." New York Call,
     19 August.
         Reading Geography and Plays aloud electrifies hearers and
perhaps foreshadows the return of an oral art.

6   D., H.V. "Books and Viewpoints." New York Globe, 19 May.
         Geography and Plays belongs shelved between Edward Lear's
Nonsense Verse and volumes in psychiatry.

7   D., K. "When Helen Furr Got Gay With Harold Moos." Vanity
     Fair 21 (October).

"Harold Moos was not a gay man but he was a very dark man, and a very heavy man and a very bald man, and of all the regularly dark men and the regularly heavy men and the regularly bald men who sat regularly there then with Helen Furr, Harold Moos was the darkest man and heaviest man and the baldest man who sat regularly there with her." [Parody of "Miss Furr and Miss Skeene"]

8   D., N.P. "A Mumbo-Jumble of the New Books." New York Globe, 19 April.
      "Nothing more interesting in literary criticism has ever happened than the comparison of Gertrude Stein with Milton, and Many Marriages and Sherwood Anderson with Pilgrim's Progress and Thomas Hardy."

9   DAVIES, JAMES. "Gertrude Stein's Vocabulary in Unclassified New Volume Astounds and Amazes Critic." Minneapolis Tribune, 23 September.
      "Somebody told Gertrude Stein in the dim, dead years of long ago that she was destined to become one of the world's geniuses; it went to her head, produced partial paralysis of the oraliferous nerve and the net result may be found in Geography and Plays."

10   DOUGLAS, GEORGE W. "Is Steinism Responsible for Modern Literature?" Philadelphia Public Ledger, 29 May.
      Having come from doubting the existence of Gertrude Stein, one comes to Geography and Plays to admit her existence but to lament her lack of lucidity.

11   [HECHT, BEN.] Review of Geography and Plays. Chicago Literary Times 1 (1 July):2.
      Stein's "object would seem to be that of taunting words to an accidental originality and allowing these tired symbols to play together, without restriction, in the hope of catching and preserving some of their relieved antics in the realm of thought and emotion."

12   JONES, RUTH LAMBERT. "The New Curiosity Shop." New York Post, 22 December.
      "If there were a Christmas there would be a Christmas mouseless dreaming in stockings and couchant red riots in the heavens jangled and pawed appellations uprisings not without chimneys and recognitions partridge-seeming pouter-pigeon perhaps floral fruition how else fitlings until nasal-gesturing-accent of departure and vociferation if there were a Christmas there would be a Christmas unless there were not." [Parody of Geography and Plays]

13   K., G.E. "Miss Stein Applies Cubism To Defenseless Prose." Baltimore Sun, 25 August.

Geography and Plays is "downright blather of the worst
sort. Probably Miss Stein isn't to blame. Persons ready for
occupational therapy usually aren't. The publishers are the
ones who really belong in the stocks."

14   L., D.K. "A Reviewer's Reveries." Detroit News, 10 June.
     The influence of Gertrude Stein in such works as Geography
and Plays is fearsome, for the English language is perfected already and not needful of polishing.

15   MARQUIS, DON. "Miss Stein's Latest." New York Herald-Tribune,
     19 May.
     One may miss the romance of Gertrude Stein, now that Geog-
raphy and Plays is respectable, not merely exotic.

16   MENCKEN, H.L. "Holy Writ." Smart Set 72 (October):144.
     "In the days before the war, when Miss Stein printed her
Tender Buttons, there was at least some charm of novelty in her
ponderous prancing. . . . But Freud and the device of stringing
meaningless phrases together are both now stale. Geography and
Plays is dreadful stuff, indeed."

17   _____. [Literary survey.] Vanity Fair 21 (August):923.
     "It is hard for me to make up a list of books or authors
that bore me insufferably, for the simple truth is that I can
read almost anything. . . . As for Lawrence and Miss Stein,
what makes them hard reading for me is simply the ineradicable
conviction that beneath all their pompous manner there is nothing but tosh."

18   "MODERN MASTERPIECES." Chicago Daily News, 11 April.
     "Suppose a cyclone took and spilt / The book that Noah
Webster built / Across the county line; / Conceive those words
so neatly listed / By some fierce brainstorm wrecked and twisted,
/ Class, that is Gertrude Stein!" [Parody of Geography and Plays]

*19 MUNSON, GORHAM B. "Stein, Tzara, Burke." All's Well 3
     (January):7-8.
          Cited: Index to Little Magazines 1900-1919, p. 1252.

20   PETTUS, CLYDE. "Chips from a Cubist Block." Atlanta
     Constitution, 14 October.
     "The cubist theory of presenting no literal likeness of an
object, but of creating a more lasting impression by picturing
one by one angles distorted according to the artist's mental
bias, might if applied to literature be expected to produce such
erratic bits of word jugglery as Geography and Plays."

*21 PRESTON, HAROLD P. "Words and Gertrude Stein." Modern Review
     1 (April):121-22.
          Cited: Index to Little Magazines 1920-1939, p. 288.

22　PULSIFER, HAROLD T.　"The Stein Songs and Poetry."　Outlook
　　134 (6 June):139.
　　　　Stein in Geography and Plays demands dissociation from re-
　　ceived meanings and nuances; she asks too much for her reward.

23　REVIEW OF GEOGRAPHY AND PLAYS.　Bookman 58 (23 September):84.
　　　　In Geography and Plays, "though futurists may deny, it
　　would seem that Gertrude Stein has used her language to conceal
　　her thoughts."

24　REVIEW OF GEOGRAPHY AND PLAYS.　Haldeman-Julius Weekly,
　　28 July.
　　　　Comparing Geography and Plays with Ulysses convinces one
　　that Stein is inferior, "an incidental detail in the work of the
　　gifted Irishman.　She seems wilful, extravagant, childish."

25　REVIEW OF GEOGRAPHY AND PLAYS.　New Rochelle (N.Y.) Standard,
　　28 August.
　　　　Praising Geography and Plays is like denying that the
　　parading king is naked.

26　REVIEW OF GEOGRAPHY AND PLAYS.　New York Town Topics,
　　2 August.
　　　　Geography and Plays is Stein's modern art:　"Modern paint-
　　ers attempted a denial of representation, and in the work of
　　Cubists and Expressionists achieved a giddy violence of color
　　and form not unlike Miss Stein's prose."

27　SHERMAN, STUART P.　"Really Quite Extraordinary."　New York
　　Evening Post Literary Review, 11 August, p. 891.
　　　　Randomly rearranging slips of paper bearing words may re-
　　veal what Stein tries in Geography and Plays--a demonstration of
　　the power of the word.

28　SITWELL, EDITH.　"Miss Stein's Stories."　Nation & Athenaeum
　　33 (14 July):492.
　　　　In Geography and Plays, "one feels . . . that there is a
　　real foundation for Miss Stein's mind, somewhere deep under the
　　earth, but that it is too deep for her to dig down to, and that
　　she herself is not capable of building upon this hidden founda-
　　tion.　She is, however, doing valuable pioneer work. . . ."

29　VAN VECHTEN, CARL.　"Medals for Miss Stein."　New York
　　Tribune, 13 May, sec. 9, p. 20.
　　　　With Geography and Plays, "if the reader would permit him-
　　self to fall under the spell of this enchantress of words, just
　　as I have often urged concertgoers to listen to Schoenberg or
　　Ornstein without thinking of Beethoven or Liszt, he would soon
　　find himself reading without much difficulty."

30 WILLARD, DONALD B. "The Latest Thing In Prose Style."
    Boston Globe, 31 October.
        "A new type of literature has burst upon the more or less
    erudite American public. It is a variety of prose narration,
    featured by short sentences, unusual punctuation, frequent repe-
    titions of ideas, and the stressing of certain words till they
    run through the mind of the reader like the whisperings of a
    guilty conscience. Miss Gertrude Stein is the person who has
    let loose this new brain-teaser."

31 WILSON, EDMUND. "A Guide to Gertrude Stein." Vanity Fair
    21 (September):60, 80.
        "Miss Stein no longer understands the conditions under which
    literary works have to be produced. There is sometimes a genuine
    music in the most baffling of her works, but there are rarely any
    communicated emotions. When Gertrude Stein succeeds in her new
    manner it is as any other poet succeeds, through coining an idea
    miraculously into words. But it is not, in the long run, I be-
    lieve, as a painter of cubist still-lifes after Braque. And, in
    any case, it is in her thought that we are chiefly interested,
    and it is precisely her thought which we now rarely get."

32 "WITH AMERICAN WRITERS IN EUROPE." New York Herald (Paris),
    9 April, p. 5.
        Long resident in Paris, Stein in her recent Geography and
    Plays reveals much of importance to her literary theories.

33 "WORDS, WONDERFUL WORDS!" Outlook, 6 June.
        Words sprinkled like pepper, according to Stein, have both
    beauty and virtue; but Geography and Plays lacks both sense and
    feeling.

34 YOUNG, F.H. "Topics of the Day." Providence Journal, 1 June.
        "Personally, we would not venture to say whether Gertrude
    Stein is a reality or only a myth. We have no definite knowledge
    that would warrant any assertion one way or the other. Our actual
    knowledge on many subjects is just as thin as that. . . . We
    are forced to accept the lady on faith, as we accept much else in
    life, but it is well to state that ours is a wavering faith."

1924

1 ANDERSON, SHERWOOD. A Story Teller's Story. New York:
    B.W. Huebsch, pp. 359, 362.
        Anderson read Tender Buttons in Chicago soon after its
    publication and saw for the first time "words laid before me as
    the painter had laid the color pans on the table in my presence."

2 "THE BARRAGE OF WORDS." Philadelphia Public Ledger, 29 June.
        "And there is that extremely repetitive fictionist,
    Gertrude Stein, who finds her strength in using the same word

over and over again, knitted together with 'anyhow.' She achieves
a tone, much in the manner of the debater who uses the same argu-
ment, shouting it a little more loudly with each repetition."

3　BUSS, KATE. "Jo Davidson and His Plastic Biographies Writ in
　　Stone." Boston Transcript, 23 February.
　　　　Davidson's statue of Gertrude Stein reveals more about the
author than do her books: "A vision above the reach of its age!"

4　COHEN, GEORGE. The Jews in the Making of America. Boston:
　　Stratford Co., p. 163.
　　　　"The tendency for innovation and renovation, those results
which follow inevitably upon the penetration of the Jew into the
various realms of human endeavor, has become visible here as elsewhere. Gertrude Stein, a Jewess, is prominent in the modern school
of impressionism and expressionism. . . ."

5　CONGER, MYRTLE. "Investigations and Oil (After Gertrude
　　Stein--With Apologies)." Saturday Evening Post, 21 June.
　　　　"Investigations like progressions arithmetical growing
larger. And larger strangely. The people pay. And it is even
so. Oil is oil and this is this. The people pay. They pay.
And pay and pay and pay. With nothing in return, nothing but
caption startling, and that is nothing. Likewise this. O ever
thus!" [Parody of Geography and Plays]

6　"FAME CONTESTS." New York Times, 24 February, sec. 2, p. 6.
　　　　Based on Stein's poem "An Indian Boy," the "humble layman
will not be presumptuous in regarding Gertrude Stein as one of
the most original writers of all times."

7　"GERTRUDE STEIN AND A ROBIN." Atlantic 133 (March):427-28.
　　　　With "Miss Furr and Miss Skeene," "if you should happen to
read a sentence of Gertrude Stein and hear a robin jabbering close
on its heels, I am sure you too would be stirred by the curious
resemblance. Heaven forfend that I should compare the supremely
civilized and bravely experimental Gertrude Stein, matronly and
superior among her Picassos, Matisses, Marie Laurencins, and
cubistic paintings, to the silly hopping of a robin. It is more
appropriate to make the robin take the onus, the flying start and
ingratiating introduction of the simile."

8　LOY, MINA. "Communication: Gertrude Stein." Transatlantic
　　Review 2, no. 3 (1924):305-9.
　　　　Stein's way of writing involves "placement and replacement
of her phrases of inversion of the same phrase sequences that are
as closely matched in level, as the fractional tones in primitive
music or the imperceptible modelling of early Egyptian sculpture."

9　　　　. "Gertrude Stein." Transatlantic Review 2, no. 4
　　(1924):427-30.

"Apart from all analyses, the natural, the debonaire way to appreciate Gertrude Stein, is as one would saunter along a country way side on a fine day and pluck, for its beauty, an occasional flower."

10   SHERMAN, STUART PRATT. <u>Points of View</u>. New York: Charles Scribner's Sons, pp. 263-68.
       Reprint of 1923.27.

11   "WHITING'S COLUMN." <u>Boston Herald</u>, 25 March.
       "We want Gertrude Stein for the national poet. We want to know that there is in some official position someone equipped and inclined to let loose all the facts presented in a way that shall be intelligible, and Miss Stein qualifies. . . . If there is no possibility of making Miss Stein national poet, then we want her elected to the Senate."

1925

1   "THE BOOK CHAT." <u>Memphis Commercial-Appeal</u>, 13 December.
       "We have an idea that Miss Stein takes an enormous amount of trouble over just such passages [as quoted]. . . . The way to read Gertrude Stein is to take a deep breath and then to race as fast as certain clergymen when they try to outdistance their congregations in response to the Psalm. . . . We tumble along with her and if we are careful not to search for a meaning a meaning may emerge. . . ."

*2   CROCKETT, MARY. "Gertrude Stein." <u>Modern Quarterly</u> 2 (1925): 233-37.
       Cited: Wilson, Robert A. <u>Gertrude Stein: A Bibliography</u>, p. 191.

*3   GRAVES, ROBERT. <u>Contemporary Techniques of Poetry: A Political Analogy</u>. London: Hogarth Press.
       Cited: Liston, Maureen R. <u>Gertrude Stein: An Annotated Critical Bibliography</u>, p. 66.

4   [HEAP, JANE.] "Comment." <u>Little Review</u> 10 (Autumn-Winter):18.
       Stein's popularity is growing on the Continent, in England, and in the United States: "Gertrude Stein is so handsome, such a mighty talker, the best host and playfellow and a first rank artist. I hope she has a hundred happy new years."

5   "INJUSTICE TO GENIUS." <u>New York Times</u>, 10 February, p. 22.
       In recognizing the beauty of words as words, Stein may have found "the corner-Stein of politics as well as literature."

6   SCUDDER, JANET. <u>Modeling My Life</u>. New York: Harcourt, Brace & Co., pp. 234-35.

Stein visited Scudder, who thought her "the discoverer of Matisse and the inventor of a new literature. . . ."

7   SITWELL, EDITH. Poetry & Criticism. London: Hogarth Press, pp. 23-24.

Stein is "bringing back life to our language by what appears, at first, to be an anarchic process. First she breaks down the predestined groups of words, their sleepy family habits; then she rebrightens them, examines their texture, and builds them into new and vital shapes."

8   STERNBERG, SADIE HOPE. "Gertrude Stein's 'Making of Americans' Is a New Year Offering of 1,000 Pages." New York Herald (Paris), 27 December, p. 9.

Publication of The Making of Americans pleases Stein, who speaks of her inspiration, writing methods, intentions, and predictions for art.

1926

1   ANDERSON, SHERWOOD. Sherwood Anderson's Notebook. New York: Boni & Liveright, pp. 47-50.

Reprint of 1922.1.

2   ARMITAGE, GILBERT. "A Word on Gertrude Stein." Oxford Magazine, 17 June, p. 584.

"When Miss Stein spoke in Christ Church last week she shattered one or two current delusions about herself pretty thoroughly. First, by pointing to the interest maintained in her works for twenty years, she proved to those who required a demonstration that she is a genuine creative artist and no charlatan. Second, in answer to a question, she said that she used all words in their common or garden meanings: which shows that she is far too sensible to try--as some of her intrepidly 'modern' admirers accused her of trying--to divorce words from meaning. She is no demented or mystical mathematician, attempting by a process of arbitrary and capricious juxtaposition of words, to build up a literature of abstract patterns."

3   "COMPOSITION AS EXPLANATION." New York Times, 24 October, sec. 2, p. 8.

Stein's recent article in the Dial proves her to be "one of the most painstaking, original and creative of contemporary authors," one who "erects a philosophical theory which, to those capable of the keen perception and reflection necessary to follow it, is irrefutable."

4   "GERTRUDE STEIN." Black & Blue Jay 6 (April).

"Not only is Gertrude Stein known as an author, but also she is known as an art critic of decided ability. . . . In addition to being an author and art critic, Miss Stein is a brilliant conversationalist, attracting to her studio the leading artists and men of letters to be found in Paris today."

5　　"GERTRUDE STEIN IN CRITICAL FRENCH EYES." Literary Digest 88 (6 February):58, 60-62.

Easy to laugh at Gertrude Stein as we find it, one must understand her serious reputation in France.

6　　"GOLDEN WORDS." New York Times, 13 December, p. 20.

Stein's poem on "Enough said" is good advice, especially for politicians in Washington, D.C.

7　　"HOGARTH ESSAYS." New Orleans Times-Picayune, 17 March.

Composition as Explanation is Stein's "irritatingly simpleminded analysis of a complex subject," accompanied by "a number of mad portrait sketches." Stein has reduced her fine intellect to "a drooling and ineffectual expression."

8　　"HOGARTH ESSAYS." Times Literary Supplement, 25 November, p. 848.

Stein's explanation in Composition as Explanation "resembles nothing so much as that curious effect which sometimes happens when there is something wrong with a Gramophone record, and the same phrase of music is repeated again and again. . . . If when this happened the progress of time was continually stopped and repeated with the phrase of time then Miss Stein's ways of writing would certainly be justifiable."

9　　"MENTAL BYWAYS." Springfield (Mass.) Republican, 21 November.

Despite Gertrude Stein's experiments with prose early in this century, her works are still unjustly ignored.

10　　MOORE, MARIANNE. "The Spare American Emotion." Dial 80 (February):153-56.

In The Making of Americans we have an extraordinary interpretation of American life: "The Making of Americans is a kind of living genealogy which is, in its branching, unified and vivid"--"a truly psychological exposition of American living."

11　　PUTNAM, SAMUEL. "Guillaume and Gertrude." Chicago Post, 18 March.

"Apolinaire and Gertrude Stein have, probably, done more than any others toward the achievement of cubism in words."

12　　REVIEW OF COMPOSITION AS EXPLANATION. Chicago Tribune (Paris), 8 November.

"Those persons (and they are many) who have been confused, not to say appalled, by the writings of Gertrude Stein, will probably not be much wiser after they have read (or tried to read) this explanation of her theory of what composition is."

13   ROSENFELD, PAUL. "Newcomers: Gertrude Stein." Saturday
      Review of Literature 2 (2 January):462-63.
         The world has been slow to recognize Gertrude Stein, but
      the recent publication of The Making of Americans marks the
      appearance of "indubitably the most monumental fiction to be
      given since the publication of Ulysses." Reprinted: 1928.23.

14   SITWELL, EDITH. Review of The Making of Americans. Criterion
      3 (April):390-92.
         Throughout The Making of Americans, Miss Stein's "unusual,
      speedy, high-pressure style, which varies its rhythm according
      to the characters she is describing, gives the impression of life
      being woven on noisy, ceaseless, yet mysterious shuttles--and
      again, of the household sounds and the noise of ordinary life by
      which we are surrounded and in which our existences are rooted."

15   STEELL, WILLIS. "An American Novel That Paris is Talking
      About." Literary Digest International Book Review 4
      (February):172-73.
         The Making of Americans is "a canvas as vastly stretched
      as the Sistine Chapel's Last Judgment, and containing, one may
      assume, as many figures, but . . . but with the kindest spirit
      imaginable for the author one couldn't call it in any sense a
      work of art. Gertrude Stein discovered heredity and made a big
      book out of it. She ought to have the credit of never losing
      sight of her theme and always sticking, limpet-like, to her
      scenario."

                              1927

1   BRICKELL, HERSCHEL. "Books on Our Table." New York Post,
      28 February.
         Reading Gertrude Stein, alleged genius is hard to spot; and
      reading her leads to dizziness.

2   CANBY, HENRY SEIDEL. "Gyring and Gimbling (or Lewis Carroll
      in Paris)." Saturday Review of Literature 3 (30 April):777,
      782-83.
         Elliot Paul tries to elucidate Gertrude Stein in transition:
      "Gertrude Stein we knew in feats of word legerdemain which had
      strange powers since some minds were fascinated by her scrambled
      sentences and others driven to wails and cursings." She is sound
      without sense, full of nonsense, making language unfit for com-
      munication. Reprinted: 1929.2; 1947.9.

3   [ELIOT, T.S.] "Composition as Explanation." Criterion 5
      (January):162.
         Stein's inability to be questioned on her literary creed
      will keep her fifty years ahead of understanding. Composition
      as Explanation is "exposition of work at once original and
      obscure."

                               21

4   FORSTER, E.M. Aspects of the Novel. New York: Harcourt,
    Brace & Co., pp. 67-68.
        Stein separated her fiction from time but fails because "as
    soon as fiction is completely delivered from time it cannot ex-
    press anything at all. . . ."

5   GOLDBERG, ISAAC. "On The World Of Books." Haldeman-Julius
    Weekly, 1 October.
        "As a headache has a critic. A Review / As a review has a
    headache. A Critic. / As a critic has a review. A Headache. /
    Bebble. / A tower, a tow-Wour, a two-woe, a tow-Whee!-er of
    Babble." [Parody of "As a Wife Has a Cow"]

6   HEMINGWAY, ERNEST. "My Own Life." New Yorker 2 (12 February):
    23.
        Hemingway broke with Stein when she locked him out of her
    apartment: "It was then that I broke with Miss Stein. I have
    never ceased to feel that I did her a great injustice and, need-
    less to say, I have never ceased to regret it."

*7 HOLMS, J.F. Review of Composition as Explanation. Calendar
    3 (April 1926-January 1927):329-32.
        Cited: Sader, Marion. Comprehensive Index to English-
    Language Little Magazines, p. 4314.

*8 M., E. Review of The Making of Americans. This Quarter 1
    (1927):275-78.
        Cited: Sader, Marion. Comprehensive Index to English-
    Language Little Magazines, p. 4314.

9   M., P.S. "Saturday Chat." Lowell (Mass.) Courier-Citizen,
    5 February.
        "Speaking of the Intellectuals and Intelligentsia, my eye
    happens to fall at this moment on a mysterious paragraph attrib-
    uted to Gertrude Stein. Do you know the works of Gertrude? If
    not you are beyond the pale--you're not a qualified member of the
    Intelligentsia. . . . If you say you do not fathom the recondite
    meanings of Gertrude's books, it only proves that you are what
    Mr. Mencken calls--at the top of a cruelly overworked voice--a
    Moron."

10 PAUL, ELLIOT H. "From a Litterateur's Notebook." Chicago
    Tribune (Paris), 22 May, p. 7.
        "Beginning with the realistic novel, Miss Stein's first
    experiment was to expand it to the utmost, as in The Making of
    Americans. Finding this not entirely satisfactory, she began
    condensing it. . . . The narrative function seemed increasingly
    childish and unimportant to her, as magazine writers turned it
    into an applied science with all the elements of quantity produc-
    tion. The next step was to generalize and conventionalize and
    otherwise simplify narrative until it scarcely obtruded from her
    composition."

11   _____. "From a Litterateur's Notebook." Chicago Tribune
(Paris), 29 May, p. 7.
Stein's "goal became the employment of words as an abstract
medium. Having stripped stories of narrative and description,
and purged characterization of incident, she proceded to another
refinement of her product and moulded her typical situations and
universal qualities into pure patterns."

12   _____. "From a Litterateur's Notebook." Chicago Tribune
(Paris), 19 June, p. 9.
Stein has a correctly limited liking for the classics,
choosing to create in a continuous present.

13   PORTER, KATHERINE ANNE. "'Everybody Is a Real One.'" New
York Herald Tribune Books, 16 January, pp. 1-2.
In reading The Making of Americans, one emerges from
spirals into understanding: "Gertrude Stein describes her function in terms of digestion, of childbirth: all these people,
these fragments of digested knowledge, are in her, they must
come out." Reprinted: 1970.34.

14   REVIEW OF THE MAKING OF AMERICANS. Dublin Magazine, n.s. 3
(January-March):68-69.
With Stein's experiments in narration, one penetrates
"jungles of unexplored experiences where progress is thwarted
at every turn."

15   RIDING, LAURA. "T.E. Hulme, The New Barbarism and Gertrude
Stein." transition, no. 3 (June), pp. 153-68.
"Completely without originality," Stein "is only divinely
inspired in ordinariness. She uses language automatically to
record pure, ultimate obviousness. She makes it capable of
direct communication not by caricaturing language in its present
stage--attacking decadence with decadence--but by purging it of
its discredited experiences." Reprinted: 1928.22.

16   _____, and GRAVES, ROBERT. A Survey of Modernist Poetry.
London: William Heinemann, pp. 204, 223, 274-75, 280-89.
Gertrude Stein "has had courage, clarity, sincerity, simplicity. She has created a human mean in language, a mathematical
equation of ordinariness which leaves one with a tender respect
for that changing and unchanging slowness that is humanity and
Gertrude Stein."

17   RODKER, JOHN. The Future of Futurism. New York: E.P. Dutton
& Co., pp. 28-31.
Stein's experiments with words are attempts to revitalize
the language; "and they are developed in recurring motifs as a
fugue might be developed or a house built up of standard units."

18   T., J.G. "More Authors Cover The Snyder Trial." <u>New Yorker</u>
     3 (7 May):69.
        "There is a man. There is a woman. There is not a man.
There would have been a man. There was a man. There were two
men. There is one man. There is a woman where is a woman is a
man. . . ."

19   "THE VIRTUE OF INTOLERANCE." <u>Saturday Review of Literature</u>
     2 (27 February):585.
        ". . . Gertrude Stein and her disciples may be perfectly
negligible phenomena, but the criticism that treats them not only
with respect but as of enormous importance is a serious matter.
It is the kind of criticism that is by the nature of the case
militant rather than persuasive, that is supercilious to tradition, and scornful of standards. . . . Surely such writing as
Gertrude Stein's could not hold attention for a day if it were
not for the smoke screen of importance which the critics have
thrown about it. Its own stupidity would have laughed it into
oblivion."

1928

1   "AMERICA HAS LITERATURE, SAYS TOURIST VAN VECHTEN." <u>New York</u>
     <u>Herald</u> (Paris), 12 September.
        Stein "is like yeast," according to Van Vechten, "the yeast
that makes the bread. Only time can disclose just how important
her own work is, but the fact remains that at present she is one
of the greatest influences of our age. According to his own ad-
mission she has greatly affected the writings of Sherwood Anderson.
She has also been important in the literary development of James
Joyce, Dorothy Richardson and others."

2   BUSS, KATE. "Gertrude Stein As a Writer And A Personality."
     <u>Boston Transcript</u>, 21 April.
        "The sooner you read [<u>The Making of Americans</u>,] this word
sonata of an American family, this Michael Angelesque structure
of your native history, the sooner will be your realization that
all the talk of the obscurity of the style of Gertrude Stein's
writing is nonsense. Her style is no more obscure than tomorrow
is obscure. Yesterday's book is clear reading today. Tomorrow's
book, then, needs but the progress of thought to elucidate a common wealth. The measure of Miss Stein's clarity may be the measure of your own imaginative intelligence."

3   CARRUTHERS, JOHN. <u>Scherezade, or The Future of the English</u>
     <u>Novel</u>. New York: E.P. Dutton & Co., p. 65.
        Joyce's "outbreaks" after <u>Ulysses</u> have been "in the manner
made familiar by Miss Gertrude Stein"--mad.

4 CHURCH, RALPH. "A Note on the Writing of Gertrude Stein."
   transition, no. 14 (Fall), pp. 164-68.
        Stein's writing is to be appreciated for form instead of
   strictly for content. The writing as writing is the subject
   matter.

5 CROSS, WILBUR L. The Modern English Novel. New Haven: Yale
   University Press, pp. 22-23.
        "Gertrude Stein and James Joyce, for all his perverse genius,
   are the bores of contemporary fiction. . . ," but Stein probably
   first invented "this manner of depicting all the layers of human
   consciousness."

6 DODD, LEE WILSON. The Great Enlightenment: A Satire in
   Verse. New York: Harper & Brothers, p. 50, and passim.
        "Lo, the poor Indian, Gertrude Stein! whose brain /
   Tangled in echolalia writes in vain. . . ."

7 FORD, FORD MADOX. "Not Idle!" New York Herald-Tribune,
   1 July.
        Stein's The Making of Americans disproves the alleged stul-
   tifying effects of Paris life and "must be one of the most volumi-
   nous of contributions to modern fiction."

8 GRACE, HARVEY. A Musician at Large. Oxford: Oxford University Press, pp. 173-79.
        "Modernist art," like Stein's, "appears to provide itself
   liberally with whatever it deserves in the way of ridicule."

9 HANSEN, HARRY. "The First Reader." New York World,
   8 September.
        In Useful Knowledge, Stein is "much better than many of the
   songs that come over the radio. Miss Stein has found her metier
   at last. She is headed for Tinpan Alley. We knew she had something in her if only she could get her words placed in suitable
   combinations."

10 HUDDLESTON, SISLEY. Paris Salons, Cafés, Studios: Being
   Social, Artistic and Literary Memoirs. New York: J.B.
   Lippincott, pp. 315-17.
        Looking like "a Cisterican monk," Stein has a cult of young
   men who worship her obscurity: "Surely it is a pity that a woman
   with the talent of Gertrude Stein should fall into such nonsense
   and should induce 'advanced' persons to accept this jumble of
   counters as glittering and precious coin of the realm."

11 HUGNET, GEORGES. "Le Berceau de Gertrude Stein." In
   Morrow's Almanack for the Year of Our Lord 1929. Edited by
   Burton Rascoe. New York: William Morrow & Co., pp. 206-8.
        "Chère Gertrude, / vous n'aviez caché / votre
   correspondence / sur papier doré / avec les habitants de Mars!"

12   LEWIS, WYNDHAM. <u>Time and Western Man</u>. New York: Harcourt,
     Brace & Co., pp. 49-52, 55-65.
         Pretending to be inarticulate and childish, Gertrude Stein
     is articulate and complex. Time is the basis of her interests,
     "the treasured key to her technical experiments." Yet Stein's
     pretended childishness is perverse; her assumed faithfulness to
     colloquialism is merely apparent. The result of Stein's fatigue,
     energy, and fatalism is "the most wearisome dirge it is possible
     to imagine . . . as slab after slab of this heavy, insensitive,
     common prose-song churns and lumbers by."

13   "LITERARY ESSAYS IN EXPLANATION." <u>Mail and Empire</u> (Toronto),
     19 January.
         Stein's <u>Composition as Explanation</u> is "like her other works.
     I do not understand one sentence of it. But it is certainly badly
     entitled. Composition it possibly is; but as explanation its
     value is minus zero."

14   McALMON, ROBERT. "Gertrude Stein." <u>Exile</u>, no. 4 (Autumn),
     pp. 70-74.
         ". . . slowly Miss Stein wishes these people who listen
     adjudgingly rather than as to an oracle were away, slowly she is
     ill at ease, and slowly she realizes suddenly that she wishes
     these people quickly away, and quickly they go, slowly control-
     ling themselves to quickly realize laughter upon relentlessly
     realizing being, surely, being outside, away from Miss Stein."
     Reprinted: 1938.3.

15   MICHAUD, RÉGIS. <u>The American Novel Today: A Social and
     Psychological Study</u>. Boston: Little, Brown & Co., p. 165.
         Despite her influence on Sherwood Anderson, Stein's <u>The
     Making of Americans</u> is "a quarry where many curious gravels can
     be found, but no statues."

16   _____. <u>Panorama de la littérature américaine contemporaine</u>.
     Paris: Kra, pp. 252-54.
         Stein dominates the new American literature through her
     experiments with prose and through her influence on other expe-
     rimenters with prose.

17   NEIHARDT, JOHN G. "Of Making Many Books." <u>St. Louis Post-
     Dispatch</u>, 23 November.
         <u>Tender Buttons</u>, Stein's "prophetic masterpiece," has
     finally been republished in <u>transition</u>. It was sadly neglected
     in 1914.

18   PORTER, KATHERINE ANNE. "Second Wind." <u>New York Herald-
     Tribune Books</u>, 23 September, p. 6.
         "If [<u>Useful Knowledge</u>] is being American I doubt it. If
     this is being making romance I doubt it. If this is owning the
     earth I doubt it." Reprinted: 1970.34.

19   RASCOE, BURTON. "The Case of Gertrude Stein." In A Bookman's
      Daybook. Edited by C. Hartley Grattan. New York: Horace
      Liveright, pp. 42-43.
          Contrary to report in 1922, Rascoe does not think that
      Stein is foolish, for her prose experiments are useful to all
      writers.

20   REVIEW OF USEFUL KNOWLEDGE. Boston Transcript, 8 December.
          "A book that is characteristic of Gertrude Stein. It is
      daring in its originality, beautiful in its make-up and cryptic
      in its contents to the nth degree."

21   REVIEW OF USEFUL KNOWLEDGE. Portland (Oreg.) Telegram,
      3 December.
          Useful Knowledge is worth twenty-five dollars in amusement
      value: "The only sad element in connection with the contempla-
      tion of Gertrude's volume of Useful Knowledge is the realiza-
      tion that innumerable printers and proofreaders must have gone gibber-
      ing mad and gained permanent homes in padded cells, as a result
      of their association with Miss Stein's Useful Knowledge in the
      process of getting it into type and into the pages of this book."

22   RIDING, LAURA. Contemporaries and Snobs. London: Jonathan
      Cape, pp. 123-99.
          Reprint of 1927.19.

23   ROSENFELD, PAUL. By Way of Art: Criticisms of Music, Litera-
      ture, Painting, Sculpture and the Dance. New York: Coward-
      McCann, pp. 111-31.
          Reprint of 1926.13.

24   SANDBURG, CARL. "From the Notebook of Carl Sandburg."
      Chicago Daily News, 9 January.
          "There are people who enjoy reading Gertrude Stein as they
      enjoy a taste of gorgonzola cheese--occasionally. Nobody cares
      what she means when she writes. . . ."

25   SCHMALHAUSEN, SAMUEL D. "Gertrude Stein: Or, Light on the
      Literary Aspects of Enuvesis." Modern Quarterly 5 (Fall):
      313-23.
          "Is Gertrude Stein original or merely mentally defective?
      Is she creative or only bilious? How do her glands behave? Is
      she endocrinologically on the blink since infancy or only since
      adolescence?"

26   SLOPER, L.A. "Bookman's Holiday." Christian Science Monitor,
      26 September.
          Merely reading Composition as Explanation is
      self-explanatory. . . .

27   WILSON, EDMUND. "Nonsense." New Republic 58 (20 February):
     21-22.
          "The only question in connection with a work of literature
     is how much we enjoy the state of consciousness to which it gives
     rise. And in connection with [Useful Knowledge], I confess that
     I find most of it very tiresome. But if I had merely said that
     it was a book of nonsense, and left it at that, I should have
     created a misleading impression."

                              1929

1   BARNEY, NATALIE CLIFFORD. Aventures de l'esprit. Paris:
     Éditions Émile-Paul Frères, pp. 230-43.
          Stein revitalizes language by synthesis of civilizations
     and idioms, assuring a return to Babel or perhaps a United States
     of Europe.

2   CANBY, HENRY SEIDEL. American Estimates. New York: Harcourt,
     Brace & Co., pp. 170-77.
          Reprint of 1927.2.

3   DRAPER, MURIEL. Music at Midnight. New York: Harper &
     Brothers, pp. 152-56.
          Paul Draper tried unsuccessfully to equal Stein by using
     random slips of paper. Muriel Draper liked Stein and thought
     "she tried to break up word habits that no longer convey any
     meaning, so long have they been used as symbols of things that
     do not exist, and so often have they been dipped in and out of
     the pools of imagined and actual experiences that lie deep in
     the history of the race."

4   EASTMAN, MAX. "The Cult of Intelligibility." Harper's 158
     (April):632-39.
          A book by Gertrude Stein does not inform the reader, pos-
     sibly because Stein knows nothing to tell. Reprinted: 1931.4.

5   "GERTRUDE STEIN'S SOLEMN QUEST FOR GENIAL OBSCURITY."
     Philadelphia Public Ledger, 5 January.
          In Useful Knowledge, Stein's "tools for freighting ideas
     are not words and combinations of words familiar to most of us,
     but apparently Miss Stein doesn't mind that. She expects her
     readers to learn her language, and, of course, whether you are
     willing to learn it depends on a number of things, few of which
     I myself can boast. It is no doubt as much a criticism of myself
     as of Miss Stein, but a page or two of hers at first makes me a
     little cross-eyed, and then puts me quite conclusively to sleep."

6   KREYMBORG, ALFRED. Our Singing Strength: An Outline of Amer-
     ican Poetry (1620-1930). New York: Coward-McCann, pp. 11,
     407, 408, 488, 567.

In poetry Stein has known and influenced poets without becoming an accessible poet herself. Hemingway and others have borrowed and developed Stein's "speech-ritual," as from "Melanctha."

7   LONDON, BLANCHE. "Gertrude Stein." New Palestine 16 (5 April):298-300.
    Rebellion and Jewish innovations in thought and style go together.

8   MORRIS, LLOYD. "Modern Style and Contemporary Writers." Galveston (Tex.) News, 17 February.
    "Four modern writers seem to have profoundly influenced contemporary literature in the element of expression or 'style.' These writers are Marcel Proust, André Gide, James Joyce and Gertrude Stein. . . . Miss Stein has attempted to exploit the secondary qualities of words; she has dissociated words from their meanings and used them as a musician might use notes for their emotional values of sound and color."

9   MUNSON, GORHAM B. Style and Form in American Prose. Garden City: Doubleday & Co., pp. 278-79.
    Stein "remains the aloof and dignified goddess of those who wish only to devote their talents to experimenting with the properties of words." Her use of time is influenced by modern painters and philosophers such as Bergson.

10 NORMAN, SYLVA. Review of Useful Knowledge. Nation and Atheneum 45 (13 April):52.
    "If Miss Stein's useful knowledge points out anything, it is that the loafing mind, equipped with language, can reach a triumph of chaotic imbecility. And for this information 207 pages are too much."

11 NOYES, ALFRED. The Opalescent Parrot: Essays. London: Sheed & Ward, pp. 51-54.
    When being daring, the Parrot chanted like Gertrude Stein.

12 PATRICE. "Gertrude Stein." Paris Comet 2 (May):26-28.
    "To appreciate Gertrude Stein it is very helpful to know her. Her personality is a short-cut to her creation. She is as American as the Covered Wagon. Herein lies the secret of her greatness. She is a contemporary American, at home in her time and from that sure poise comfortably able to consider and evaluate every other one."

13 REVIEW OF AN ACQUAINTANCE WITH DESCRIPTION. Times Literary Supplement, 18 July, p. 578.
    "It may be possible to read an entirely meaningless conjunction of words, but Miss Stein tantalizes us with occasional sentences that seem to have an ordinary meaning, and this makes

it all the easier for the ordinary reader to expect from her
what other literature gives, and naturally to be disappointed."

14   REVIEW OF USEFUL KNOWLEDGE. New Statesman 33 (13 April):22.
     "Hitherto we have been accustomed to see charlatanism adopt
modes which, though perhaps uncomfortably esoteric, were more or
less designed to capture our interest, to excite, titillate and
shock. Miss Stein knows better. She refuses every concession;
she bores us mercilessly and immoderately; and for that reason
and no other reaps considerable applause."

15   REVIEW OF USEFUL KNOWLEDGE. Times Literary Supplement,
     25 April, p. 342.
     "Though it is easy enough to assume that most writing which
is apparently and superficially sense is really nonsense, it is
harder so to put on one side what appears to be simple nonsense
as if it were quite simply nonsense. Nevertheless, we are in-
clined to think that this effort should be made."

                              1930

1   BRION, MARCEL. "Le Contrepoint poètique de Gertrude Stein."
     L'Échanges 3 (June):122-28.
         In her poetry Stein expands conventions and traditional
tastes and creates an art of austerity and renewal.

2   FAŸ, BERNARD. "Portrait de Gertrude Stein." La Revue
     Européenne, May-June, pp. 592-99.
         Stein has been a great revolutionary, but not in a polit-
ical sense. Rather she has revolutionized the literary understanding of words. Reprinted: 1931.5.

3   HUBBELL, LINDLEY WILLIAMS. "A Letter to Gertrude Stein."
     Pagany 1 (Spring):37.
         Poem honoring Stein.

4   HUGNET, GEORGES. "Virgil Thomson." Pagany 1 (January-March):
     37-38.
         Thomson and Stein--composer and librettist--are working
together on a musical.

5   JOSEPHSON, MATTHEW. Portrait of the Artist as American.
     New York: Harcourt, Brace & Co., p. 294.
         Stein is part of modern expatriation in Europe--"a brilliant
legation of American talent." Such pioneers in reverse as Stein
are followed by "the myriads of disciples, camp-followers, and
sutlers who have all variously fled from their severe, ungrateful
country."

6   MANSFIELD, KATHERINE. <u>Novels and Novelists</u>. Edited by
     J. Middleton Murray. New York: Alfred A. Knopf, pp. 283-85.
          Reprint of 1920.1.

*7   RIDING, LAURA. <u>Experts Are Puzzled</u>. London: Jonathan Cape,
     pp. 95-110.
          Cited: Liston, Maureen R. <u>Gertrude Stein: An Annotated
     Critical Bibliography</u>, p. 70.

8   WAKEFIELD, ELEANOR. "Stormy Petrel Of Modernism Is Patriotic."
     <u>New York World</u>, 18 May.
          "After living 20 years in Paris Gertrude Stein, apostle of
     ultra-modernistic writing, still considers herself the 'most
     utterly Americanized' person in the world. The mere mention of
     the word 'expatriate' drives her to uncontrollable rage. . . ."

9   WILLIAMS, WILLIAM CARLOS. "The Work of Gertrude Stein."
     <u>Pagany</u> 1 (Winter):41-46.
          "To be most useful to humanity, or to anything else for
     that matter, an art, writing, must stay art, not seeking to be
     science, philosophy, history, the humanities, or anything else
     it has been made to carry in the past. It is this enforcement
     which underlies Gertrude Stein's extension and progression to
     date." Reprinted: 1932.13; 1954.26.

                              1931

1   BALD, WAMBLY. "La Vie de Bohème." <u>Chicago Tribune</u> (Paris),
     7 April.
          Gertrude Stein said in an interview, "The natural line of
     descent is the big four: Poe to Whitman to James to myself. I
     am the last." Of her writing, she said: "You might learn that
     American writing is signalized by the consistent tendency toward
     abstraction without mysticism. There is no mysticism in my work."

2   C., R.M. "Books, Books, Books." <u>New Yorker</u> 7 (21 February):
     58-60.
          The Plain Edition of Stein's works "ought to help do away
     with a lot of this futile pointing at her, either with pride or
     the finger of scorn."

3   CURRIE, GEORGE. "Passed in Review." <u>Brooklyn Eagle</u>,
     25 February.
          Stein "was born to the da-da school of the arts. And the
     da-das are now extinct. The magnum opus before us [<u>Lucy Church
     Amiably</u>] is a volume from the grave of literature. And it cer-
     tainly reads like the ravings of a disembodied genius of a corpse."

4   EASTMAN, MAX. <u>The Literary Mind: Its Place in an Age of
     Science</u>. New York: Charles Scribner's Sons, pp. 63-64.
          Reprint of 1929.4.

                              31

5   FAŸ, BERNARD. <u>Les Romanciers américains</u>. Paris: Éditions
      Denoël et Steele, pp. 371–78.
      Reprint of 1930.2.

6   GRAMONT, ELIZABETH de. "Écrivains anglais vue de Paris."
      <u>La Revue Hébdomadaire</u> 29 (July):317–38.
      Stein loves Paris and her paintings and laughs when asked
about returning to America. Stein is full of vitality and
creativity.

7   H., B.K. "The Sideshow." <u>Providence Journal</u>, 4 February.
      "My copy of <u>Lucy Church Amiably</u> is one of the very first to
reach America, and I am am enormously proud of it, because it
symbolizes the ultimate whoozit of Miss Stein's genius. . . .
It doesn't mean ANYTHING--not even to Miss Stein."

8   HUDDLESTON, SISLEY. <u>Back to Montparnasse: Glimpses of</u>
      <u>Broadway in Bohemia</u>. Philadelphia: J.B. Lippincott Co.,
      pp. 89, 116, 122, 125, 127, 257.
      Jo Davidson thought of Gertrude Stein as always interesting.
Huddleston resented Stein's experiments being condemned, not
valued as new and valid approaches.

9   KNIGHT, GRANT C. <u>The Novel in English</u>. New York: Richard R.
      Smith, pp. 27, 358, 362.
      Stein's novels fit no known form, being totally
uncommunicative.

10   LEWIS, WYNDHAM. <u>The Apes of God</u>. London: Grayson & Grayson,
      pp. 420–21.
      Stein, possibly a genius though a woman, is a "stammerer"
who "writes like an idiot."

11   LONDON, BLANCHE. "The Career of a Modernist." <u>New York</u>
      <u>Jewish Tribune</u>, 6 March, pp. 2, 6.
      "If Miss Stein has been audacious, her revolt in her sphere,
like that of other Jewish rebels in the arts, has paved the way
for many creative writers. . . . Those who appreciate her work
need no explanation of it. To others, who scoff at and cannot
be persuaded to enjoy modernism in literature, all explanation
is futile. However, it is generally conceded that Miss Stein has
altered for the modern world the whole face and complexion of
English prose."

12   REVIEW OF <u>LUCY CHURCH AMIABLY</u>. <u>Boston Transcript</u>, 11 March.
      <u>Lucy Church Amiably</u> is a "novel" of "refined irony; so
refined, in fact, that most persons who look at it will not get
the point at all, and most of the rest will not be interested
even if they do get it."

13 SHIPLEY, JOSEPH T. The Quest for Literature: A Survey of
    Literary Criticism and the Theories of the Literary Forms.
    New York: Richard R. Smith, pp. 128, 285, 412, 427, 480-83.
        Stein demands total artistic freedom in the widest romantic
    tradition; she uses real words but employs meaning "to shade
    toward progressions."

14 STEFFENS, LINCOLN. The Autobiography of Lincoln Steffens.
    New York: Harcourt, Brace & Co., pp. 883-84.
        Stein and Pound "both encouraged the younger artists to
    despise the old forms and the old stuff, to rebel, break away
    and dare." Stein "was another powerful revolutionary leader
    who was content to be herself, do her own work, but when the
    young men and women came to her, she gave them all they would
    take."

15 W., S.M. "Two Unusual Novels and the Enigmatic Lenin."
    Harvard Crimson, 6 May, sec. 2, pp. 1, 3.
        Lucy Church Amiably must be appreciated without great study
    or frustration, for Stein writes to appeal directly to the senses.

16 WILSON, EDMUND. Axel's Castle: A Study in the Imaginative
    Literature of 1870-1930. New York: Charles Scribner's Sons,
    pp. 1, 24, 25, 129, and passim.
        With Stein one verges into the psychology of humans, for
    her prose experiments are with word procession instead of with
    literal meaning. Especially in her early work she influenced
    more storytellers of the traditional stripe.

1932

1   A[DAMS], F[RANKLIN] P. "The Conning Tower." New Bedford
    (Mass.) Mercury, 13 August.
        "Billy Phelp's chief abhorrence / Is the name of D.H.
    Lawrence. . . . / His eye will be dissolved in brine / If you
    but mention Gertrude Stein."

2   BEACH, JOSEPH WARREN. "The Twentieth Century Novel: Studies
    in Technique. New York: Century Co., pp. 528, 540.
        Perhaps Stein's Tender Buttons and Geography and Plays
    influenced Joyce. These works are "amusing, amazing, and some-
    times significant." The Making of Americans is superior, for
    here Stein avoids the "riddling" method of writing.

3   BUTTERFIELD, J.L. "The Common Round." Vancouver (B. C.)
    Daily Province, 19 September.
        "Miss Stein is undoubtedly mad. And so are the people who
    affect to see a purity of language and an attempt to make language
    more expressive in her ravings."

4   COATES, R.M. "Books, Books, Books." New Yorker 8
     (20 February):69-70.
        With Lucy Church Amiably, "one may read it for the intri-
cate delicate embroidery of its style. One may read it for the
peculiar evasive beauty of some of its passages, or for one's
interest in the author's way of probing the oddities of words.
But one should never read it--or for that matter the writings
of any other of the 'moderns'--for its plot."

5   DuPOY, ELLEN ALIX. "Gertrude Stein Gives Views on How to
     Write." Chicago Tribune, 4 June.
        How to Write shows Gertrude Stein with "no patience with
the school of thinking called subconscious thinking. It has, she
says, a tendency to sacrifice intensity and exactness to mere
rhythm. Nothing is real thinking that leads one away from the
thing to be thought of, and this is what that sister of subconscious thinking, associational thinking, does. For example, take
James Joyce."

6   KNIGHT, GRANT C. American Literature and Culture. New York:
     Ray Long & Richard R. Smith, p. 451.
        Although Anderson learned from Stein to use "the truth of
naiveté" in his writings, he avoids--one is glad to see--her
obscurity.

7   "LITERATURE: A BRAINSTORM." Tulsa Tribune, 29 July.
        "Gertrude Stein has it, but we defy anybody to tell us what
it is. Miss Stein, our readers may or may not be interested in
knowing, is regarded as something of a literary genius by those
whose minds were unbalanced during long high school periods of
picking Shakespeare to pieces with dotty professors looking for
hidden meanings, and who wound up as admirers of Eugene O'Neill.
She writes, or maybe it would be more accurate to say that she
mumbles on the typewriter. She writes things that the New York
Intelligentsia simply rave about."

8   McCARTHY, DESMOND. Criticism. New York: G.P. Putnam,
     pp. 260-72.
        Without blaming Gertrude Stein for "indulging in automatic
writing," one should blame people who encourage her. Only a self-
indulgent, childish age could produce or value her publications.

9   McINTYRE, O.O. "New York Day by Day." New York American,
     7 July.
        "Greenwich Village never turned out a more complex literary
figure than Gertrude Stein. . . . She was first of the weird
literary hedge flowers the Village nurtured and her epileptic
essays brought that elusive twin yearning--fame and fortune."

10   P., I.M. "Turns With a Bookworm." New York Herald-Tribune,
     25 September.

". . . Gertrude Stein's babblings are infantile rather than mystical; to be short about it, they haven't any rhythm at all, but 'time,' the maddening beat of a metronome, which is scansion, meter, not rhythm. . . . For anyone who needs a metronome, Gertrude Stein might be useful, though dangerous."

11   "SCENERY AND GEORGE WASHINGTON." Nation 135 (27 July):67.
      "Whatever mere academicians may say, we are convinced that Miss Gertrude Stein is not actually loony. If she were, then she would have her lucid intervals and she could not put so many words together without having them occasionally say something according to the rules of grammar and the processes of logic. Consider for example her latest composition 'Scenery and George Washington.'"

12   WARD, A.C. American Literature 1880-1930. New York: Dial Press, pp. 194-96.
      "Those who fail to discover the marks of true genius upon Gertrude Stein's writing may at least value her as a literary purge, and find her justified in the new orientation of poetry for which she is to some extent responsible. Those who dislike modernist verse will insist that she has helped to degrade poetry. . . ."

13   WILLIAMS, WILLIAM CARLOS. A Novelette and Other Prose (1921-1931). Toulon: Imprimarie F. Cabasson, pp. 103-10.
      Reprint of 1930.9.

1933

1   ADAMS, JOHN R. Review of The Autobiography of Alice B. Toklas. San Diego Union, 17 September.
      "The book is a very fine one, filled with humor and wisdom, and it is so obviously intelligent and well written that it ought to go a long way towards silencing the unintelligent ridicule of Gertrude Stein's experimental writings."

2   ADLOW, DOROTHY. "Alice B. Toklas On Picabia." Panorama, December, p. 3.
      "It was helpful, Alice B. Toklas, to read the commentary in your life story upon the thorny subject of contemporary art. Light has been shed upon darksome matters, overshadowing trees have been felled, intrusive weeds plucked so that none but the finest blooms survive. The rue de Fleurus has spoken."

3   [AGEE, JAMES.] "Stein's Way." Time 22 (11 September):57-60.
      "Plain readers are not apt to go to Gertrude Stein, with or without introduction. Mahomets in their own right, they insist that Mountain Stein should come to them. And now [with The Autobiography of Alice B. Toklas] at last the mountain has come. At

one long-deferred bound she has moved from the legendary borders
of literature into the very market-place, to face in person a
large audience of men-in-the-street."

4   "ALICE VS. GERTRUDE IN RARE NEW BOOK." Washington (D.C.)
     Daily News, 31 August.
         The Autobiography of Alice B. Toklas is "rare material,
and the author's stylistic conversion becomes a victorious individuality. She writes with more crystalline clarity than the
one-syllable purveyors of pot-boilers."

5   "AMERICANS IN PARIS." Wings 7 (September):14-15.
         Stein lives in Paris, loves conversation and reading, and
is not at all an expatriate.

6   ANDERSON, SHERWOOD. "Gertrude Stein's Kitchen." Wings 7
     (September):12-13, 26.
         Reprint of 1922.1.

7   "AUTHORS AND BOOKS." Golden Book 18 (November):4A.
         The Autobiography of Alice B. Toklas "does justice to
[Stein's] career both as a writer and as a personality, and
it is full of good gossip."

8   B., O.S. "Gertrude Stein Writes an Autobiography." Boston
     Transcript, 20 September, p. 2.
         The Autobiography of Alice B. Toklas is written in "the
rambling, repetitive style of the oral raconteur," perhaps in
the "gay contralto voice we imagine may resemble Gertrude Stein's
when she is happy."

9   BAISDEN, FRANK M. Review of The Autobiography of Alice B.
     Toklas. Chattanooga Times, 10 September.
         "The autobiography is witty, conversational and deals
almost exclusively with the personalities grouped about Miss
Stein. The impression is given (with some truth) that Gertrude
Stein was, and is, a Gibraltar of modernism--a rock of prudential
stability about which the pilots of the new movement dropped
anchor."

10   BECKER, MAY LAMBERTON. "The Reader's Guide." New York
     Herald-Tribune, 19 November.
         "If I were a book-collector instead of one whose books
might be said to collect me, I would make it my business to get
together all the more important works of everyone who appears at
full length in Miss Stein's incomparable memoirs [The Autobiography of Alice B. Toklas], and every book of importance written
about them. It would be a prudent proceeding."

11   "THE BOOK BOAT." Memphis Commercial-Appeal, 10 September.
         "We take it that you know who Gertrude Stein is, was and
has been; and if you don't you should and reading The Autobiography

of Alice B. Toklas will be a good way of finding out. . . . If
we can lay hands on a copy we'll give you a more connected
account of it later. . . . It is certain to be one of the most
important books of the season."

12   "BOOKS IN BRIEF." Christian Century 50 (20 September):1179-80.
       The Autobiography of Alice B. Toklas is interesting about
the life of Gertrude Stein and artists in France early in this
century, but the book does little to explain Stein's or the
artists' goals.

13   "BRAIN ANATOMY." Newsweek 2 (9 September):29.
       Stein's The Autobiography of Alice B. Toklas is "a book for
anyone interested in the art of this century, and for those who
like to meet Bohemians in print. The writer of memoirs is apt
to talk only about himself, even when he is describing other
people; with Gertrude Stein, this is not the case. While her
book tells in detail of her efforts to get in touch with a public which could never make head nor tale of her obscure and confused style, the bulk of it concerns the interesting men and
women who met at her house. Like the great Sam Johnson, Miss
Stein's eccentric, egoistic personality has had a much wider
influence than her works."

14   BROMFIELD, LOUIS. "Gertrude Stein, Experimenter With Words."
       New York Herald-Tribune Books, 3 September.
       The Autobiography of Alice B. Toklas will undoubtedly be
a great success: "Gertrude Stein has always wanted to write for
a large public. Being caviar never interested her, and now it
appears that her desire is to be achieved. . . . It is both
interesting and important that with this book the intelligent
reading public will be able to discern the source of an influence which hitherto has gone almost unrecognized, an influence
which has filtered down through writer after writer until it
might be said with a great deal of truth that it has set aside
American writing (and by this I mean words and sentences) from
all others in this century. Today one can pick up a book and
by the writing of a page tell whether it is written by an American or an Englishman. It seems to me that one powerful influence, emanating from 27 rue de Fleurus, is largely responsible."

15   BURTON, RICHARD. "The Crier Among the Books." Town Crier
       (New York), November.
       The Autobiography of Alice B. Toklas is "expressed in a
style childish in its banal simplicity, its lack of proper punctuation, and at times its chaos of sentence construction. The
naif egotism of it is so colossal as to make one gasp--or smile."

16   BUTCHER, FANNY. "Gertrude Stein Writes a Book in Simple
       Style." Chicago Tribune, 2 September, p. 8.

When Butcher met Stein in France the reporter left still not understanding Stein's writings but sure "that for one day I had been with a mind so many faceted, so brilliant, so intense, as I had never before met." Now The Autobiography of Alice B. Toklas proves that Stein can write clearly: "No book that I have read for months has given me the sheer pleasure in its writing that this book has."

17   C., E.J. Review of The Autobiography of Alice B. Toklas. America 50 (28 October):90.
       Despite syntactic and stylistic lapses, Stein's autobiography is full of her unusual observations and psychological insights.

18   "CABBAGES AND KINGS." Newburyport (Mass.) News, 11 September.
       Regarding The Autobiography of Alice B. Toklas, "we were interested to read the critical opinion the other day that Gertrude Stein, outstanding among modern writers, is said to be responsible for clearing much of the 'rubbish' from present-day writing. She is credited with influencing other writers to make their produce simpler--more concise. A sample of her writing proves the truth of this contention."

19   CAIRNS, HUNTINGTON. "Ex Libris." Baltimore Sun, 9 September.
       "For the present volume [The Autobiography of Alice B. Toklas] Gertrude Stein has abandoned the eccentric style of writing which she has cultivated for the past score or more years. Her style in the Autobiography is simple and straightforward and puts little strain upon the reader. It is, however, undistinguished and its syntactical aspects more than disconcerting."

20   CANTWELL, ROBERT. "Books and Reviews." New Outlook 162 (October):62.
       The Autobiography of Alice B. Toklas by Gertrude Stein "tells almost every thing anyone would want to know about her, including her tastes, prejudices, friendships, quarrels and clever sayings."

21   CHESTERTON, G.K. All I Survey: A Book of Essays. New York: Dodd, Mead & Co., pp. 62-68.
       Stein's jokes on readers will probably cause her to be quickly forgotten. Rather than Stein, W.S. Landor will be seen as progenitor of English prose of the new period.

22   COLUM, MARY M. "Mr. Crane, Miss Stein, and Expression." Forum 90 (November):334.
       "I confess that this Autobiography of Alice B. Toklas is the first work of Gertrude Stein that I have ever been able to understand, and I commend the ingenuity of it to any one who wants to write a book praising himself and making himself the

unabashed hero. . . . Miss Stein herself emerges as a very
intelligent woman, easily flattered, with a lot of physical
energy, and a certain amount of American Rotarianism; but a
woman who was undoubtedly a good art critic and probably a
picture-dealer of genius."

23   CURRIE, GEORGE. "Passed in Review." Brooklyn Eagle,
      6 September.
      "You will read this Autobiography through without fascina-
tion. You will discover you have come under the sway of a mind
which likes to meddle in other creatures' affairs, a compelling
mind intent upon having its own way. You will discover, also,
that it is a mind which can have its small moments, as witness
the bland ignoring of James Joyce, its most slavish pupil."

24   CURRIER, ISABEL R.A. "The Autobiography of a Genius."
      Worcester Telegram, 3 September, p. 6.
      The Autobiography of Alice B. Toklas "is very entertaining.
It tells all about Gertrude Stein, and her discovery of Picasso,
and her discovery of Matisse, and her discovery of Ernest
Hemingway, and her regret at the discovery of Ernest Hemingway,
and her discovery of Gertrude Stein."

25   CURTISS, MINA. Review of The Autobiography of Alice B.
      Toklas. Atlantic, November, "Bookshop."
      "Along with The Autobiography of Benjamin Franklin and The
Education of Henry Adams [Stein's autobiography] raises the question of why three books so essentially American, so revealing of
the American mind and temper, should have been written by Americans who drew so much of their sustenance both physical and
spiritual from Europe, and particularly from France."

26   DAWSON, FRANCES. "No Modern Trends in Gertrude Stein's
      Original Biography." St. Louis Globe-Democrat, 14 October.
      "The scoffers should read [The Autobiography of Alice B.
Toklas], for [Stein] has ably demonstrated that she can, if she
chooses, write other than heterodox prose."

27   DeSELINCOURT, BASIL. "The Real Gertrude Stein." Observer
      (London), 15 October.
      The Autobiography of Alice B. Toklas shows Gertrude Stein
as a stylist and--finally--a "massive and a lovable character.
She would have been great if she had not diminished herself by
eccentricities, by pushing and calling for the place which should
have fallen to her."

28   DuPOY, ELLEN ALIX. "New Poem of Gertrude Stein Given Praise."
      Chicago Tribune, 21 October, p. 15.
      After lunch Stein gave DuPoy a copy of Before the Flowers
of Friendship Faded Friendship Faded. This book is "a valuable
handbook for the poet who is interested in the basic principles

underlying his art and it is a volume to be read with delight by the layman who delights in poetry for its own sake."

29   FADIMAN, CLIFTON. "Books." New Yorker 9 (2 September):46-47.
           In The Autobiography of Alice B. Toklas, Stein "gives the whole show away. She is the Radcliffe aesthetic bluestocking, very arty, very snobbish, totally sheltered from life . . . with a dilettante passion for the 'advanced,' pathetically reminiscent of the most artificial gestures of the nineties. She is a tuft-hunter of no inconsiderable talents, possessing all the naïve arrogance of a wealthy, spoiled, very bright child and obviously endowed with the ability to impress herself upon impressionable people, particularly when they are at an impressionable age. There is no doubt that she is sufficiently eccentric to get away with the Mahatma pose, especially in the semi-infantile environment of avant-garde Parisian artistic society."

30   FAGIN, BRYLLION. "A Groundling Laughs at a Genius." Panorama, December.
           Stein "has lived in Europe for such a long time and mingled either with Europeans or with expatriate Americans that of actual American life pulsating through her pages there is little. At its best and clearest, as in Three Lives, her work is isolated, ivory tower, microscopic, arty. Of mundane problems of toil and conflict, aspiration and defeat, passion and prejudice and deed enacted against the complex of shifting forces in a changing land there is [in The Autobiography of Alice B. Toklas] no inkling."

31   FAŸ, BERNARD. "'A Rose Is a Rose.'" Saturday Review of Literature 10 (2 September):1-3.
           The Autobiography of Alice B. Toklas finally proves that Stein can write clearly, beautifully, freshly: "It seems as if all her work, all her experiments and trials had stirred up in her a more precise appreciation of all the qualities and of all the possibilities of the English language."

32   FERGUSSON, FRANCIS. "The Individualists." Hound and Horn 7 (October-December):148-52.
           In The Autobiography of Alice B. Toklas, Stein had advantage of being her "own Boswell"; here "the worshipful atmosphere of genius is maintained, yet the genius herself does the writing. . . ."

33   "'FOUR SAINTS IN THREE ACTS.'" New York Times, 31 December, sec. 9, p. 8.
           The Stein-Virgil Thomson Four Saints in Three Acts will premiere on 8 February. The composer has chosen black faces to sing Stein's intriguing lines.

34   "FRIENDS LIVE IN STEIN BOOK." Detroit Free Press, 10 September.

"Anyone who thinks of Gertrude Stein only in terms of <u>As a Wife Has a Cow a Love Story</u>, for example, will miss a lot of humor, philosophy and information about people if he fails to read <u>The Autobiography of Alice B. Toklas</u>. . . ."

35   G., J.P. "Some of the Mysteries of an Eccentric Writer Revealed in Autobiography." <u>Kansas City Star</u>, 20 September.
        With <u>The Autobiography of Alice B. Toklas</u>, we have a "narrative as provocative to literary curiosity, as clarifying of a mystical vogue in literature as in art. . . ."

36   GANNETT, LEWIS. "Books and Things." <u>New York Herald-Tribune</u>, 1 September, p. 15.
        "You can read the autobiography of Gertrude Stein, if you will, as a study of a violent personality; as a history of modern French painting and painters; or as a gossip book, a sort of <u>Mirrors of Modern Art</u>. If it attains popularity--and Miss Stein obviously expects it to be her first popular success--it will be as a gossip book. No such frank gossip book has appeared for years."

37   "GEORGE ANTHEIL IN PRINT." <u>Trenton Times-Advertiser</u>, 3 September.
        The <u>Autobiography</u> is an "odd book, of course, but an interesting one--if you can swallow that weary, bored and lofty tone of Miss Stein, who would rather write around in circles or cubes or squares than follow conventional forms. She has, to her credit, a discerning eye, a flair for expressive (albeit unintelligible) words and an uncanny mind for situation and slick dialogue."

38   "GERTRUDE STEIN." <u>Art Digest</u> 8 (15 October):22.
        Stein's ideas about art and artists give <u>The Autobiography of Alice B. Toklas</u> extraordinary interest.

39   "GERTRUDE STEIN'S BIOGRAPHY." <u>Variety</u>, 19 September.
        The <u>Autobiography</u> is "a book of chatter and gossip. Miss Stein, perhaps the most important writer of the day, in the book gossips about the people she's met. She seems to have met everyone of importance in the past and present generation."

40   "GERTRUDE STEIN'S NEW BOOK HEADS LIBRARY COLLECTION." <u>Ossining</u> (N.Y.) <u>Citizen-Register</u>, 22 September.
        "If the reader will not enjoy hearing of Gertrude Stein in this autobiography of a secretary he will at least quicken to the names which march across the pages as this woman tells of the events and the people of the present day who are so far removed from the greater herd that they are almost legendary."

41   "GERTRUDE STEIN'S REMINISCENCES." <u>Springfield</u> (Mass.) <u>Union and Republican</u>, 3 September.

"The result in the case of [The Autobiography of Alice B. Toklas] is an oddly naive and apparently unedited style, a sort of writing which turns back on itself, interpolates, mixes times and dates so that the reader in the end has no very clear idea of the chronology of Gertrude Stein's development but instead an organic sense of the person she was and is."

42   GORMAN, HERBERT. "Reading and Writing." New York Post, 1 September.
       The Autobiography of Alice B. Toklas "becomes, in essence, a history of the revolutions from Cézanne, through cubism to surrealism and even beyond."

43   GRAY, JAMES. "Grotesque Book Gives Insight on Gertrude Stein." St. Paul Dispatch, 7 September.
       As fatuous as Queen Victoria and thinking of herself as a Delphic oracle, Stein in The Autobiography of Alice B. Toklas makes points about modern art--but points less important than she believes.

44   HALL, THEODORE. "Miss Stein Looks Homeward." Washington (D.C.) Post, 8 October.
       The Autobiography of Alice B. Toklas is "an altogether delightful book, rich as a plum-pudding with good-humored, amusing and sensible tidbits."

45   HAMNETT, NINA. Laughing Torso: Reminiscences. London: Constable & Co., pp. 188-89.
       Talking with Stein made Hamnett nervous, during the years when Stein was writing The Making of Americans.

46   HANSEN, HARRY. "The First Reader." New York World-Telegram, 1 September.
       The Autobiography of Alice B. Toklas is a remarkable phenomenon. Its frankness is appealing; its very honesty is something rarely attained. Evidently Gertrude Stein has followed closely the advice of her teacher, William James, 'Keep your mind open,' and her own determination to make exact use of her eyes."

47   HOBBY, OVETA CULP. Review of The Autobiography of Alice B. Toklas. Houston Post, 19 November.
       Stein's autobiography is "a very readable, sporadically brilliant and fascinating story of life on the rue de Fleurus" and "represents a compromise in style, to say the least, for the salty old woman."

48   HONE, J.M. "The Toklas Memoirs." Week-end Review (London), 14 October.
       In The Autobiography of Alice B. Toklas "we have a book which should please even the running reader: it has really a

rich humanity about it, and peculiarities of manner are more or less limited to the deliberate monotone of the narrative, to novelties of punctuation and to a miserly use of capital letters."

49   HUBBELL, LINDLEY WILLIAMS. "The Plain Edition of Gertrude Stein." Contempo 3 (25 October):1, 4.
      "Until this year the public has steadfastly refused to read Miss Stein, preferring to deride her at a safe distance; but during recent months the tide has turned with a vengeance, and it is apparent that the reading public, having thoroughly digested the work of her followers and imitators, are turning their attention, at long last, to the far more impressive original." Now the public can read Lucy Church Amiably, Before the Flowers of Friendship Faded Friendship Faded, How to Write, and Operas and Plays.

50   HUTTON, DOUGLAS ENGLISH. "Gertrude Stein's Autobiography in 'Toklas.'" San Francisco Call-Bulletin, 23 September.
      The Autobiography of Alice B. Toklas is "written with a simplicity and a charm seldom encountered, a charm which you can understand when you reflect on the worn path that many distinguished disciples have beaten to [Stein's] atelier in Paris."

51   "INTEGER VITAE." New Statesman and Nation 6 (14 October): 450, 452.
      In The Autobiography of Alice B. Toklas, "every ingredient of happiness is here: intellectual friendship, creation, distress, more creation, publication. It is a flower. It is also a perfect piece of narrative. And the whole book is like this, from beginning to ending delightful, and brilliant with sincerity."

52   J., C.K. Review of The Autobiography of Alice B. Toklas. Apollo 18 (November):328.
      "Under the thin disguise of an autobiography of her friend and companion, Alice B. Toklas, Gertrude Stein gives her readers a lively account of artistic life in Paris before and since the War."

53   JACKSON, JOSEPH HENRY. "Gertrude Stein Reveals Self in Autobiography But Only Between Lines." San Francisco Chronicle, 8 October.
      The only reason to read The Autobiography of Alice B. Toklas is to learn the facts about Stein's life.

54   JORDAN-SMITH, PAUL. "I'll Be Judge You Be Jury." Los Angeles Times, 10 September.
      The Autobiography of Alice B. Toklas is "the one book by G.S. that an ordinary person can read. It is the first one I have ever read through, and I have found it quite amusing. It might have been written by a bright, honest child of 12 and shows a great advance over the previous work of the author. . . . I commend this volume to all who have hitherto been confused by

the work of this curious American woman. In fact, she is here
revealed as a humorous and kindly old lady."

55   KINGSBURY, EDWARD M. "Gertrude Stein Articulates at Last."
     New York Times Book Review, 3 September, p. 2.
         "Some heartless and incurable skeptics have ventured to
express doubt or denial of the existence of Alice B. Toklas.
From the followers of the school of Betsy Prig the good will
shrink in horror. In [The Autobiography of Alice B. Toklas]
full justice is done with pen and pencil to the subject of its
title, which in a sense is pleasant fiction. In fact, the book
is by and about a writer at once famous and obscure, who has a
growing audience of the fittest and of whose works, in her own
language, the world cannot be long deprived. . . ."

56   KNICKERBOCKER, WILLIAM S. "Stunning Stein." Sewanee Review
     4 (October-December):489-99.
         The Autobiography of Alice B. Toklas is foolishness and
simple-mindedness posing as writing and literary art.

57   L., B. Review of The Autobiography of Alice B. Toklas.
     Lowell (Mass.) Telegram, 8 October.
         "It is hard to place the book in its proper niche. One
might say that it is a saga of the beginning of modern art; or
of experimental English modern writing; or the story of the
social life of American expatriates on the Continent. It is
better to say that it embraces these three ideas and includes
delicious gossip, witticisms, and wisdom, couched in long rhyth-
mical, soothing sentences. The punctuation is free and easy and
so the reader does a little creative reading on his own and is
triply repaid for his efforts."

58   "L'Actualité littéraire à l'étranger." Les Nouvelles
     Littéraires, 29 July.
         Operas and Plays lacks the playful rhythm of some of
Stein's recent works and creates great communications problems.

59   LEVY, HENRY W. "Belles Lettres." American Hebrew & Jewish
     Tribune, 3 November.
         The Autobiography of Alice B. Toklas will be Stein's popu-
lar book, for here she is interested in actuality instead of in
mere creation of abstraction.

60   "LITERATURE TO DOGGIE'S LAPPING RHYTHM." Des Moines Register,
     7 September.
         "In all fairness it would appear to the bewildered reader
[of The Autobiography of Alice B. Toklas] then, that the order
of genius should be: Basket, Stein, Picasso and Whitehead. We
will await breathlessly the autobiography of the poodle."

61   LOVEMAN, AMY. "The Autobiography of Alice B. Toklas."
     <u>Book-of-the-Month Club News</u>, October.
          Whatever one's personal opinion of Gertrude Stein, her
     autobiography is clearly written, entertaining, and lucid.

62   LUTZ, MARK. "Gertrude Stein Autobiography Is Lively Series
     of Memoirs." <u>Richmond News-Leader</u>, 23 September.
          The <u>Autobiography</u> is "not a sentimental journey backward."
     Instead, the memoirs are "a lively remembrance of things past.
     [Stein's] reminiscences of Paris and the painters and writers of
     the last three decades or so are fresh and vigorous, original and
     honest; they are to be read whether or not you care a hang for
     any of the personalities who move through them. There is no
     other book quite like it, and there may never be if Miss Stein
     does not turn around and write the things she left out of <u>The
     Autobiography of Alice B. Toklas</u> in a volume to be called, let
     us say, <u>The Autobiography of Gertrude Stein</u>."

63   McBRIDE, HENRY. "Lively Local Exhibitions Are Previewed for
     Coming Winter." <u>New York Sun</u>, 14 October.
          <u>The Autobiography of Alice B. Toklas</u> is perhaps responsible
     for an improved tone in art discussions and exhibitions lately.

64   MacDONALD, ANN SPRAGUE. "The Business Woman's Bookshelf."
     <u>Independent Woman</u>, November.
          "In a time when few books are gay, Alice B. Toklas comes
     [in <u>The Autobiography</u>] to delight and amaze us with her brilliant
     and scintillating wit. But the book is far more than a mere
     amusing autobiography--it is literature of a high order, one of
     the most intrinsically important works of the year."

65   MARTIN, W.A. Review of <u>The Autobiography of Alice B. Toklas</u>.
     <u>Buffalo News</u>, 9 September.
          "Out of the dark seed of such books as <u>Geography and Plays</u>,
     <u>The Making of Americans</u> and other pieces that have amused and
     bemused simple literal folk has blossomed a masterpiece which is
     crystal clear in style, exuberantly alive, strangely fascinating
     and filled with the miracle of laughter."

66   MASLIN, MARSHALL. "All Of Us." <u>Dayton Journal</u>, 3 November.
          "Some reviewers criticize Gertrude Stein's [<u>The Autobiog-
     raphy of Alice B. Toklas</u>], call the writing bad, sneer at it.
     The Browser doesn't agree. He thinks she wrote it precisely,
     surely, with a fine talent for adjusting her manner to her mate-
     rial, and he thinks the world lost some excellent writing when
     Miss Stein decided to be a force in literature, instead of a
     creating force all by herself."

67   "MEMOIRS BY PROXY." <u>Spectator</u> 151 (13 October):496.
          <u>The Autobiography of Alice B. Toklas</u> is "as fascinating as
     a marionette show: the characters are not intended to excite the

sympathy or dislike of the reader: the scandals and quarrels are
related in a detached and matter-of-fact tone which makes the
reader forget that he is reading of the intimate affairs of
people who are still alive."

68   "MISS GERTRUDE STEIN." Times Literary Supplement, 9 November,
      p. 767.
           Sometimes in The Autobiography of Alice B. Toklas Stein is
      less than intellectually clear, but "in spite of all this the
      book is amusing and readable. . . . And, however much one may
      think that Miss Stein's experiments in writing are unfruitful,
      it cannot be denied that her attitude to the arts is entirely
      honourable."

69   "NEWS OF BOOKS." New York Times, 31 August, p. 15.
           The Autobiography of Alice B. Toklas is "less strangely
      titled and less strangely written than many of [Stein's] other
      works."

70   O., R.G. "The Crimson Bookshelf." Harvard Crimson,
      11 October.
           The Autobiography of Alice B. Toklas has "deep, rich humor"
      that separates Stein from "the stretches of the lunatic fringe."

71   O'D., G.M. "Of Books." Observer 2 (October-November):11-12.
           "Whatever one thinks of Gertrude Stein's earlier work, any-
      one at all interested in the artistic evolutionary processes of
      our age must be grateful to her for producing in The Autobiogra-
      phy of Alice B. Toklas one of the most interesting books of the
      century in its field."

72   "OBSCURANTS." New York Times, 9 April, sec. 4, p. 4.
           Stein and Joyce share credit for obscurantism in recent
      literature.

73   P., I.M. "Turns with a Bookworm." New York Herald-Tribune
      Books, 1 October, p. 19.
           The egotistical Miss Stein is amazingly interesting in her
      new work: "If a baby could write a book it would resemble The
      Autobiography of Alice B. Toklas."

74   P., R. "In Tender Slippers." Christian Science Monitor,
      9 September, p. 12.
           "The faux naif note which has caused [Stein's] writing to
      be compared to that of Gentlemen Prefer Blondes is even more
      apparent here [in The Autobiography of Alice B. Toklas], where
      the words are allowed to have a perfectly coherent meaning, than
      in her other work, but the consciousness of a sophisticated in-
      tellect behind it reminds one that it is only the indulgence of
      an entertaining drollery. And the matter itself, the gossip
      about the extraordinary number of the great, the near-great and

the pseudo-great with whom Miss Stein has been intimate, the
repeated witticisms and criticisms and portraits and anecdotes,
the neat, barbed thrusts of the description as well as the affec-
tionate warmth of much of it, constitute a continuously lively
chronicle of a vivid and important aspect of twentieth-century
life."

75   PATERSON, ISABEL. "Books and Things." New York Herald-
     Tribune, 11 July.
        ". . . there is a persistent rumor or theory that Gertrude
Stein is the actual author of the Autobiography, and we are told,
though not authoritatively, that Alice B. Toklas is a real person,
but that is not her real name; so the question of authorship is
doubly obscure. It seems to be two other fellows."

76   PATTERSON, CURTIS. Review of The Autobiography of Alice B.
     Toklas. Town and Country, 1 October, p. 50.
        The Autobiography is nostalgic, set in "the pleasant
fairyland of the past," one of "I-knew-him-when" books.

77   PIERSEL, GUTHRIE. "Gertrude Stein's Autobiography Is 'Furor
     Scribendi.'" Bloomington (Ill.) Pantagraph, 10 September,
     p. 13.
        "Not even Samuel Johnson, with his dictatorial pronounce-
ments and egotism, would have had the courage to write a biography of Boswell and make it all about Samuel Johnson. [Stein's]
vision evidently is not complete, and in her own words the words
are flat. Even more than the writings of Lord Riddell, [The
Autobiography of Alice B. Toklas] seems to be a furor loquendi,
a fury of speaking, or should I say furor scribendi?"

78   "PREJUDICIAL BOOKS." Tulsa World, 22 October.
        "A peculiarly useless and, it seems to many, atrocious
abuse of the biographical or autobiographical revival is the
perpetration of a book [The Autobiography of Alice B. Toklas]
by Gertrude Stein. Who she is and what she has done we have no
idea, but it seems she fed a lot of American expatriates in Paris.
Somehow she took a notion to write her story. There was a commo-
tion. The heavy review sections of the big papers actually took
the thing seriously and undertook to impress the readers with the
idea that it was something original and worth while. Some skeptical newspaper editors who have examined it cannot see a bit of
excuse for the book or the hogwash revivalists who touted it.
Apparently, it was an all-around piece of literary racketeering."

79   PUTNAM, SAMUEL. "Amusing With Malice." New York Sun,
     2 September.
        "This is an age of Last Things, no doubt of that. Gertrude
Stein, first of the Atlantic Monthly, and then a book-club selection for September." With the success of The Autobiography of
Alice B. Toklas, Stein will be abandoned by the "Palpitant Few
[who] will have to find a new Isis now."

80   RENNELS, MARY. Review of The Autobiography of Alice B. Toklas.
      Cleveland News, 9 September.
            Stein herself "I can understand and enjoy which, I must
      admit, is more than I can say for her writing, even knowing, as
      I do, that she has been a great influence on all modern writers."

81   REVIEW OF THE AUTOBIOGRAPHY OF ALICE B. TOKLAS. Augusta (Ga.)
      Herald, 10 September.
            "For those interested in the modern movement in art, music
      and literature and in the literary group that inhabits Paris and
      works there this book will be a treasure house."

82   REVIEW OF THE AUTOBIOGRAPHY OF ALICE B. TOKLAS. Booklist 30
      (October):47.
            "A biography of Gertrude Stein, written by herself as
      though it were the autobiography of her secretary, Alice B.
      Toklas. This device has allowed her to write with a certain
      detachment not possible in an autobiography, and with the sim-
      plicity and apparent lack of sophistication proper to her
      secretary."

83   REVIEW OF THE AUTOBIOGRAPHY OF ALICE B. TOKLAS. Christian
      Century 50 (20 September):1179.
            In spite of the material about artists in Paris, Stein
      gives little of these artists' goals.

84   REVIEW OF THE AUTOBIOGRAPHY OF ALICE B. TOKLAS. Covington
      (Ky.) Post, 19 September.
            "Lurking, for more than 20 years in a Cretan labyrinth of
      'elemental abstraction,' Gertrude Stein, at 54, has at last
      emerged to seek a share of the popular recognition hitherto
      denied her by a writing style that has elicited little save
      profane guffaws from the majority of the reading public, its
      critics, and its more intelligent writers."

85   REVIEW OF THE AUTOBIOGRAPHY OF ALICE B. TOKLAS. Durham (N.C.)
      Herald, 17 September.
            "At last Gertrude Stein comes away from her repetitive
      wrangle of words and writes for an audience to read. No more
      does she say the tree the tree the tree the cow the cow the cow
      the cow--no one gets the connection between the tree the cow and
      me but I do. She is writing the autobiography of Alice B. Toklas,
      sister as much to Lilith as she is to Gertrude Stein."

86   REVIEW OF THE AUTOBIOGRAPHY OF ALICE B. TOKLAS. Les Nouvelles
      Littéraires, 16 December.
            "Of great importance to us in our artistic life is the
      appearance of [Stein's autobiography], which with events that
      are historical, such as the banquet for Rousseau, make this book
      such a lovely narrative."

87   REVIEW OF <u>THE AUTOBIOGRAPHY OF ALICE B. TOKLAS</u>. <u>Opinion</u>,
      November.
            Stein's autobiography is "in reality a novel concerned with
      Gertrude Stein, her salon and her home life. It is witty, irrev-
      erent, and, strange to say, quite understandable."

88   REVIEW OF <u>THE AUTOBIOGRAPHY OF ALICE B. TOKLAS</u>. <u>Parnassus</u> 5
      (December):26.
            "The value of this book as a document in the history of
      American culture and its relations to the independents of Paris,
      for the two decades, 1910-1930, cannot be overlooked."

89   REVIEW OF <u>THREE LIVES</u>. <u>Christian Century</u>, 50 (8 November):
      1410-11.
            With Stein, "it is easy to believe, as competent critics
      say, that some popular writers have learned much from the study
      of her style. They might learn from it how to keep very close
      to nature in its simplest forms, how to dispense with all verbal
      ornament and sentimentality, how to write sentences and paragraphs
      and whole chapters as flat as a Nebraska landscape or a tune of
      three notes, how to get on with a very small vocabulary by the
      patient and unencumbered repetition of the same few words."

90   SCHMALHAUSEN, SAMUEL D. "The Plain Edition of Gertrude
      Stein." <u>Contempo</u> 3 (25 October):1, 4.
            "If Gertrude Stein is a genius, then I'm a Checko-
      Slovakian. But if I'm a genius, then Gertrude Stein is a
      Schizophrenic." How can anyone like Stein while the world's
      problems are unsolved?

91   SELBY, JOHN. "The Literary Guidepost." <u>Sioux City</u> (Iowa)
      <u>Journal</u>, 3 September.
            ". . . <u>The Autobiography of Alice B. Toklas</u> is merely
      Gertrude Stein's oblique way of writing about herself; of writing
      a book that most unbiased readers will feel deserves to hang very
      high in the biographical firmament, perhaps, indeed, out of
      sight."

92   SULLIVAN, FRANK. "The Autobiography of Alice B. Sullivan."
      <u>New Yorker</u> 9 (1 July):13-14.
            "I said to myself, 'Well, if Alice B. Toklas can have her
      autobiography written, I guess Alice B. Sullivan can, too,' so I
      called up my very dear friend, Frank Sullivan, and asked him if
      he would come directly over and write my autobiography. He did,
      and this is my autobiography, by Frank Sullivan."

93   "'THREE LIVES,' WORK BY GERTRUDE STEIN, TO BE ISSUED AGAIN."
      <u>Chicago Tribune</u>, 19 August, p. 8.
            Bernard Faÿ introduces the new printing of <u>Three Lives</u>,
      which now "simply cries to be read."

94   "TOKLAS AND STEIN." Macon (Ga.) News-Telegraph, 24 September.
        "There is not a dull sentence in [The Autobiography of
Alice B. Toklas]. It makes such easy and delightful reading
that one is apt to forget that it is an important description
of a woman of tremendous vitality and originality who has had
more influence, perhaps, on modern artists and writers than any
other living person."

95   "TOPICS OF THE TIMES." New York Times, 2 July, sec. 4, p. 4.
        One may recall fondly Stein's disparagement of the Germanic
genius for organization.

96   TROY, WILLIAM. "A Note on Gertrude Stein." Nation 137
        (6 September):274-75.
        ". . . among books of literary reminiscences Miss Stein's
[The Autobiography of Alice B. Toklas] is one of the richest,
wittiest, and most irreverent ever written. . . . But if it
were only this it would be an even less characteristic book by
Miss Stein than it is; others could have given us these facts,
but only Gertrude Stein can give us Gertrude Stein. And the
deepest interest of the book lies in the insight it gives us
into the genesis of the mind and sensibility reflected in
Gertrude Stein's other and more characteristic books."

97   VAN DOREN, CARL. Review of The Autobiography of Alice B.
        Toklas. Wings 7 (September):5-7.
        Stein's book is "the memoirs of a place and an age. It is
to be expected that it will be very widely read by persons eager
now for the first time to be made acquainted with that charming
world. It is certain that it will long be read as the classic
work dealing with its theme."

98   VAN VUREN, FLOYD. Review of The Autobiography of Alice B.
        Toklas. Milwaukee Journal, 5 August.
        "In writing his autobiography [of] Robinson Crusoe, Defoe
. . . did not write mostly of himself. Nor did he, as Gertrude
did in her autobiography of Alice, declare himself one of the
world's few bona fide geniuses."

99   W., F.A., Jr. "New Books on Art." American Magazine of Art
        26 (November):519.
        "Whether or not Gertrude Stein is the first twentieth cen-
tury writer, she has [with her Autobiography] succeeded in writing an intensely American book, American somehow because of its
Spanish, French, Italian, Russian, German, and British characters
and its continental scene--and not in spite of all these things.
It is American in attitude yet not vulgarized by the spectacular;
most of all American in the flow of its language. It is a good
book."

100   W., S.   "Gertrude Stein's Autobiography of Alice B. Toklas."
      Philadelphia Enquirer, 2 September.
          "Here is real bohemia with a thousand passing glances."

101   W., S.H.   "Heigh-Ho, Gertie!"   Lowell (Mass.) Telegram,
      26 November.
          "A rose is a rose is a rose is a rose, / No matter what
      others may say or suppose. / You may think what you like, put
      your thumb to your nose, / Still a rose is a rose is a rose is
      a rose."

102   WALTON, EDA LOU.   "Gertrude Stein."   Scribner's 94 (October):
      n.p.
          "In the Autobiography the reader has a collection of many
      famous people as alive and vital as Miss Stein herself. Reading
      the book is a real experience, an education in modern art and in
      modern writing."

103   WATHEN, LAWRENCE J.   "Early Work of Gertrude Stein Is Repub-
      lished."   Dallas Times-Herald, 26 November.
          "It may be that Three Lives is a landmark in American fic-
      tion. Certainly its vitality after a quarter of a century is an
      indication that it has merit. Those who read this with an open
      mind, or even those who will not read Miss Stein unprejudiced,
      cannot but recognize a powerful work of art."

104   _____.   "Gertrude Stein Reveals Herself In Autobiography."
      Dallas Times-Herald, 24 September.
          "Gertrude Stein is articulate! And that is something anal-
      ogous to the Sphinx speaking. The culture hounds will finally be
      able to read and perhaps to understand a bit of the work of a
      writer whose previous literary efforts have been classed as un-
      intelligible. Without a doubt, The Autobiography of Alice B.
      Toklas is one of the most important books of the year."

105   WELLS, CAROLYN.   "Gertrude Stein."   Chicago Herald, 18 May.
          Stein's autobiography is "as delightful as I anticipated.
      I almost never read biography, it being by nature fallacious,
      but I knew this one would be sincere. And it is."

106   "WHICH IS WHICH?"   Telegraph (London), 29 September.
          The fake attribution of authorship and the strange style
      make The Autobiography of Alice B. Toklas "as curious an auto-
      biographical book as has ever appeared."

107   WILDES, HARRY EMERSON.   "Of Making Many Books."   Philadelphia
      Public Ledger, 1 September.
          Although candidly not great, The Autobiography of Alice B.
      Toklas is "indeed enthralling to those who like literary gossip
      and especially to those who hunger after news of the exotic."

108   WILLIAMS, STANLEY T. <u>American Literature</u>. Philadelphia: J.B. Lippincott, p. 151.
     Representative of unfortunate phenomena is "hysterical experimentation, as in the typographical antics of Gertrude Stein. . . ."

109   WILSON, EDMUND. "27 rue de Fleurus." <u>New Republic</u> 76 (11 October):246–47.
     The <u>Autobiography of Alice B. Toklas</u> "has something of the character and charm of a novel--a novel of which the subject is the life which Miss Stein and Miss Toklas have made together in Paris, the salon over which they have presided, the whole complex of ideas and events of which they have become the center: a social-artistic-intellectual organism."

110   WYETH, OLA M. "Gertrude Stein's Autobiography." <u>Savannah News</u>, 22 October.
     ". . . I am wondering if [Stein's autobiography] isn't in some measure an acknowledgment that she has been too extreme, as, while it contains some of the mannerisms of her more bizarre works and an occasional sentence must be read twice before the reader gives it the right inflection, it is in general written in as fresh, pure, and effective prose as one could wish and creates a personality--that personality being Gertrude Stein herself--which is so alive, so vital, and so genuine that many who will read it will do so as I did--read other things she has written and try to understand them, because they like her so much."

111   Y., B. "Gertrude Stein's Life." <u>Chicago Herald</u>, 16 September.
     "Essentially Gertrude Stein is a writer's writer but her <u>Autobiography</u> is a book which will please many, especially those interested in modern art and the people who contributed to its development."

1934

1   AIKEN, CONRAD. "We Ask for Bread." <u>New Republic</u> 78 (4 April):219.
     The <u>Making of Americans</u> is "a complete esthetic miscalcula-tion: it is dull; and although what it seeks to communicate is interesting, the cumbersomeness of the method defeats its own end." A "miracle of proofreading" of such dullness, "merely to think of it is almost to die of exhaustion." Reprinted: 1958.1.

2   "ALAS." <u>Scholastic</u> 25 (17 November):20.
     Although the ordinary person thinks that Stein writes non-sense, she embarks soon on a tour of literary America.

3   ALSOP, JOSEPH W., Jr. "Gertrude Stein Likes to Look At
     Paintings." New York Herald-Tribune, 2 November, pp. 1, 18.
        At Stein's lecture to the Museum of Modern Art, "the con-
     gregation looked a little puzzled, but still respectful. . . .
     Puzzlement or no puzzlement, there were rounds of delight ap-
     plause over and over again all through the performance. The
     truth is that with Miss Stein there is never a dull moment.".

4   _____. "Gertrude Stein Says Children Understand Her." New
     York Herald-Tribune, 3 November.
        "Gertrude Stein, the leading literary enigma of her age,
     began the large task of explaining herself to the world in a lec-
     ture on the 'Gradual Making of The Making of Americans' last
     night at the McMillan Academic Theater of Columbia Univer-
     sity. . . . If her endeavor was scarcely crowned with the
     laurels of complete success last night, at least the audience's
     delighted response to her personality should have made her trip
     worth the trouble to her."

5   _____. "In Words Gertrude Stein Finds Emotions." New York
     Times Book Review, 25 November, p. 5.
        ". . . I found hardly a comprehensible paragraph in all of
     Portraits and Prayers. And so the book gave me less than no
     pleasure." Perhaps "the trouble lies in Miss Stein's abnormal
     sensitivity to words and arrangements of words, so strong that
     such a conglomeration as this . . . stirs in her real and meaning-
     ful emotion. Surely Miss Stein has misapprehended the very na-
     ture of words."

6   ANDERSON, SHERWOOD. "Gertrude Stein." American Spectator 2
     (April):3.
        Contrary to the idea of B.F. Skinner that Stein writes
     "automatically," she is instead a crafter of words who has
     opened doors to others' experimental approaches to writing.
     Reprinted: 1934.7.

7   _____. No Swank. Philadelphia: Centaur Press, pp. 81-85.
     Reprint of 1934.6.

8   ATHERTON, GERTRUDE. "Works vs. Play." New York American,
     6 December.
        Contrary to Stein's dislike of conventional punctuation,
     the ordinary reader in America demands such aid in reading in a
     busy life.

9   BAKER, GLADYS. "Literary Phenomenon Visits U.S." Birmingham
     (Ala.) News-Age-Herald, 2 December.
        "For the first time in my experience as a New York news-
     paper correspondent a celebrity has come to America whose right
     to fame defies analysis. . . . It is said that only 10 men in
     the world are able to explain the Einstein theory of relativity.

I doubt if that many individuals actually understand Gertrude
Stein's method of abstruse literary expression."

10   BEER, THOMAS. "Playboy: To Alice B. Toklas." American
      Mercury 32 (June):180-81.
            A reflection on Toklas shows that she errs in saying that
      John Reed was not familiar with Spain.

11   "BOOK MARKS FOR TODAY." New York World-Telegram, 14 November.
            In 1922 Stein borrowed from the American Library in Paris
      all the new books by Harold Bell Wright, Oliver Curwood and Rex
      Beach.

12   BORLAND, HAL. "Of Making Many Books." Philadelphia Public
      Ledger, 8 February.
            The Making of Americans is "merely another freak, perhaps
      not written as such but certainly achieving that status. There
      may be music in [Stein's] words, but it is the music of 'Chop-
      sticks' repeated interminably in various keys."

13   BRICKELL, HERSCHEL. "Books on Our Table." New York Post,
      22 November.
            Stein "has never written what seemed to me more utter rub-
      bish than appears in Portraits and Prayers, and it is my con-
      sidered opinion that no contemporary writer has written as much
      rubbish as Miss Stein."

14   "BRIEFER MENTION." Commonweal 19 (6 April):644.
            The Making of Americans "gives the impression of indulging
      in naiveté for its own sake, and in mystification for the sake of
      something else--just what remains uncertain. There are striking
      passages, mostly of reflection; but the whole is a drain on time
      and sympathy which the average reader will find himself unable to
      stand."

15   BROUN, HEYWOOD. "It Seems to Me." New York World-Telegram,
      7 November.
            "Chiefly I am moved to the support of Gertrude Stein be-
      cause I bridle at the popular habit of making some member of a
      minority group a joke on no better basis than the lack of will-
      ingness to conform. . . . There is in my mind a definitely
      heroic quality in the individual who sets off to discover some
      new passage to the Indies."

16   BROWN, JOHN MASON. "The Play." New York Post, 21 February.
            "Because of its music, its intention, and the magnificent
      feats in singing and maintaining poker-faces, which its colored
      actors perform, [Four Saints in Three Acts] is passably inter-
      esting as novelty. The only pity is that Miss Stein has been so
      determined to be the villain of the piece."

17   BRYANT, HELEN. "At Last! At Last!" <u>Greenwich Villager</u>,
      15 February, p. 10.
          <u>The Making of Americans</u> is long and "contains many words
      all put together in a certain way just as the drops of water in
      the sea are all put together in a certain way." On this book
      "the reader floats easily and pleasantly if he likes to float,
      for Gertrude Stein has a lively sense of rhythm and it is some-
      times very pleasant to read books with a lively sense of rhythm."

18   BURKE, KENNETH. "Two Brands of Piety." <u>Nation</u> 138
      (28 February):256-58.
          <u>Four Saints in Three Acts</u> in performance "was superb in
      its devices for ocular ingratiation. . . . Stein's nonsense, as
      reinforced by Thomson, has established its great musicality."

19   "BUT A STEIN IS A STEIN IS A STEIN." <u>New York Times Book
      Review</u>, 18 November, p. 10.
          <u>Portraits and Prayers</u> is "unadulterated Steinese. He who
      has not yet acquainted himself with Miss Stein's verbal acrobat-
      ics in their purest and most uncompromising form is here accorded
      the fullest opportunity." Yet there is "nothing in this book to
      merit more than five minutes' attention of a reasonably honest
      and intelligent mind."

20   "BUT IS IT ART?" <u>Commonweal</u> 19 (23 February):453.
          With <u>Four Saints in Three Acts</u> "the obscurity of its book
      and the eccentricity of its ballet and stage directions will
      simply arrest many in a state of personal irritation."

21   BUTCHER, FANNY. "Book Presents Gertrude Stein as She Really
      Is." <u>Chicago Tribune</u>, 10 February, p. 14.
          ". . . the great, brilliant amateur of modernity in her
      special field," Gertrude Stein in <u>The Making of Americans</u> now
      demonstrates "perfect sense." Read "slowly and with intelli-
      gence," this book clarifies "what all the word grenading has
      been about."

22   _____. "English Letters to Flower Next in U.S.: Gertrude
      Stein." <u>Chicago Tribune</u>, 26 November, p. 4.
          Last night Gertrude Stein lectured at the Arts Club on
      "What Is English Literature," declaring that the next flowering
      would be in America: ". . . some of the time everybody under-
      stood; much of the time fewer understood, but there were always
      a few who understood all of the time."

23   _____. "Stein Lectures May Clear Up Thick Writing." <u>Chicago
      Tribune</u>, 10 November, p. 12.
          Stein declared that "the modern play should reunite audi-
      ence and play"; she will lecture for two weeks in Chicago after
      she returns on November 24.

24   CANBY, HENRY SEIDEL. "Cheating at Solitaire." <u>Saturday
      Review of Literature</u> 11 (17 November):290.
            "I have never before reviewed a book I have not read. I
      have always tried to read Gertrude Stein since her earliest pub-
      lications and I have always failed. I have tried in [<u>Portraits
      and Prayers</u>], though not so hard as before, because I anticipated
      failure. My eye goes over the smooth rhythms, but my brain
      ceases to function." Reprinted: 1936.4.

25   _____. "Dressmakers for Art." <u>Saturday Review of Literature</u>
      10 (24 March):572.
            <u>Four Saints in Three Acts</u> as an opera "meant nothing,
      means nothing, and could mean nothing in itself to anyone but
      a practising psychologist. Not even the rules that govern non-
      sense stand in the way of a complete anarchy of suggestive but
      unintelligible sound."

26   CANE, MELVILLE. "Appeal to Gertrude." <u>New Yorker</u>,
      3 November.
            "Gertrude--there's a good old scout! / What's it what's it
      all about? / Hear a tortured hemisphere / Begging you to make it
      clear. / Drop a clue or slip a hint / Touching on the what-you-
      print, / What-you-print and what-there's-in'it."

27   CHEW, SAMUEL C. "O Heart, Rise Not up Against Me As a Wit-
      ness." <u>Yale Review</u>, n.s. 23 (Winter):392-93.
            <u>The Autobiography of Alice B. Toklas</u> "is a very entertain-
      ing book, too long, too generously inclusive of all the people
      who, Miss Stein thinks, are . . . entitled to its pages because
      they obtained admission to 27 rue de Fleurus; too anecdotic and
      too chaotic; but valuable for its vivid characterization of
      notable people and for its equally vivid picture of a 'movement,'
      a 'period,' a 'moment' in the world of genuinely creative art,
      seen from the vantage point of its very centre."

28   CHOTZINOFF, SAMUEL. "Four New Operas in One Week." <u>Town and
      Country</u>, 1 March.
            <u>Four Saints in Three Acts</u> was presented properly by a good
      company--"devout, zealous, rhapsodic and, apparently, all-knowing."

29   COLEMAN, ARTHUR. "After Seventeen Years Gertrude Stein's
      Novel Is Published in America." <u>Dallas News</u>, 18 February.
            <u>The Making of Americans</u> "will not be read by many; we are
      too impatient a people, and it can not be comprehended with one
      eye on the baby and half a mind on the radio; but the serious
      lover of the art of expression in words will go back to it again
      and again, seeking to penetrate its inner significances."

30   "DIAGNOSIS: THE DOCTOR MAKES AN ANALYSIS OF GERTRUDE STEIN."
      <u>Newsweek</u> 4 (8 December):24.

The editor of the Journal of the American Medical Association thinks that Gertrude Stein might suffer from palilalia, "a frequent hangover from encephalitis, better but less correctly known as 'sleeping sickness.'"

31   "THE DOWAGER'S NOTEBOOK." Chicago Herald & Examiner,
      8 November.
      At Stein's first interview in Chicago, "those of us who came, perhaps, to scoff, a little found ourselves not exactly remaining to pray . . . but at least to admire."

32   DuPOY, ELLEN ALIX. "Author Tells of a Visit to Gertrude
      Stein." Chicago Tribune, 13 October, p. 12.
      Operas and Plays shows Stein liking words "too well to be tactful with them." Her "search for the right word is to her pure adventure, and that is what she is--an adventuress at large among words and an indefatigable one."

33   E., M.M. Review of The Making of Americans. Centaur, May,
      pp. 26-28.
      "There is intelligence in the book and there is sometimes foolishness, there is humor and kindness and there is no contempt. It is the kind of book that is never quarreling with itself, that is always sure what kind of book it wants to be."

34   EGLINGTON, LAURIE. "Gertrude Stein Reveals Reactions to Home
      Country." Art News 33 (3 November):3-4.
      When interviewed, Stein speaks in a voice "which is mellow, like old port. Even the slightest remark played a part in the rhythm of her speech. . . . The effect is naturally to soothe and to make one feel the rhythm rather than the sense of what she said, although the latter was perfectly clear."

35   ELDRIDGE, PAUL. Review of The Making of Americans. Oklahoma
      City Oklahoman, 25 February.
      In her long novel, Stein is not merely eccentric: "She is, on the contrary, a sincere artist saying in a new way something individual to us about the making of Americans."

36   ERNEST, CLIFFORD. "Gertrude Stein Gets Reporters That Way
      Too." Chicago Daily News, 8 November.
      In Chicago for the premiere of Four Saints in Three Acts, Stein "explained little and denied much. She never conceded that she uses the stream of consciousness method in literary style, as James Joyce did in Ulysses, nor is her composition of the cult of Dadism, the literary nihilism of two decades ago."

37   FADIMAN, CLIFTON. "Books." New Yorker 9 (10 February):78-79.
      "With The Making of Americans, this department can offer not the least assistance. Dimly I grasp that this is a sort of novel, a generalized history of an American family. Also I have

read far enough to realize that Miss Stein is a past master of
making nothing happen very slowly."

38 _____. "Books." New Yorker 10 (17 November):86.
    "... if you would like to meet Miss Stein's friends with-
out benefit of grammar, or watch Carl Van Vechten impaled on a
sharp phrase, you had better leap for Portraits and Prayers. I
do not know which of these pieces . . . are portraits and which
prayers. Perhaps most of them are prayers; they have the shrill,
incantatory quality of the rituals of a small child at solitary
play."

39 FAŸ, BERNARD. "Gertrude Stein et ses souvenirs." Le Figaro,
    27 October.
    Because Stein innovated in words and style, the public from
1904 to 1933 viewed her as a charlatan. Publication of her memoirs was necessary for the public to take her seriously as an
artist.

40 FERGUSSON, FRANCIS. "The Making of Gertrude Stein."
    Saturday Review of Literature 10 (17 February):489.
    In The Making of Americans one finds "a prose from which
all the suggestiveness, many of the familiar denotations, and all
the commonsense light have been removed. The words are English,
but they are used in a special limited sense like the technical
vocabulary of some new science. [Stein] would never call a spade
a spade; she would invent a phrase that would turn it into a
diagram of itself."

41 FLUTTERBYE, Mme. "In Mayfair." New York Journal, 17 November.
    Yesterday at the Ritz "Miss Stein captured her audience by
her frankness, humor and total lack of artificiality . . . [and]
she talked to everyone just as if they were intimate friends.
She rested a pair of steel-rimmed spectacles on the bridge of
her nose while she read from her notes . . . and from time to
time, as if for emphasis, she rubbed her left hand through her
short cropped grey hair."

42 "FOUR SAINTS IN THREE ACTS 1 OF MANY." New York Sun,
    6 November, p. 6.
    At a Christmas Relief Fund lecture, Stein's explanation of
Four Saints in Three Acts "constituted a little journey into the
literary fourth dimension of her heavens, practically all of whom
registered either amusement or bewilderment, and sometimes the
two alternately or even at the same time."

43 "FREEDOM OF CHOICE." Commonweal 21 (16 November):95.
    Stein's lecture on pictures was a success in New York:
"Some claim she is exhibiting the release of Nirvana; some that
she knows the vitality of art; some that she is a dilettante
amusing decadent exploiters; some that she points a new and
revolutionary way."

44   GANNETT, LEWIS. "Books and Things." <u>New York Herald-Tribune</u>,
        7 November.
        "Gertrude Stein is a jolly, bright-eyed, wholly natural,
likeable, laughing human being; I met her and liked her--and
Alice B. Toklas--at Random House's party for her last week. She
insisted so amiably, so without pose, so convincingly, that her
prose really makes sense to any one who can read with his ears
as well as his eyes, that I tried very hard to make sense of
<u>Portraits and Prayers</u>. I regret to report failure."

45   GARDNER, VIRGINIA. "Stein Arrival Exciting Time to Committee."
        <u>Chicago Tribune</u>, 8 November, p. 19.
        Stein and Toklas arrived yesterday, an hour late, for the
Chicago premiere of <u>Four Saints in Three Acts</u>. Stein pinched
the cheek of a questioner who wondered "whether her work could
be called self-conscious unconsciousness."

46   "GERTRUDE STEIN ARRIVES AND BAFFLES REPORTERS BY MAKING HER-
        SELF CLEAR." <u>New York Times</u>, 25 October, p. 25.
        "Miss Stein surprised interviewers by speaking a language
everyone could understand," and she spoke none of her famous non-
sensical lines. She denied that her writings were insane but
refused to discuss politics.

47   "GERTRUDE STEIN BREAKS INTO OPERA." <u>Literary Digest</u> 117
        (3 February):21.
        With <u>Four Saints in Three Acts</u>, "since the words of the
opera convey no coherent story much depends on the choreography.
It thus becomes a ballet of action with a singing accompaniment."

48   "GERTRUDE STEIN, CHAMPION OBSCURANTIST AT 60, IS COMING BACK
        TO U.S. AFTER 30 YEARS ABROAD." <u>New York World-Telegram</u>,
        6 October.
        Stein's lectures "will deal with literature, especially
her own work, which she sincerely considers as a cornerstone of
modern American literature."

49   "GERTRUDE STEIN COMES HOME, WORDS AND THOUGHTS ASKEW."
        <u>New York Sun</u>, 24 October, pp. 1, 15.
        "Gertrude Stein and Alice B. Toklas both together and not
like together in boats traveling alike but different, oh how
different got to America, back to America today."

50   "GERTRUDE STEIN COMES TO BROADWAY." <u>Literary Digest</u> 117
        (10 March):22.
        Whether <u>Four Saints in Three Acts</u> "is the inspiration for
a new school of opera is difficult to predict. It was a unique
experience and likely to remain so.

51   "GERTRUDE STEIN: HER WORDS 'DO GET UNDER THEIR SKIN.'"
        <u>Newsweek</u> 4 (27 October):24.

Gertrude Stein has returned to the United States:
"Masculine-looking, dressed in weird, baggy clothes, woolen
socks, and 'sensible' shoes, she sits back resembling Jo
Davidson's monolithic statue of her. Crazy about arguments,
she chatters ceaselessly while the audience flies into impas-
sioned contradiction."

52   "GERTRUDE STEIN HOME AFTER THIRTY-ONE YEARS." Literary Digest
      118 (3 November):34.
         Stein came home to America "a large, warm, witty woman, who
      likes her groceries and admits she does." Toklas was "a small,
      thin-faced, mouse-like woman."

53   "GERTRUDE STEIN, HOME, UPHOLDS HER SIMPLICITY." New York
      Herald-Tribune, 25 October.
         Sort of a "matron saint" in Paris, Stein has come home to
      explain her art and accept the laurels due her.

54   "GERTRUDE STEIN IN GREENWICH." New York Times, 4 November,
      sec. 2, p. 8.
         Stein and Toklas are guests of Alfred Harcourt in Greenwich,
      Conn., and attended the Yale football game.

55   "GERTRUDE STEIN IS RETURNING IN FALL TO LECTURE." New York
      Herald-Tribune, 14 June.
         Although Stein "has not agreed definitely to make the tour,
      she wishes to return to this country and is willing to stay as
      long as her lectures make it necessary."

56   "GERTRUDE STEIN LIKES PREPOSITION, BUT QUESTION MARK IS HER
      POISON." New York Herald-Tribune, 17 November.
         "Piloted a little breathlessly by Miss Alice B. Toklas,
      Miss Gertrude Stein hurried around town yesterday spreading en-
      lightenment concerning her esoteric style, observing that a play
      was like a landscape and a landscape like a play, and confessing
      that of the sundry parts of speech she liked prepositions best
      of all."

57   "GERTRUDE STEIN MAY RETURN TO U.S." Chicago Herald & Examiner,
      7 December.
         The idea that Stein may return to live in America causes
      pleasure, for most artists save money desperately to leave
      Chicago.

58   "GERTRUDE STEIN, PROPHET." New York World-Telegram,
      3 November.
         "Gertrude Stein comes to America a mortal of rare importance,
      understandable best to those who can step out of the literary con-
      ventions as easily as Miss Stein steps out of her Paris home for
      a walk around the neighborhood. It is possible that Gertrude
      Stein, living on alien soil, far from Yankee inhibitions and

being fundamentally not fantastic but as solid and real as a
ditchdigger or a child weaving dreams and rhythms in her fancy,
has contributed to a super-literature, which, she says, is for
the great-grandchildren."

59   "GERTRUDE STEIN REBUKES CRITIC AT PARIS DINNER." New York
       Herald-Tribune, 4 January.
          To a doubter Stein stated: "Present day geniuses can no
       more help doing what they are doing than you can help not under-
       standing it, but if you think we do it for effect and to make a
       sensation, you're crazy."

60   "GERTRUDE STEIN RUNNETH OVER AND OVER. . . ." Philadelphia
       Record, 16 November.
          After lecturing an hour on writing, Stein "spent just ten
       minutes squelching befuddled questions of her audience. Finally
       she bowed off the stage like a chuckling school-marm, leaving
       her bejeweled audience feeling like a bunch of children who
       went up on the stage to try to fool the magician."

61   GILDER, ROSAMOND. "Prepare for Plays." Theatre Arts Monthly
       18 (May):385-86.
          Four Saints in Three Acts is a good example of current
       drama that relies on "explanation, exposition and the airing of
       personal opinion."

62   GILMAN, LAWRENCE. "Music." New York Herald-Tribune,
       21 February.
          With Four Saints in Three Acts, "one rather regrets,
       indeed, that Mr. Thomson (evidently a good and loyal friend)
       should have chosen to tie his Muse to the fame of so clearly
       dated a figure as the sibylline Gertrude."

63   GOLDBERG, ISAAC. "A Stein On The Table." Panorama, April,
       p. 8.
          Stein's present popularity, revealed by The Autobiography
       of Alice B. Toklas, is a phenomenon based on advertising and
       promotion rather than on merit: "As a literary phenomenon,
       despite all statements to the contrary, Gertrude Stein's influ-
       ence has been nil. She has been a social influence in the lit-
       erary careers of certain young Americans; that is all."

64   GRAY, JAMES. "Gertrude Stein's U.S. Visit in Fall Awaited
       Eagerly." St. Paul Dispatch, 16 July.
          ". . . because she is such an absolutely unique figure,
       it will be much more stimulating and refreshing to hear Gertrude
       Stein on any subject than to hear, as we have had to do,
       Christopher Morley making bad puns about Shakespeare and Ben
       Jonson, or Louis Untermeyer consuming an hour with inferior
       vaudeville gags."

65   GREGORY, ALEXANDER. Review of The Making of Americans.
      Debate Magazine, April.
          In The Making of Americans Stein is unscientifically and
      inaccurately remarking about language, creating a private com-
      munication in a private world.

66   H., H. "Four Saints' Acts Is Acts in 30 Acts." New York
      Times, 9 February, p. 22.
          The premiere of Four Saints in Three Acts in Hartford satis-
      fied all expectations of a bizarre performance: "The fabulous
      rumors of an all-Negro cast singing in tan-face and costumed in
      cellophane; of a libretto whose words were unintelligible and an
      opera whose stage directions were set to music. . . ."

67   H., N. "Hypnotic Writing." New York Sun, 17 February, p. 17.
          In The Making of Americans, "Miss Stein's prose has the
      ability to lull the reader into a kind of hypnotic trance, and
      you find yourself ten pages gone and you have forgotten every
      word of it."

68   HALL, THEODORE. "No End of Books." Washington Post,
      15 November.
          Gertrude Stein, "I now see, is one of our prime humorists.
      Monday night, she gave a talk over the air, voicing some of the
      Steinian axioms in a smooth, rather sing-song voice, which was
      calculated to take in all but the wary."

69   HANSEN, HARRY. "The First Reader." New York World-Telegram,
      8 February.
          In comparison with such an author as Joseph Conrad, Stein
      in The Making of Americans creates merely headache.

70   _____. "The First Reader." New York World-Telegram,
      8 November.
          The only clear sentence in Portraits and Prayers is the
      dedication.

71   HARTWICK, HARRY. The Foreground of American Fiction. New
      York: American Book Co., pp. 37, 123, 139, 140, 141, 142,
      158, 380.
          Stein is part of literary expressionism--based "on the
      principle that every man's style should be as unique as his
      fingerprints."

72   HENDERSON, W.J. "American Opera Keeps Struggling." American
      Mercury 32 (May):104-5.
          "This music lover does not think Four Saints worth so much
      [intellectual] labor of the soul. It is a good show, it has a
      certain emotional quality which cannot be described, and it
      transforms undefinable speech and action into something spe-
      cious and plausible."

73   HEWETT, AINSLIE. "The Making of Gertrude Stein." Louisville
     Courier-Journal, 18 February.
         Surely Henry James and William James are responsible for
     Stein's wordiness in The Making of Americans.

74   HICKOK, VIRGINIA. "Tea With Gertrude Stein." Profile, July,
     pp. 5, 25.
         Being reduced to babble at Stein's talk, the author recalls,
     ". . . in another five minutes we were all sitting on the floor,
     chattering like monkeys . . . exactly like them."

75   HILL, EDWIN C. "Human Side of the News." New York Journal,
     19 October.
         "A dark, plump woman of sixty, whose masculine features
     are attenuated by a decidedly mannish haircut, is due soon to
     step off a trans-Atlantic liner in New York and to receive col-
     umns of notices from the press and the magazines. She brings a
     message which will be greeted with laughter, praise, scorn,
     interest and disdain, all depending on the person who receives it."

76   HOFMAN, W.J.V. "Contemporary Portraits: Gertrude Stein."
     Literary America 1 (December):17-19.
         Stein is visiting America, confounding the critics, pleas-
     ing the audiences, and forcing Americans to think about art.

77   HYNDS, REED. "Gertrude Stein in 'Portraits and Prayers.'"
     St. Louis Star-Times, 16 November.
         Despite the unclarity of Portraits and Prayers, Stein "is
     a phenomenon for which we may be thankful. She has been an ec-
     centric figure, one live and exciting; quixotic and stimulating--
     in a field all too often dull and prosaic. And--to many--she has
     been a great, good joke. The world needs colorful characters of
     her sort."

78   "IF YOU WERE IN NEW YORK." Arts and Decoration 42 (December):
     50.
         "The nearest thing to a dignified riot that has hit these
     shores in some time was the disembarking of Miss Gertrude Stein,
     lately of Paris, France, and Four Saints in Three Acts. She
     spoke at the Colony Club one evening--the first time in America--
     to a group of the members of the Museum of Modern Art. . . . It
     was, as far as anyone could see, a scoop for the museum . . . and
     for anyone who could get a ticket."

79   ISAACS, EDITH J.R. "Theatre Magic." Theatre Arts Monthly
     18 (April):246-48.
         Four Saints in Three Acts was the month's "pleasantest
     event": "There are still a great many intelligent people who
     think that the victory of Four Saints was won by Gertrude Stein.
     But, though many of them are under thirty, they are very old peo-
     ple." For the music and staging redeemed Stein's "often ugly and
     unsingable" lyrics.

80   K., M.L. "Gertrude Stein and the Pigeon." New York Times,
      8 November, p. 22.
          Pigeons would be pleased to have Stein throw seeds to them.

81   KAUFMAN, SAMUEL. "Today's New Books." Brooklyn Times-Union,
      3 December.
          In Portraits and Prayers, "the personages dealt with could
      hardly resent anything the author said of them, for they will
      never know. The book seems to be written in an intricate code
      for which no key is furnished."

82   KING, BILL. "All-American Stein." New York American,
      20 November.
          At her lecture to the Radcliffe College faculty, "Miss
      Stein seemed a bit familiar to the football writers. They agreed
      that she would look a lot like Pop Warner if that sage of the
      gridiron was as short as Andy Kerr and had a closer haircut."

83   KIRNON, HODGE. "Seeing Difference." New York Times,
      2 November, p. 22.
          Negroes, contrary to Stein's claim, certainly can see dif-
      ferences in photographs of similar objects and, compared to
      Edna St. Vincent Millay, Stein writes "twaddle."

84   KIRSCHTEN, ERNEST. "Stein Smile Wins Radcliffe and Words
      Bring Laugh." Boston American, 20 November.
          Stein "has poise. She is perfectly at ease, and she has
      the gift of making every one who hears her feel that she is an
      old and dear friend. Her voice is friendly. Her eyes have a
      cheerful sparkle. And there is that smile. It cannot be re-
      sisted. Hollywood could learn much from her."

85   KLEIN, NORMAN. "Gertrude (Tender Buttons) Stein Arrives,"
      New York Post, 24 October, pp. 1, 3.
          "That grand old expatriate from life and the American
      scene, Gertrude Stein, sixtyish, returned to these shores after
      thirty-one cloistered years in Paris. She brought with her
      Alice B. Toklas, her queer, birdlike shadow."

86   KRUTCH, JOSEPH WOOD. "A Prepare for Saints." Nation 138
      (4 April):396, 398.
          "Four Saints in Three Acts is a success because all its
      elements--the dialogue, the music, the pantomime, and the spark-
      ling cellophane decor--go so well with one another while remaining
      totally irrelevant to life, logic, or common sense."

87   KYES, JOHN F. "Four Saints in Three Acts--An Opera of If,
      When and But." Musical America, 25 February.
          The Hartford premiere of Four Saints in Three Acts "at
      least demonstrates that music, motion, color, such as artists
      can devise, do in themselves offer a fabric of enjoyment and

even illusion, though utterly unsupported by conventional opera props of plot, lucid speech, and hectic action."

88   "LA STEIN'S LITTLE JOKE." Music News, 15 November.
     Because plots do not matter in opera, Stein and Thomson in Four Saints in Three Acts perhaps are creating a "mental debauch."

89   "LITERARY SNOBBERY." New York Times, 6 February, p. 18.
     Stein continues to function after the vogue of obscurantism, "protecting a vested interest, like a losing trolley line that keeps going because it has a franchise."

90   LOVEMAN, AMY. "Clearing House." Saturday Review of Literature 11 (22 December):388.
     List of Stein books recommended to readers.

91   LUTZ, MARK. "Literal Reading Suggested For Portraitures By Stein." Richmond News-Leader, 15 November.
     The portraits in Portraits and Prayers "all are typical. In each you will find the essence of the sitter and all that Miss Stein knows about him, with all the obscuring and confusing outerness pared away."

92   McCULLOUGH, JOHN M. "Stein Is Stein and Art Is Art, Alas, Alas!" Philadelphia Inquirer, 16 November, p. 5.
     You either take Stein as she is or "maybe you'll tip your hat to a Philadelphia lamp-post, which professes an inner consciousness made only of sundry watt-hours of electric current and a cast iron constitution."

93   MacDIARMID, HUGH. At the Sign of the Thistle. London: Stanley Nott, pp. 33-56.
     By eliminating the cult of personality from her writings, Stein opens ways to creation of a pure literature.

94   McEVOY, J.P. "Letters I Would Love to Mail." New York American, 6 March.
     "A letter a letter I will write should write can write a letter to you I am writing a letter to you and that's that. . . ."

95   MANNES, MARYA. "Vogue's Spotlight." Vogue, 15 March.
     In Four Saints in Three Acts, "I am torn, now, between wondering whether the opera would have been twice as good if the words had had sense, and suspecting that logic and intelligibility would have ruined it."

96   MATTHEWS, T.S. "Gertrude Stein Comes Home." New Republic 81 (5 December):100-101.
     Stein's triumphal return to the U.S. proves that even in hard times people want circuses. Mere publicity does not, she could learn, equal importance. Reprinted: 1935.38.

97   "MISS KING DISCUSSES GERTRUDE STEIN'S ART." <u>Bryn Mawr College News</u>, 21 February, pp. 1, 4.
     "One should start to understand Gertrude Stein by parallels. Living in Paris, in the midst of painting, she could not help being affected by the successive influences which affected painting"--impressionism, Cézanne, and cubism.

98   "MISS STEIN A WOW." <u>New York Sun</u>, 1 November.
     "Miss Gertrude Stein may take a lot of understanding, but New Yorkers apparently are determined to make the attempt. On the eve of her first lecture here Miss Stein finds herself in the enviable position of a smash hit, a sell-out--in another word, a wow."

99   "MISS STEIN CANCELS 2 LECTURES SCHEDULED AT U. OF C. CAMPUS." <u>Chicago Tribune</u>, 16 November, p. 21.
     Stein will not lecture at the University of Chicago on 27-28 November, as scheduled, because the sponsors have allowed more than 500 people to purchase tickets for each lecture.

100   "MISS STEIN PUZZLE TO PSYCHIATRISTS." <u>New York Times</u>, 29 November, p. 29.
     In a current issue of the <u>Journal of the American Medical Association</u>, Gertrude Stein is accused of indulging in abnormal behavior for her seemingly meaningless and random verbiage.

101   "MISS STEIN RETURNS TO HER NATIVE LAND." <u>Nation</u> 139 (7 November):521.
     Arriving for an American tour, Stein "was genial to reporters, gasped amiably at the New York skyline, and was not ashamed of considerable ignorance of American affairs. . . . We admire and like her, and wish her a merry and profitable home-coming."

102   "MISS STEIN SPEAKS TO BEWILDERED 500." <u>New York Times</u>, 2 November, p. 25.
     "Gertrude Stein made her American debut as a speaker last night before an audience that packed the ballroom of the Colony Club, listened intently for nearly an hour to the frequently puzzling involutions and repetitions of her diction and went away afterward to argue."

103   "MISS STEIN USES SAINTS AS SCENERY." <u>New York Times</u>, 17 November, p. 13.
     Stein explained that the saints in <u>Four Saints in Three Acts</u> are background figures with not much else to do but converse. Later at a Columbia University lecture she won her audience with a lecture on grammar in literature.

104   MITCHELL, JOSEPH. "Gerty Gerty Stein Stein Is Back Home Home Back." <u>New York World-Telegram</u>, 24 October, pp. 1, 2.

"Gertrude Stein, 60, a good-natured lady with a masculine haircut, large eyes and a grouse-hunter's cap, whose poems and novels composed of weirdly disassociated words have been compared to Cab Calloway's hi-de-ho and with the ravings of a victim of schizophrenia, arrived from Paris today. . . ."

105   MOFFETT, INDIA. "Audience Eyes a Simple Gown at Stein Opera." Chicago Tribune, 8 November, p. 19.
       The best Chicago society at the premiere of Four Saints in Three Acts were ignored as all looked at Stein, "short-haired, simply gowned."

106   MOORE, EDWARD. "Leave Common Sense at Home and You Can Enjoy This Opera." Chicago Tribune, 8 November, p. 19.
       ". . . the most discussed musical entertainment of the last quarter century," Four Saints in Three Acts opened in Chicago last night: "Dismiss the canons of what is ordinarily termed common good sense when you go to see it and let yourself drift into another world."

107   _____. "New Opera Has Fine Music but Lacks Meaning." Chicago Tribune, 4 March, sec. 7, p. 4.
       Four Saints in Three Acts, "a distinct curiosity," has attracted American intelligentsia even though the libretto "avowedly does not make sense. . . ."

108   MURRAY, MARIAN. "'Four Saints' Cheered at World Premiere." Hartford Times, 9 February.
       Yesterday's premiere of Four Saints in Three Acts "uses tradition as a spring board and leaps into uncharted waters which Hartford found very pleasing."

109   NASH, OGDEN. "They Don't Speak English in Paris." New York American, 22 March.
       "I wish that I could get in line / And shout the praises of Gertrude Stein. . . ."

110   NATHAN, GEORGE JEAN. "The Theatre." Vanity Fair 42 (May):49.
       In Four Saints in Three Acts, Stein holds "that the meaning and sense of words are of infinitely less significance than their sound and rhythm"; but Stein in practice does not produce beauty but cacaphony.

111   NELSON, JOHN HERBERT. Review of The Autobiography of Alice B. Toklas. American Literature 5 (January):392-94.
       Full of anecdote and judgment--even of the author--The Autobiography "mirrors the vigorous mind and the strong and engaging personality which have left their imprint on those with whom she has associated."

112   "NEW STEIN EFFORT PUZZLE TO READER." <u>Detroit Free Press</u>,
      18 February.
      "Gertrude Stein has written in <u>The Making of Americans</u>
another of those books which may be quite clear to her but which,
to a raft of fairly discriminating persons, will be just a sticky
hodgepodge."

113   P., F.W. "Reflections on Intelligibility vs. Miss Stein."
      <u>Philadelphia Inquirer</u>, 24 February.
      It is unwise to expect a public to be educated to under-
stand a work of art that cannot explain itself. Only members of
the Stein fan club will claim understanding of <u>The Making of
Americans</u>.

114   "PALILALIA AND GERTRUDE STEIN." <u>Journal of the American
      Medical Association</u> 103 (1 December):1711-12.
      Peculiarities in <u>Four Saints in Three Acts</u> make one wonder
whether Stein is subject to charges of hoaxing or of palilalia--
"a form of speech disorder in which the patient repeats many
times a word, a phrase or a sentence which he has just spoken."

115   "PERFECTING LANGUAGE." <u>New York Times</u>, 19 November, p. 16.
      Stein seems inconsistent in eschewing punctuation, for she
keeps apostrophes for possessives and periods for demarcation of
sentences. She even uses a semicolon and is revealed as impure
of innovation.

116   "PRINCETON DAZED BY GERTRUDE STEIN." <u>New York Times</u>,
      6 November, p. 23.
      "After the lecture" at Princeton University, "Miss Stein
left the platform and her listeners left the hall apparently
with the realization that their education, their education had
been sadly neglected, neglected."

117   REDMAN, BEN RAY. "Stein." <u>New York Herald-Tribune</u>, 11 March.
      Stein's <u>The Making of Americans</u> is "capable of plunging the
reader into a troubled sleep. The soporific effect of her prose
is undeniable, but the slumber she produces is not sound."

118   REVIEW OF <u>THE AUTOBIOGRAPHY OF ALICE B. TOKLAS</u>. <u>Literary
      America</u> 1 (April):33.
      "Though perhaps not a new heaven and earth so poignantly
needed has Miss Stein created, but certainly the lady has dropped
upon our heads--some very receptive ones--an original literary
style."

119   REVIEW OF <u>FOUR SAINTS IN THREE ACTS</u>. <u>Booklist</u> 30 (June):306.
      In Stein's "most baffling manner," this libretto is
"probably of interest only to those who have seen the performance, or to students of this author's work."

120   REVIEW OF FOUR SAINTS IN THREE ACTS. Musical Educators'
       Journal, December.
            "Four Saints in Three Acts will not please you if you look
       for a Tosca or Die Walküre. No, indeed. But if you can accept
       it for what it is, there's bound to be some measure of enjoyment
       in it for you."

121   REVIEW OF THE MAKING OF AMERICANS. Booklist 30 (March):222.
            A popularly printed edition of The Making of Americans is
       "the story of an American family and of their relationship with
       members of their group, told with a wealth of detail, but some-
       what abridged for this edition. Its appeal is chiefly literary;
       in spite of the interest aroused by The Autobiography of Alice B.
       Toklas it is not likely to be popular as a story."

122   REVIEW OF THE MAKING OF AMERICANS. Catholic World 139
       (April):87-88.
            ". . . Gertrude terrible terrible awful Gertrude do stop
       hear a stop stop stop mercy mercy. . . ."

123   ROGERS, W.G. "Local Color." Springfield (Mass.) Union,
       31 October.
            "Miss Stein speaks for the living artist better than anyone
       else can because she speaks her own language . . . a language
       which is her own personal medium, the peculiar, unique response
       to her own search for the only possible way of saying the things
       which she alone of all possible persons has been driven to say.
       Before she is a mouthpiece for painting, she is a writer."

124   _____. "Stein Sits Listening to America After Thirty-One
       Years' Absence." Springfield (Mass.) Union, 11 November.
            "What America thinks of [Stein] is not particularly impor-
       tant, because her personal integrity is beyond the need of praise
       and impervious to misunderstanding. It is important, though,
       that America should not fail itself, should not be less than
       itself to the listening and the seeing of this American who has
       remained true to her American-ness during 31 (or rather 60)
       years."

125   ROSENFELD, PAUL. "Prepare for Saints." New Republic 78
       (21 February):48.
            "For all its lousiness, Four Saints in Three Acts, as it
       is called, definitely attests the simpiternal attractiveness and
       power of the Catholic religion, its mysteries, its ritual, the
       figures of its illustrious champions; assuring them all a future
       which present conditions might appear to belittle."

126   "SAINTS IN CELLOPHANE." Time 23 (19 February):35.
            The sets and costumes for Four Saints in Three Acts were
       intriguing, but, as usual, the Gertrude Stein text "provided the
       controversy."

127   SCHNEIDER, ISADOR. "Home Girl Makes Good." <u>New Masses</u> 13
      (27 November):21-22.
            "I am sure of course that Miss Stein enjoys her own work,
      but I am not sure that she understands it. Perhaps, if she con-
      sidered the phenomenon of herself, which has occupied her all
      these years, considers it as a Marxist would, she might under-
      stand it. But she would not find it amusing. She would in fact
      find it terrifying. And she would know, at last, why she is the
      only success among the escapists."

128   SCHRIFTGIESSER, KARL. "Gibberish Of Gertrude Stein Seen As
      Attempt To Freshen Language." <u>Washington Post</u>, 23 December.
            ". . . I do not think all that Miss Stein has written is
      gibberish; I do not believe that she is the perpetrator of a lit-
      erary hoax; nor do I swallow all the kind things that have been
      said about her. . . . Miss Stein seems to me to be a fairly sim-
      ple person, quite possible of understanding, whose importance as
      a writer lies almost entirely in her way of saying whatever it
      is she has been trying to say."

129   SEELEY, EVELYN. "Alice Toklas Hides in Shadows of Stein."
      <u>New York World-Telegram</u>, 25 October.
            Toklas "is not exactly plain; she is unusual looking.
      Gertrude Stein, speaking of her in a vivid red gown, found her
      exotic. She did not look exotic but mouselike, in her gray fur
      cloak and her little astrakhan cap pulled low over her brow. Her
      hair was dark and curly, her eyes gray and rather sad. Her voice
      seemed tired. She was nervous."

130   _____. "Stein, the Bohemian, Doesn't See Our Life." <u>New
      York World-Telegram</u>, 13 November.
            Stein "has captured our imagination for a time, given us a
      passing nostalgia for our own enchanted Bohemian days which we
      grew out of reluctantly but to which we would not return. But
      she also makes us wonder, as she walks down the Avenue--so un-
      related to our contemporary life:--'If nobody baked a cake would
      you put frosting on it?'"

131   SELDES, GILBERT. "Delight in the Theatre." <u>Modern Music</u> 11
      (March-April):138-41.
            With <u>Four Saints in Three Acts</u>, "I prefer that part of the
      method of <u>James Joyce</u> in which he packs ten meanings into a word
      to the method of Gertrude Stein by which she strips all meaning
      from words. Yet the opera pleased me more than all but half a
      dozen in the traditional repertory. It has fantasy and vigor.
      It can be taken as a gigantic piece of mystification and a huge
      joke; it certainly should not be taken without laughter. It has
      taste and liveliness, humor and feeling."

132   "SHORTER NOTICES." <u>Catholic World</u> 139 (April):123-24.
            After reading <u>The Making of Americans</u>, "what the reviewer
      felt when this stein splashed into the stream of consciousness:

Gertrude Stein verbosity boldness nonsense originality intelligentsia claque paid advertising furors vogue prestige excitement critics friendly public buffaloed sales pressure booksellers
happiness. . . ."

133   "SHORTER NOTICES." Nation 138 (11 April):421–22.
        Reading The Making of Americans is like "listening to a
piece of music on one of those modern gramophones which automatically play the same record over and over again without
stopping."

*134   SIMON, ABBOTT. "Gertrude Stein and the Critics." Clionian
        (April):7.
        Cited: Bulletin of Bibliography 18 (May–August 1943):12.

135   SITWELL, EDITH. Aspects of Modern Poetry. London:
        Duckworth, pp. 215–26.
        Gertrude Stein and James Joyce caused the rebirth of lit-
erary language in the modern age. Stein achieved superb power
over prose rhythm, creating "extraordinary complexity and
subtlety."

136   SKINNER, B.F. "Has Gertrude Stein a Secret?" Atlantic 153
        (January):50–57.
        Assuming that Gertrude Stein practices automatic writing
and "considering the freedom that Miss Stein has given herself,
I do not think that the result is very striking, although this
is clearly a debatable point." Yet, "I do not believe in the
importance of the part of Miss Stein's writing that does not make
sense. On the contrary, I regret the unfortunate effect it has
had in obscuring the finer work of a very fine mind." Stein's
clear, unautomatic writings may be enjoyed "without puzzlement."

137   SKINNER, RICHARD DANA. "The Play." Commonweal 19 (9 March):
        525.
        Four Saints in Three Acts "achieves form" although it
lacks coherence and progression and although the "affectations
of Miss Stein's verbiage are enough in themselves to make one
suspect an attempt at sensation mongering and the use of the
Negro cast merely augments this suspicion."

138   SOSKIN, WILLIAM. "Reading and Writing." New York American,
        8 February.
        "Frankly, The Making of Americans puts me to sleep. I
resent the need to follow Miss Stein through the intestinal
convolutions of her sentences and the glacier-like development
of her paragraphs in order to derive a not too subtle meaning
from them."

139   _____. "Reading & Writing." New York American, 14 November.
        Stein seemed pleased that a person claimed that Tender
Buttons was a cure for melancholia.

140   SPENCER, THEODORE. Review of The Making of Americans.
      Atlantic 154 (September):"Bookshelf."
           Stein handicaps herself in her novel by "refusing to use
      her senses" to create people, situations, conversations--reality.

141   STEVENS, GEORGE. "Syllabus of Syllables." Saturday Review
      of Literature 10 (3 March):519.
           With Four Saints in Three Acts, "four sybils in three acts
      sounds tinkling sounds brass but a sybil is not a symbol alas.
      Pigeons on the grass alas is pigeon English."

142   "STEIN IN PERSON." Vanity Fair 43 (September):13.
           With rumors that Stein and Toklas may tour America, "please,
      Miss Stein and Miss Toklas, don't disappoint us: we do be ex-
      pecting you!"

143   "STEIN LIKES STEIN OPERA." New York Times, 9 November, p. 24.
           Stein expressed herself "completely satisfied" with the
      Chicago performance of Four Saints in Three Acts.

144   "STEIN OPERA." Newsweek 3 (17 February):37-38.
           The premiere of Four Saints in Three Acts last week had
      the authority of Stein and Thomson and the "soft Negro voices
      had just the right quality, but much of what they were saying
      would have been incomprehensible even if Miss Stein had not been
      the author."

145   STORM, JOHN. "If Magpie in the Sky on the Sky Cannot Cry,
      Why Did Gerty Stein Come Home?" Cleveland News, 6 November.
           Stein and Toklas "are in this country for a lecture tour
      and at every stop, no doubt, her interviewers will be stirred to
      write silly sentences in satire. But deep in their hearts, they
      won't be so sure. They won't be sure whether the joke is on her
      or on themselves."

146   STRUNSKY, ROBERT. "Gertrude Stein." New York Sun,
      17 November.
           "If the business of writing has any purpose at all it is
      to communicate with the greatest possible clarity the ideas and
      sensations which make up the perishable experience of mankind.
      Once these lines of communication are impaired or go dead, as
      they do in Miss Stein's latest book [Portraits and Prayers], it
      is time to call in the embalmers."

147   "TENDER BUTTONS." New Yorker 10 (13 October):18-19.
           "Gertrude Stein is 'pleasantly pleased,' she wrote to a
      literary friend a week or so ago, that she is coming over here
      to lecture. In fact, she's already written her lectures, she
      said. . . . In case you're interested, we have learned a few
      things about her that she may not tell in her lectures"--her
      habits of sleeping, dining, bathing, driving, quarreling, and
      dressing.

148   THOMPSON, RALPH. Review of The Autobiography of Alice B.
        Toklas. Current History 39 (January):xii.
            "The style is artful, consciously naive, at times pompous,
        but it is never boring or obscure, and is often highly amusing."
        This book "should convince even the most skeptical that Miss
        Stein is gifted and has something to say."

149   "TOPICS OF THE TIMES." New York Times, 26 October, p. 20.
            It is fortunate that a conservative movement in art and
        literature comes in time for Gertrude Stein to cash in on the
        popularity of The Autobiography of Alice B. Toklas, itself by
        comparison to earlier works a model of clarity."

150   _____. New York Times, 3 November, p. 14.
            Determined to seek her lecture after learning that Stein
        would address no more than five hundred people, the league of
        those affected by public relations sought tickets.

151   _____. New York Times, 1 December, p. 12.
            The Journal of the American Medical Association medical
        terms used to describe Gertrude Stein's verbal aberrances are
        nothing to remove obfuscation.

152   TOURTELLOT, ARTHUR BERNON. "A Backward Glance at Literary
        1934." Boston Transcript, 29 December.
            ". . . Miss Stein's works, up to The Autobiography of
        Alice B. Toklas, are themselves lifeless and spiritless weights.
        Her writings, nevertheless, grew on her until they became so
        deliberately the logs of an experiment of doubtful value that
        they sacrifice the classification of art to the more mechanical
        one of science. Now, I am afraid, she is convinced that the
        mode of expression that has been developed through succeeding
        ages is a less adequate one than she herself could continue."

153   "TWO STEINS." New York Times, 1 January, p. 22.
            Perhaps B.F. Skinner has applied too scientific a rigor to
        Stein's so-called automatic writings, not recalling that Stein
        is writing poetry.

154   "U.VA. TO HEAR TALK BY POET." Richmond News-Leader,
        24 October, p. 1.
            "Miss Stein is bringing a definitive explanation of that
        enigmatic, repetitive prose, so defiant of grammar, which has
        probably set more literary, club-lady and college-student tongues
        to wagging than any other development in the field of creative
        writing the last two decades."

155   VAN VECHTEN, CARL. "On Words and Music." New York Times,
        18 February, sec. 9, p. 2.
            Anyone "who brings to a performance of Four Saints in
        Three Acts more than a kind of receptive passivity, a complete
        relaxation of the perceptions, is making a mistake."

156   W., E.K. "Music." <u>Opinion</u>, March.
      "<u>Four Saints in Three Acts</u> more nearly approximates the
spirit of William Blake than any other. It has recaptured it
alive, authentic, unharmed, and enclosed it alive in bars of
intellectual sophistication."

157   WARREN, LANSING. "Gertrude Stein Views Life and Politics."
      <u>New York Times Magazine</u>, 6 May, pp. 9, 23.
      "A visit to Miss Gertrude Stein in her studio in the Rue
de Fleurus is like consulting a Grecian sibyl. But, as Miss
Stein says of Avila and Barcelona in her opera, there's a difference. Many of Miss Stein's statements have an irrefutable
terseness, though that terseness may conceal mystifying ambiguity
such as characterized the sibylline utterances."

158   WATTS, RICHARD, Jr. "Sight and Sound." <u>New York Herald-
      Tribune</u>, 4 March.
      <u>Four Saints in Three Acts</u> is "grand fun, particularly to
those who think opera librettos are silly anyway."

159   "WELCOME, GERT!" <u>Panorama</u>, November.
      "Gertrude Stein is in America, lecturing. As a Gertrude
is a Stein, a lecturer."

160   "WHAT IS AN OIL PAINTING?--GERTRUDE STEIN LETS IT OUT."
      <u>Baltimore Sun</u>, 29 December, pp. 20, 5.
      A breathless audience at the Museum of Art learned from
Stein that an oil painting is an oil painting.

161   WILSON, EDMUND. "One Being Musing Dosing." <u>New Republic</u> 81
      (26 December):198.
      "There is nothing new to say about Miss Stein. She is a
first-rate literary talent to whom something very strange and
probably unfortunate has happened--perhaps it is the basic
emptiness of the life of the artistic foreigner in Paris" that
makes a dull book of <u>Portraits and Prayers</u>.

162   YOUNG, STARK. "Might It Be Mountains?" <u>New Republic</u> 78
      (11 April):246.
      With <u>Four Saints in Three Acts</u>, "the spell, invention and
contagion of it blow about your cerebral and sensory responses
as a garden blows before your eyes, ears and mind; so that in
the theatre there is present and at your service the substance
at least for adult pleasure."

163   _____. "One Moment Alit." <u>New Republic</u> 78 (7 March):105.
      <u>Four Saints in Three Acts</u> "is the most important event of
the theatre season: it is the first free, pure theatre that I
have seen so far." Not for content but for living in itself is
this opera a delight and surprise.

164   _____. "Reading Lesson." <u>Theatre Arts Monthly</u> 18 (May):
       354-57.
       Much of the success of <u>Four Saints in Three Acts</u> is due to
the choreography, which is often pictorially conceived.

1935

1   "ADOPTING A HOME." <u>Chicago Herald & Examiner</u>, 12 March.
       At the University of Chicago, Stein "made the announcement
yesterday that her next return to Europe will be to close up her
Paris home, where for almost thirty years writers painters and
sculptors have trooped," in order to come to live in America,
perhaps in Chicago.

2   BACON, PEGGY. "Facts about Faces: Gertrude Stein." <u>New
       Republic</u> 82 (13 March):120.
       Stein's face is a "well shaped masculine head chopped from
a big block, vigorously modeled, striking as Stonehenge, posed
as an image, carrying a close skull-cap of short thick iron-gray
hair. . . ."

3   BEARDSLEY, HARRY M. "James Joyce <u>vs</u>. Gertrude Stein." <u>Real
       America</u> 6 (February):43, 76-77.
       "The truth is there is little in the Stein works to inter-
pret. She hasn't much to say. In conversation, she seems to
impart a significance to her words that evaporates when they are
cast into type. She is not a trained observer. She is not ener-
getic enough to think through to the heart of an idea or to en-
gage in research to find support for her theories."

4   BILLY, ANDRÉ. "Les Livres de la semaine." <u>L'Oeuvre</u>,
       12 February.
       Always entertaining but occasionally inaccurate in data,
<u>The Autobiography of Alice B. Toklas</u> is a great document for
modern art.

5   BRAQUE, GEORGES. Testimony. In <u>Testimony Against Gertrude
       Stein</u>. The Hague: Servire Press, pp. 13-14.
       "Miss Stein understands nothing of what went on around her.
I have no intention of entering into a discussion with her, since
it is obvious that she never knew French really well and that was
always a barrier. But she has entirely misunderstood cubism
which she sees simply in terms of personalities."

6   BURKE, KENNETH. "The Impartial Essence." <u>New Republic</u> 83
       (3 July):227.
       Stein's literary theory in <u>Lectures in America</u> is "(a) the
first draft of a critical credo, (b) complicated by the co-
presence of its revision, (c) further vitiated by the fact that
the revisionary process was not applied to all its parts."

7   B[UTCHER], F[ANNY]. "Stein Lectures to Americans Are Pub-
     lished." Chicago Tribune, 11 December.
        Publication of Narration and Lectures in America makes "a
     complete record of the public utterances of the most spectacular
     literary visitor of our day. No writer for years has been so
     widely discussed, so much caricatured, so passionately
     championed."

8   C[ANBY], H[ENRY] S[EIDEL]. "Belles Lettres." Saturday
     Review of Literature 13 (21 December):18.
        With Narration, "there is a good deal of shrewd common
     sense in these lectures—for those who know how to get it out.
     Whether there is anything more is difficult to say."

9   CHAPERON, The. "Gertrude Stein, Alice Toklas Pay Surprise
     Visit to Chicago University 'Mirror' Show." Chicago American,
     2 March.
        Stein and Toklas attended a performance of Mirror at the
     University of Chicago.

10   CONRAD, LAWRENCE. "Gertrude Stein in America." Landmark 6
     (June):303-6.
        In America Stein evoked much admiration, admiration far
     beyond her merit.

11   DEUTSCH, BABETTE. This Modern Poetry. New York: W.W.
     Norton & Co., pp. 138-40.
        Bored by music and handicapped by "lack of feeling for
     verbal texture," Stein "approaches words with the excitement of
     a child to whom grammar is a discovery, and the futility of much
     of her work is the result of her own intellectual poverty."

12   ELDRIDGE, DeWITT. "A Valentine for Gertrude Stein."
     University of Virginia Magazine 93 (January):2-4.
        Stein's visit to the University of Virginia ought to be
     marked and celebrated; perhaps disease or malaise causes South-
     erners to neglect famous speakers.

13   "END PAGES." Story 6 (May):2, 98.
        Stein's American tour was immensely successful, for
     Stein proved to be a warm and entertaining person.

14   EVANS, A. JUDSON. "Gertrude Stein Reaches Town! And She's
     Lucid, Lucid, Lucid." Richmond Times-Dispatch, 6 February,
     pp. 1, 9, 17.
        "Gertrude Stein, the enigmatic word painter, whose prose
     and poetry have been the delight of litterateurs and the dismay
     of lay readers, arrived in Richmond yesterday for a series of
     three lectures and conversed in her hotel suite with disarming
     lucidity."

15   _____. "Gertrude Tells All About All But Audience Just Can't
      Take It." Richmond Times-Dispatch, 7 February, pp. 1, 6.
            After last night's lecture, "the audience in general con-
      fessed--almost to a woman--that Miss Stein had left them palely
      loitering; mere metaphysicians meandering along the stream of
      consciousness, measureless to man, down to a psychopathic sea."

16   FAŸ, BERNARD. "Gertrude Stein: Poète de l'Amérique." Revue
      de Paris 42 (15 November):294-96.
            Gertrude Stein has long lived in Paris and loved France,
      but her subject-matter and interests are products of her love
      for America, making her the most American of American writers.

17   FLETCHER, JOHN GOULD. "A Stone of Stumbling." American
      Review 5 (June):379-84.
            In Lectures in America, "Miss Stein knows perfectly well
      what she is talking about. But what she is talking about has
      nothing whatever to do with modern literature or indeed with any-
      thing beyond literature for the nursery. She has oversimplified
      her problem without clarifying it." Her "stupidity . . . may per-
      haps account for her popularity at this moment with many other
      people in the United States."

18   GANNETT, LEWIS. "Books and Things." New York Herald-Tribune,
      14 March.
            "The best thing in Gertrude Stein's new book, Lectures in
      America, is Carl Van Vechten's photograph of Miss Stein herself,
      looking like a bright-eyed robin who has just pulled an extra
      long earthworm out of the spring soil."

19   "GERTRUDE AVERS SHE IS 'MARRIED, MARRIED' TO 'BEAUTIFUL' U.S.A."
      Chicago Tribune, 13 May.
            At her return to Paris, Stein declared her intention of
      returning someday to beautiful America.

20   "GERTRUDE STEIN ADORES U.S. BUT NOT CALIFORNIA." New York
      Herald-Tribune, 30 April.
            "Gertrude Stein was back in New York yesterday after a re-
      discovery of America, which seemed to have delighted her far
      more than Columbus's pioneer work could have him. . . . She
      simply did not care for California."

21   "GERTRUDE STEIN BEGINS HER LECTURE IN N.E. WITH TALK AT
      CENTURY CLUB HERE." Springfield (Mass.) Union, 8 January,
      pp. 1, 4.
            In town to speak on how she wrote The Making of Americans,
      Stein diagnosed America as recovering but doubtful of paying the
      medical bills.

22   "GERTRUDE STEIN COMING HOME." San Francisco News,
      19 February.

"Gertrude Stein is coming home--on a lecture tour. The Oakland girl who made good in Paris and New York is about to discover whether or not poets as well as prophets are without honor in their own country."

23   "GERTRUDE STEIN GETS CLEW FOR BOOK IN DOGS." New York
      Herald-Tribune, 2 December.
           ". . . her next book would be called A Geographical History
      of America. It will be based on her personal observations of
      last summer's activities of three members of her household--the
      celebrated Alice B. Toklas, her companion; Pepe, six-pound
      Chihuahua terrier; and Basket, a French poodle which, like Miss
      Stein, is both affable and woolly."

24   "GERTRUDE STEIN PUT ON RECORD." New York Sun, 23 April.
           On 24 April Gertrude Stein's voice will be phonographically
      recorded.

25   "GERTRUDE STEIN RAPS MODERN MUSEUM WITH WINDOWLESS EXHIBITION
      HALLS." Springfield (Mass.) Union, 24 January.
           "From as far away as Pittsfield and Worcester, persons
      came last night in the worst blizzard since 1920 to form the
      crowd which filled the Springfield Museum of Fine Arts for the
      lecture on pictures by Gertrude Stein, author, and owner of one
      of the best-known private collections of paintings."

26   "GERTRUDE STEIN TELLS PARIS SHE IS WED TO AMERICA." New York
      Times, 13 May, p. 8.
           In Paris, interviewed about her U.S. tour, Stein said, "it
      was like a bachelor who goes along fine for twenty-five years
      and then decides to get married. That is the way I feel--I mean
      about America."

27   GILBERT, DOUGLAS. "U.S. is 'Violent and Gentle,' Miss Stein's
      Parting Shot." New York World-Telegram, 4 May, pp. 1, 4.
           Pleased with her tour, Stein sailed for Europe today, full
      of comment about the contradictory elements of her native land.

28   HECHT, LUCILLE. "Gertrude Stein's Conquest of the Midwest."
      Real America 6 (February):40-42.
           Stein had become "high hat" by the time of her Chicago
      lectures and she did not always get along well with her "managers."

29   HEMINGWAY, ERNEST. Green Hills of Africa. New York:
      Charles Scribner's Sons, pp. 65-66.
           Stein learned from Hemingway how to write dialogue; then
      she became "jealous and malicious," probably due to her excessive
      ambition.

30   JEWELL, EDWARD ALDEN. "Extra Muros, Murals, and America."
      New York Times, 3 March, sec. 8, p. 7.

One wonders how Gertrude Stein will answer the attacks published in Testimony Against Gertrude Stein.

31   JOLAS, EUGENE. Preface to Testimony Against Gertrude Stein. The Hague: Servire Press, p. 2.
Responses to Stein's statements in The Autobiography of Alice B. Toklas "invalidate the claim of the Toklas-Stein memorial that Miss Stein was in any way concerned with the shaping of the epoch that she attempts to describe. There is unanimity of opinion that she had no understanding of what really was happening around her, that the mutation of ideas beneath the surface of the more obvious contacts and clashes of personalities during the period escaped her entirely."

32   JOLAS, MARIA. Testimony. In Testimony Against Gertrude Stein. The Hague: Servire Press, pp. 8-12.
"It is interesting to speculate as to just why Miss Stein should have chosen to create in [The Autobiography of Alice B. Toklas] false impressions which she knew to be such. Why has she sought to belittle so many of the artists whose friendship made it possible for her to share in the events of this epoch? The answer is obvious."

33   LOCKRIDGE, RICHARD. "No Question Marks." New York Sun, 5 April.
With Lectures in America, "Miss Stein dwells happily in concord with Miss Stein, devotions are prayerfully offered up to genius and it is all a religious ceremony upon which, it seems to me, no outsider should intrude."

34   LUTZ, MARK. "Gertrude Stein Finds U.S. Visit Charming." Richmond News-Leader, 1 January, pp. 1, 4.
"Gertrude Stein is finding her American trip one continuous Christmas tree. . . . Although Miss Stein has lived away from America for more than three decades, she has lost none of her Yankee enthusiasm."

35   _____. "Those Who Failed to Hear Miss Stein May Now Read." Richmond News-Leader, 13 April.
". . . the reader who listens as he reads Lectures in America will get to know the real literary and artistic credo of the author. Then he may decide for himself if Miss Stein is writing, as many persons of high judgment have maintained, what may be the super-literature of this generation's great-grandchildren."

36   M., F. Review of Lectures in America. Boston Transcript, 17 April, p. 2.
Lectures in America does "make one think," for Stein "has studied deeply and seriously the things she talks about, but she does not use the conventional literary form and we still remain skeptical as to her manner being an improvement."

37 MATISSE, HENRI. Testimony. In <u>Testimony Against Gertrude
    Stein</u>. The Hague: Servire Press, pp. 3-8.
        <u>The Autobiography of Alice B. Toklas</u> "is composed, like a
    picture puzzle, of different pieces of different pictures which
    at first, by their very chaos, give an illusion of the movement
    of life. But if we attempt to envisage the things she mentions
    this illusion does not last. In short, it is more like a harle-
    quin's costume the different pieces of which, having been more or
    less invented by herself, have been sewn together without taste
    and without relation to reality."

38 MATTHEWS, T.S. "Gertrude Stein Comes Home." In <u>Essay Annual
    1935</u>. Edited by Erich A. Walter. Chicago: Scott, Foresman
    & Co., pp. 351-54.
        Reprint of 1934.96.

39 "MISS STEIN SAILS." <u>New York American</u>, 5 May.
        "The American people are very violent and gentle at the
    same time," said Stein. "They like excitement and violence and
    in manners and ways they are very gentle. To other people, they
    are very gentle. In their pleasures they are very violent and
    excitable."

40 "MISS STEIN VISITS STEFFENS." <u>Monterey</u> (Calif.) <u>Peninsula
    Herald</u>, 9 April.
        In California to lecture, Stein visited Lincoln Steffens,
    Charlie Chaplin, and Upton Sinclair.

41 NATHAN, GEORGE JEAN. <u>Passing Judgments</u>. New York: Alfred A.
    Knopf, pp. 171-76.
        If words and sense do not matter in opera, Stein should
    compose texts in true nonsense syllables. Until Stein writes
    clearly, she will be "the Helen Kane, the Boop-a-doop girl, of
    modern literature."

42 "PASSION IN LITERATURE." <u>New York Times</u>, 25 August.
        "In a recent interview Gertrude Stein refers to Emerson as
    one of the passionate writers. Although Miss Stein's personal
    literary style looks like an emotional orgy she has a vigorous
    critical mind. Her description of Emerson proves it."

43 PEPLE, G.A. "A Rose." <u>Richmond Times-Dispatch</u>, 13 February.
        "A rose is a rose, is a rose is a rose. / Does any one
    doubt it? I hardly suppose / You could find one so stupid, and
    so I will close-- / A rose is a rose, is a rose, is a rose."

44 PRESTON, JOHN HYDE. "A Conversation." <u>Atlantic</u> 156
    (August):187-94.
        "If I had seen her a year ago I should have expected a
    legend, but I had learned to expect a woman, and I came to find
    something more--more, I mean, than one who had been a fountainhead

not so much for herself as for others and certainly for all the young Americans who were writing in Paris after the war."

45   REVIEW OF LECTURES IN AMERICA. Booklist 31 (July):371.
      "Ostensibly an exposition of the author's theories about writing, art, and music, but baffling and to most readers generally unenlightening."

46   SALMON, ANDRÉ. Testimony. In Testimony Against Gertrude Stein. The Hague: Servire Press, pp. 14-15.
      With The Autobiography of Alice B. Toklas, "the scandalous part of the book took us somewhat by surprise. After all we were all young at that time and had no thought of possible later echoes of our actions. I am not angry but I think Gertrude Stein went too far when she made all these things public. Furthermore, there is great confusion of dates, places and persons in her book."

47   SCHWARTZ, HARRY. Checklists of Twentieth Century Authors, Third Series. Milwaukee: Casanova Booksellers, pp. 18-19.
      List of books by Gertrude Stein.

48   "SOMEONE CALLED STEIN SAILS WITH ALICE B. TOKLAS." New York Herald-Tribune, 5 May.
      Toklas allowed Stein only a brief chat with reporters and stated that Stein would not return to the U.S.

49   STEARNS, HAROLD E. The Street I Know. New York: Lee Furman, p. 301.
      Stearns believed that, after The Autobiography of Alice B. Toklas, he did not need to add to Stein's accounts of her institutional place in Paris. She did not, as author, deserve much attention.

50   STRAUSS, HAROLD. "Miss Stein's Lectures." New York Times Book Review, 14 April, p. 12.
      "Far be it from us to discourage any one from dipping into Lectures in America. If you like to play with pretty theories you will find a bucketfull here on which you can try your wits. But if by any chance you should come to understand one of them, you will have changed it into your theory, and then it could not possibly be Gertrude Stein's any longer. It's not a bad pastime."

51   TREADGOLD, PAUL. "A Note on Gertrude Stein." Programme, 19 June, pp. 12-13.
      Stein's method of gaining immediacy is to write directly from observation; from listening and talking, not from remembering. What appears to be repetition in her work is the result.

52   TZARA, TRISTAN. Testimony. In Testimony Against Gertrude Stein. The Hague: Servire Press, pp. 12-13.

"Underneath the 'baby' style [of <u>The Autobiography of</u>
<u>Alice B. Toklas</u>], which is pleasant enough when it is a question
of simpering at the interstices of envy, it is easy to discern
such a really coarse spirit, accustomed to the artifices of the
lowest literary prostitution, that I cannot believe it necessary
for me to insist on the presence of a clinical case of
megalomania."

53   WILLIAMS, WILLIAM CARLOS. "A 1 Pound Stein." <u>Rocking Horse</u>
     2 (Spring):3-5.
         "My own feeling is that Stein has all she can do in tack-
     ling the frontier of stupidities bound in our thoughtless phrases,
     in our calcified grammatical constructions and in the subtle
     brainlessness of our meter and favorite prose rhythms--which
     compel words to follow certain others without precision of
     thought." Reprinted: 1954.26.

54   WINTER, ELLA. "Gertrude Stein Comma." <u>Pacific Weekly</u> 2
     (12 April):172-73.
         ". . . Gertrude Stein is a path-breaker, a revolutionary
     and a torch for those who feel like not using or putting up with
     the using of anything that to them is particularly degrading.
     Gertrude Stein is a revolutionary in writing and in thinking and
     in feeling and so she is a revolutionary."

55   WOODBURN, JOHN. "Aloft With Miss Stein in Verbal Fog."
     <u>San Francisco Chronicle</u>, 20 January.
         "This reviewer has experimented and discovered that a
     great deal of <u>Portraits and Prayers</u> is written in reversible
     English. That is, it may be read backward as well as forward
     without appreciably altering the context."

56   "YOUTH UNDERSTANDS SAYS GERTRUDE STEIN AS SHE SAILS FOR
     FRANCE." <u>New York Times</u>, 5 May, p. 33.
         Stein was pleased with Americans on her tour but "had made
     no plans for another visit."

<u>1936</u>

1   BEIMFOHR, MARY. "Mrs. Beimfohr Probes the Puzzle of Miss
     Stein." <u>Evanston News-Index</u>, 12 March.
         In <u>Narration</u>, "there is not a word in these lectures which
     will cause anyone to reach for the dictionary, but one's range
     of ideas may widen if one reads these lectures as a collaborat-
     ing attention-giver."

2   BISHOP, JOHN PEALE. "Homage to Hemingway." In <u>After the</u>
     <u>Genteel Tradition: American Writers Since 1910</u>. Edited by
     Malcolm Cowley. New York: W.W. Norton & Co., pp. 193-95.

Stein's intentions and means are interesting; her results are often tiresome. By the time of the Stein-Hemingway relationship, Stein no longer had content in her writing. Only later, in the guise of Alice B. Toklas, could Stein again find subject-matter.

3   BOYNTON, PERCY H. <u>Literature and American Life: For Students of American Literature</u>. Boston: Ginn & Co., pp. 731, 862.
Even before Stein, Henry James had written obscure passages. From Stein and from Sherwood Anderson did Hemingway learn disillusionment as a literary pose.

4   CANBY, HENRY SEIDEL. <u>Seven Years' Harvest: Notes on Contemporary Literature</u>. New York: Farrar & Rinehart, pp. 159-63.
Reprint of 1934.24.

5   DAVIES, HUGH SYKES. Review of <u>Narration</u>. <u>Criterion</u> 15 (July):752-55.
With <u>Narration</u>, Stein has shown that she has "disregarded her limitations" and "attempted tasks which she does not understand, and which she could hardly perform even if she understood them. This book on narration marks the nadir--if we are lucky--of this sad decline in honesty."

6   EAGLESON, HARVEY. "Gertrude Stein: Method in Madness." <u>Sewanee Review</u> 44 (April-June):164-77.
Stein has led herself blindly into noncommunication, a poor dead-end for a writer who has "shrewdness of observation, a satiric and at the same time sympathetic humor, and a philosophical profundity that is unexcelled by any other modern writer."

7   FLINT, F. CUDWORTH. "Contemporary Criticism." <u>Southern Review</u> 2 (Spring):208-13.
In <u>Narration</u>, "one must regard Miss Stein as something of a sorceress--a frank sorceress, eminently agreeable to expounding, to the profit of her audience, the secrets of her sorcery; but in the long run, a person from whom one must escape. I shall perhaps say no and yes and perhaps no."

8   FORBES, CONSTANCE. "Woman With A Load of Words." <u>Daily Express</u> (London), 13 February.
"Tea with gertrude stein tea with gertrude stein with gertrude stein. She drinks hot water she drinks hot water. In a Berkshire village tea with gertrude stein stein strange stein myths all gone all gone."

9   GOLD, MICHAEL. <u>Change the World!</u> Foreword by Robert Forsythe. London: Lawrence & Wishout, pp. 23-26.
Despite Stein's popularity, Marxists "refuse to be impressed with her own opinion of herself. They see in the work

of Gertrude Stein extreme symptoms of the decay of capitalist
culture. They view her work as the complete attempt to annihi-
late all relations between the artist and the society in which
he lives."

10   HABICH, WILLIAM. "The Words Go Round and Round." Louisville
      Courier-Journal, 26 January.
          Read aloud, Narration "again reveals that S[tein] words
      not only go 'round and around but also up and down, in and out,
      over and across, and through and through and through to the sub-
      conscious conveying abstract ideas that it would be impossible
      to convey through any other method."

11   HALDANE, CHARLOTTE. "Gentlemen Prefer." English Review 62
      (May):528-30.
          Gentlemen Prefer Blondes was fun until one found The Auto-
      biography of Alice B. Toklas, which is "all about a girl called
      Gertrude Stein. . . ."

12   HECHT, LUCILLE. "Gertrude Stein's Magnificent Hoax." Real
      America 6 (January):8-11, 70.
          Not everyone in Chicago jumped aboard the bandwagon to
      welcome Stein as a lioness of literary matters.

13   IMBS, BRAVIG. Confessions of Another Young Man. New York:
      Henkle-Yewdale House, 301 pp.
          Imbs, Toklas, and Stein were great friends in Paris until
      Toklas announced that the association with Imbs was over, osten-
      sibly because of the young man's "colossal impertinence."

14   LANE, JAMES W. "The Craze for Craziness." Catholic World
      144 (December):306-9.
          "Miss Stein's idea . . . like that of other devotees of the
      craze for craziness, is to astonish, and it is not astonishing
      that they do astonish. The craze-for-craziness people have that
      idea as their end-all and be-all."

15   LAUGHLIN, JAMES, IV. "About Bilignin and Literature and the
      GBM." In Gotham Book Mart Catalogue 36. New York: Gotham
      Book Mart, pp. 1-2.
          Stein never knew why literary fame, for her, became fickle.

16   _____. "New Words for Old." Story 9 (December):105, 107, 110.
          Stein's career since Three Lives shows a decline into
      "denial of conventional meaning, believing that a wholesale
      'scrambling' of the familiar, expected groupings would break
      down the corresponding associative links in the reader's mind."
      Reprinted: 1937.19.

17   LUHAN, MABEL DODGE. Movers and Shakers. New York: Harcourt,
      Brace & Co., pp. 26, 27, 38, 74, 75, and passim.

The 1913 <u>Arts and Decoration</u> essay helped Stein into public awareness: "From that year, when her essence was poured into the public consciousness, she has crept through it like a slow, inevitable tincture coloring prose and verse."

18   MASSEE, J., Jr. "Today's Book." <u>Macon</u> (Ga.) <u>Telegraph and News</u>, 26 January.
      "Miss Stein's discussions lead into the realms of metaphysics and philosophy and physics, all in the simplest language of everyday usage. If you don't like Gertrude Stein, be sure to read <u>Narration</u>."

19   MOORE, MARIANNE. "Perspicuous Opacity." <u>Nation</u> 143 (24 October):484, 486.
      "<u>The Geographical History of America</u> is offered as a detective story. . . . A detective story is a conundrum, and this one has 'content without form' and is 'without a beginning and a middle and an end. . . .' The repeatings and regressions are . . . sometimes for emphasis, sometimes a method of connecting passages, sometimes a musical refrain, sometimes playful, And, one adds, sometimes a little inconsiderate and unaccomodating. . . . But the book is a triumph, and all of us, that is to say a great many of us, would do well to read it."

20   "THE NEW BOOKS." <u>Saturday Review of Literature</u> 15 (14 November):38.
      <u>The Geographical History of America</u> "runs to 207 pages and has a lot of words in it. Some of it appeared in the <u>Saturday Evening Post</u>, a fact of interest to literary historians. It has an introduction by Thornton Wilder, so very soft, so very Susie."

21   OKIE, WILLIAM. "Literature and Stuff." <u>UCLA Daily Bruin</u>, 6 April.
      Stein's <u>Narration</u> is "among the clearest of her writings, and whatever doubts remain in the reader's mind spring from the profundity of the author's thought, not from any malicious intent to dupe. Miss Stein has pondered her subject deeply; she rightly expects the reader to do the same. For this no author need be defended."

22   REVIEW OF NARRATION. <u>Booklist</u> 32 (March):196.
      <u>Narration</u> is "written in [Stein's] characteristic, individual idiom."

23   ROSENFELD, PAUL. <u>Discoveries of a Music Critic</u>. New York: Harcourt, Brace & Co., pp. 297-302.
      <u>Four Saints in Three Acts</u>, performed in 1934, is "a tidbit for 'sophisticated' audiences of the sort which we have recently begun developing . . . a thirty-minute vaudeville stunt stretched out to the length of eighteen saints in four acts and two and a half hours."

24   S., R. "Crossword Puzzle." New York Sun, 30 October.
         Perhaps people do buy such books as The Geographical History
     of America; publishers surely profit somehow from such books.

25   SHIPP, CAMERON. "Gertrude Stein Writes Clearly About Writing."
     Charlotte News, 26 January.
         Narration "is not for the hammock reader, but it is im-
     peratively a book for the writer and the connoisseur."

26   SLOCOMBE, GEORGE. The Tumult and the Shouting. New York:
     Macmillan Co., p. 227.
         Slocombe met Stein when she modeled for Jo Davidson. He
     found the sculpture not kind enough: "She is, despite her dis-
     illusionment over Hemingway (vide The Autobiography of Alice B.
     Toklas), a very kind person."

27   VOLLARD, AMBROISE. Recollections of a Picture Dealer. Trans-
     lated by Violet M. MacDonald. Boston: Little, Brown & Co.,
     pp. 66, 136-38.
         Vollard liked Stein's personality, one "in which the artist
     predominates. She writes for her own pleasure; if fame has come
     to her, it is certainly not because she has sought it."

                                 1937

1   ALSOP, JOSEPH, Jr. "Gertrude Stein on Writing." New York
     Herald-Tribune Books, 10 January, p. 2.
         Stein's Geographical History of America is a fascinating
     book, "since the thesis it expresses is her reason for her de-
     parture from the common literary forms."

2   "AUTHORS OF THE WEEK." Saturday Review of Literature 17
     (4 December):56.
         Biographical sketch.

3   BARRY, IRIS. "Gertrude Stein Came Home." New York Herald-
     Tribune Books, 12 December, p. 6.
         The main attraction of Everybody's Autobiography is that
     the book is written by an intensely happy woman.

4   BROWN, STERLING ALLEN. The Negro in American Fiction.
     Washington, D.C.: Associates in Negro Folk Education,
     pp. 111-12.
         In "Melanctha," Stein's characters talk alike in very man-
     nered dialogue.

5   BUTCHER, FANNY. "Three Unusual Women Live in These Volumes."
     Chicago Tribune, 11 December, p. 15.
         Not to be read rapidly, Everybody's Autobiography is "in-
     teresting and true."

6   CLEATON, IRENE, and CLEATON, ALLEN. Books and Battles: Amer-
     ican Literature 1920-1930. Boston: Houghton Mifflin Co.,
     pp. 36, 40-46, 50, and passim.
           Stein's obscurity became her trademark to those unsympa-
     thetic to her method. After The Autobiography of Alice B. Toklas
     she was ready to lay it away in mothballs; "in all probability
     the only further reference that will be made to her is as a mon-
     umental literary curiosity of the nineteen-twenties."

7   DANIELS, ROY. "Drifted Words." Canadian Forum 16 (February):
     27.
           Concerning The Geographical History of America: "Lift up
     the Stein, 'tis brimming full,/ And take a deep and hearty pull,
     / For here's to capture if we can / America and Art and
     Man. . . ."

8   DESFEUILLES, PAUL. "La Grammaire et la poésie d'après
     Gertrude Stein." Yggdrasil, 23 October, pp. 115-17.
           Stein's poetry is like Morse Code--dry, novel, stylized.

9   DICKINSON, ASA DON. The Best Books of the Decade 1926-1935:
     A Later Clue to the Literary Labyrinth. New York: H.W.
     Wilson Co., p. 144.
           "A favorite student of William James at Radcliffe, [Stein]
     is known specially for her early appreciation of and friendship
     with Picasso, Matisse and other moderns, and for her supposed
     strong influence on Ernest Hemingway. In some of her writing
     she chooses words for sound and rhythm rather than for sense."

10   EDSTROM, DAVID. The Testament of Caliban. New York: Funk &
     Wagnalls Co., pp. 239-40.
           After meeting the Steins in Florence, Edstrom often visited
     the salon in Paris: "I do not suppose Gertrude could guess how
     many times I came into their large studio with my nerves raw with
     anguish and gained relief at just seeing her, stolid, fat, Buddha-
     like, sitting in a corner with a grin on her face."

11   ELIAS, ROBERT H. "Letters." Story 10 (February):108-9.
           In Story for January, 1937, Zolotow has misjudged Gertrude
     Stein's writing: "Mr. Zolotow has implied that Stein has no end
     in view. It is not the end that is lacking, but that the end has
     been systematically misconceived. Gertrude Stein's value as a
     writer lies in her revolt against that logical classification
     known as realism, where the individual is characterized by the
     common; but her failure is in thinking that it is possible to
     give an absolute individuality significance as divorced from
     logical order."

12   FADIMAN, CLIFTON. "Books." New Yorker 13 (4 December):
     115-16, 118.
           "I awoke one night from a deep dream of peace and found
     that unaware I had just finished Everybody's Autobiography, a

new book by Gertrude Stein. Confusedly, I found myself murmuring
some lines which I must have made up in my slumber, much as
Coleridge did in the case of 'Kubla Khan.'"

13 FLETCHER, JOHN GOULD. Life Is My Song: The Autobiography.
    New York: Farrar & Rinehart, pp. 298, 313.
        "I had met Miss Stein in Paris as early as 1913, had read
    some of her work in a magazine then published by Alfred Stieglitz,
    and I was not ready--nor am I ready now--to accord her the epithet
    of 'genius.'"

14 FRANK, WALDO. In the American Jungle: 1925-1936. New York:
    Farrar & Rinehart, p. 186.
        Gertrude Stein is the "ridiculous" sister of Leo Stein,
    not too different in prose from her brother's weird ideas of art.

15 "GERTRUDE STEIN IN A LUCID MOOD." Philadelphia Record,
    11 December.
        "The Gertrude Stein of Everybody's Autobiography is the
    Gertrude Stein of The Autobiography of Alice B. Toklas, in other
    words, the Gertrude Stein of the relatively lucid moments, who
    can be understood at least part of the time."

16 HARRIS, WILLIAM B. Review of Everybody's Autobiography.
    Boston Transcript, 4 December, p. 3.
        Quite articulate about the effect on herself of an American
    tour, Stein in her second autobiography is warm and witty.

17 HUMANN, RAY. "Stein Stumper." Academic Observer 51
    (February):23.
        Crossword puzzle.

18 JACK, PETER MUNRO. "Gertrude Stein Continues the Story of
    Her Life." New York Times Book Review, 5 December, p. 7.
        In Everybody's Autobiography, "the pleasant purling of
    Miss Stein's prose brings us by degrees to her American tour
    three years ago and what she thought about everybody and every-
    thing. Easy to read and easy to forget, it is now obvious that
    Miss Stein's chief asset in writing is her colossal egotism, and
    her chief deficiency is her inability to create character. . . .
    Her mind is acute and lively, as intelligent a recording instru-
    ment as one could wish for; but it is extraordinarily limited,
    and almost purely parasitical."

19 LAUGHLIN, JAMES, IV. New Directions in Prose and Poetry.
    Norfolk, Conn.: New Directions.
        Reprint of 1936.16.

20 LEVY, HARRIET L. "Neighbors (including Alice Toklas)."
    Menorah Journal 25 (April):187-90.

Alice Toklas spent her youth caring for male relations in California, where her sensitivities were not appreciated by the family. Reprinted: 1947.26.

21   LEWIS, SINCLAIR. "The Gas Goddess." Newsweek 10 (13 December): 36.

In Everybody's Autobiography, Stein answers the pressing questions "as to whether she is (1) crazy; (2) joking; or (3) contributing new rhythms to an outworn English literary style. She reveals the whole thing as a lovely racket."

22   LOGGINS, VERNON. I Hear America: Literature in the United States since 1900. New York: Thomas Y. Crowell Co., pp. 7, 8, 12, 13, 97, and passim.

If a new prose is being invented in America, Gertrude Stein is the creator, for "there is not a stylistic device employed by Hemingway and his numerous followers which had not been first worked out and used by Gertrude Stein. According to existing standards, she is not a poet nor a story-teller, but she is a creative thinker. She has discovered new functions for words. So ardent believers in her discoveries have called her the mother of modern American literature and its one great genius."

23   LUCHA, MARGARET. "Gertrude Stein." Academic Observer 51 (February):4.

"Choosing words for sound rather than sense, creating an ever moving rhythm of distraction to the reader, [Stein] remains (to us 'umble folks) the eighth wonder of the world."

24   MARINI, MYRA. "Being Dead Is Something." New Republic 89 (20 January):365.

After reading The Geographical History of America, "I protest 'with tears in my eyes' that the writer of 'Melanctha' persists in handing us her experimental nonsense. Taking the broadest view possible of the value of experimentation in literature, it is still doubtful whether she has contributed anything valuable by her breaking down of language."

25   McCOLE, C. JOHN. Lucifer at Large. New York: Longmans, Green & Co., pp. 137, 153, 154, 157, and passim.

Stein taught Hemingway to write careful conversation, but from Stein he learned "repetitious phrases, drab monotones, sheer echolaic passages, four-letter words, and overly frequent pronouns."

26   "MENCKEN DERIDES ROOSEVELT VOICE." New York Times, 21 October, p. 25.

H.L. Mencken declared that Gertrude Stein is a "quack. She has no ideas and she can't express 'em."

27   MULLER, HERBERT J. Modern Fiction: A Study of Values. New
      York: Funk & Wagnalls, pp. 10, 16, 311, 313, 314, 315, 396,
      397.
           Stein forgot that "words are by mankind at large inevitably
      associated with meanings. . . ." She used a private language and
      increasingly retreated from meaning.

28   RASCOE, BURTON. "Self-Confidential." Saturday Review of
      Literature 17 (4 December):11, 56.
           With Everybody's Autobiography, "I have never read a book
      in my life that had more words and less in it than this one, un-
      less it was another book by Gertrude Stein. But if you take a
      page at a time of her, occasionally, you may find something that
      strikes you as pretty damn funny."

29   REVIEW OF EVERYBODY'S AUTOBIOGRAPHY. Booklist 34
      (15 December):144.
           "Although ostensibly a sequel to The Autobiography of
      Alice B. Toklas, covering the past five years, Gertrude Stein
      writes this in the first person, and brings in her early life,
      experiences in France, and anecdotes of her many friends."

30   RICKEL, WILLIAM. "Some New Books." Wilmington (Del.) Star,
      28 November.
           In Everybody's Autobiography, "you meet, in its 300 pages,
      nearly all the important writers, painters, philosophers and
      educators of our time. They are only the background for the
      most marvelous of all manifestations: Gertrude Stein."

31   SILLEN, SAMUEL. "Obituary of Europe And Gertrude Stein."
      New Masses, 7 December.
           Currently obsessed with money and a theory of money, in
      Everybody's Autobiography Stein shows that "the mama of dada is
      going gaga."

32   "SUCCESS STORY." Time 30 (6 December):91.
           Between the lines of Everybody's Autobiography is a picture
      of Gertrude Stein and Alice Toklas "dashing animatedly over the
      country [the U.S.A.], telling eminent personages what's what,
      patting the U.S. on the back for its friendliness, curiosity,
      generosity."

33   VAN GHENT, DOROTHY. "Gertrude Stein and the Solid World."
      In American Stuff. New York: Viking Press, pp. 218-22.
           Stein "writes of a solid world" and "has attempted to
      cancel the gaps between one thing and another, between space
      and time, between past and present, between concept and precept."

34   WILLIAMS, DORIS. "Milk Will Not Sour." Academic Observer
      51 (February):7.
           Parody of Stein.

35 ZOLOTOW, MAURICE. "Letter." Story 10 (January):196-7.
    Stein "has mighty little to show for thirty years of expe-
riments . . . except more experiments. So she has garnered a
meagre crop of figs."

1938

1 GASSER, HANS ULRICH. "Pablo Picasso." Weltwoche (Zurich),
    29 April.
    Among the first to appreciate Picasso's art, Stein has
tried to assess this Spaniard's accomplishments.

2 GRAMONT, ELIZABETH de. Memoirs. Paris: Éditions Bernard
    Gramont, pp. 344-50.
    "Gertrude Stein has lived in France for thirty-seven years.
She has written for twenty-seven years. Her books, her essays,
her stories, her poems appear in English; but the French ignored
them and her completely; and suddenly success has come like thunder. Great trees shake with the thunder and Gertrude Stein is a
great tree, a vigorous oak."

3 McALMON, ROBERT. Being Geniuses Together: An Autobiography.
    London: Secker & Warburg, pp. 133-42.
    Reprint of 1928.14.

4 MACAULAY, ROSE. "Aspects of the Novel." The Writings of E.M.
    Forster. New York: Harcourt, Brace & Co., pp. 229-30.
    Stein damages writing and words: ". . . she is a philis-
tine, a barbarian, a Vandal, practically a butcher. . . ." Her
experiments destroy the precision of language.

5 McB[RIDE], H[ENRY]. "Gertrude Stein Writes in French."
    New York Sun, 28 May.
    Stein's French explanation of Picasso is blunt, amusing,
and often startling.

6 "MISS STEIN ON PICASSO." Times Literary Supplement,
    26 November, p. 751.
    Stein, under the spell of Picasso or his art, has in
Picasso added to the legend. Perhaps his art indeed influenced
her own.

7 PACH, WALTER. Queer Thing, Painting: Forty Years in the
    World of Art. New York: Harper & Brothers, pp. 14, 116, 143.
    Pach could not understand what the Steins, when he knew
them, could see in the early works of Matisse. The Steins had
helped keep Matisse from starving.

8 "PEOPLE." Time 32 (28 November):38.
    Stein has completed a libretto for another opera, this one
"a Steinish version of Faust."

9   STEFFENS, LINCOLN. <u>The Letters of Lincoln Steffens</u>. 2 vols.
     Edited by Ella Winter and Granville Hicks. New York:
     Harcourt, Brace & Co., pp. 594, 615, 904.
          To Steffens, Stein was a "cubist writer," well-sculpted by
     Jo Davidson: "That suggests philosophy and repose, understanding,
     a sense of proportion and applied knowledge, which is wisdom."

10   TIETJENS, EUNICE. <u>The World at My Shoulder</u>. New York:
     Macmillan Co., pp. 205, 206, 207.
          Stein by telegram helped Tietjens to find a lovely villa
     to rent in Italy.

                              1939

1   BECHTEL, LOUISE SEAMAN. "Gertrude Stein for Children."
     <u>Horn Book</u> 15 (September):286-91.
          <u>The World Is Round</u> is a charming book from a literary
     master--this time writing for children. Reprinted: 1959.4;
     1970.3.

2   BECKER, MAY LAMBERTON. "Books For Young People." <u>New York
     Herald-Tribune Books</u>, 24 September, p. 6.
          "Pure delight, simple pleasure, is what little children
     will get as they listen, a chapter or so at a time, to <u>The World
     Is Round</u>. So will the adult who reads it to them, unless his
     mind is too stiff to bend with the rhythm."

3   BENÉT, ROSEMARY CARR. "The Children's Bookshop." <u>Saturday
     Review of Literature</u> 21 (18 November):22.
          <u>The World Is Round</u> may not appeal to many children, but
     "young readers will find this is certainly not like their other
     books."

4   BIDDLE, GEORGE. <u>An American Artist's Story</u>. Boston: Little,
     Brown & Co., pp. 205, 210-11.
          Biddle and Stein argued about his talent as an artist: "I
     argued with her coldly. I think she called me a lawyer. We
     parted not entirely on unfriendly terms."

5   BUELL, ELLEN LEWIS. "By Gertrude Stein." <u>New York Times
     Book Review</u>, 12 November, pp. 10, 20.
          With publication of <u>The World Is Round</u>, "it is a pleasant
     duty to report that Miss Stein seems to have found her audience,
     possibly a larger one than usual."

6   BURNETT, WHIT. <u>The Literary Life and the Hell with It</u>.
     New York: Harper & Brothers, pp. 99-106.
          Stein captivated America on her lecture tour. She believed
     that the contents of <u>Story</u> were too realistic for her taste; yet
     she cherished the writings of P.G. Wodehouse.

7 CHILDREN'S BOOKS." Catholic World 150 (December):373.
        In The World Is Round, Stein "can write about boys and
girls and even lions and mountains with delicate sensitiveness
and a nice touch of humor. We personally feel she can express
herself much more clearly than many people who have less to
express. . . ."

8 F., H. Review of Picasso. Apollo 29 (January):40.
        In Picasso, "the pity is that if the author had not pre-
served this infantile manner of expression one would be able to
appreciate her often shrewd remarks· on the artist with much less
difficulty."

9 FADIMAN, CLIFTON. "Books." New Yorker 15 (18 February):68-69.
        Stein's "little monograph, Picasso . . . is as interesting
a book as she has ever done, though I admit that my prejudice in
its favor derives from the happy circumstance that I seem to
understand probably everything she says."

10 _____. "Books." New Yorker 15 (25 November):72.
        With The World Is Round, "certainly, few children will have
the patience to read the book to themselves, and evidently Miss
Stein does not expect them to. Other minor difficulties are that
the volume has an odd and slightly disagreeable smell and that it
is printed in blue type on a violent rose paper, a color combina-
tion which gave me spots before the eyes in no time at all."

11 FEIBLEMAN, JAMES. In Praise of Comedy: A Study in Its Theory
        and Practice. New York: Macmillan Co., pp. 179, 188, 236-41,
        250, 258.
        Stein comically confuses "the categories of actuality as
an indication of their ultimate unimportance, and as a warning
against taking them too seriously." Her formula is to juxtapose
seemingly meaningful words to tantalize readers toward absent
meaning--"a subtle variety of the comedy of meaninglessness."

12 "FOR THE LITTLE ONES." New York Sun, 16 September.
        The World Is Round is "printed on rose-colored paper and
is as clear as a painting by Dali."

13 "GERTRUDE STEIN FOR CHILDREN." Chicago Tribune, 30 September,
        p. 12.
        The World Is Round will be loved by children because "it
has one quality which always delights them--its words jingle
like bells."

14 GORMAN, HERBERT. "A Picasso Is a Picasso Is a--." New York
        Times Book Review, 5 March, p. 9.
        In Picasso, "Miss Stein, with various darts to the right
and left to explain some of her own conceptions of art, has
followed Picasso rather closely through his career and gives

her readers an excellent idea of the growth, regressions and
progressions of the Spanish painter."

15   HAPGOOD, HUTCHINS. A Victorian in the Modern World. New York:
      Harcourt, Brace & Co., pp. 120, 122, 166, 215, 245, and passim.
          Even when Hapgood met Gertrude Stein in Heidelberg, early
      in her life, he sensed her immense ego. Although he now thinks
      her early writing childish, Hapgood admits the influence of this
      work on other writers. He later disapproved of both her writing
      and her lifestyle.

16   HINKS, ROGER. "Profile of Picasso." Spectator 162
      (17 February):271-72.
          In Picasso, Stein has qualifications "to write the one
      really illuminating book about the most significant and the most
      perplexing artist now alive. And she has, in fact, written a
      curiously attractive, yet at the same time most unsatisfactory
      essay, about her favourite painter."

17   MACKENZIE, CATHERINE. "Children and Parents." New York
      Times, 24 September, sec. 2, p. 8.
          Stein's The World Is Round gives children a book in which
      they can fully enjoy the sounds of words.

18   McMAHON, PHILIP. "New Books on Art." Parnassus 11 (April):
      29.
          Stein's Picasso, "not too far in the future . . . may well
      be judged a basic volume in the art movement that is still aston-
      ishing called modern. It is intelligible, straightforward, wise,
      and sympathetic."

19   MONGAN, AGNES. "Stein on Picasso." Saturday Review of
      Literature 19 (18 March):11.
          With Picasso, "when Miss Stein undertakes the interpreta-
      tion of Picasso's work, as years ago Picasso in his now famous
      portrait of Miss Stein undertook his interpretation of the writer,
      the appearance of her essay--its length is a scant fifty pages--
      becomes at least a minor event in both the literary and artistic
      worlds."

20   MOORE, A.C. Review of The World Is Round. Horn Book 15
      (September):294.
          The World Is Round, if read aloud, is "genuine child stuff
      rather than something about children, or for children--the kind
      of thing children say when they are free from superimposed tradi-
      tion. . . . We have need of gaiety and a return to childhood in
      these grave days."

21   MORRIS, GEORGE L.K. "Further Testimony." Partisan Review 6
      (Spring):126-27.

It is ironic that Stein may be best liked for her art
criticism instead of for her literary efforts. In Picasso, the
illustrations do not compliment Picasso.

22   "PUZZLE BOOK." Times Literary Supplement, 30 December, p. 758.
        Although The World Is Round is for children, "we doubt if
any children will be helpless enough to endure such a campaign
of trial and error father than a few pages, and those only for
the pleasurable opportunity of exposing their parents' inability"
to explain the text.

23   REES, GARNET. "Notes on Books." Journal of the Royal Society
        of Arts, 13 January, pp. 247-48.
        "For sheer interpretive criticism, Miss Stein's [Picasso]
is outstanding. She has followed with sympathetic understanding
and a rare discretion the struggle in Picasso's work. She does
not intrude herself, but allows her intuition to be an unassuming
guide."

24   REVIEW OF PICASSO. Booklist 35 (15 March):229.
        "Except for a few seemingly irrelevant arguments, this is a
brief, straightforward account of the artist's life and family,
and of the influences which affected his different styles and
periods of painting."

25   REVIEW OF PICASSO. Guardian (Manchester), 22 November, p. 7.
        Picasso is a short book and "well illustrated; it is a
revealing book. In other words, if the reader can put his pre-
judices about what is and what is not English prose in his pocket
he will learn from Miss Stein quite a good deal about Picasso."

26   REVIEW OF PICASSO. Springfield (Mass.) Republican,
        19 February, sec. E, p. 7.
        Stein's Picasso is "the work of an ardent disciple, blend-
ing delphic generalizations, anecdotes, intuitive impressions and
scattered interpretations. Her style gives no difficulty to any
person who has read letters with a minimum of punctuation."

27   REVIEW OF THE WORLD IS ROUND. Booklist 36 (1 January):180.
        The World Is Round is "an interesting experiment in rhythm
and word patterns. . . . The author has used a minimum of punctuation. There are flashes of spontaneous humor and much of the
writing is pure poetry, but the format as well as the unusual
manner of punctuation will limit its appeal. . . . Most effective if read aloud."

28   REVIEW OF THE WORLD IS ROUND. Springfield (Mass.) Republican,
        17 December, sec. E, p. 7.
        "Miss Stein gives the impression that with a little closer
approximation to sense she could write nonsense for children,
but this effort is not impressive."

29   "ROSE IS A GERTRUDE." Time 34 (9 October):76.
     The World Is Round shows that "long and serious practice has given witty Miss Stein a mastery over itty language that puts most children's writers in the shade."

30   S., E.C. "Pablo, According to Gertrude." Christian Science Monitor, 11 March, "Weekly Magazine," p. 11.
     In Picasso, "Gertrude Stein is almost continuously clear" and says of her subject "many shrewd things."

31   "SHORTER NOTICES." Nation 148 (29 April):508.
     Picasso is an "appealing book, just, perceptive, and close to the artist. Handsomely printed, it completes what was begun in Portraits and Prayers and adds an indispensable item for the appreciation of the least predictable of modern painters."

32   STANTON, JESSIE, and STEELE, ELLEN. Review of The World Is Round. New Republic 101 (13 December):237.
     With The World Is Round, "quite young children will like the fantasy and rhythm; older ones who can play with words may enjoy the unusual idiom for its own sake."

33   SWAN, NATHALIE. "Stein on Picasso." New Republic 99 (5 July):259.
     With Stein's Picasso, "as a critical explanation of the artist's place in society, her definition is trivial and limited. . . . The ivory tower has its uses but they must be differentiated from the functions of a padded cell."

34   SWEENEY, JAMES JOHNSON. "Criticism With Myopia." Kenyon Review 1 (Summer):327-30.
     In Picasso, "Miss Stein's appreciation profits from the effort, if only a superficial one on her part, to evoke the spiritual climate of Picasso's period and our own which demands formal arrangements just as fresh for its expression as Cézanne's period did."

35   TAYLOR, PRENTISS. Review of Picasso. Magazine of Art 32 (July):430.
     "This is an interpretive chronicle of Picasso's emptying and renewing of himself, a process he has used with more vigor and resourcefulness than any other contemporary painter. It is a fascinating study of his realism. . . ."

36   "TYRONE POWER SELECTS . . . THE WORLD'S 10 MOST INTERESTING WOMEN." Look 3 (11 April):4.
     "Gertrude Stein. No other woman has so influenced art and letters as has this dynamic expatriate. Even those who do not accept her style agree she has influenced an important school of literature."

37   ULRICH, DOROTHY LIVINGSTON. "Gertrude Stein in Summer."
      Avocations 3 (February):309-15.
           Visiting Stein and Toklas in Bilignin revealed to Ulrich
      much of Stein's personality and life purpose: "It was only by
      meeting her and hearing her talk that I became convinced of her
      essential sincerity despite the evidence of showmanship in some
      of her work."

38   W., G. Review of Picasso. Gazette des Beaux-Arts 21
      (February):127.
           In Picasso Stein has shown excellent "American" taste for
      the master.

39   "WILLIE & HENRY & ROSE." New York World-Telegram, 19 September.
           ". . . who would quarrel with the Greeks or Chinese for
      speaking their own language? Miss Stein may select any audience
      she chooses, of any age, any I.Q., any psychiatric notice. This
      time [with The World Is Round] it is the children."

40   WILSON, EDMUND, and HACKETT, CHAUNCEY. "Slightly Pied Pipers."
      New Republic 101 (20 December):266-67.
           Wilson had trouble finishing The World Is Round; Hackett
      felt that Stein had become a child to interest a child.

                                  1940

1   A., D. "Books and Books." Chicago Herald-American, 21 July.
           In Paris France, the "voice of the France of yesterday
      speaks through these pages, the voice of a France that Miss Stein
      knew and loved for forty years, the voice of a France that died
      the other day at Compiegne."

2   BODENHEIM, MAXWELL. "To Gertrude Stein." Poetry 57
      (December):193.
           "You twirl umbrellas, cryptograms of sound, / Like some
      old princess on a wistful tour. . . ."

3   BOWEN, STELLA. Drawn from Life. London: Collins Publishers,
      pp. 117, 123, 171-72.
           Bowen and Stein met in 1924: "I found her a very common-
      sensible person, of a robust and earthly disposition, ever ready
      with domestic advice."

4   BREGY, KATHERINE. "War." Commonweal 32 (23 August):373.
           Paris France "is the most stimulating book Miss Stein has
      given us--a book in which she is vastly more interested in her
      subject than in herself. And like everybody else, in loving
      something more than herself she finds all that is best in
      herself."

5   "BRIEFLY NOTED." New Yorker 16 (13 July):68.
      Paris France is a "charming but now melancholy recital of
the customs and qualities of France by an American who has known
them since 1900. Dilettante in spots, though much of the book
seems fresh and sagacious. Not hard reading."

6   B[UTCHER], F[ANNY]. "Gertrude Stein Writes a Book in a Clear
     and Moving Prose." Chicago Tribune, 26 June, p. 23.
      Paris France is Stein's "subtle distillation of a people,
of their psychology and of their way of life, a way of life in
the last few weeks wiped suddenly and tragically off the face of
the earth in its outer manifestations."

7   CHAMBERLAIN, DOROTHY. "Her France, Her Paris." New Republic
     103 (22 July):123-24.
      "For its literary quality, for its nostalgic pictures of
life in France, and for the lesson to be learned from the fal-
lacies of an intellectual class and the weaknesses that democracy
has tolerated, Paris France is a book you should read."

8   FADIMAN, CLIFTON. "Books." New Yorker 16 (19 October):87.
      What Are Masterpieces proves that "at this late date there
is very little to say about Miss Stein, and Miss Stein will say
it."

9   FLANNER, JANET. "History Tramps Down the Champs Élysées."
     New York Herald-Tribune Books, 23 June, p. 1.
      Paris France is Stein's "hommage à la France, to the France
which was, until a month ago. It is one of her saddest and fun-
niest, deepest and easiest books to read. It is audibly written
in her clear conversational style."

10   FORBES-BOYD, ERIC. Review of Paris France. Christian Science
     Monitor, 13 July, p. 11.
      As Stein does not in Paris France go to her accustomed ex-
tremes of style, the present book may be easily understood.

11   "FRANCE: A TRUE PICTURE IN TERMS OF STEIN." Times Literary
     Supplement, 25 May, p. 252.
      With Paris France, "Miss Gertrude Stein's work is not
every one's meat, but it is indubitably every one's cocktail, to
be slowly sipped until the required intoxication occurs. It will
be a delicate intoxication, a gentle relinquishing of the inhibi-
tions, but once the bouquet of the wine is fully savoured the
habit may be established so that perhaps in future nobody will
be able to do without her."

12   GANNETT, LEWIS. Review of Paris France. Boston Transcript,
     14 June, p. 11.
      Paris France is "a love letter to France, written in the
perfectly intelligible and effectively rhythmic English of which

Miss Stein when she wishes to be understood is capable." Yet, with war now on, "nothing which was written eight months ago seems to stand the sun without fading."

13   "GERTRUDE STEIN'S PARIS." Newsweek 16 (8 July):35.
        In Paris France, Stein writes "as she talks--brilliantly, disconnectedly always with an underlying flow of sense. Which is not always the way she writes."

14   GODFREY, ELEANOR. "Long Live The Phoenix." Canadian Forum
        20 (September):190.
        "Paris France well repays those who have struggled with Gertrude Stein in her attempt to revitalize the English language. Her prose has a fresh simplicity that gives one the feeling of hearing as well as reading. Paris France is almost devoid of mannerisms, yet it has an oblique individuality that reflects a highly trained, acutely sensitive intelligence."

15   "IN BRIEF." Nation 151 (23 November):512.
        With publication of What Are Masterpieces, "it is perhaps superfluous at this date to say that Miss Stein's writings not only are stimulating but actually mean something."

16   L., J. "John Pratt's Cheerful Inventions." Art News 39
        (21 December):9.
        When Stein toured America she called Pratt "the best draftsman in America"; now he has modeled her in papier-mâché.

17   MELLQUIST, JEROME. "And Paris." Commonweal 33 (29 November):
        148.
        What Are Masterpieces is "charming, but principally a Stein item."

18   _____. "France and Its Paintings." Kenyon Review 2
        (Autumn):480-81.
        In Paris France, Stein's "little vignettes of land and peasant and even the quays along the Seine, evoke not only Paris, but that old stone-grey, rich, infinitely mottled human environment where the race for a thousand years has lived so much of its art and thought."

19   MILLETT, FRED B. Contemporary American Authors: A Critical
        Survey and 219 Bio-Bibliographies. New York: Harcourt,
        Brace & Co., pp. 19, 66, 94-95, 179, 593-96.
        Stein's Three Lives is important for the author's "sensitivity to the inner lives of her characters" and led away from objective realism and naturalism.

20   MURDOCH, WALTER. Collected Essays. Sydney, Aust.: Angus &
        Robertson, pp. 190, 216, 218-22, 369, 493.

Joyce and Stein are not insane, "merely silly." They do work out a nihilistic theory of literature, and this theory is "entirely false."

21   "NICE OLD GERTRUDE STEIN." Time 36 (8 July):69.
       In Paris France are "pictures, one of them is an 18th-Century script drawing of Voltaire one is by Sir Francis Rose. The Germans are in Paris but would they like Gertrude Stein's writing about Paris and the French. Would they yes would they."

22   O'BRIEN, JUSTIN. "Miss Stein and France." Nation 151
       (27 July):76.
       "With all its charm and flavor and superficiality, Paris France is a pathetic little book. It is pathetic because, obviously designed as propaganda of the nicer sort, it fails to achieve its end. The larger public having been frightened away by the author's reputation and style, it will be read and enjoyed only by the initiates, the small minority who know both Miss Stein and France."

23   "PARIS FRANCE." Atlantic 166 (August):"Bookshelf."
       "Miss Stein's forty years in France have given her a love for the French people and a knowledge of them equally profound; and in this brilliant small book she has distilled the essence of her insight and affection."

24   REVIEW OF PARIS FRANCE. Booklist 36 (15 July):427-28.
       "Written during the present war but before the invasion of France, this is an affectionate characterization of the Paris Gertrude Stein knows and loves. Her impressions of the French are entertaining and moving; she pays equal attention to trivial and important things, from hats to war."

25   STEARNS, HAROLD E. "Gertrude Stein's France." Saturday
       Review of Literature 22 (13 July):6.
       With Paris France, "for once Miss Stein is concise, forthright, clear, and articulate--almost as if she hadn't time to bother to be anything else, almost as if she had forgotten to be literary."

26   VAN DOREN, CARL. The American Novel, 1789-1939. Rev. ed.
       New York: Macmillan Co., pp. 324, 338-40, 341, 381.
       The Making of Americans is Gertrude Stein's "vast cadenced interlocking saga." No expatriate except physically, Stein "was as obstinately American as Fenimore Cooper had been." Her "importance, so far as literature was concerned, lay less in her actual writings than in her reforming influence on the tones and cadences of prose."

27   VAN VECHTEN, CARL. "Gertrude Stein." In We Moderns. New
       York: Gotham Book Mart, p. 63.

"Gertrude Stein rings bells, loves baskets, and weaves handsome waistcoats. . . . In the matter of fans you can only compare her with a moving picture star in Hollywood and three generations of young writers have sat at her feet. . . . For her a rose is a rose and how!"

28   WILCOX, WENDELL. "A Note on Stein and Abstraction." Poetry
      55 (February):254-57.
         Stein refines a growing fascination with description sans naming: "In her mind as she writes there is almost always a subject but that subject is often as not her own private property. She writes about it but does not name it, or names it in such a way that its physical context cannot be guessed. The excitement is in words themselves, in the movement and interplay of the words."

29   WOODS, KATHERINE. "Civilization and the French." New York
      Times Book Review, 23 June, pp. 1, 13.
         Paris France "as a whole is, of course, devoted, in every sense of that word, to France, the guardian, whether in its capital or in its towns and villages, of the quality of civilization in the minds and spirits of man. It is Gertrude Stein's expression of understanding and gratitude. And in being completely Gertrude Stein's expression it is no less poignantly objective and clear."

1941

1   "ABSTRACT PROSE." Time 37 (17 February):99-100.
         Here are suggestions for Ida: "Read it with care, but require no sense of it that it does not yield. Read it aloud. Read it as poetry must be read or must be listened to: several times. Read it for pleasure only. If it displeases you, quit."

2   AUDEN, W.H. "All about Ida." Saturday Review of Literature
      23 (22 February):8.
         "Ida is not about IDA, but about Dear Ida. Who is Dear Ida? Why, everybody knows Dear Ida, but not everybody knows whom they know."

3   BEACH, JOSEPH WARREN. American Fiction: 1920-1940. New
      York: Macmillan Co., pp. 51, 71, 83.
         Stein introduced young authors to the world of art in Paris after World War I, leading them to imitate painting as they wrote.

4   BIRNEY, EARLE. "Fiction and Diction." Canadian Forum 21
      (April):28.
         "Unless my eyes have deceived me all these years, Ida does not even inexactly reproduce any other reality known to man. As for the inner verities, no doubt the book is chock-full of them,

but the dilettantish babble of babytalk which serves Miss Stein
for a language got in the way of this reviewer whenever he tried
to get his trembling hands on any of them."

5   BROOKS, PHILIP. "Notes on Rare Books." New York Times,
     30 March, p. 22.
         The Haas-Gallup catalogue of Stein's works provides "a
brief and authentic record" of the author's literary achievement."

6   BROOKS, VAN WYCK. Opinions of Oliver Allston. New York:
     E.P. Dutton & Co., pp. 186, 231, 238-40, 254.
         Allston noted Stein's return to intelligibility in her
later works. He liked the emotional content of Three Lives and
deplored Stein's attempts to purge literature of content, blaming
her exile in Europe and her dissociation from ordinary human contact—ultimately Stein became "infantile."

7   CARGILL, OSCAR. Intellectual America: Ideas on the March.
     New York: Macmillan Co., pp. 177, 221, 276, 287, and passim.
         Stein perhaps scheduled her 1934 tour of America because
decadence and obscurity were waning in public interest. The
"supreme egocentric of the most perfect clique of egocentrics,
she probably felt there was a lack of drum-pounding in America. . . ." The failure of Stein's writing was her adoption of
automatic writing as literature. Her final merit will be her
humor.

8   GANNETT, LEWIS. "Books and Things." New York Herald-Tribune,
     15 February.
         Ida is "rather like modern poetry" but "it has somewhat
more rhythm and a great deal more charm. Miss Stein conveys,
as do the progressive-school children, a sense that she really
enjoys writing, and doesn't care a bit whether you, or her publisher, know what she is talking about or not."

9   GILDER, ROSAMOND. "A Picture Book Of Plays and Players,
     1916-1941." Theatre Arts 25 (August):599.
         In Four Saints in Three Acts, "all the performers—saints,
choruses, dancers, compères and comères alike—conveyed a sense
of exaltation which, heightening the dramatic significance, in
no way lessened the satiric impact."

10   GOLD, MICHAEL. The Hollow Men. New York: International
     Publishers, pp. 75-76.
         When Stein declared that money distinguishes the human from
the animal, she revealed herself as "too politically naive and
personally arrogant to hide behind hypocrisy" and not motivated
by literature but by avarice.

11 HAAS, ROBERT BARTLETT, and GALLUP, DONALD CLIFFORD. A Cata-
    logue of the Published and Unpublished Writings of Gertrude
    Stein. New Haven: Yale University Press, 64 pp.
        Primary bibliography.

12 HANSEN, HARRY. "The First Reader." New York World-Telegram,
    15 February.
        ". . . I find that parts of Ida, Miss Stein's 'first novel
    in 11 years,' do seem to make sense, although I can't get inter-
    ested in Ida herself."

13 HAUSER, MARIANNE. "Miss Stein's Ida." New York Times Book
    Review, 16 February, p. 7.
        "Ida, Miss Stein's first novel in eleven years, is not her
    most eccentric work, though it surely is a queer enough book.
    One might call it a short novel, a long poem, or a modern fairy
    tale; or a painting in words, reminding one of a Dali rather
    than of a Picasso."

14 LEVINSON, RONALD B. "Gertrude Stein, William James, and
    Grammar." American Journal of Psychology 54 (January):124-28.
        "It is . . . intellectual concern with linguistic experimen-
    tation, though one may deny the success of the experiments, which
    may supply a clue for distinguishing the products of Miss Stein's
    literary workshop from those early automatic fruits of [William
    James'] Harvard laboratory of Psychology."

15 LITTELL, ROBERT. "Outstanding Novels." Yale Review, n.s. 30
    (Spring):xiv.
        Littell endured a wrecked car while reading Ida: "I regard
    this as an omen of some kind, and have abandoned my search for
    the key to what may very well be the door beyond which lies the
    future of American literature."

16 MANN, KLAUS. "Two Generations." Decision 1 (May):71-74.
        Stein and Carson McCullers would disagree about literary
    art, McCullers thinking Stein's Ida less valuable than her essays
    and Stein disliking the would-be psychology of Reflections in a
    Golden Eye.

17 MAXWELL, ELSA. "Potatoes Without Punctuation." New York
    Journal, 31 December.
        "I have always been fascinated by Gertrude. Maybe it is
    because we do a lot of the same things . . . in different ways.
    I have also made it a point, however, to punctuate my nonsense."

18 "MISS STEIN'S WORK SHOWN. New York Times, 30 April, p. 17.
        With a singing of Four Saints in Three Acts, an exhibition
    of Stein's work opened at Columbia University Library.

19   O., O. "What Has Gertrude Done Now?" Boston Transcript,
     15 February, p. 1.
          With Ida, "it is easier for Gertrude Stein to write a book
     than not a book well why should it be and not be about the
     Duchess of Windsor."

20   ROSHER, DONALD G. "Einstein Is Fine, But Zwei Is Too Many."
     Chicago Daily News, 16 April.
          In regard to Ida, "Read Stein with abandon; look for no
     concrete sense that is not obviously there as far as you are
     concerned."

21   S., E.C. Review of Ida. Christian Science Monitor, 22 March,
     p. 12.
          The ambitious reader might understand Ida, for Stein "puts
     together words that were never before associated in just such
     arrangements and yet they make sense in a personal way, by means
     of Gertrude's all-her-own style. There are times when you think
     you have the clue to her aims, and then you wonder."

22   SAWYER, JULIAN. Gertrude Stein: A Bibliography. New York:
     Arrow Editions, 162 pp.
          Primary bibliography.

23   SWEENEY, JAMES JOHNSON. "Picasso and Iberian Sculpture."
     Art Bulletin 23 (September):192-93.
          Repainting Stein's face, Picasso "gave it a formal, mask-
     like character," with features like an Iberian bas-relief "Negro
     Attacked by a Lion."

24   WILSON, EDMUND. The Wound and the Bow: Seven Studies in
     Literature. Boston: Houghton Mifflin Co., p. 217.
          Stein contributed to Hemingway's understanding of the
     colloquialism of the American language.

                                1942

1   [AGEE, JAMES.] "Woman With a Hoe." Time 40 (27 July):83-84.
          In wartime France Gertrude Stein and Alice B. Toklas are
     rusticated but safe from persecution as Jews.

2   BONNEY, THÉRÈSE. "Gertrude Stein in France." Vogue 110
     (1 July):60-61, 70.
          Stein "wrote that she had decided not to leave France
     'because it would be awfully uncomfortable.' That is all the
     reason she gives. But I think she stayed because she owed France
     a great gratitude and like Matisse, Dufy, Bonnard, Maillol, and
     Lurcat, felt that she must stay with her friends there. Like
     everybody else in France today, she is very busy accommodating
     herself to everything, digging potatoes, writing. . . ."
     Reprinted: 1942.3.

3   _____. Vogue's First Reader. Introduction by Frank
       Crowninshield. New York: Julian Messner, pp. 228-31.
       Reprint of 1942.2.

4   CERF, BENNETT. "Trade Winds." Saturday Review of Literature
       25 (5 September):20.
            Boxes for Gertrude Stein are being returned from France
       undelivered. Concerning Stein's books, "we always print an
       edition of exactly twenty-five hundred copies of a new Gertrude
       Stein book. The demand is constant. We rarely have fifty copies
       left over. We never have to reprint."

5   "GERTRUDE STEIN." In Twentieth Century Authors. Edited by
       Stanley J. Kunitz and Howard Haycroft. New York: H.W. Wilson
       Co., pp. 1337-38.
            Influenced by modern art, Stein's work is abstractionist;
       her personal manner is "downright and plain-spoken."

6   GREEN, JULIAN. Memoirs of Happy Days. New York: Harper &
       Brothers, pp. 226-27.
            Green was taken by his father to the Stein studio, where
       the modern art confused and frightened him.

7   HAINES, GEORGE, IV. "Forms of Imaginative Prose: 1900-1940."
       Southern Review 7 (1942):766-69.
            Stein, "having . . . translated the individual perspective
       into verbal terms . . . is free to relate all things to each
       other in the word, and in word relationships."

8   HARPER, ALLANAH. "A Magazine and Some People in Paris."
       Partisan Review 9 (July-August):316.
            Harper met Stein in Paris and got lectured to about modern
       art.

9   KALLEN, HORACE M. Art and Freedom. New York: Duell, Sloan
       & Pearce, pp. 29, 464, 800, 801, 802, 803.
            Tender Buttons is "a mutation upon the Imagist practice,"
       and this book was "to the Imagist anthology what Cubism was to
       post-Impressionism or Picasso to Gauguin. [Stein's] verses may
       be judged to own a cubist contagion."

10   KAZIN, ALFRED. On Native Grounds: An Interpretation of
       Modern American Prose Literature. New York: Reynal &
       Hitchcock, pp. 167, 192, 195, 207, 214-15, and passim.
            Stein learned her writing art from fifteen years of "devo-
       tion to the independent vision of modern French painting"--an
       esthetic which she taught to Sherwood Anderson and Ernest
       Hemingway.

11   PEARSON, NORMAN HOLMES. "The Gertrude Stein Collection."
       Yale University Library Gazette 16 (January):45-47.

Van Vechten has given the Yale University Library a valuable collection of Gertrude Stein materials.

12   POURRAT, HENRI. "Faite de terre." <u>Dépêche de Toulouse</u>, 3 January.
     <u>Paris France</u> is delicious, enchanting, and wise about France.

13   SCHLAUCH, MARGARET. <u>The Gift of Tongues</u>. New York: Modern Age Books, pp. 240-44.
     Stein "sacrifices more than most writers are willing to do in order to gain musical quality and immediacy." Her reward to the reader for such collaboration does not repay the effort, resulting mostly in a "snobbish pleasure."

*14   SCHORER, CALVIN E. "A Life Is a Life Is a Life." <u>Trend</u> 1 (April):23-24.
     Cited: <u>Index to Little Magazines</u>, 1940-1942, p. 164.

1943

1   "THE LITERARY LIFE." <u>Time</u> 41 (3 May):55.
     The manuscript of <u>Mrs. Reynolds</u> has reached New York from France: "The publisher said he could make nothing of it, thought it could probably be read from either end, decided to publish it."

2   SAWYER, JULIAN. "Gertrude Stein (1874--): A Check-list comprising Critical and Miscellaneous Writings about her Work, Life and Personality from 1913-1924)." <u>Bulletin of Bibliography</u> 17 (January-April):211-12.
     Secondary bibliography.

3   _____. "Gertrude Stein (1874--): A Check-list comprising Critical and Miscellaneous Writings about her Work, Life and Personality from 1913-1943." <u>Bulletin of Bibliography</u> 18 (May-August):11-13.
     Secondary bibliography.

4   TAVERNIER, RENÉ. "Les Arbres--a Gertrude Stein." <u>Signes</u> [Lyon]: Confluences, pp. 13-17.
     Poem dedicated to Stein.

1944

1   ADAMS, J. DONALD. <u>The Shape of Books to Come</u>. New York: Viking Press, p. 12.
     Too much credit has been given to Gertrude Stein for teaching simplicity and repetition as prose devices. Reprint of 1944.2.

2   _____. "Speaking of Books." New York Times Book Review,
     16 January, p. 2.
     Reprinted: 1944.1.

3   "BOOK IS A BOOK." New Yorker 20 (19 February):18-19.
          "There are four people in New York who have read the manu-
     script of Gertrude Stein's new novel. Three of the people do
     not matter at all well hardly at all but the fourth is us and
     that is a good thing because we can tell you all about Gertrude's
     new novel. The name of the novel is Mrs. Reynolds."

4   CERF, BENNETT. Try and Stop Me: A Collection of Anecdotes
     and Stories, Mostly Humorous. New York: Simon & Schuster,
     pp. 85, 128-31.
          Cerf and colleagues at Random House published Stein without
     understanding her prose, being able to count on selling 2500
     copies of any one work by her.

5   "FINDS GERTRUDE STEIN SAFE." Chicago Herald-American,
     2 September.
          Eric Sevareid has reported that Stein lives simply and
     safely in southern France.

6   GANNETT, LEWIS. "Gertrude Stein Returns to Paris; Nazis
     Looted Home but Left Art." New York Herald-Tribune,
     29 December.
          Stein and Toklas "found their apartment on the Left Bank
     stripped of its linen, blankets and kitchen pots by Gestapo
     agents who searched it during the occupation; but not a picture
     had been touched, and Miss Stein is blissful."

7   "GERTRUDE STEIN FOUND; JUST FINISHING A BOOK." New York Times,
     2 September, p. 9.
          Eric Sevareid has found Stein in southeastern France, safe
     but thinner, finishing a book called Wars I Have Seen.

8   "THE LIBERATION OF GERTRUDE STEIN." Life 17 (2 October):83-84.
          "Racing north with a Seventh Army unit, LIFE Photographer
     Carl Mydans stopped off at Culoz, a pretty little village in
     southeastern France, to call on a world-famous 70-year-old
     American lady author. Though the Nazis knew and denounced her
     literary work and though German officers lived right in her
     house during the occupation, they never recognized the lady as
     Gertrude Stein."

9   NOYES, NEWBOLD, Jr. "Star War Writer Interviews Gertrude
     Stein in South France." Washington Star, 5 September.
          "We had come a long way to find her. All morning we drove
     through shady lanes and country so freshly liberated the people
     looked at us strangely, unsure as to whether or not we were Ger-
     mans. Miss Stein was well off the beaten track. If she had not
     been, we might never have found her at all."

10   RÖNNEBECK, ARNOLD. "Gertrude Was Always Giggling." <u>Books
     Abroad</u> 18 (October):3-7.
         "I suppose it would be easy to imitate Wordsworth or even
     Shelley or the bombast of Victor Hugo in type, but very difficult
     to imitate convincingly Gertrude Stein because her style is her
     <u>meaning</u> and you can't imitate meaning if it is not your own.
     Gertrude Stein <u>does</u> write the way she talks and she always did
     that thing that way."

                              1945

1   ANTHEIL, GEORGE. <u>Bad Boy of Music</u>. Garden City, N.Y.:
     Doubleday, Doran, pp. 151, 157, 159-61.
         Stein and Joyce were the sought-after authors in Paris--
     among writers of exotic prose.

2   BARNES, DJUNA. "Matron's Primer." <u>Contemporary Jewish
     Record</u> 8 (June):342-43.
         "For a number of years Gertrude Stein has been read with
     considerable consternation, admiration and annoyance. [<u>Wars I
     Have Seen</u>], like the earlier <u>Autobiography of Alice B. Toklas</u>,
     is comprehensible. I remain uneasy as to the validity of the
     medium."

3   BENEDICT, LIBBY. "The Disillusionment That Calls Itself
     Objectivity." <u>New York Times Book Review</u>, 20 May, p. 4.
         With <u>Wars I Have Seen</u>, "could anyone, even in 1943, main-
     tain that a war won against Nazi fury would not be a lost war?
     To see it as a victorious war does not mean to extol war, or to
     love it. One can loathe war to the bottom of one's heart. One
     can pray every moment of the day for war's end. But to say that
     it must of necessity be a lost war, when the beast that has been
     unleashed in a nation is annihilated by avowed and sincere fight-
     ers for civilization--that is irresponsible cynicism."

4   BRADLEY, J. CHAPMAN. "Bible Still a Best Seller." <u>New York
     Times</u>, 3 September, p. 22.
         Contrary to Stein's assertion that U.S. soldiers use few
     Bibles in Europe in the war, the facts are otherwise.

5   BREIT, HARVEY. "Books." <u>Mademoiselle</u>, May, pp. 193, 243.
         "Joyce's Dublin and its inhabitants made Joyce's method
     as much as the method made the city and its citizens. But Culoz
     and its people failed to modify Miss Stein. Miss Stein's tech-
     niques were made in a warm dream in a cool bed in a long ago day
     in a far away land far away long ago as you know completely and
     entirely as you know it must be."

6   BROMFIELD, LOUIS. <u>Pleasant Valley</u>. New York: Harper &
     Brothers, p. 204.

                              108

Bromfield's dog "nearly destroyed a famous dog, the handsome white poodle called Basquette, belonging to Gertrude Stein."

7   BUCKNELL, PHILIP H. "Crystal Unclear Gertie Stein Tells Off
     Off Reich GIs Off GIs." Stars and Stripes, 4 August.
        Brewsie and Willie is "a contemporary Gettysburg Address.
The soldiers talk about the Germans and the French, jobs and
Gallup Polls and pin-up girls, the last depression and the next,
and what to do about them, England and Industrialism and Negroes
and children. The ideas have the same simplicity and clarity
that made [Stein's] Composition as Explanation one of the most
important discussions in esthetics in our time. The language,
the grammar, is so real, so well heard, so contemporary, and so
funny . . . that any sentence is a paradigm of modern American
usage. And the sound is so real. Reading, one is there, present.
That is if one reads listening to it."

8   BURNS, BEN. "Double-Talk-Prose; Common-Sense Talk." Chicago
     Defender, 27 October, p. 11.
        "The only pioneers left in America are Negroes and Jews.
From famed Gertrude Stein, world-renowned author, whose name has
been written indelibly in the history of literature, comes that
blunt assertion. The aged Paris novelist insists that American
Negroes, because they are persecuted people, are 'one of the few
peoples in the United States still pioneering.'"

9   BUTCHER, FANNY. "Gertrude Stein Gives Some Lucid Observations
     on War." Chicago Tribune, 11 March, sec. 6, p. 9.
        America's most famous literary figure to have lived through
the war and occupation, Stein in Wars I Have Seen tells the "story
of those last weeks and of the arrival of the Americans [in] as
factual writing, as vivid conventional recital as any of you will
ever read."

10   CORBETT, Sgt. SCOTT. "Give Me Land." Yank 2 (11 November):17.
        Stein said, "the trouble is, Americans aren't land-crazy
any more. That's what the pioneers were, land-crazy, and that's
what all Frenchmen are and always have been, because they know
that owning a place of your own is what gives you independence
and lets you stand on your own feet, and nobody is rich unless
he owns his own land."

11   COURNOS, JOHN. "This Week's Book." Philadelphia Bulletin,
     17 March.
        With Wars I Have Seen, "you cannot help asking: if Miss
Stein can write like other people when she is moved, why the
deuce does she still show a tendency to renege when writing in
a more tranquil, more deliberate mood?"

12   COWLEY, MALCOLM. "Gertrude Stein for the Plain Reader."
     New York Times Book Review, 11 March, pp. 1, 22.

In <u>Wars I Have Seen</u>, "nobody else, among all the writers who have told us about life in occupied France, has made the story so intimate, homely, immediate, as if a squad of Germans were quartered in your own kitchen. . . ." Apart from the autobiographical books, however, Stein has produced many books "monumental in their dullness, so many pyramids and Parthenons consecrated to a reader's apathy."

13   _____. "How Do We Talk American?" <u>New Republic</u> 113
       (9 July):50-51.
       "At the very end of her new book, <u>Wars I Have Seen</u>," Stein "descends from the great problems of war and peace, on which her remarks are sometimes rather silly, to the smaller but no less complicated problem of creating an American style in speech and writing."

14   _____. "The Middle American Style: D. Crockett to E.
       Hemingway." <u>New York Times Book Review</u>, 15 July, pp. 3, 14.
       Stein developed the colloquial American prose style in
       <u>Three Lives</u>—a bridge from the prose of Mark Twain to that of
       Ernest Hemingway and Sherwood Anderson.

15   FARBER, MARJORIE. "Autobiography Continued." <u>Partisan Review</u>
       12 (Spring):257-59.
       <u>Wars I Have Seen</u> is Stein's naive defense of her aid to
       other writers and her experiences in two world wars.

16   F[ITTS], D[UDLEY]. "Brief Comments." <u>Kenyon Review</u> 7
       (Autumn):721-22.
       "Like all of those books by Miss Stein which are written in
       the English language, <u>Wars I Have Seen</u> has the plain virtues of
       honesty, sympathy, and good humor."

17   "From 'Business English' To Gertrude Stein." <u>Saturday Evening</u>
       <u>Post</u> 217 (12 May):112.
       <u>Wars I Have Seen</u> is "a great book, which tells practically
       everything about how people act when waiting for a war to get
       itself over, but the average reader will need conditioning in
       order not to miss conventional punctuation. To get basic training for Gertrude Stein, we suggest a few days reading the reports
       of investigating committees, reinforced by some fast work among
       the rules of the Internal Revenue Bureau."

18   GANNETT, LEWIS. "Books and Things." <u>New York Herald-Tribune</u>,
       6 March.
       "I love Gertrude Stein. I love to hear her talk, like a
       bright, excited child, mixing oracular nonsense with fresh childlike wisdom, all tumbling out with the delighted kaleidoscope
       inconsecutiveness of memory. Sometimes I've wanted to argue with
       her, but no one ever argues with Gertrude Stein, one just listens
       to the flood. And I like to read Gertrude Stein when she writes
       as she talks, as she does in <u>Wars I Have Seen</u>.

19   GHALI, PAUL. "G.I. Is a G.I., So Gerty Stein Turns Her
     Talents Upon Them." Chicago Daily News, 5 December, sec. A,
     p. 2.
        "Gertrude Stein has emerged from this war unchanged. Four
     years of concealment in German occupied France have preserved her
     beautifully. Those who knew her before say she looks even better
     now. . . . She has the same hatred of the common, the same irri-
     tation of the banal, and the same teeny-weeny bit of inclination
     to scandalize. Gertrude is surely not aging. Maybe it is the
     world around her which has aged."

20   "A GI is a GI Is a. . . ." Newsweek 26 (3 September):30-31.
        Stein has begun a book about the GI, Brewsie and Willie,
     making her a sort of "Left Bank Ernie Pyle."

21   HACKETT, FRANCIS. "Books of the Times." New York Times,
     8 March, p. 21.
        "Luckily, [as in Wars I Have Seen by Stein] when her emo-
     tions grip her, she throws off the swaddling clothes, and the
     faithful reader moves into a full world that has air in it as
     well as intimacy. Hers is a powerful personality, but it needed
     the American Army to liberate her."

22   JOHNSON, WENDELL. "Yes Dear People Here It Is About Gertie
     It Certainly Is." Chicago Sun, 11 March.
        Neither insane nor silly, Gertrude Stein has produced an
     unusual book in Wars I Have Seen.

23   [KNAUTH, PERCY.] "Gertie & the G.I.'s." Time 45 (16 April):
     26-27.
        Stein has returned to Paris and spoken to groups of sol-
     diers from America: "This Stein is easier to understand when
     she is talking than when she is writing, but there still remains
     a considerable gap between her mind and that of the average Amer-
     ican soldier in this war."

24   _____. "War Is A War Is a War." Life 18 (16 April):14, 17-18.
        At a recent speech Stein gave to American soldiers in Paris,
     some members of the audience "are still trying to figure out the
     Steinian views on life, humanity and the war which the little old
     lady expounded with such energy and directness. . . . Miss
     Stein's delivery was in fact so forceful, even though she re-
     mained seated on the platform through most of her lecture, that
     those who tried to argue with her were left hanging in the air."

25   LAMPORT, SARA. "Gertrude Stein, A Movie Hater, Poses for One."
     New York Herald (Paris), 1 November.
        "Gertrude Stein, who 'hates movies,' posed Tuesday for an
     hour of A 1 film effort, and will appear in the cast of the
     soldier-made documentary The Sergeant Sees the City."

26   MacKAY, S/Sgt. GEORGE. "Gertie, Maggie Enliven Orly Field
      Lecture Series." <u>Paris Air Courier</u>, 25 August.
         Stein "talked to GI's over here about themselves; their
responsibilities to the world, now and later; about their bad
manners in foreign countries; about the possibility of their
failure as salesmen of the democratic ideal. She didn't talk
in her 'repetitious, apparently artless style,' but in good old
Allegheny, Penna., American. She mowed 'em down--and she got
away with it."

27   MAUROIS, ANDRÉ. <u>Études américaines I</u>. New York: Éditions
      de la Maison Française, pp. 9-19.
         Stein understood the French and loved them but remained
always the free American.

28   MILL, ANTONIO SABATE. "Gertrude Stein, futuro universal de
      la novella." <u>Destino</u> (Barcelona), 31 March.
         "Today America achieves, with Gertrude Stein, major liter-
ary expression. And who knows whether, with her, a new orienta-
tion of reality in the twentieth-century novel?"

29   MILLIET, ANTOINE. "Wars I Have Seen." <u>Le Coq Bugiste</u>,
      1 September, p. 2.
         <u>Wars I Have Seen</u> merely reconfirms the mutual adoption of
France and the United States.

30   O., T.M. "Gertrude Ends Exile In War." <u>Kansas City Star</u>,
      17 March.
         "Gertrude Stein's <u>Wars I Have Seen</u> is a masterpiece of
clarity compared with much of her work. Its prose has a sing-
song quality that is definitely childish but, once you get
accustomed to it, rather fascinating."

31   REDMAN, BEN RAY. "The Importance of Being Earnest."
      <u>Saturday Review of Literature</u> 28 (10 March):8, 30.
         <u>Wars I Have Seen</u> "is a good book, a very good book, and it
would be a great pity if any readers were put off it by Gertrude
Stein's reputation for willful obscurity and nonsensicality.
For this book makes sense, all the way through. . . . Whatever
else may be said of it, Gertrude Stein's prose is now a mature,
flexible, wonderfully useful instrument."

32   REVIEW OF <u>WARS I HAVE SEEN</u>. <u>Booklist</u> 41 (1 April):222
         "Written in France during the Nazi occupation, the book
begins in 1943 as a rather random set of reminiscences and reflections on wars the author has read about or lived thru.
Gradually the air of detachment is replaced by more personal
feeling about the war around her. . . ."

33   REVIEW OF <u>WARS I HAVE SEEN</u>. <u>Bulletin from Virginia Kirkus'
      Bookshop Service</u> 13 (15 January):24.

"Perhaps this is the shot in the arm that war reporting needs--though I question it. Here, with a slight increase in intelligibility, but equal eccentricity, is the mistress of the marathon, her indefatigable retreats and repetitions, her aberrational associations. . . ."

34   REVIEW OF WARS I HAVE SEEN. Radcliffe Quarterly, May, pp. 27-28.
     "There is no particular construction to the book--at least if there is I missed it; just this stream of conversation, anecdotal and reflective and pretty darned interesting. It leaves you with the feeling of a warm and vital person."

35   "ROSE STILL ROSE IN MISS STEIN'S CHILDREN'S BOOK." New York Herald-Tribune, 15 September, sec. 2, p. 1.
     "Gertrude Stein has adopted a policy of appeasement toward literary critics. Sundry critics for many years, in their desperation to interpret Miss Stein's alliterative sentences to befuddled readers, have compared them to selections from Mother Goose, Alice in Wonderland and other children's classics. Miss Stein has [in The World Is Round] met that challenge and written a book for children."

36   S., E.C. Review of Wars I Have Seen. Christian Science Monitor, 6 March, p. 12.
     In Wars I Have Seen, Stein is difficult but interesting, apparently expressing her thoughts just as they come to her.

37   SCHWARTZ, DELMORE. "Gertrude Stein's Wars." Nation 160 (24 March):339-40.
     Wars I Have Seen is not in Stein's obscure style from the earlier days, but "Miss Stein has made the long journey without losing any of her possessions or prepossessions, her prose rhythm, her fascination with herself, or her love of unqualified generalization about the inner essence of anything and everything."

38   SCOTT, W.T. "Gertrude Stein's Particular Warfare." Providence Journal, 11 March.
     Wars I Have Seen is as "alive as highpowered electric cable, it is as exciting--and exhausting--as going on a drunk. It is sometimes illiterate, occasionally perverse, and it contains an erratic blend of nonsense . . . and of brilliant analysis."

39   "STEIN ON WAR." Time 45 (12 March):45, 100.
     ". . . those with the patience to read Wars I Have Seen slowly may discover an uncommon charm and perception."

40   "STEIN SCREENED." News and Review (London), 22 November.
     "Gertrude Stein has won fame over three generations as the short, stumpy high-priestess of staggered, repetitive poetry. . . . Last week she made her screen debut in Paris in The Sergeant Sees

the City. Mannish, 71-year-old Miss Stein appears as one of the leading intellectuals visited by a culture-hungry GI in Paris."

41   SULZBERGER, C.L. "GI Novel Written by Gertrude Stein." New York Times, 25 August, p. 13.
      Gertrude Stein in France is "writing a new novel called Brewsie and Willie which is about GI's and how they worry and how she worries about them and how they worry together about their worrying."

42   T., W.P. "The Heart of the Business." Infantry Journal, May.
      Wars I Have Seen, "peculiar English and all, speaks for itself; and surfeited with personal-narrative war books as I am, I say that here is one of the best."

43   TAYLOR, HOWARD. "Gertrude Stein's Diary Of Life in Fallen France." Philadelphia Inquirer, 11 March.
      "Anyone who will forget Miss Stein's eccentricities and tackle Wars I Have Seen without prejudice will find it a stimulating and memorable experience."

44   THOMSON, VIRGIL. "Gertrude Stein's France in War." New York Herald-Tribune Weekly Book Review, 11 March, p. 2.
      Wars I Have Seen "is really the most charming and the most realistic picture imaginable of a life that has been closed to our knowledge for more than four years. Stories from France are beginning to come through now, but none is so convincing as Miss Stein's. It must have been like that there; it would not have been any other way. It is a true picture."

45   TUBBS, VINCENT. "Gertrude Stein Talks for Afro." Baltimore Afro-American, 28 July.
      "'The American colored man has reached a turning point where he must become spiritually independent of the white man if he is to solve the complexing problems that beset his race,' says Gertrude Stein, American-born, internationally-known writer who courageously weathered four years of Nazi occupation of France."

46   WAHL, JEAN. "Miss Stein's Battle." New Republic 112 (19 January):396-98.
      Out of the prison of occupied France, Stein has written her version of The Enormous Room—a narrative "beautiful and very moving in parts, with many marvelous simple stories."

47   WEEKS, EDWARD. "A woman preoccupied." Atlantic 175 (April): 129, 131.
      In Wars I Have Seen Stein's "chronicle meanders rather like Salvador Dali on a bicycle; yet it is always clear in its focus, for in the meandering the world is seen to be revolving around Gertrude Stein. . . ."

48 WILSON, EDMUND. "Books." New Yorker 21 (17 March):83-84.
     "The new book by Gertrude Stein--Wars I Have Seen--has a
kind of journalistic interest that none of her other books has
had and may possibly get a wider circulation. . . . If you start
reading at page forty, say, you will find yourself involved in a
development--an alternation of comments on history with anecdotes
of daily life--which gradually becomes exciting and, finally,
exhilarating."

49 WRIGHT, RICHARD. "Gertrude Stein's stay is drenched in
     Hitler's horrors." New York PM, 11 March.
     Having learned authentic written speech from "Melanctha,"
Wright found Wars I Have Seen clear testimony to Stein's relevance and power of political observation.

                              1946

1   "ALICE TOKLAS HEIR OF GERTRUDE STEIN." New York Times,
     11 August, p. 46.
     In Baltimore, Stein's will reveals bequests to Toklas, the
Metropolitan Museum of Art and Yale University Library.

2   BARR, ALFRED H., Jr. Picasso: Fifty Years of His Art.
     New York: Museum of Modern Art, pp. 37, 50, 59, 254, 256,
     and passim.
     The Steins were encouraging, discerning buyers of
Picasso's art; but Gertrude Stein was incorrect often in dis-
cussing Picasso's artistic history.

3   BERNSTEIN, CHARLES. "Science Is Dead." Occident, Winter,
     pp. 27-30.
     ". . . it certainly is nice and a relief to read Wars I
Have Seen and find no causes and effects and extra nice to find
not one prediction in this world of predictions."

4   BINGAY, MALCOLM W. "She Kept Us Fooled." Chicago Daily News,
     7 August, p. 7.
     Stein "wrote foolishly for a purpose: to attract attention
and to kid the pants off the phony highbrows who took her stuff
seriously."

5   BOGAN, LOUISE. "Great-Aunt Gertrude, Half-Asleep."
     Washington Post, 28 July, pp. 6, 25.
     With The First Reader and Three Plays, "one leans against
Great-Aunt's ample aproned lap. Great-aunt is half asleep and
so is the listening child. What comes through from this combi-
nation of the old speaker and the young listener does not sound
particularly sensible, in print. But how clever Great-aunt is
in the choice of what she weaves so oddly together! Her stories
are full of ancient metamorphoses, horrible surprises, shocks

and terror, as well as gentler subjects and themes, like food, animals, flowers and vegetables."

6   "BRIEFLY NOTED." New Yorker 22 (9 November):124.
    In Selected Writings of Gertrude Stein, "every phase of the author's style, from the queerest to the most limpid, is represented, and every period of her career. Mr. Van Vechten has made it possible for new readers to become easily acquainted with the work of this eccentric and remarkable woman and for old readers to get a well-rounded view of it."

7   BUTCHER, FANNY. "Gertrude Stein Reports What She Heard GIs Say." Chicago Tribune, 21 July, pp. 3, 7.
    Brewsie and Willie is clear writing from Stein, proving her "a past master at recording American idiomatic talk."

8   _____. "The Literary Spotlight." Chicago Tribune, 11 August, sec. 4, p. 9.
    Stein is dead, but ultimately history will credit her most with that "quality of thinking clearly and translating her thoughts into communication with other minds. . . ."

9   _____. "Miss Stein's Clear and Opaque Prose." Chicago Tribune, 27 October, sec. 4, p. 25.
    Publication of Selected Writings of Gertrude Stein "is a timely contribution to the world's understanding of one of its most spectacular literary artists."

10 CERF, BENNETT. "Trade Winds." Saturday Review of Literature 29 (14 July):14.
    Cerf enjoyed Stein's chiding people for being foolishly Communist.

11 "COME ALL OVER PATRIOTIC." Time 48 (5 August):102.
    ". . . between the lines of babytalk, Brewsie and Willie is a serious lecture on the postwar responsibilities of America's younger generation."

12 COWLEY, MALCOLM. "An American Patriot By Remote Control." New York Herald-Tribune Weekly Book Review, 21 July, p. 5.
    In Brewsie and Willie, Stein has a subject dear to Americans and important to hear--the lesson to live well and fully and independently. The wonder is that a political naif like Gertrude Stein has expressed such political wisdom.

13 _____. "Gertrude Stein, Writer or Word Scientist?" New York Herald-Tribune Weekly Book Review, 24 November, p. 1.
    Publication of Selected Writings of Gertrude Stein causes one to imagine her as a scientist in a laboratory, separate from mankind and society, researching the quality of words: "With three or four exceptions, the books that record her experiments

are unreadable; and yet they have exercised a wide influence on American writing. . . . Her style is like a chemical useless in its pure state but powerful when added to other mixtures. American prose has changed its whole direction partly because of Gertrude Stein."

14 DESFEUILLES, PAUL. Une Fervente de la répétition: Gertrude Stein. Paris: Mirefleurs, 31 pp.
      The essential character of Stein's use of psychology is the importance which she gives to repetition. Through apparently perpetual restatements, her style demonstrates this dominant preoccupation.

15 DOOLEY, WILLIAM GERMAIN. "Double-Talk in The Museum World." New York Times Book Review, 15 September, p. 2.
      In What Are Masterpieces Stein was correct in stating that the creation of too few masterpieces in any art is due to too much talk by would-be artists.

16 FREEMANTLE, ANNE. "Letter." Commonweal 45 (20 December): 253-54.
      Contrary to recent opinion, Stein "is always, it seems to me, aware . . . of the entire dependence of the word--of every word ever written--on the Word, and of its existence only within this framework and within the terms of that relationship."

17 _____. "Mom in the Kitchen." Commonweal 45 (25 October): 33-35.
      "It is very difficult to estimate [Stein's] effect upon the English language, or upon English literature, because she is so solid and single a character that, now she is recently gone, there is a great gap, a hole torn in the earth where the tree fell, and it may be some time before the importance of her impact can properly be evaluated."

18 [FLANNER, JANET.] "Letter from Paris." New Yorker 22 (10 August):36-37.
      "To Gertrude Stein's old friends here [in Paris], her death was the last chapter in her private history's concordance with the important things going on in France. She had lived in France for forty years, had worked for it in its two greatest wars, and had received public acclaim here during the period between them; she had met and welcomed our Army during the liberation; and she left the scene as international statesmen began talking over the second peace."

19 GALLUP, DONALD. "Gertrude Stein Analyzes American Soldiers." Dallas News, 28 July, sec. 4, p. 5.
      Brewsie and Willie is a "strange but stimulating mixture of Nineteenth Century theory and Twentieth Century fact, of Stein and GI. The American soldiers in France awaiting redeployment are presented with telling accuracy through the medium of their conversation."

20   "GERTRUDE STEIN DIES IN FRANCE, 72." New York Times, 28 July,
      p. 40.
          Dead of a "run-down condition," Stein "could and did write
      illegibly at times, [yet] her distinction rested on her use of
      words apart from their conventional meaning. . . ."

21   "GERTRUDE STEIN LEAVES PICASSO PORTRAIT TO MET." Art News 45
      (September):8.
          "As unpredictable as Gertrude Stein herself was the desig-
      nation in her will of the Metropolitan" to receive her Picasso
      portrait.

22   "GERTRUDE STEIN'S BURIAL DELAYED." New York Times, 31 July,
      p. 27.
          Alice Toklas has announced that Stein's body will be in
      the American Cathedral Church until burial in Paris.

23   GREEN, JULIAN. "Souvenirs de Gertrude Stein." Le Figaro,
      10 August.
          "I can see her only in the image of a mountain or a
      menhir, something unshakable that gives the race so much of
      its spirit; and when, with a familiar gesture, she separated
      with a finger her short grey hair and when she turned on me her
      tranquil glance which held a great sweetness, I can not but have
      a secret admiration for this shadowless woman which doubt seemed
      never to have attacked."

24   GROSSER, MAURICE. "Gertrude Stein's Autobiography of Joe."
      Atlanta Journal, 28 April, p. 34.
          In Brewsie and Willie, "Miss Stein I am afraid has written
      a Classic of Literature. I know of nothing else that has this
      particular texture, sense, or sound, and I imagine that this book
      will change English writing even more than her other works and
      conversation have already done."

25   HUTCHENS, JOHN K. "Plain Talk From Gertrude." New York Times
      Book Review, 20 January, p. 24.
          Soon Brewsie and Willie and an anthology of Stein's other
      writings will be issued by Random House, to whose Bennett Cerf
      Stein recently wrote, "What the hell is the matter with you?"

26   K., H. "The World of Gertrude Stein." Punch, 20 February.
          Wars I Have Seen is "a fascinating book. In other books,
      written in other times, Miss Stein's peculiar style has not con-
      ciliated all readers, and has induced acute nervous irritation
      in some. But it seems perfectly suited to her present
      theme. . . ."

27   LAUGHLIN, JAMES. "Miss Stein and 2 G.I.s." Chicago Sun Book
      Week, 4 August, p. 6.
          Brewsie and Willie may not be an absolutely accurate trans-
      cription of GI dialogue, but it is fascinating Gertrude Stein
      dialogue.

28 LERMAN, LEO. "A Wonderchild for 72 Years." Saturday Review
of Literature 29 (2 November):17-18.
Selected Writings is the summation of Stein's career: "So
this source of strength, this deep well of wisdom, this grand-
mother was a wonderchild for seventy-two years, an authentic
wonderchild. That meant she was a prodigy and she behaved ac-
cordingly and was fawned upon and never fawned."

29 LEWIS, LLOYD. "There's Nobody Like Gertrude." Chicago Sun
Book Week, 3 February.
"You have heard [Stein] called a poseur, tricking the intelligentsia with her literary hocus-pocus. Then when she talks you
see honesty transparent in her grave, bright face, and something
perhaps superior to honesty--candor."

30 MAUK, J.F. "Gertie Forgot Her Paragraph Marks Again."
Washington Post, 28 July.
In Brewsie and Willie, Stein is "dull, affected and long-
winded! Except for an occasional epigrammatic half-truth, tossed
in to dazzle less brilliant minds, she says nothing that has not
been said better by editorial writers and columnists."

31 "MILESTONES." Time 48 (5 August):87.
Gertrude Stein has died--"grizzled matriarch of the stut-
tering sentence . . . whose literary doubletalk was as confusing
as amusing. . . ."

32 MILLER, PERRY. "Steinese." New York Times Book Review,
3 November, pp. 6, 30.
"It is time now for a comprehensive estimate of [Stein's]
place in modern literature and for defining her real influence
on her contemporaries. When it is made, I wager, it will bear
out the truth of her own contention that she disliked the ab-
normal because to her it seemed obvious and that she was always
seeking normality because she imagined normality would be more
complicated and interesting."

33 "MUSEUM WITHOUT WINDOWS." Time 48 (26 August):42.
Stein has left her portrait by Picasso to the Metropolitan
Museum.

34 "OBITUARY." Times (London), 29 July, p. 6.
Stein was "perhaps the earliest and, after James Joyce,
the most celebrated of the modern writers to attempt a new style
of English composition, a style destructive of a great deal of
normal usage and convention." Applying modern psychology to
writing, Stein has "an essential simplicity and directness of
mind, a spontaneity of thought on the pristine level of the
child's consciousness"; and "in seeking to reproduce it she
gave expression to the continuous, repetitive, and associative
process by which thought is translated into words."

35   "OBITUARY NOTES." <u>Publishers' Weekly</u> 150 (3 August):484-85.
      "Gertrude Stein, one of the most controversial figures in
contemporary literature, died in the American Hospital outside
of Paris on July 27 at the age of 72."

36   PAUL, ELLIOT. "Gertrude Stein, Alas." <u>Esquire</u> 26 (July):
      62, 189-93.
      "Miss Stein is a preposterous woman. . . . She is con-
ceited, overbearing, frivolous, selfish, egotistical, unimportant. Her friends will add that she is stimulating, full of
common sense, that she has a zest for life and lives it well.
Anyone will have to admit that she has held more than her share
of the public attention nearly half a century and is still going
strong."

37   PAULDING, C.G. "Let Them Talk and Talk." <u>Commonweal</u> 44
      (2 August):384-85.
      "It has become at last possible to write about a book by
Gertrude Stein because nobody in his senses thinks any more that
she is a joke." The problem with <u>Brewsie and Willie</u> is that the
GI talk gets nowhere and the GI worries remain unresolved.

38   POORE, CHARLES. "GI Conversation Piece, Translated into the
      Steinese." <u>New York Times Book Review</u>, 21 July, p. 7.
      Stein's <u>Brewsie and Willie</u> is "a book about what the GI's
talked about, or rather what she would like to think they talked
about, for Miss Stein is a very powerful character and things are
apt to change dizzily when translated into the Steinese."

39   RAGO, HENRY. "Gertrude Stein." <u>Poetry</u> 69 (November):93-97.
      Stein has died: ". . . she often said that a writer should
never do what he knows he can do. She applied this maxim by
losing interest in anything once she saw that she could do it.
If this explains her failure, it would be well for her literature
to have more of its failures issue from such wholesome intention. But having chosen, she gave us too a rich gift of fantasy
and playfulness, a refreshment of our language, and a new appreciation of formal prose."

40   REVIEW OF <u>BREWSIE AND WILLIE</u>. <u>Bulletin from Virginia Kirkus'</u>
      <u>Bookshop Service</u> 14 (1 March):122.
      In <u>Brewsie and Willie</u>, "Miss Stein is at her most lucid and
liberal, and making sense on both scores most of the time."

41   REVIEW OF <u>SELECTED WRITINGS OF GERTRUDE STEIN</u>. <u>Booklist</u> 43
      (15 November):84.
      ". . . the volume is an advisable purchase for libraries
that have not been able to buy the separate works of the widely
discussed American writer."

42 REVIEW OF <u>SELECTED WRITINGS OF GERTRUDE STEIN</u>. Bulletin from
    <u>Virginia Kirkus' Bookshop Service</u> 14 (15 October):538.
        "The originality of [Stein's] ideas, the simplicity of her
    conception of style, much of her best work is here available in
    one volume."

43 ROGERS, JOHN WILLIAM. "Understanding Gertrude Stein."
    <u>Chicago Sun Book Week</u>, 11 August.
        Only faintly do people now understand Gertrude Stein; some-
    day she shall be explained as more than just "a vastly colorful
    and interesting person."

44 S., L.W., and E., L.S. "In Memoriam: Gertrude Stein, 1898."
    <u>Radcliffe Quarterly</u> 30 (August):21.
        "When her Radcliffe friends think of Gertrude Stein, it is
    of a good companion with a genuine warmth of interest in those
    about her. She knew how to enjoy life and could lead others to
    enjoy it with her. She has always been like a magnet to young
    people who loved intellectual freedom. . . ."

45 "THE SHAPE OF THINGS." <u>Nation</u> 163 (10 August):142-43.
        "Hearing that Gertrude Stein is dead is like hearing that
    Paul Bunyan has been eaten by his ox Babe. Certainly she is not
    really dead: legends never die, and Miss Stein has made herself
    into an American legend more lasting than anything Barnum himself
    ever created. . . . The world will be a duller place without
    her; her sins harmed no one; at this moment she is sitting in
    the Elysian Fields talking to Samuel Johnson, the only man who
    could ever be her match."

46 SIGAUX, GILBERT. "Gertrude Stein." <u>La Gazette des Lettres</u>,
    3 August, pp. 6, 8.
        "Her writing effort deserves serious study. Let us say
    briefly that G. Stein sought total expression in deliberately
    sacrificing sense to the music of language. Rhyme, assonance,
    alliteration, in short <u>verbal</u> values were chief with her, more
    and more. . . . In appearance naive, her work is a concerted,
    solid reality. . . ."

47 SMITH, HARRISON. "A Rose for Remembrance." <u>Saturday Review
    of Literature</u> 29 (10 August):11.
        Gertrude Stein has died: "It is not unlikely that if she
    had lived and had continued to write for another few years she
    would have disciplined her theories to meet the necessities of
    a continued terse and lucid prose form, without wandering off
    into the maze of repeated words and the whimsy of sentences
    without punctuation."

48 SQUIRES, J[AMES] RADCLIFFE. Review of <u>Brewsie and Willie</u>.
    <u>Chicago Review</u> 1 (Summer):171-72.

"Even if Stein's portrait of the GI mind is faithful, and
I doubt that it is, Brewsie and Willie which ignores fairly bio-
logical self-beliefs of man, is still a bad book. Brewsie and
Willie died in a drawing room before it was born."

49   "TRANSITION." Newsweek 28 (5 August):54.
     "Among the first to recognize Picasso, Matisse, and other
modern French painters, Miss Stein made her Left Bank apartment
a meeting place for a generation of artists and writers."

50   VAN VECHTEN, CARL. "Pigeons and Roses Pass, Alas." New York
     Post, 9 December.
     With Stein's work, "all of it was part of her, some of it,
no doubt, less well done than the rest, but all of it a kind of
testimony to her mind, her temperament, yes, her genius. She
may one day stand in marble on a pedestal and watch Paris and
the world go by, but in a sense she stood on a pedestal all her
life. Three Lives would give her a position as a great writer;
there is sufficient evidence that she was a great woman as well."

51   WARSHOW, ROBERT S. "'Gerty' and the G.I.'s." Nation 163
     (5 October):383-84.
     "The funniest thing is that in reading Brewsie and Willie
one even feels a twinge of that unreasonable philistine irrita-
tion [Stein] aroused so often when she deserved it less. For
she has escaped again; worry and think, she said, and then died,
expatriating herself so effectively this time that one cannot
hope to reach her with our murmur: yes, that's what we have
been doing, worrying and thinking."

52   WEYAND, NORMAN. "Letter." Commonweal 45 (20 December):253.
     A Jesuit asks what Anne Freemantle meant on 25 October in
equating Stein's "word" with the Word.

53   WILSON, EDMUND. "Books." New Yorker 22 (15 June):77.
     The title characters of Brewsie and Willie "grow vague,
and we see that Miss Stein is vague, too. But she is intelligent
as far as she goes and--what is cheerful news just now--she is
quite free. . . ." In Brewsie and Willie the "monotony and the
repetitious characteristics of Gertrude Stein become a little
tedious, yet they have the justification of appropriateness to
the endless repetitions of soldier conversation and the stultify-
ing monotony of soldier life. . . ."

54   WOODBURN, JOHN. "Words in Their Meaning." Saturday Review
     of Literature 29 (27 July):13.
     Brewsie and Willie is "a kind of recording, with the muta-
tions through which art transcends simple reporting, of the conversations of G.I.'s as they talked in Miss Stein's apartment in
Paris and when she visited them in troop centers."

55   WRIGHT, RICHARD. "American GI's Fears worry Gertrude Stein."
      New York PM, 21 July, sec. M, pp. 15-16.
           Regarding Brewsie and Willie, "Gertrude Stein received the
      GIs like a mother. She talked with them and learned to know them
      with an objectivity which, perhaps, few people in America can
      muster. I think that I can say that really she saved some of
      them. . . ."

56   YARMON, MORTON. "Gertrude Stein Sizes Up America." New York
      Herald (Paris), 10 April.
           Stein does not expect a great expatriation movement after
      World War II, but she does predict a new Lost Generation.

57   "YES AND NO." Time 47 (25 March):67.
           The premiere of Yes Is For a Very Young Man took place in
      Pasadena, California: "Whether, afterwards, those who got in
      had a clearer idea of Yes than those who did not, remained a
      moot point."

                                1947

1   ADVERTISEMENT. New York Times, 11 December, p. 25.
           "Our name isn't Gertrude so we can't say: 'A shirt is a
      shirt, is a shirt--' and expect to arouse enthusiasm--but when
      we tell you they're Arrow Luster Stripe Shirts, well therein
      lies a story. . . ."

2   ALFRED, WILLIAM. "Epitaph (Lyric in Memory of Gertrude Stein)."
      In Atlantic Prize Papers 1946-1947. Boston: Atlantic Monthly,
      p. 13.
           "I asked my question of two nations / till I was out of
      heart and breath: / who like me would not love patience / and
      expatriate to death?"

3   BABCOCK, FREDERIC. "Among The Authors." Chicago Tribune,
      12 January, sec. 4, p. 4.
           "Ever since Gertrude Stein came to these unenlightened
      shores to tell us about literature I've had an idea that her
      performance was one of the great hoaxes of all time and that
      those who pretended to understand her writings were pseudo-
      intellectuals. . . . But I hesitated to say so in print, lest
      it be proved that I was too dumb to appreciate her artistry."

4   "BRIEF MENTION." American Literature 18 (January):347.
           Van Vechten has chosen wisely for Selected Writings of
      Gertrude Stein, but "his brief Introduction could have been
      profitably expanded to twice or three times its length."

5   "BRIEFLY NOTED." New Yorker 23 (22 November):130.
        With Four in America, "the idea sounds promising, but the
     pieces are in one of the author's less popular styles: the
     vacuous-repetitive-vague."

6   BRINNAN, JOHN MALCOLM. "Little Elegy for Gertrude Stein."
     Harper's 194 (January):75.
        "Pass gently, pigeons on the grass, / For where she lies
     alone, alas, / Is all the wonder ever was."

7   BRODIN, PIERRE. Écrivains américains du vingtième siècle.
     Paris: Horizons de France, pp. 27-44.
        "Gertrude Stein is not merely an original poet and an in-
     novator in literary technique. Beneath her appearance of naivete
     and obscurity she has ideas. She criticizes implicitly the false
     gleam of American civilization and explicitly the styles of au-
     thoritarianism and the primacy of materialism. She sides with
     humanity and freedom. . . . This American on the rue de Fleurus
     has represented and expressed the most comprehensive and human
     in the American ideal."

8   BURGUM, EDGAR BERRY. The Novel and the World's Dilemma.
     New York: Oxford University Press, pp. 8, 157-83, 246.
        The irony of Stein's career is that she knew the major
     authors to come without influencing them in literary style and
     that her public acceptance was for non-experimental writing done
     later in her life: ". . . she could no longer be considered a
     writer of importance, but she had become a woman of the people."

9   CANBY, HENRY SEIDEL. American Memoir. Boston: Houghton
     Mifflin Co., pp. 332-34.
        Reprint of 1927.2.

10   CLEMENS, CYRIL. "A Chat With Gertrude Stein." Hobbies
     42 (October):145, 150.
        "Gertrude Stein and I were having tea together upon her
     last visit to St. Louis. In appearance she was a woman of
     splendid physique and extraordinary grace. Her close cropped
     hair, fine Roman features, well tanned complexion, and deep grey
     eyes with their sparkle and dance made an immediate impression
     upon the observer. What perhaps impressed me more than anything
     else was her complete self-possession--such as one sees in very
     few people, especially women."

11   CLIFFORD, WILLIAM. "Hommage to Gertrude Stein." Nassau Lit
     105 (Winter):25-28.
        "It has been claimed that Gertrude Stein will be remembered
     more for her warm, vastly human personality than for her writings.
     In these writings she has been found to be cold and disrespectful
     of the reader, immensely conceited and egotistical, and an author
     who, until her last days, never considered any subject outside of

herself. I know she was human; I doubt if she was any more con-
ceited than she had a right to be."

12　EMPSON, WILLIAM. Seven Types of Ambiguity. Rev. ed. London:
　　Chatto & Windus, p. 7.
　　　　It is not yet possible to understand Stein's method, and
she "implores the passing tribute of a sigh."

13　EVANS, OLIVER. "Gertrude Stein as Humorist." Prairie
　　Schooner 21 (March):97-101.
　　　　". . . Gertrude Stein's humor never descends to the merely
slapstick. . . . Hers, of course, is a subtler intelligence:
she has taken the best elements of American humor and refined
them, combining them also with other elements, and the final
product, the particular brand of humor which is Stein's alone,
is a literary phenomenon of more than passing interest and
importance."

14　FITTS, DUDLEY. "Toasted Susie Is My Ice-Cream." New York
　　Times Book Review, 30 November, p. 5.
　　　　"Is Four in America readable? That depends on the reader."
Yet, Four in America is "the sincere work of a consummate artist
and profound intelligence," "a book for the youthful minds of
people young and old who are eager to investigate what lies
around the corner. What lies there may be useless; it is something to have gone and seen."

15　FREEMANTLE, ANNE. "Expatriates End." Commonweal 47
　　(12 December):229-30.
　　　　"Gertrude Stein and Henry Miller are two excellent examples
of the antean American, of the American that must go back every
so often and kiss the old European earth. For both, it would
seem that the normal breathe in, breathe out, of the creative
artist can only take place on a bi-continental level, and that
for neither is patriotism pur et simple enough. . . ."

16　GAGECY, EDMOND M. Revolution in American Drama. New York:
　　Columbia University Press, pp. 23, 110-11.
　　　　Four Saints in Three Acts was "purely aesthetic drama,
divorced from realism, depending for its effects upon a fusion
of the arts."

17　GALLUP, DONALD. "The Gertrude Stein Collection." Yale
　　University Library Gazette 22 (October):21-32.
　　　　With the growth of the Stein collection at Yale University,
"hardly before in the history of English and American literature
and in the annals of manuscript collecting has an important
writer been so completely represented in one Library by manuscript material, and few accumulations of correspondence have
covered such a span and been so comprehensive."

18   GANNETT, LEWIS. "Books and Things." <u>New York Herald-Tribune</u>, 26 December.
      <u>The Mother of Us All</u> in printed form reveals no meaning. Neither did the author, Gertrude Stein.

19   GRAY, JAMES. "Competent Priestess." <u>Saturday Review of Literature</u> 30 (22 November):30-31.
      "In none of her books as well as in this one did [Stein] manage to communicate [her] warmth to the page. In <u>Four in America</u> she took a reader inside her mind with an air of almost maternal confiding. She shared the intricacies of her own mental process, wooing, cajoling, tempting the imagination on."

20   HACKETT, FRANCIS. <u>On Judging Books: In General and in Particular</u>. New York: John Day Co., pp. 83-85.
      Reprint of 1945.21.

21   HAGGIN, B.H. "Music." <u>Nation</u> 164 (31 May):667.
      Compared to <u>Four Saints in Three Acts</u>, "the words of <u>The Mother of Us All</u> have less poetic imagery and music, and more rational meaning. . . . But Thomson's method is the same--by which I don't mean that he uses it mechanically; on the contrary, one is delighted by the attentiveness and freshness of attack at moment after moment that produce, so simply and often artlessly, the results that are so witty, so touching, so good."

22   HAGUE, ROBERT A. "A Pleasant Evening With Gertrude S. and Virgil T." <u>New York PM</u>, 9 May.
      <u>The Mother of Us All</u> is "blessed with warmth and humor, touched alike with simple sentiment and ingenuous wit. It is nearly always entertaining; it is often gently moving, at times achieving a very real poignancy; and all of it has a charm and a flavor that are peculiarly--and beguilingly--its own."

23   HART, H.W. Review of <u>Four in America</u>. <u>Library Journal</u> 72 (15 October):1468.
      "Portions of this work, which is written in Miss Stein's most experimental manner, may seem like prattle to the general reader, but it is part of the record of an important literary career. . . ."

24   HOFFMAN, FREDERICK J.; ALLEN, CHARLES; and ULRICH, CAROLYN F. <u>The Little Magazine: A History and a Bibliography</u>. Princeton: Princeton University Press, pp. 82, 174, 248, 275, and passim.
      Among the many periodicals willing to publish the work of Stein were <u>transition</u>, <u>Close-up</u>, <u>Rogue</u>, <u>Pagany</u>, <u>Rocking Horse</u>, <u>Larus</u>, and <u>The Transatlantic Review</u>.

25   LANEY, AL. <u>Paris Herald: The Incredible Newspaper</u>. New York: D. Appleton-Century Co., pp. 4, 152-55.
      Elliot Paul and Eugene Jolas claimed to understand the work of Gertrude Stein, which they eagerly published in France.

26　LEVY, HARRIET LANE. 920 O'Farrell Street. New York:
　　Doubleday & Co., p. 23.
　　　Reprint of 1937.20.

27　"THE LITERARY LIFE." Time 50 (24 November):51.
　　　Alice B. Toklas, contrary to rumor, has no plan to move
　back to California.

28　LOHMAN, SIDNEY. "Concerning Radio Row." New York Times,
　　25 May, sec. 2, p. 9.
　　　Thomson himself will conduct the first radio performance
　of Four Saints in Three Acts.

29　"LOTS OF FUN." New Yorker 23 (31 May):19-20.
　　　The Yale exhibit of Stein memorabilia is open and "we don't
　know when we've been permitted to poke about in a more distin-
　guished grab bag of letters, drawings, manuscripts, and photo-
　graphs, and only the fact that Miss Stein saved receipted bills
　for the repair of her Ford as assiduously kept us from thinking
　she'd banked a shade too self-consciously on their and her
　importance."

30　MORRIS, LLOYD. "Gertrude Stein's Method." New York Herald-
　　Tribune Weekly Book Review, 30 November, p. 19.
　　　Four in America by Stein is "unlikely to promote her to the
　more elevated ranks of the philosophical hierarchy. It makes her
　a candidate for a place in homely and comfortable circles."

31　"NOT FOR THE TIMID." Time 50 (17 November):110, 113.
　　　"Gertrude Stein had leisure, intelligence, curiosity and
　quite a bit of gall. She never got tired of playing games with
　language. She preferred to live in Europe, but America and Amer-
　icans always fascinated. Four in America is an inquiry about the
　American soul as exemplified in four great men. . . ."

32　PHELAN, KAPPO. "The Stage & Screen." Commonweal 46 (30 May):
　　167-68.
　　　The Mother of Us All "was wholly a delight and in perform-
　ance and working-out admirable."

33　PORTER, KATHERINE ANNE. "Gertrude Stein: A Self-Portrait."
　　Harper's 195 (December):519-28.
　　　Stein was not "opposed to ideas, but . . . she was not
　interested in anybody's ideas but her own, except as material
　to put down on her endless flood of pages. Like writing, opin-
　ion also belonged to Miss Stein, and nothing annoyed her more--
　she was easily angered about all sorts of things--than for any-
　one not a genius or who had no reputation that she respected, to
　appear to be thinking in her presence." At her death she was
　trying to "unfold" like a "wooden umbrella"--but too late.
　Reprinted: 1952.8; 1970.34.

34   PUTNAM, SAMUEL. Paris Was Our Mistress: Memoirs of a Lost & Found Generation. New York: Viking Press, pp. 4, 9, 13, 14, 89, and passim.

      Stein frightened Putnam, reminding him of "the cigar-smoking Amy Lowell." Stein looked like Caesar and defended her prose and genius as haughtily.

35   RASCOE, BURTON. We Were Interrupted. Garden City, N.Y.: Doubleday & Co., pp. 187–88.

      Hemingway introduced Rascoe to Stein, who gave him her one-page history of literature. To Rascoe, Stein's "connection with either painting or literature seemed remote. . . ." He suspected her of ignorance of others' writings.

36   REVIEW OF FOUR IN AMERICA. Bulletin from Virginia Kirkus' Bookshop Service 15 (15 October):596.

      "An important book because Miss Stein is an important fig-ure in our literary scene. Important also because [Thornton] Wilder's introduction is one of the finest pieces of literary criticism to be written in our decade. There's a Stein clique."

37   SAWYER, JULIAN. "A Key to Four Saints in Three Acts." New Iconograph, Fall, pp. 30–41.

      In Four Saints in Three Acts, Stein has said much in few words and "has brilliantly succeeded in resolving the distant periods and locales of her text into an authentic Aristotelian synthesis of his well-known unities."

38   SEVAREID, ERIC. Not So Wild a Dream. New York: Alfred A. Knopf, pp. 89, 90, 457–62.

      Far from being amusing, Stein was profound and wise in talk; at the end of World War II Sevareid found Stein living in provin-cial France, full of perceptions of war and Germans.

39   SIMON, ROBERT A. "Musical Events." New Yorker 23 (17 May): 103–4.

      The Mother of Us All turns out to be "an original, enter-taining, and provocative libretto," and "Mr. Thomson's musical setting for the libretto is right on every count."

40   SLOPER, L.A. "Nonsense." Christian Science Monitor, 22 November, Magazine section, p. 17.

      Seals of approval by Thornton Wilder and the University of Chicago do not prevent Four in America from being nonsense.

41   SMITH, CECIL. "Gertrude S., Virgil T., and Susan B.," Theatre Arts 31 (July):17–18.

      "If the libretto kept to its own best level as persistently as the music does, The Mother of Us All might be singled out as the best of the American operas. Perhaps it is anyway, despite its unevenness and its soggy finale. . . ."

42 _____. "Sounds of Spring." <u>New Republic</u> 116 (2 June):33.
   <u>The Mother of Us All</u> "is not exciting, but it is interesting, witty, and reasonably intelligible, and it could well be
produced by local operatic organizations across the country."

43 SOBY, JAMES THRALL. "Gertrude Stein And The Artists."
   <u>Saturday Review of Literature</u> 30 (24 May):34-36.
   Yale's display of Stein materials is fascinating, but "I
suppose the question of Miss Stein's intrinsic quality as a
writer is still debated, but there can be no doubt about her
influence. She was, in fact, a sort of Typhoid Mary of prose
style, infecting in some degree a lively percentage of those who
came within range of her wondrously commonsensical mind."

44 "STEIN SONG." <u>Time</u> 49 (19 May):47.
   At Columbia University's performance of <u>The Mother of Us
All</u>, "just about everything from the U.S.'s historical kitchen
was on stage."

45 STEIN, LEO. <u>Appreciation: Painting, Poetry and Prose</u>.
   New York: Crown Publishers, pp. 152-67.
   Too much fantasy has been published about 27 rue de Fleurus.
The facts are more "veridical."

46 STIEGLITZ, ALFRED, III. "Camera Work Introduces Gertrude
   Stein to America." <u>Twice a Year</u>, no. 14-15 (Fall-Winter),
   pp. 192-95.
   Mrs. Edward Knobloch encouraged Stieglitz to publish
Stein's early work in <u>Camera Work</u> in 1912, and the issue "did
create a great stir. A great stir primarily amongst the literary
folks. Stieglitz was cracking a joke this time."

47 "'SUSAN B' IN THREE ACTS." <u>Newsweek</u> 29 (19 May):94.
   <u>The Mother of Us All</u> includes a pantheon of American heroes
and heroines and "time out for a discussion of wealth and poverty,
marriage, political fame, a dream sequence, and two romances."

48 WATTS, RICHARD, Jr. "Writing Out Loud." <u>New Republic</u> 117
   (17 November):28.
   "There are entertaining conceptions in <u>Four in America</u> if
you have the patience to dig for them. Yet, save for the addicts,
this is a dull and exasperating book, because a little less way-
wardness could have made it so much better and more amusing. So
could James Thurber."

49 WILDER, THORNTON. "Gertrude Stein Makes Sense." <u>'47</u> 1
   (October):10-15.
   "Miss Stein's writing is the record of her thoughts, from
the beginning, as she 'closes in' on them. It is <u>being written</u>
before our eyes; she does not, as other writers do, suppress and
erase the hesitations, the recapitulations, the connections, in

order to give you the completed fine results of her meditations.
She gives us the process."

50　　WITHAM, W. TASKER. Panorama of American Literature. New York:
　　　　Stephen Daye Press, pp. 246, 247-48, 249-50, and passim.
　　　　　　Despite the prevailing idea that Stein "wrote gibberish,"
indeed "that is far from true. Her sentences are grammatically
correct, and her vocabulary is simple and colloquial. The reader
has the sense of being in the presence of a friendly woman who
loves to talk and who talks exceedingly well."

1948

1　　ACTON, HAROLD. Memoirs of an Aesthete. London: Methuen,
　　　　pp. 46, 47, 132, 147, 160-63, and passim.
　　　　　　"Gertrude Stein was said to lead a school of disorganiza-
tion and her work was supposed to be connected with insanity.
As a person, however, she was highly organized, and saner than
most of us."

2　　BUNKER, ROBERT. Review of Four in America. New Mexico
　　　　Quarterly Review 18 (Winter):471-72.
　　　　　　In Four in America Stein demonstrates little but the ability
to improvise history and writing.

3　　CONNOLLY, CYRIL. Enemies of Promise. Rev. ed. New York:
　　　　Macmillan Co., pp. 59, 65.
　　　　　　Three Lives had wide influence, especially on Sherwood
Anderson and Ernest Hemingway: "It was a simplification, an
attack on order and meaning in favour of sound but of sound
which in itself generated a new precision."

4　　COWIE, ALEXANDER. The Rise of the American Novel. New York:
　　　　American Book Co., pp. 721, 751, 753, 853.
　　　　　　Perhaps Stein learned her "continuous present" from Henry
James. She sought "the texture of experience, not to interpret
life in its totality."

5　　CUPPY, WILL. "Mystery and Adventure." New York Herald-
　　　　Tribune Weekly Book Review, 9 May.
　　　　　　Blood on the Dining Room Floor is good literary lunacy:
"Suitable for collectors of Gertrude Stein, or, for that matter,
collectors of anything."

6　　EVANS, OLIVER. "The Americanization of Gertrude Stein."
　　　　Prairie Schooner 22 (March):70-74.
　　　　　　"When one considers the range of the late Gertrude Stein's
published writings . . . one is immediately impressed by the fact
that they reveal a sensibility which is profoundly and uniquely
American. . . . In a deeper and wider sense, one is conscious

130

in all her works of a substratum of thought and feeling which is peculiarly American. The attitudes, whether stated or implied; the humor; even the very accents and cadences of her language-- all these bear unmistakable witness of the author's nationality."

7   FREEDLY, GEORGE. Review of The First Reader and Three Plays.
    Library Journal 73 (15 April):653.
        "Miss Stein's plays are hardly playable nor are they in- tended to follow any conventional dramatic form. The volume as a whole has considerable charm and all of the much discussed and celebrated Stein style."

8   FREEMANTLE, ANNE. "Whodunits, in a Variety of Keys." New York
    Times Book Review, 1 August, p. 13.
        Blood on the Dining Room Floor is Stein's "only murder mys- tery, and strikes a balance between her earlier realism, that, for example of Three Lives, published in 1905 [sic], where she was chiefly concerned with creating character, and her Brewsie and Willie of 1942 [sic], where she was trying above all to con- vey and to epitomize emotion."

9   GALLUP, DONALD C. "A Book Is a Book Is a Book." New Colophon
    1 (January):67-80.
        Because Stein's account in The Autobiography of Alice B.
    Toklas is inaccurate and incomplete regarding publication of Three Lives, study of her papers at Yale reveals the facts (and difficulties) of Stein's first book publication.

10 _____. "Picasso, Gris, and Gertrude Stein." In Picasso Gris
    Miro. San Francisco: San Francisco Museum of Art, pp. 15-23.
        ". . . just as Gertrude Stein herself drew upon Picasso and Gris and their pictures for intellectual nourishment and inspira- tion to such an extent that it becomes almost impossible to con- ceive of her work as existing independently of theirs, so the encouragement, understanding, and publicity which she gave to them in return were vital factors in their eventual achievement."

11 _____. "The Weaving of a Pattern: Marsden Hartley and
    Gertrude Stein." Magazine of Art 41 (November):256-61.
        Correspondence of Marsden Hartley and Gertrude Stein from 1912 to 1934 demonstrates that one artist at least never fell out with Stein: "Altogether the letters document with a great deal of detail the story of this friendship and are eloquent of the encouragement which Miss Stein gave and the esteem in which she was held by one of the foremost American artists of the twentieth century."

12 "GENERAL." New Yorker 24 (6 March):100.
        The First Reader and Three Plays--"about a dog that wanted to learn to read, some careless butter, and other cryptic mat- ters, combined with three miniscule plays--appears to add up to nothing. On second consideration, it seems to add up to the same."

13   GLOSTER, HUGH M. Negro Voices in American Fiction. Chapel
     Hill: University of North Carolina Press, pp. 105, 107, 159,
     162, 264.
         Stein influenced the modern interest in Negro life by such
     authors as Carl Van Vechten.

14   GRAMONT, ELIZABETH de. "Gertrude Stein." Revue Hébdomadaire
     47 (February):344-50.
         Stein lived in Paris for many years, being friends with
     the great in literature and art.

15   GROSSER, MAURICE. Painting in Public. New York: Alfred A.
     Knopf, pp. 5, 18, 160, 164, 182, 186.
         Stein's comments on modern art as to be looked at and
     painters as workmen are always useful. She also illustrates the
     relationship of poet to painter.

16   HERBST, JOSEPHINE. "Miss Porter and Miss Stein." Partisan
     Review 15 (May):568-72.
         Katherine Anne Porter's analysis of Gertrude Stein is mis-
     leading and false. Porter would have Stein's "life experience
     [as] little more than the glutton dream of a greedy egomaniac;
     her quarrels, personal stigmata." The true Stein was truly
     otherwise.

17   KAZIN, ALFRED. "From an Italian Journal." Partisan Review
     15 (May):555-57.
         Leo Stein continues to struggle in advanced age with
     Gertrude: "They had transferred the cultural rivalry in that
     prosperous Jewish family to Europe and worked it in and out of
     the expatriate life, making Paris and Florence new outposts for
     an old ambition."

18   KIRSTEIN, LINCOLN. The Sculpture of Elie Nadelman. New York:
     Museum of Modern Art, pp. 10-11, 16, 24, 26.
         Leo bought some Nadelman drawings and a plaster piece in
     1908 for the salon he shared with Gertrude Stein: "Gertrude
     kept the plaster for twenty years, when it was cast in bronze."

19   McAFEE, THOMAS. "Gertrude Stein." Prairie Schooner 22
     (March):14.
         "Because the words were so foamed up / as if one whipped
     them in a cup, / she took the words and told them be! / . . ."

20   PEARSON, NORMAN HOLMES. "Gertrude Stein." Yale Review 37
     (Summer):743-45.
         In Four in America, "it is in the aspect of creativity
     that Miss Stein finds her common denominator among the four
     Americans she has chosen. They offer a broad scope: religion,
     art, invention, statesmanship, painting, and writing. . . .
     Miss Stein was not interested in being distracted by the specific;
     it was the spirit of fiction that concerned her most."

*21   PIVANO, FERNANDA. "Introduzione a uno studio su Gertrude
       Stein." La Rassegna d'Italia 3 (August):827-40.
       Cited: MHRA Bibliography for 1948, p. 229.

22   ROGERS, W.G. When This You See Remember Me: Gertrude Stein
      in Person. New York: Rinehart & Co., 247 pages.
          "In addition to her very special contributions to litera-
      ture, there are spread through all [Stein's] writing, for the
      delectation of the diligent new reader, a diversity of rhythms,
      many profound and searching observations, much wit, and extremely
      quotable remarks, of exactly the kind for which she chided Ernest
      Hemingway. But some books abound in discouraging pages, and
      other volumes, it seems to me, are more notebooks than finished
      work, even though to her they were complete; they are the incep-
      tion, not the development, of ideas, more interesting after you
      know Gertrude Stein than when you are trying to make her
      acquaintance."

23   SAWYER, JULIAN. "Gertrude Stein: A Bibliography, 1941-48."
      Bulletin of Bibliography 19 (May-August, September-December):
      152-56, 183-87.
          Supplementary primary bibliography.

24   _____. "Gertrude Stein (1874-1946): A Check-list comprising
      Critical and Miscellaneous Writings about her Work, Life and
      Personality from 1913-1948." Bulletin of Bibliography 19
      (January-April):128-31.
          Secondary bibliography.

25   SITWELL, Sir OSBERT. Laughter in the Next Room. Boston:
      Little, Brown & Co., pp. 273-74.
          In 1929, Edith and Osbert Sitwell went with Gertrude Stein
      to her lecture at Oxford, where the wiser students appreciated
      Stein's remarks.

26   SUGRUE, THOMAS. "With No Stein Unturned." New York Herald-
      Tribune Weekly Book Review, 7 March, p. 2.
          In The First Reader, "the last fragments of her work[,]
      Miss Stein is concerned almost wholly with the joyful sound of
      Anglo-Saxon words, with the rhythm of thought as it breaks and
      spills into speech, with the lovely patterns of sound and idea
      which cluster around the edges of awareness. The joy of the
      reader is obvious in every matching pair of words, and it is a
      joy which finds easy access to a reader's mind."

27   YOUNG, STARK. Immortal Shadows: A Book of Dramatic Criticism.
      New York: Charles Scribner's Sons, pp. 150-51.
          Reprint of 1934.162.

1949

1   BARNES, HOWARD. "Gertrude Stein's Last: A Resistance Epi-
    logue." New York Herald-Tribune, 12 June.
       Yes Is for a Very Young Man "is not a distinguished piece
    of theater but it is very much worth seeing."

2   BERENSON, BERNARD. Sketch for a Self-Portrait. Bloomington:
    Indiana University Press, pp. 44-46.
       The Stein family prodded Berenson to become an art critic.
    Picasso revealed to Berenson that the Steins had exploited him in
    his early career.

3   BERNSTEIN, LEONARD. "Music and Miss Stein." New York Times
    Book Review, 22 May, pp. 4, 22.
       Stein's great importance has been those whom she influenced,
    but Last Operas and Plays reveals a neglected comic side in her
    pieces for theater. She is in libretti what Thomson is in music--
    a great simplifier toward modernism.

4   DESFEUILLES, PAUL. "Gertrude Stein et le 'vrai présent.'"
    Le Bayou 40 (Winter):31-39.
       Stein's work--seeking the "true present"--we read with
    pleasure, laughter, balance, happy life.

5   FARRELLY, JOHN. "Homespun Sibyl." New Republic 120 (16 May):
    18-19.
       With Last Operas and Plays, "much of [Stein's] later writ-
    ing reads like coterie talk--full of private jokes, private allu-
    sions, private names. One can appreciate this exclusiveness. . . .
    But privacy is a delicate thing, requiring infinite tact. The
    temptation in privacy, for an artist, is to withdraw from the pub-
    lic view and perform for the keyhole."

6   GALLUP, DONALD. "Always Gtrde Stein." Southwest Review 34
    (Summer):254-58.
       Letters to and from Gallup and Stein resulted in a meeting
    in France and Stein's giving her unpublished manuscripts to Yale
    University.

7   "GENERAL." New Yorker 25 (9 April):122-23.
       Last Operas and Plays proves that, with Van Vechten's intro-
    duction, "Gertrude Stein is more fun to read about than to read."

8   GOLDRING, DOUGLAS. Trained for Genius: The Life and Writings
    of Ford Madox Ford. New York: E.P. Dutton & Co., pp. 228,
    230, 248, 249, 255, 256.
       Pound gave Ford entrée to Stein's circle of admirers and
    friends; Van Wyck Brooks deplored the influence of Ford and Stein
    as esthetic snobs.

9   HAGGIN, BERNARD H. Music in the Nation. New York: Sloane,
      pp. 71-72, 297.
         Thomson's music in Four Saints in Three Acts explicates
Stein's words.

10   HAINES, GEORGE, IV. "Gertrude Stein and Composition."
      Sewanee Review 57 (Summer):411-24.
         Stein's death must not end her influence on modern thought
regarding individualism and community.

*11   HARUYAMA, YUKIO. "G. Stein." Amerika Bungaku, March.
         In Japanese. Cited: MHRA Bibliography for 1949, p. 259.

12   HENRY, CONSTANCE. "The Bookshelf." Theatre Arts Monthly 33
      (July):11.
         Stein's operas and plays are often insufferable, bewilder-
ing, pointless, infuriating, private; and only a few are
worthwhile.

13   MILLER, ROSALIND S. Gertrude Stein: Form and Intelligibility.
      New York: Exposition Press, 162 pp.
         "Gertrude Stein, in one sense, has failed because her
critics have failed. Either her writing has been dismissed as
unintelligible or her critics have been so keen in judging her
work by the detail that they have failed to evaluate the whole.
Ignoring her all-important critical volumes, they have concen-
trated on her form without taking into consideration her content. . . . Stein is a writer so much a part of twentieth-century
literature--private, abstract, experimental--that even if our perspective is still too limited to determine the final merit of an
author, Gertrude Stein must one day be recognized as one of the
leading exponents of the new forms."

14   PHELAN, KAPPO. "The Stage & Screen." Commonweal 50 (24 June):
      271.
         In Yes Is for a Very Young Man, if the purpose is a French-
U.S. comparison, "one wonders why she chose to title her piece as
she did, and why she should have given over most of it to a character whose motives are as slippery as they are proved. As for
the familiar syntax and the usual wholehearted humor which is the
general signature of this author's work, there is no evidence in
the play."

15   REDMAN, BEN RAY. "Word-Intoxicated Woman." Saturday Review
      of Literature 32 (2 April):18-19.
         With Last Operas and Plays, "it is a safe bet at almost any
odds, I think, that all but Miss Stein's most devoted admirers
will condemn this collection as a scandalous waste of paper,
printer's ink, and binder's cloth. And there are strong reasons
for such a judgment; reasons that can, indeed, be countered only
by oblique arguments. It is true that the bulk of the writing in
this book is, in the most exact meaning of the word, nonsense."

16   ROGERS, W.G. "Gertrude Stein Hovering." <u>New York Herald-
      Tribune Weekly Book Review</u>, 3 April, p. 6.
         Regarding <u>Last Operas and Plays</u>, if the reader's "effort is
great, his reward is sometimes close, literally, to fabulous.
Levitated, as it were, shunted magically from real to unreal,
he is introduced into unimagined experiences. Miss Stein's abra-
cadabra works; her open-sesame opens doors."

17   SIMON, JEAN. <u>Le Roman américain au xx° siècle</u>. Paris:
      Boivin et Cie, pp. 98-99.
         Stein is important although most of her work is unreadable.
By teaching disciples the rigor of composition, Stein encouraged
a pure literary art.

18   TILTON, ELEANOR M. "Gertrude Stein's Amusing and Confusing
      Plays." <u>Philadelphia Inquirer Books</u>, 27 March, p. 1.
         As revealed in <u>Last Operas and Plays</u>, Stein "seemed to be
a writer whose creative work was more necessary than good. Nevertheless, I think she was a writer who will be discovered and rediscovered at separate intervals."

19   WYATT, EUPHEMIA VAN RENSSALAER. "The Drama." <u>Catholic World</u>
      169 (August):388-89.
         In <u>Yes Is for a Very Young Man</u>, "the repetition that
strengthens the speeches of one or two of the characters blurs
the others and in the end, it seems to be only Gertrude Stein
who is doing the talking. Some of the dialogue is surprisingly
natural and forceful, rather on the order of Maeterlinck but
without the curious, elusive tension which he knew so well how
to build."

                              1950

1   BOURDET, DENISE. "Images de Paris: Sixième arrondissement."
      <u>Revue de Paris</u> 57 (March):139-41.
         Stein and her dwelling in Paris represent a muse at the
beginning of a new age.

2   BRADDY, HALDEEN. "The Primitive in Gertrude Stein's
      'Melanctha.'" <u>New Mexico Quarterly Review</u> 20 (Autumn):358-65.
         "Melanctha" is primitive because Stein completely omits
specific cultural features and implies aboriginal sexual mores:
"Without resources to folklore, superstition, spirituals, or
dialect--the stock-in-trade paraphernalia of the regional writer--
the novelist has with her original style limned in full detail
the humble background of Melanctha Herbert."

3   COMMAGER, HENRY STEELE. <u>The American Mind: An Interpretation
      of American Thought and Character Since the 1880's</u>. New Haven:
      Yale University Press, pp. 127-28.

Destined to be forgotten because it is based on "the quag-
mire of futility," the literature of Stein and other writers of
the "cult of irrationality" debased reason and rationality.
Stein "dabbled in primitivism, she experimented with the association of words and sound, she related literature to the art
of the motion picture; she was original and creative and could
be sincere."

4   [FITTS, DUDLEY.] "Q.E.D." New York Times Book Review,
    24 December, p. 11.   .
       With Q.E.D., "it is the style that will interest the crit-
    ical reader most. As in Three Lives (but decreasingly so there-
    after), it is effortless, lucid talk. The sprawling sentences,
    on the face of things so hopeless in their disarray, their calcu-
    lated disregard of punctuation and syntax, speak from the page."

5   GALLUP, DONALD C. "The Making of The Making of Americans."
    New Colophon 3 (1950):54-74.
       The tangled publication history of The Making of Americans
    and the public indifference and resentment of the huge book dis-
    couraged Stein: "its publication could hardly have been attended
    by more numerous and varied misfortunes, continued over a greater
    number of years."

6   GARVIN, HARRY RAPHAEL. "Gertrude Stein: A Study of Her Theory
    and Practice." Ph.D. dissertation, University of Michigan,
    271 pp.
       "Gertrude Stein's achievement in creative literature lies
    not in her intellectual ideas or thematic conceptions but in her
    technical innovations in the novel and in 'portrait-writing.'
    Close analysis of her major novels . . . reveal[s] a pervasive
    originality in her varied use of repetition, 'imitative form,'
    and a Steinian tone and time-sense." Summarized: Dissertation
    Abstracts International 10 (1950):210-11.

7   GIFFORD, ERNEST. "Reader Be Damned." Saturday Review 33
    (27 May):23-24.
       Gifford asked Stein why she did not talk as she wrote; and
    Stein became uncomfortable in discussing whether art should,
    above all, communicate.

8   "HOW TO BE A QUEEN." Time 55 (26 June):76-77.
       Meyer Kupferman's setting of Stein's words for In a Garden
    made "a one-act opera as stylish, Steinish, charming and listen-
    able as any summer audience could want to hear."

9   ISAACS, E.J.R. "Four Saints in Three Acts." Theatre Arts
    Anthology: A Record and a Prophecy. Edited by Rosamond
    Gilder et al. New York: Theatre Arts Books, pp. 626-27.
    Reprint of 1934.79.

*10   JANZON, ÅKE. "Gertrude Stein." Bonniers Litterära Magasin
      7 (September):528-31.
          In Swedish. Cited: Liston, Maureen R.. Gertrude Stein:
      An Annotated Critical Bibliography, p. 91.

 11   KOCH, VIVIENNE. William Carlos Williams. Norfolk, Conn.:
      New Directions, pp. 209-10, 211.
          In his first collected stories, Williams showed the influ-
      ence of Stein's "cadenced, clear, syntactically functional prose."

 12   "LIBRARY HONORS GERTRUDE STEIN." New York Times, 10 January,
      p. 27.
          The New York Public Library will open an exhibit of Stein's
      manuscripts, scores, and memorabilia.

 13   POUND, EZRA. The Letters of Ezra Pound, 1907-1941. Edited
      by D.D. Paige. New York: Harcourt, Brace & Co., pp. 227, 277.
          In 1930 Pound was pleased to have some Cummings poems to
      read: "Ever a pleasure to have something to decipher that ain't
      Jim [Joyce] or oedipus Gertie." In 1936 he called Joyce "the
      greatest forcemeat since Gertie."

 14   STEIN, LEO. Journey Into the Self: Being the Letters,
      Papers & Journals of Leo Stein. Edited by Edmund Fuller.
      Introduction by Van Wyck Brooks. New York: Crown Publishers,
      pp. 3-9, 10, 18, 19, and passim.
          Leo Stein describes his life with Gertrude in Paris and the
      coming of their estrangement.

 15   TYLER, PARKER. "An Elegy for Gertrude Stein." Poetry New
      York, no. 2 (1950), pp. 9-10.
          Stein "was a natural enemy of furbelow. Her existence
      implied the broad bottom of an ocean-liner, an architectural
      mass of being beyond the mere function of motherhood. Her real
      medium was not conjugation or fertility; it was empathy. In her,
      empathy became sibylline."

                                1951

  1   ALDRIDGE, JOHN W. After the Lost Generation: A Critical Study
      of the Writers of Two Wars. New York: McGraw-Hill Book Co.,
      pp. 13-17, 19, 86.
          Stein taught her disciples "how to make the most of their
      'lostness,' how to develop, as had Sherwood Anderson, an idiom
      that would be true of their time and truly their own." Her lit-
      erature became ever more divorced from reality, lost in an ab-
      sorption with self.

  2   ANDERSON, MARGARET. The Fiery Fountains: The Autobiography.
      New York: Hermitage House, p. 122.

                                138

When Stein expected celebrity treatment from Gurdjieff, she was ignored. He thought her too vain and settled.

3   BARR, ALFRED H., Jr. Matisse: His Art and His Public. New York: Museum of Modern Art, pp. 21, 37, 41, 56-58, and passim.

Leo Stein's interest in Matisse was more strong and analytical than was Gertrude's: "The friendship with the four Steins was of the greatest value to Matisse," for through the Steins he met collectors and other artists.

4   BAUR, JOHN I.H., Revolution and Tradition in Modern American Art. Cambridge: Harvard University Press, pp. 36, 131.

Leo and Gertrude Stein brought together in Paris most of the artists later to be known as great. The Stein family generously bought paintings by needy artists.

5   BEATON, CECIL. Photobiography. New York: Doubleday & Co., pp. 175-79.

Edith Sitwell introduced Beaton to Stein and Toklas, and he became fond of both and photographed them occasionally.

6   BOGAN, LOUISE. Achievement in American Poetry, 1900-1950. Chicago: Henry Regnery Co., pp. 30, 58-59, 120.

With Tender Buttons, Stein's "experiments, in which logical meaning is definitely eliminated, are the first of the kind to reach America and to be caught up by the poetic experimentalists who were then functioning."

7   CORY, DONALD WEBSTER. The Homosexual in America: A Subjective Approach. New York: Greenburg Publishers, p. 169.

Stein has written about "the homosexual temperament."

8   COWLEY, MALCOLM. Exile's Return: A Literary Odyssey of the 1920's. New York: Viking Press, pp. 3, 9, 110, 119, 148, 275, 286.

Stein enjoyed teaching her disciples, as did Pound, and hiding the keys to her almost-nonsensical writing.

9   DAVIDSON, JO. Between Sittings: An Informal Autobiography. New York: Dial Press, pp. 174-75.

In 1923 Davidson did his statue of Stein--"a sort of modern Buddha." He and Stein and Toklas were close friends; only Stein could read her own compositions well aloud.

10   FRANKENBERG, LLOYD. "Gertrude Stein's Reality." New York Times Book Review, 30 September, p. 5.

Two is "a collection of early 'portraits' done between 1908 and 1912. It is both the best and the worst book with which, as she might have said, to be beginning reading Gertrude Stein."

11 GALLUP, DONALD C. The Making of "The Making of Americans."
    New Haven: Yale University Press, 21 pp.
        Reprint of 1950.5.

12 GROSSER, MAURICE. The Painter's Eye. New York: Rinehart &
    Co., pp. 35-36, 163-64, 168, 213.
        When even writers began artistic "composition," composition
    itself became the subject of Stein--"composition in sound."

13 HARRIMAN, MARGARET CASE. The Vicious Circle: The Story of
    the Algonquin Round Table. New York: Rinehart & Co.,
    pp. 149-52.
        Stein's basic humor, under her formidably bizarre appear-
    ance, charmed the Round Table members.

14 HERON, MICHAEL. "A Note on Gertrude Stein." Envoy 4
    (January):72-76.
        "Gertrude Stein has left a large legacy of thought and in-
    vention. Her ideas may take years to assimilate." She was one
    of those who "led the way."

15 HOFFMAN, FREDERICK J. The Modern Novel in America, 1900-1950.
    Chicago: Henry Regnery Co., pp. 76-88, 109-10.
        "Miss Stein was more interested in the isolated sentence,
    in its rhythm and its succession of meanings for the thing it is
    describing. She could have little to do with the problems of
    structure; nor could she go beyond a certain point in her influ-
    ence upon modern fiction," leading unwise writers to do no more
    than repeat endlessly.

16 McBRIDE, HENRY. "Pictures for a picture of Gertrude."
    Art News 49 (February):16-18, 63.
        The shame is that Stein cannot dominate in person the dis-
    play of her paintings, for her collection is as important as any
    collection ever formed.

17 MORRIS, LLOYD. "She Disconnected Quality From Subject."
    New York Herald-Tribune, 28 October, sec. 6, p. 12.
        In Two, "readers who are unacquainted with [Stein's]
    writings may find these early examples of interest. For the
    already initiated they hold no surprises; they can be described
    as merely more of the same."

18 PICTURES FOR A PICTURE OF GERTRUDE STEIN AS A COLLECTOR AND
    WRITER ON ART AND ARTISTS. New Haven: Yale University Press,
    43 pp.
        Catalogue of art associated with Stein.

19 ROGERS, W.G. "Sound Keeps on Sounding." Saturday Review 34
    (29 September):16-17.
        The work in Two is "in the style of The Making of Americans,
    but it is more intense, compact and rewarding."

20   SUTHERLAND, DONALD. <u>Gertrude Stein: A Biography of Her Work</u>.
      New Haven: Yale University Press, 218 pp.
           Because Stein's work is so little biographically oriented,
      readers have thought her writing unemotional. But with Stein,
      "the excitement of it was mental, but the intellect was, popu-
      larly and to the educated, dead." Stein's subjects were quite
      important but not publicly important. Soon, perhaps, Stein's
      work will be seen as "as immediate and exciting as anything
      America has produced in this century."

21   TAUBMAN, HOWARD. "Records: Americana." <u>New York Times</u>,
      9 December, sec. 2, p. 12.
           Of <u>Gertrude Stein Reads Gertrude Stein</u>:   "To a Stein
      devotee it may all seem clear and logical. To the irreverent
      some of it may be hard going. I confess I got lost following
      her most intricately simple phrases. There are places where she
      stumbles over some of her tongue twisters. And there are some
      passages where you think the needle stuck in the same groove.
      Her voice and reading style are disarming."

22   WHICHER, GEORGE F. "Gertrude Stein and Her Experimental
      Techniques." In <u>The Literature of the American People: An
      Historical and Critical Survey</u>. Edited by Arthur Hobson
      Quinn. New York: Appleton-Century-Crofts, pp. 864-66.
           Stein "was the best kind of democrat, a democrat who knew
      what she wanted and was able to get things done. Ever since her
      death her ideas have continued to exert an influence."

23   WILLIAMS, WILLIAM CARLOS. <u>The Autobiography of William Carlos
      Williams</u>. New York: Random House, pp. 171, 186, 241, 253-56,
      and passim.
           Stein found the key to modernism in literature by her
      "objective use of words." When Williams and Stein met he
      offended her by commenting unfavorably on the many unpublished
      manuscripts she had accumulated.

24   WILSON, EDMUND. "Books." <u>New Yorker</u> 27 (15 September):
      125-26, 129-31.
           Stein seemed "a great iceberg of megalomania that lay
      beneath [the pleasant] surface and on which, if one did not
      skirt around it, conversations and personal relations might
      easily crash and be wrecked." With <u>Q.E.D.</u>, one may know Stein's
      tension and reserve; but the story will be valuable for its reve-
      lations more than for its "limpidity."

<u>1952</u>

1   BROOKS, VAN WYCK. <u>The Confident Years: 1885-1915</u>. New York:
      E.P. Dutton & Co., pp. 181, 212, 309, 392, and passim.

Stein's literary standard was personal and subjective;
only if something "affected her pleasantly" did she like it.
Her fame rose when her artistic and literary friends became
well known; then to her flock she presented "assurance in a
sick and jittery world."

2   DEUTSCH, BABETTE. <u>Poetry in Our Time</u>. New York: Henry Holt
    & Co., pp. 113-14, 197, 221.
        The apparent resemblance of Cummings' work to Stein's is
    illusory, for Stein eschewed connotation; her influence is upon
    novelists, not poets.

3   ENKVIST, NILS ERIK. "Gertrude Stein." <u>Finsk Tidskrift</u> 152
    (July-December):69-75.
        In Finnish. Seen but not translated.

4   GALLUP, DONALD. "Carl Van Vechten's Gertrude Stein." <u>Yale
    University Library Gazette</u> 27 (October):77-86.
        Van Vechten's collection of letters from Stein and of her
    publications after 1914 forms a major addition at the Yale Univer-
    sity Library.

5   HAVIGHURST, WALTER. Review of <u>Mrs. Reynolds</u>. <u>Saturday Review</u>
    35 (4 October):35-36.
        <u>Mrs. Reynolds</u> is "a tantalizing and exasperating book,
    which can also be exhilarating in the measure that a reader
    likes to be thrown upon his own resources."

6   "OLD PIGEONS." <u>Time</u> 59 (28 April):42.
        <u>Four Saints in Three Acts</u> "seemed a mighty old, effete and
    expatriate piece of Americana to represent U.S. culture at Paris."

7   PIVANO, FERNANDA. "Gertrude Stein, pioniera di un secolo."
    <u>Il Pensiero Critico</u> (March):14-45.
        Stein through prose experimentation linked the nineteenth
    and twentieth centuries. Reprinted: 1961.10.

8   PORTER, KATHERINE ANNE. <u>The Days Before</u>. New York:
    Harcourt, Brace & Co., pp. 36-60.
        Reprint of 1927.13; 1928.18; 1947.33.

9   PRESTON, J.H. "Conversation with Gertrude Stein." In <u>The
    Creative Process: A Symposium</u>. Edited by Brewster Ghiselin.
    Berkeley: University of California Press, pp. 164-72.
        Reprint of 1935.40.

10 REID, BENJAMIN. "Gertrude Stein's Critics." <u>University
    Review of Kansas City</u> 19 (Winter):121-30.
        Stein is adored or hated; critics should be more moderate
    and reasoned.

11   ROGERS, W.G. "Stein Stories, Lifelike in Their Way." New
     York Herald-Tribune Book Review, 28 September, p. 7.
          In Mrs. Reynolds, "because this is disorderly, because it
     seems aimless, because so much rich material goes to waste, it
     is like life."

12   ROSENFELD, ISAAC. "Pleasures And Troubles." New York Times
     Book Review, 21 September, pp. 6, 28.
          Scholarly interest such as that in Mrs. Reynolds is sad-
     dening: it shows Stein's decline from any popular audience to
     a narrowly academic audience.

13   RUDIKOFF, SONYA. "Clarity and Force in Gertrude Stein."
     Hudson Review 5 (Spring):148-54.
          Two demonstrates that Stein "was never wholly in or wholly
     out of her books, but her ambiguous presence determined their
     forms. The self she took as a center was fundamentally passive:
     it welcomed all phenomena, recorded them minutely, but took no
     action with regard to them. The self was passive because any
     other attitude might deprive it of possibility."

14   "STEIN'S LAST NOVEL." Time 60 (22 September):114, 116.
          Mrs. Reynolds proves that Stein "began as a literary in-
     novator, helping to break the crusts of conventional literary
     language. But she took her experiments too seriously and, like
     many another pioneer, refused to budge from her first discovery.
     Her manner became a mannerism, her breakthrough a limitation.
     In her last novel, the old revolutionary proves a rather garru-
     lous bore."

15   SUTHERLAND, DONALD. "A Lady of Letters." New Republic 127
     (6 October):26.
          Mrs. Reynolds "offers little obscurity by anybody's lights
     and is enormously funny very often, as often as terrible, like
     war. If not Gertrude Stein's greatest novel, it is surely her
     handsomest so far and most human."

16   TÉRIADE, E. "Matisse Speaks." Art News Annual 21 (1952):50.
          Matisse took a Negro statue to Stein's studio, where he
     discussed it with Picasso . . . and the Negro influence entered
     modern art.

17   VAN VECHTEN, CARL. "Some 'Literary Ladies' I Have Known."
     Yale University Library Gazette 26 (January):97-116.
          Van Vechten had nothing to do with publishing Three Lives,
     but he long enjoyed Stein's trust and friendship. Reprinted:
     1955.21.

18   WATT, DOUGLAS. "Musical Events." New Yorker 28 (26 April):
     121-24.

In <u>Four Saints in Three Acts</u>, "Thomson has used Miss Stein's firm procession of simple words with striking ingenuity, making them dance to a variety of rhythms and bend to countless emotional impulses, but it is also true that he was given a great deal of freedom by the nature of the text. Miss Stein presented him with a wide field, dotted with strange growths, and he obviously had the time of his life romping in it."

19   WIGGIN, LAWRENCE A. "In Defense of Joyce & Stein." <u>Saturday Review</u> 35 (29 November):23-24.
     Contrary to some statements, Stein's unconventional writing is not unrealistic; one may simply listen unobserved to children's talk to hear the validity of her works.

20   WILSON, EDMUND. <u>The Shores of Light: A Literary Chronicle of the Twenties and Thirties</u>. New York: Farrar, Straus & Young, pp. 116, 118, 119, 234, 575-86.
     Reprint of 1933.109.

1953

1   ANDERSON, SHERWOOD. <u>Letters of Sherwood Anderson</u>. Edited by Howard Mumford Jones and Walter B. Rideout. Boston: Little, Brown & Co., pp. 85, 86, 87, 88, 146, and passim.
     Anderson wrote Stein in 1921 to seek her aid for Hemingway. He thereafter praised her friendship and early literary example for himself.

2   BROOKS, VAN WYCK. <u>The Writer in America</u>. New York: E.P. Dutton & Co., pp. 24, 63, 71, 82, 92, 115, 128.
     Anderson lost his literary way when Stein and other esthetes bedazzled him, but Stein early recognized--as did Anderson--the limitation on reality in writing.

3   CLURMAN, HAROLD. "Theater." <u>Nation</u> 176 (25 April):353.
     The dramatic <u>Brewsie and Willie</u>, based on Stein's story, is a "rambling yet unified stretch of dialogue which is both naturalistic and stylized" and which "has caught and interpreted for us the basic homelessness of the G.I. at the end of the last war, and through him the basic confusion in all of us."

4   CROSBY, CARESSE. <u>The Passionate Years</u>. New York: Dial Press, pp. 224-25.
     The Crosbys and Stein met once, in 1928, so that Stein could see the books published by Crosby and the Crosbys could see Stein's pictures by Picasso. Caresse met Stein once again, in 1934, through Francis Rose.

5   GALLUP, DONALD, ed. <u>The Flowers of Friendship: Letters Written to Gertrude Stein</u>. New York: Alfred A. Knopf, 403 pp.

"The reader will find bits of information upon a variety of subjects: [Stein's] family background and her education; her taste and interest in art, her salon and the people who came there; the rapid growth of her celebrity as a personage and her long, slow struggle for recognition as a serious writer; her influence on other writers and what they learned from her; her warmth and sympathy and understanding, and her knowledge of human nature; her deep, passionate longing after glory and how she finally achieved it."

6   LEWIS, SINCLAIR. The Man from Main Street: Selected Essays and Other Writings, 1904-1950. Edited by Harry E. Maule and Melville H. Cane. New York: Random House, pp. 130, 131, 166, 210.
         Stein is a hoaxtress, misleading the easily misled.

7   MEYER, AGNES E. Out of These Roots: The Autobiography of an American Woman. Boston: Little, Brown & Co., pp. 79-82.
         Meyer liked Leo Stein but "conceived an immediate antipathy for his sister Gertrude," because Gertrude was too masculine. At the Stein salon, it was Leo who was respected and brilliant, not Gertrude.

8   ROGERS, W.G. "And a Fact Is a Fact." New York Times Book Review, 8 November, p. 24.
         Bee Time Vine "belongs on your Stein shelf. But it must be confessed that many of these pages have all of Miss Stein except the distinguishing, unforgettable edge, all of her except the very best. These seem to be exercises, or notebooks."

9   TAVERNIER, RENÉ. "'La France est mon chez moi.'" Rapports 72 (March):21-28.
         For her insatiable generosity, culture, vitality, courage, and friendship, Gertrude Stein deserves to be remembered by France.

1954

1   BARRY, JOSEPH A. "Cooking as Culture." New Republic 131 (29 November):17.
         The Alice B. Toklas Cookbook describes the Stein-Toklas love: "If anything, the experiences they shared were not divided but rather doubled by their sharing of them, and each was to contain the total to which each had contributed."

2   BUTCHER, FANNY. "Recipes and Reminiscences by Alice B. Toklas Herself." Chicago Tribune Magazine of Books, 28 November, p. 4.
         "Intriguing as many of the recipes sound, what really fascinates the reader is the series of reminiscences which makes up

more than half the book. . . . It is a special charm of this
unorthodox cookbook that the reader never is sure whether the
people in it recall the recipes or the recipes the people. You
never can tell what excitement will pop up on the next page."

3   CUNLIFFE, MARCUS. The Literature of the United States.
     Baltimore: Penguin Books, pp. 87, 214, 216, 232-37, and passim.
        Stein aimed at uncluttered art and abstract expression. Her
     work suffers less from dullness and obscurity than from repetition.
     With Twain, Stein is a great "formative influence upon American
     prose. One might say facetiously that he is its father, and she
     its mother."

4   "A DISH IS A DISH IS A DISH." Time 64 (22 November):110-11.
        ". . . what gives the Cook Book its special charm is the
     stream of Alice's prattle, in which the recipes appear like
     floating islands, in no special order."

5   FENTON, CHARLES A. The Apprenticeship of Ernest Hemingway.
     New York: Farrar, Straus & Young, pp. 103, 145, 147, 150,
     and passim.
        Copying Stein's manuscript of The Making of Americans was
     invaluable to Hemingway's development of a prose style, teaching
     him to compose fiction as carefully as great artists compose
     paintings.

6   FIRMAGE, GEORGE JAMES. A Check-list of the Published Writings
     of Gertrude Stein. Amherst: University of Massachusetts,
     8 pp.
        "This check-list is being issued by the English Department
     of the University of Massachusetts as part of a program to cele-
     brate the 80th anniversary of Gertrude Stein's birth."

7   GARVIN, HARRY RAPHAEL. "Sound and Sense in Four Saints in
     Three Acts." Bucknell Review 5 (December):1-11.
        Being the best of Stein's portraits and plays, Four Saints
     in Three Acts offers insight into Stein's complex sense of
     "language, rhythm, perception, and poetry."

8   "GERTRUDE STEIN'S UNPUBLISHED WORKS." Times Literary Supple-
     ment, 5 February, p. 90.
        Two and Mrs. Reynolds are new collections of Stein works,
     and nothing now available will change current estimates of the
     author's place. With Stein, "honesty of intention is not enough
     and . . . looking into one's consciousness and then writing is
     not enough."

9   HELM, EVERETT. "Virgil Thomson's Four Saints in Three Acts."
     Music Review 15 (May):127-32.
        Four Saints in Three Acts as music is unique: "It is an
     amusing opera, and it is also much more than that. Like the text

on which it is written, it is entertaining and at the same time
a work of art. In a sense it can be judged only by itself, for
there is no other work like it."

10   JACKSON, JOSEPH HENRY. Review of The Alice B. Toklas Cookbook.
      San Francisco Chronicle, 19 November, p. 23.
           Despite the difficulty of saying anything new about cooking,
      Toklas has entertained well in her Cookbook.

11   KNIGHT, GRANT C. The Strenuous Age in American Literature.
      Chapel Hill: University of North Carolina Press, pp. 86, 186.
           Three Lives was a pioneering work, for one life was devoted
      to a Negro. And Q.E.D. remains a startling work on lesbianism.

*12   LAS VERGNAS, RAYMOND. "Lettres anglo-américaines: Gertrude
      Stein." Hommes et Mondes 9 (September):313-15.
           Cited: American Literature 27:151.

13   LANE, MARGARET. Review of The Alice B. Toklas Cookbook.
      New Statesman and Nation 48 (4 December):752.
           Entertaining as Toklas's cookbook is, it is not for daily
      use in the kitchen so much as for reading about Gertrude Stein.

14   LÖTSCHER, HUGO. "Gertrude Stein." Welt der Kunst,
      6 February.
           One of the lost generation, Stein today is regularly asso-
      ciated with literature and art; yet a good study of her life is
      lacking, for she is still the object of mere fascination and
      cult.

15   McCASLIN, WALT. "Good Cookery, Good Talk By Alice Toklas."
      Dayton News, 12 December.
           "It should be said at the onset that this is more a book
      for the reader than a book for the cook--the busy American cook,
      at least. . . . Here is a highly civilized, thoroughly enjoyable
      book--every page steeped in the character of provincial France,
      the whole garnished with the kind of charming eccentricity one
      would have expected to find in the Toklas-Stein menage."

16   "NEWS OF FOOD." New York Times, 22 November, p. 26.
           The Alice B. Toklas Cookbook is as interesting for Toklas's
      memories as for the classic French cuisine that the book
      demonstrates.

17   "PEOPLE." Time 64 (4 October):44.
           The Alice B. Toklas Cookbook results from the "gay old
      time" that Toklas and Stein had in their kitchen. Perhaps the
      famous fudge could explain some of Gertrude's hashed lines.

18   REVIEW OF THE ALICE B. TOKLAS COOKBOOK. Booklist 51
      (15 December):167.

"An unusual mixture of both exotic and comparatively simple recipes, interspersed with delightful essays on French life and cuisine which also offer indirect glimpses of the author's association with Gertrude Stein."

19   "A ROSE IS NOT A COOK." Cedar Rapids Gazette, 19 December,
          "Fortunately, for clarity, [Toklas'] recipes never include passages like a fowl is a fowl is a fowl. . . . Her book makes tasty reading but I doubt whether many Americans will know for sure what some of her dishes taste like. They belong to the cook who can spend loving hours in a kitchen surrounded by exotic herbs, tempting wines, foods particularly native to France. And a fat pocketbook!"

20   S., I. "Unique Cookbook With French Touch." Worcester (Mass.) Telegram, 21 November.
          "Observation to a writer is what skill and fresh ingredients are to a cook. Alice B. Toklas, famed companion of the late Gertrude Stein, happily combines both in an interesting and informative mélange that will appeal to gourmets."

21   STOUT, REX. "To Cook Is to Cook." New York Times Book Review, 21 November, p. 26.
          In The Alice B. Toklas Cookbook are "mentions of Gertrude Stein--Stein anecdotes, her pronouncements on food and cooking, her reactions to people and things"--along with great French recipes!

22   TATE, ALLEN. Sixty American Poets 1896-1944. Rev. ed. Washington, D.C.: Library of Congress, pp. 121-27.
          "Miss Stein's poetry differs from her prose chiefly by being shorter."

23   TENAND, SUZANNE. "Gertrude Stein: Écrivain de chez nous." Visages de l'Ain, April-May, pp. 16-24.
          Bored by America, Stein graced France and loved the country and the people. A dilettante, Stein nevertheless was sincere in her writing.

24   "VERSE." New Yorker 30 (6 March):119-20.
          With Bee Time Vine, Stein's "instinctive feeling for the color and weight of words and phrases, and her touching delight in life's little jokes, just as often . . . push the material over onto the side of poetry, in spite of much that is trivial, tiresome, and downright peculiar."

25   VICKERS, JOHN. "Theatre." San Francisco Argonaut, 8 October, p. 16.
          A performance of Doctor Faustus Lights the Lights may present difficulties with Stein's version of the Faust story, but "you will be the recipient of a rewarding emotional experience."

26 WILLIAMS, WILLIAM CARLOS. Selected Essays. New York: Random House, pp. 113-20, 162-66.
Reprint of 1930.9; 1934.48.

27 WILLIS, KATHERINE TAPPERT. Review of The Alice B. Toklas Cookbook. Library Journal 79 (15 December):2453.
Toklas's cookbook "is indeed a book for cooks, but even more for all who love life, and good writing, and above all France, and the U.S.A."

1955

1 "ALICE TOKLAS RECIPES." Houston Post, 13 February.
"Interspersed with the memories are a succession of recipes and menus, some so prosaic that they might have come from an Iowa kitchen instead of an atelier in Paris. Others whet the appetite by a mere reading. Still others are fantastic and far-fetched. There never seemed to be a dull moment for Miss Toklas, whether she was in the parlor admiring a new Picasso, or in the kitchen at work on a stew."

2 BARO, GENE. Review of The Alice B. Toklas Cookbook. New York Herald-Tribune Book Review, 13 February, p. 8.
This is "more than an abundant collection of excellent and tempting recipes; it is also a way of life as practiced oh so well by Miss Toklas and her dear friend Gertrude Stein. . . . Thus, a cookbook that is delightful by way of its fine food has been made doubly pleasurable by the addition of shrewd worldly comment, by reminiscences, personalities, anecdotes, by the strong characters of the Misses Stein and Toklas."

3 "BRIEFLY NOTED." New Yorker 30 (5 February):116.
In The Alice B. Toklas Cookbook the recipes are fine, "but it is the author's salty comments and her contagious feeling for good cooking that give the book its zest."

4 CARPENTER, FREDERIC I. American Literature and the Dream. New York: Philosophical Library, pp. 185, 187, 188.
To Hemingway in Paris talks, Stein was "a trained philosopher," one who may have led him to Bergson's interest in time.

5 FADIMAN, CLIFTON. Party of One: The Selected Writings of Clifton Fadiman. Cleveland: World Publishing Co., pp. 85-97.
Gertrude Stein is the woman that Fadiman would most hate being on a deserted island with. He is anesthetized by Stein and puzzled by his anesthesia. She influenced greater writers in a time of intense experimentation. Perhaps Stein will be more appreciated when Americans tolerate humor and eccentricity.

6 GARVIN, HARRY R. "Stein's 'Lipchitz.'" Explicator 14 (December):#18.

"Lipchitz" is in Stein's "third style, wherein she tries to capture the sculptor's essence.

7　HEISSENBÜTTEL, HELMUT. "Reduzierte Sprache: Über ein Stück von Gertrude Stein." Augenblick 1 (1 January):1–16.
　　As A Wife Has a Cow illustrates quite well the need to study Stein's work for both content and style, both literarily and linguistically. Reprinted: 1966.8.

8　HOFFMAN, FREDERICK J. The Twenties: American Writing in the Postwar Decade. New York: Viking Press, pp. 43–44, 156–59, 217–18, and passim.
　　Stein's influence is hard to determine precisely. She did contribute to writing a sense of high art, of impressionism, of textual complexity to equal psychological complexity.

9　LIVINGSTON, J.A. "Gert Stein's Money Is Money Is Escape From Pile of Debt." Philadelphia Bulletin, 31 March, p. 36.
　　"Gertrude Stein's version of money was contemporaneous with President Roosevelt's tenure in the White House. [The Banker] Arthur resented Roosevelt. He doesn't resent Eisenhower. He resents free and easy lenders. He associates them with free and easy spenders."

10　LUEDERS, EDWARD. Carl Van Vechten and the Twenties. Albuquerque: University of New Mexico Press, pp. 5, 22, 55, 56, 58–59, and passim.
　　Van Vechten always championed the work of Stein, keeping it in public view until its merit was discovered, serving as "a middleman between eccentric artist and reluctant public."

11　MACKALL, LAWTON. "Jesse, Casseroles, and the Virgins." Saturday Review 38 (12 February):39.
　　The Alice B. Toklas Cookbook is a relief to hungry dieters and a lament to dieticians, a book with the "mesmeric quality of a personality as impervious to circumstances as a wooden Indian and as perceptive as Argus."

12　MELLOW, JAMES. "Gertrude Stein and the Cone Collection." Arts Digest 29 (15 January):6–7, 21, 33.
　　Although Stein was "a forceful personality at the beginnings of modern art, she somehow remained on the outside of it, observant and dispassionate, content to assume a passive role. She put forth in print and in random conversations her individual opinions upon the art of painting in our time, but she did not advance herself as one of its muses, nor did she make any claims to a fine discrimination." Yet the Cone Collection testifies to her achievement in art.

13　PAUL, ELLIOT. Understanding the French. New York: Random House, pp. 21–22, 63, 127.

Stein and Toklas loved Belly and finagled through the
French government to rent a summer house there: "Gertrude Stein
did Provence more good than James or Dickens did."

14 RADOM, EDYTH. "A Cook is a Cook." Hartford Courant,
　　2 January.
　　"The informality and almost-sporadic style of [Toklas'
cookbook] with its interspersed recipes makes really entertaining,
informal and informative reading. It's a book for epicures and
food stylists despite the fact that many of the recipes are prac-
tical and usable."

15 RICHARDS, ROBERT FULTON, ed. Concise Dictionary of American
　　Literature. New York: Philosophical Library, pp. 214-15.
　　"Through her examples and direct contact with many younger
writers and through their influence in turn on others," Stein
"had an enormous influence on contemporary literature, out of
all proportion to the quantity or popularity of her own work."

16 ROGERS, W.G. "Nothing, But Something." New York Times Book
　　Review, 23 October, p. 12.
　　The pieces in Painted Lace are the "splinter production of
those thrilling years, the chips which fell as [Stein's] major
works were hewn out. Some of them are excellent."

17 SIEVERS, W. DAVID. Freud on Broadway: A History of Psycho-
　　analysis and the American Drama. New York: Hermitage House,
　　pp. 243-45, 256.
　　"Of all playwrights, the one who apparently set out to
suppress the conscious as rigidly as the pre-Freudians suppressed
the unconscious was Gertrude Stein, who has been represented on
Broadway only by the opera, Four Saints in Three Acts. . . ."

18 SPILLER, ROBERT E. The Cycle of American Literature: An
　　Essay in Historical Criticism. New York: Macmillan Co.,
　　pp. 184, 191-92, 201, 206.
　　Experimenting in free-form prose, Stein always dwelled on
the continuous present and saw irrationality and primitivism as
"a sophisticated escape from reality rather than, as in Dreiser
and the more simple naturalists, an effort to track life to its
sources."

19 SPRIGGE, ELIZABETH. "Gertrude Stein's American Years."
　　Reporter 13 (11 August):46-52.
　　Sprigge muses about the mind and personality of Stein as
she visits the places in the U.S. where Stein lived.

20 UNTERMEYER, LOUIS. Makers of the Modern World. New York:
　　Simon & Schuster, pp. 406, 407, 458-67, 567, 717, 718.
　　Stein "was always trying 'a new thing in a new way,'
even though her departures, which suggested constant change,

were constantly the same only more so. She did not mind goading and worrying the reader as long as she worried him into wakefulness. As a communication her work was a failure."

21   VAN VECHTEN, CARL. <u>Fragments from an Unwritten Autobiography</u>. New York: Yale University Press, pp. 19-24. Reprint of 1952.17.

22   WHITE, WILLIAM. "Only One, Only One, Only One." <u>Wolf Magazine of Letters</u> 21 (June):4.
     The British publisher A.C. Fifeld imitated Stein's odd style when he rejected for publication one of her manuscripts.

1956

1   BLÖCKER, GÜNTER. "Die Muse der veloren Generation." <u>Merkur</u> 10 (July):720-24.
     The legendary Stein in Paris helped invent the modern novel, demonstrating the possibilities of nonrepresentational forms of reality. Reprinted: 1957.3.

2   BROWN, MORRISON. <u>Louis Bromfield and His Books: An Evaluation</u>. London: Cassell & Co., pp. 55, 57, 147.
     Stein was a "close friend of the Bromfields and came to visit them" in France. Bromfield "thought she had one of the keenest minds he had ever encountered and he enjoyed conversations with her just as she apparently enjoyed them with him."

3   FOWLIE, WALLACE. "The State of Change." <u>Saturday Review</u> 39 (22 December):20-21.
     In <u>Stanzas in Meditation</u>, "the aphoristic style and the conciseness of the formulas express the energy of the writer's consciousness, which appears almost excessive."

4   GRIS, JUAN. <u>Letters, 1913-1927</u>. Collected by Daniel-Henry Kahnweiler. Translated and edited by Douglas Cooper. London: n.p., pp. 6, 12, 13, 14, 18, and passim.
     Stein arranged loans for Gris, expecting pictures in return; later Stein called the loans a gift. She once thought of writing a ballet with Gris, and they exchanged letters from 1914 to 1927.

5   HARRIMAN, MARGARET. <u>Blessed Are the Debonaire</u>. New York: Rinehart & Co., p. 224.
     Stein spent one Christmas Eve at the Algonquin Hotel in New York City and loved tree-trimming.

6   HAYES, RICHARD. "The Making of Us All." <u>Commonweal</u> 64 (28 September):634-35.

The Mother of Us All, "though here the landscape is less private [than in Four Saints in Three Acts], is indeed that great public athaneum of nineteenth-century American life, oracular and rotund, full of a spacious and rhetorical eloquence, the monument to an age of didacticism and moral passion."

7   LEACH, WILFORD. "Gertrude Stein and the Modern Theatre." Ph.D. dissertation, University of Illinois, 203 pp.
    Stein's "idea of the theatre is primarily that it is an event during which an arrangement of 'things' may be seen and heard; such elements as plot, conflict, story, are structural devices that may or may not be appropriate to the 'emphasis' present in modern existence, rather than part of the unchanging basic nature of theatre." Summarized: Dissertation Abstracts International 17:434.

8   McBRIDE, HENRY. "Soufflé for Alice." Art News 54 (February): 30, 63-64.
    The Alice B. Toklas Cookbook is "more than a cook book. It is a diplomatic coup of the first order," good for French morale.

9   PEARLÈS, ALFRED. My Friend Henry Miller. Preface by Henry Miller. New York: John Day Co., p. 22.
    Miller "had made a hit with Gertrude Stein, the babble-queen of the rue Fleurus."

10 PHELPS, ROBERT. "The Uses of Gertrude Stein." Yale Review 45 (June):600-603.
    With five volumes out of hitherto unpublished Stein writing, "I am not sure what use, beyond titilation, most of Gertrude Stein's writing has for those of us who only read. But I cannot foresee a time when some of its aspects will not itch and tease writers themselves beyond what they already know, and out into that openness of mind where their own originality can quicken. And this is as large and honorable a use, for all of us, as any writer can hope to have."

11 SALMON, ANDRÉ. Souvenirs sans fin, II. Paris: Gallimard, pp. 56, 57, 58, 62.
    Stein soberly invents a style of her own, paying no attention to the passing parade of life.

12 TAYLOR, WALTER FULLER. The Story of American Letters. Chicago: Henry Regnery Co., pp. 393, 400.
    Stein was partly playful in describing the "lost generation" as such. She enjoyed playing Paris sponsor to Hemingway.

<u>1957</u>

1   ASHBERRY, JOHN. "The Impossible." <u>Poetry</u> 90 (July):250-54.
        <u>Stanzas in Meditation</u> is "no doubt the most successful of
    [Stein's] attempts to do what can't be done, to create a counter-
    feit of reality more real than reality. And if, on laying the
    book aside, we feel that it is still impossible to accomplish the
    impossible, we are also left with the conviction that it is the
    only thing worth trying to do."

2   BENSE, MAX. "Kosmologie und Literatur: Über Alfred N.
    Whitehead und Gertrude Stein." <u>Texte und Zeichnen</u> 5 (1957):
        512-25.
        Stein sought in poetic form an exploration of meaning as
    Whitehead did in philosophical form.

3   BLÖCKER, GÜNTER. <u>Die Neuen Wirklichkeiten: Linien und
    Profile der Modernen Literatur.</u> Berlin: Argon Verlag,
        pp. 232-40, and passim.
        Reprint of 1956.1.

4   "EXPERIMENT IN DESTRUCTION." <u>Times Literary Supplement,</u>
        8 February, p. 82.
        <u>Stanzas in Meditation</u> is "about as long as <u>Paradise Lost</u>
    but not so good. . . . That this volume, and introduction,
    should be issued by a responsible University Press, is an aston-
    ishing monument to academic gullibility."

5   FLANNER, JANET. <u>Men & Monuments.</u> New York: Harper &
    Brothers, pp. xx, 82-84, 131, 132, 138, and passim.
        The Steins had unerringly good taste in buying French art.
    Gertrude Stein befriended Matisse, Braque, Picasso. Her interest
    in art centered on the generation that, she said, ended in 1914.

6   GUHL, DALE. "Stein." <u>New York Times Book Review</u>, 21 April,
        p. 16.
        Stein was filled with a "somethingness," whether it was
    "a belief in her own work or her own genius or merely a desire
    to have others believe in them. . . ."

7   HINCHLIFFE, ARNOLD P. "American Writing." <u>Times Literary
    Supplement</u>, 22 February.
        Stein "saw that by the twenties American writers had an
    American language, and the problem was what to do with it. She
    proceeded therefore, to translate the specious present of William
    James into literary terms, and her emotional paragraphs, repeti-
    tions and excessive use of gerund constructions are all devices
    to convey particular experience in a precise manner."

8   JOYCE, JAMES. <u>Letters, II.</u> Edited by Richard Ellman. New
    York: Viking Press, pp. 55, 188, 216, 351.

Hemingway quoted Stein as deriding the alleged poverty of
Joyce. Joyce's brother hated seeing the presumed competition of
Joyce and Stein. Joyce resented Bennett Cerf's apparent prefer-
ence for Stein's work over Ulysses.

9   LOWE, FREDERICK W., Jr. "Gertrude's Web: A Study of Gertrude
     Stein's Literary Relationships." Ph.D. dissertation, Columbia
     University, 369 pp.
        "This study examines the relationship between Gertrude
Stein's salon and her effect, as a writer and salonière, on
Americans who joined her circle. The salon, at 27 rue de Fleurus,
Paris, served throughout her career as a rallying point or a symbol for the avant garde of American literature. Its changes re-
flect, as a microcosm, the changing characteristics of the American
expatriate movement." Summarized: Dissertation Abstracts International 17:1766.

10   McDONALD, GERALD D. Review of Stanzas in Meditation. Library
     Journal 82 (1 March):679.
        At the time of Stanzas in Meditation Stein reached the peak
of her innovation and afterwards wrote conventionally: "It is
clearly poetry, is less abstract than many may suppose, and has
its own peculiar sensory and intellectual stimulus."

11   MICHELSON, HERB. "Gertrude Stein: An Appraisal." New York
     Mirror, 16 November.
        "Gertrude Stein was a genius--perhaps the least understood
genius of her time, but still a real genius. Gertrude Stein was
a fad--her works were a chunk of the revolution in art and literature 35 years ago."

12   MILLETT, FRED B. "Book Reviews." American Literature 29
     (May):222-23.
        Publication of Painted Lace denies potential publication
to unsubsidized "valuable scholarly manuscripts."

13   ROGERS, W.G. "Lovely Paper, Lovely Pens." New York Times
     Book Review, 24 November, p. 12.
        "Occasionally, in the six earlier posthumous volumes of her
works, [Stein's] admirers had the uneasy feeling that going on
was the only thing that did matter. But [Alphabets and Birthdays]
most happily contains much standard Stein."

14   SHAPIRO, KARL. "Poetry in 1956." Prairie Schooner 31
     (March):15-16.
        Stanzas in Meditation reveals that "from translations from
the Persian, Greek, Latin, and what-not, it's no great hop to
Gertrude Stein, who perfected a kind of pidgin King's English. . . . She wrote as a poet would if a poet had never
had a dream or a sleepless night."

15   SOBY, JAMES THRALL. Modern Art and the New Past. Introduction by Paul J. Sachs. Norman: University of Oklahoma Press, pp. 47-48, 84, 98, 107-12, 113, 121.

Stein is among the few American writers to be concerned deeply with art, as illustrated by her Papers at Yale. If U.S. painting becomes important to the world, Stein will deserve praise.

16   SPRIGGE, ELIZABETH. Gertrude Stein: Her Life and Work. New York: Harper & Brothers, 277 pp.

Stein had "enormous vitality, an unfailing zest for living and a searching interest in human beings which, expressed in a candid gaze, a compelling voice and hearty laughter, gave her great magnetism. In early days people used to go to her house to see the pictures, but later they went for herself; and she knew an enormous number of interesting contemporaries in every field. Most men and women found her enchanting company, but to a few she seemed merely eccentric and self-centered; for many she had great humour, others found in her none at all."

17   STEWART, ALLEGRA. "The Quality of Gertrude Stein's Creativity." American Literature 28 (January):488-506.

Because Stein's vision does not depend on her subject-matter, her concern is esthetically intensified: "It is for this reason that Gertrude Stein's writings give the appearance of triviality, and convey an impression of fragmentariness and inconsequentiality. But this is only on the surface. Like Henry James, she knew that it is the quality of life in the work of art that really counts."

18   WILLIAMS, WILLIAM CARLOS. The Selected Letters of William Carlos Williams. Edited by John C. Thirwall. New York: McDowell, Obolensky, pp. 113, 121, 129, 142-43, 144, 252, 271.

Williams did not approve of Stein's simple-minded verbal experiments, but he credited her and Joyce with drawing attention to the word. He liked The Autobiography of Alice B. Toklas.

19   WRIGHT, RICHARD. Pagan Spain. New York: Harper & Brothers, pp. 1-2.

In her last days, Stein encouraged Wright to visit Spain, as she had done early in her life.

1958

1   AIKEN, CONRAD. A Reviewer's ABC: Collected Criticism of Conrad Aiken. Introduction by Rufus A. Blanshard. New York: Meridian Books, pp. 364-67.

Reprint of 1934.1.

2   CANNELL, KATHLEEN. "The Lucid and Friendly Gertrude Stein."
     Providence Journal, 3 August.
         "A reader wishing to tackle Gertrude Stein on his own could
     hardly do better than begin with Alphabets and Birthdays. It
     presents a cross section of this author's work and can serve as
     an introduction to more difficult volumes."

3   CLURMAN, HAROLD. Lies Like Truth: Theatre Reviews and
     Essays. New York: Macmillan Co., pp. 120-21.
         The dramatic form of Brewsie and Willie is "a rambling yet
     unified stretch of dialogue which is both naturalistic and
     stylized."

4   FLANNER, JANET. "Recipes of Alice B. Toklas." New Republic
     139 (15 December):20.
         Aromas and Flavors is "a remarkable new cook book with a
     split personality, containing two hundred precisely detailed and
     delicious recipes by Miss Alice B. Toklas of Paris, accompanied
     by useful annotations by Mrs. Poppy Cannon of House Beautiful,
     which will often help the American kitchenette gourmet to avoid
     the bother of cooking anything like as well as Miss Toklas."

5   FOSTER, JEANNETTE H. Sex Variant Women in Literature: A
     Historical and Quantitative Survey. London: Frederick
     Muller, pp. 247-51, 255, 269, 334.
         The conclusion of Q.E.D. is probably that "such an emo-
     tional game could never be worth the candle."

6   GASS, WILLIAM H. "Gertrude Stein: Her Escape from Protective
     Language." Accent 18 (Autumn):233-44.
         "In her effort to escape a purely protective language and
     make a vital thing of words, Gertrude Stein unsettled the whole
     of prose. Her abstractions enlarged the vocabulary of exciting
     words and made for some of the dullest, flattest, and longest
     literature perhaps in history. . . . None of her contemporaries
     had her intellectual reach, few her persistence and devotion,
     though many had more industry and insistence on perfection."
     Reprinted: 1970.15.

7   GLASGOW, ELLEN. Letters of Ellen Glasgow. Edited by Blair
     Rouse. New York: Harcourt, Brace & Co., pp. 173, 174.
         In 1935, Glasgow looked forward to meeting Stein and
     being polite even if Stein did not appeal to her. Then, after
     the meeting, Glasgow wrote: "Though I do not take Miss Stein's
     prose seriously, her personality won me, and we became very good
     friends."

8   HEWITT, LOUISE. "Alice B. Toklas' Recipe Book Makes for
     Refreshing Reading." Shreveport Times, 2 November.
         Aromas and Flavors is not just a superb cookbook; it is
     also a mirror of the life led by Stein and Toklas in Paris.

9   NEVILLE, HELEN. "The Portrait of Gertrude Stein."
     Commentary 25 (March):260.
          "It doesn't look like her. It's much too new. / She
     needs to die a little more, to be / reclaimed by that which
     made her, which she made."

10   REID, B.L. Art by Subtraction: A Dissenting Opinion of
     Gertrude Stein. Norman: University of Oklahoma Press,
     244 pp.
          Compared to other writers of her age, Stein is "pathetic--
     no other word suffices. To her pathetic narrowing must be com-
     pared their burgeoning inclusiveness; to her fortuitous form,
     their organic form; to her art-for-art insulation from life,
     their hot immerson in it; to her drab, cacaphonous emptiness,
     their proliferation of the possibilities for beauty, meaning,
     and passion in language." Having subtracted from her art all
     traditional elements of literature, Stein wrote books with "no
     beauty, no instruction, no passion. All that is finally there is
     Gertrude Stein mumbling to herself."

11   REVIEW OF AROMAS AND FLAVORS. Kirkus Reviews 26 (15 September):
     733.
          "The dishes range from the exotic and esoteric (perfumed
     goose or shrimps with oranges) to the staunch and hearty (beef-
     steak in the Polish manner or white sauce). Delectable recipes
     with clear instructions, this culinary guide is guaranteed to
     whet the appetite of even the most orthodox epicure."

12   SAARINEN, ALINE B. The Proud Possessors: The Lives, Times
     and Tastes of Some Distinguished American Art Collectors.
     New York: Random House, pp. 15, 174-205, 210, 215, and
     passim.
          "Gertrude, Leo and Michael and Sarah Stein were not col-
     lectors of modern masterpieces. . . . They acquired many fasci-
     nating and illuminating paintings, but only a very few were of
     the first order of magnitude. Yet the impact of the Steins was
     formidable. They altered the whole atmosphere of modern art.
     After the Steins no self-respecting intellectual could ignore
     it." Reprinted in part: 1958.13.

13   _____. "The Steins in Paris." American Scholar 27 (August):
     437-48.
          Reprint in part of 1958.12.

14   SHATTUCK, ROGER. The Banquet Years: The Arts in France.
     New York: Harcourt, Brace & Co., pp. 25, 37, 54-56, 196,
     268, 269.
          Stein lived quite ordinarily in Paris, although she wrote
     excitingly of the artistic ferment there.

15 SOBY, JAMES THRALL. Juan Gris. New York: Museum of Modern
    Art, pp. 9, 10, 11, 13, 35, and passim.
         "To Gertrude Stein in particular much credit must go for
    [Gris'] ascending fame. She wrote about him and his art more
    warmly than about any other artist with the exception of Picasso;
    she cajoled or bullied many visitors to her celebrated apartment
    on the rue de Fleurus into taking him seriously as a cubist of
    the first rank."

16 TURGEON, CHARLOTTE. "Favorite Dishes of Gertrude Stein and
    Others." New York Times Book Review, 7 December, p. 60.
         Toklas's two cookbooks reveal her--finally--to be "an
    energetic and independent person in her own right."

17 YALDEN-THOMSON, D.C. "Obscurity, Exhibitionism, and Gertrude
    Stein." Virginia Quarterly Review 34 (Winter):133-37.
         Stanzas in Meditation and Alphabets and Birthdays demon-
    strate again that, despite her obscurantism and showing off,
    Stein needed to experiment as she did. To create--not recreate--
    was her purpose in writing.

18 WALTHER, ELISABETH. "Notizen über Gertrude Stein."
    Augenblick 3 (3 January):45-51.
         Unknowingly Stein influenced later artists and philosophers
    with her theory of literature--even Sartre and his Existentialism.

19 WILLIS, KATHERINE TAPPERT. Review of Aromas and Flavors.
    Library Journal 83 (1 December):3449.
         "Buy this book for every collection and if an imaginative
    cook finds it, great will be the pleasure. The past and the
    present meet in methods and ingredients."

                              1959

1   LES ANNÉES VINGT: LES ÉCRIVAINS AMERICAINS À PARIS ET LEURS
    AMIS, 1920-1930. Paris: Centre Culturel Américain, pp. 43-46.
    Primary bibliography.

2   BALDANZA, FRANK. "Faulkner and Stein: A Study in Stylistic
    Intransigence." Georgia Review 13 (Fall):274-86.
         "William Faulkner and Gertrude Stein represent, in their
    contrasts, the baroque way of proliferation and the romanesque
    way of simplicity; but in their similarities they represent a
    common achievement of putting to paper by means of unconsciously
    shared stylistic devices the tone and rhythm of primitively in-
    transigent obsession."

3   BEACH, SYLVIA. Shakespeare and Company. New York: Harcourt,
    Brace & Co., pp. 27-29, 31, 32, 33, 82, 125, 136, 165, 206.

Stein and Toklas patronized Beach's library in Paris: "Gertrude was always teasing me about my bookselling, which appeared to amuse her considerably." Of the two women, "Alice had a great deal more finesse than Gertrude. And she was grown up: Gertrude was a child, something of an infant prodigy."

4   BECHTEL, LOUISE SEAMAN. "Gertrude Stein for Children." In *A Horn Book Sampler on Children's Books and Reading*. Edited by Norma R. Fryatt. Introduction by Bertha Mahoney Miller. Boston: Horn Book, pp. 128-32.
        Reprint of 1939.1.

5   BRINNAN, JOHN MALCOLM. *The Third Rose: Gertrude Stein and Her World*. Boston: Little, Brown & Co., 427 pp.
        "In a writing career that lasted more than forty years, Gertrude Stein separated literature from history, from sociology, from psychology and anthropology, even from knowledge itself. As a poet, she destroyed the connecting tissues that hold observed realities together and, as a writer of novels, she attempted to remove from the body of literature the very sinew and bone of narrative. She preached that literature was an art not necessarily dependent upon any of these, and she practiced what she preached."

6   CANNELL, KATHLEEN. "A Rose Is a Rose Is a Rose Is a Rose." *Providence Journal*, 4 October.
        A Novel of Thank You is "replete with words, combined with many names in the endless, hypnotically repetitive, slightly varied rhythms which to Gertrude Stein identified individual characters."

7   EASTMAN, MAX. *Great Companions: Critical Memoirs of Some Famous Friends*. New York: Farrar, Straus & Cudahy, pp. 47-48, 70-72.
        Eastman had remained ignorant of "Gertrude Stein and her__ as silly--"equivalent in every respect except sincere passion to the ravings of a lunatic." Hemingway never really learned from Stein how to write prose.

8   FitzGIBBON, CONSTANTINE. *Paradise Lost and More*. London: Cassell, pp. 98-102.
        In 1945 an army captain, FitzGibbon met Stein through the offices of Francis Rose. He enjoyed food and paintings and Stein and Toklas.

9   "FIVE GOURMETS IN SEARCH OF GOOD FOOD." *Saturday Review* 42 (7 February):22.
        "A friend and companion to Gertrude Stein, Miss Toklas earned her reputation as a great cook in a country where such accolades are not easily won."

10   HART, RICHARD. Review of <u>A Novel of Thank You</u>. <u>Library Journal</u> 84 (1 February):519-20.
      "Most readers will find nothing but chaos in the text; admirers of Miss Stein will cherish one more early example of her stream of words, associations and images, dreams in a private world."

11   HOOVER, KATHLEEN, and CAGE, JOHN. <u>Virgil Thomson: His Life and Music</u>. New York: Thomas Yoseloff, pp. 9, 27, 48, 57-66, and passim.
      <u>Four Saints in Three Acts</u> is valuable to the history of music because Thomson treated Stein's text as though it were easily comprehensible: "The inverted shock produced by this anti-modern treatment of an ultra-modern libretto precipitated a reaction against the turgidity of much American music of the time."

*12   KRETZOI, CHARLOTTE M. "Gertrude Stein: Zsákutca." <u>Világirodalmi Figyelö</u> 5 (1959):229-31.
      In Hungarian. Cited: <u>MHRA Bibliography</u> for 1962, p. 404.

13   LOEB, HAROLD. <u>The Way It Was</u>. New York: Criterion Books, pp. 62-64, 89, 109, 129, 142, and passim.
      Loeb's first thought at seeing Stein's manuscripts was that "Gertrude was attempting to achieve with words an effect akin to that which musicians realize by ordering sounds and painters by integrating forms and colors. I did not think it could be done." Loeb did accept and publish several of Stein's works.

14   POPE, RICHARD L. "Gertrude was a stein was a stein." <u>Artesian</u> 4 (Winter):20-30.
      Stein "did not conform. She went her own direction and explored new ways. To some that is virtue in itself. She was original, provocative, and stimulating that is to say her enduring contributions outweigh her eccentricities."

15   R., J.W. "'Novel' By Gertrude Stein Published in Yale Series." <u>New Haven Register</u>, 11 January.
      <u>A Novel of Thank You</u> "is very representative Gertrude Stein; whatever other significance it has may have to wait until the contemporary language catches up to Miss Stein's innovations."

16   RAY, CYRIL. Review of <u>Aromas and Flavors</u>. <u>Spectator</u>, 25 December, p. 940.
      Toklas has been corrupted in cooking by such conveniences as electric blenders and short-cut recipes.

17   REVIEW OF <u>AROMAS AND FLAVORS</u>. <u>Booklist</u> 55 (1 January):232.
      "Like the earlier <u>Alice B. Toklas Cookbook</u> this contains an intriguing collection of both exotic and simple recipes, set down

exactly as the uncompromising Miss Toklas wrote them, but clari-
fied for the American housewife by Poppy Cannon's comments and
suggestions for substitutions."

18   REVIEW OF AROMAS AND FLAVORS. Greensboro Daily News, 3 May.
      "In this delightful small book . . . [Toklas] shares some
amazing cooking experiences with her readers. It is a book for
the gourmet and for those who have real appreciation for the
delicacy, the aroma, the taste of fine foods."

19   "SATURDAY REVIEW GOES TO THE KITCHEN." Saturday Review 42
      (7 February):35.
      Aromas and Flavors "is a book for browsing, for preparing
special, beautiful, delicately flavored dishes in the best tradition of French cuisine."

20   SMITH, A.E. "On Gertrude Stein." One Institute Quarterly 2
      (Summer):83-90.
      Only frightened critics and scholars have denied Stein's
homosexuality and its importance to her writing. Q.E.D. may be
the earliest homosexual novel ever written.

21   SMITH, T. HENRY. "Ode: Walking in Snow: To Gertrude Stein."
      Virginia Quarterly Review 35 (Fall):581-84.
      "Hello, Miss Stein. And, when you left your chair / beside
the fire, walking in the snow, / you made discovery of prayer for
fun, / that once upon a time. Hello, hello, / Miss Stein
hello. . . ."

22   SCHNEPS, MAURICE. The Woman at St. Lô. Tokyo: Cross
      Continent, pp. 117-20.
      In conversation Stein was not brilliant as a philosopher.

23   YOUNG, PHILIP. Ernest Hemingway. Minneapolis: University
      of Minnesota Press, pp. 28, 29, 31.
      "Up in Michigan" was unappealing to Stein because of its
plot of seduction. Stein was one of the few people to accuse
Hemingway of "smelling of museums."

                              1960

1   COATES, ROBERT M. The View From Here. New York: Harcourt,
      Brace & Co., p. 213.
      Joyce and Stein were too retiring to be part of Paris café
life. Stein did not get in her lifetime credit for "introducing
an almost mathematical lucidity (the classic influence, as distinguished from Joyce's, the romantic influence), into the treatment of the English language."

2   De ACOSTA, MERCEDES. <u>Here Lies the Heart</u>. New York:
     Reynal & Co., pp. 68, 120, 342–43.
         Alice B. Toklas is "beautifully modest, religiously humble,
     sensitive to an extreme, artistic, full of awareness, alert,
     tactful, forceful, unswerving to principle, generous and kind."

3   HASSAN, IHAB N. "Love in the Modern American Novel: Expense
     of Spirit and Waste of Shame." <u>Western Humanities Review</u> 14
     (Spring):153.
         In "Melanctha," Stein wrote "as perfect a love story as
     Americans had seen, though few Americans were in the mood then
     to follow the painful poetry, the endless beginnings, the slow
     knotting and unknotting of love in that work."

4   HOWARD, LEON. <u>Literature and the American Tradition</u>. Garden
     City, N.Y.: Doubleday & Co., pp. 260–62.
         Stein chose a style of "calculated simplicity" to communi-
     cate "her profound knowledge of people as well as things." When-
     ever Stein becomes obscure the fault lies in her obsession with
     total abstraction.

5   KAHNWEILER, DANIEL-HENRY. "Erinnerungen an Gertrude Stein."
     <u>Augenblick</u> 5 (1960):1–10.
         Kahnweiler knew Gertrude and Leo Stein as customers for
     the cubist art in his shop; later he became quite close to
     Gertrude Stein and Alice Toklas.

6   NORMAN, CHARLES. <u>Ezra Pound</u>. New York: Macmillan Co.,
     pp. 199, 245–46, 265, 322, 448.
         Pound and Stein shared an interest in Japanese art but
     could not remain friends.

7   PARRY, ALBERT. <u>Garrets and Pretenders: A History of</u>
     <u>Bohemianism in America</u>. Rev. ed. New York: Dover Publica-
     tions, pp. 192, 272, 336, 339.
         Stein's obscurity became joke material in literary circles,
     although little magazines sought her for contributions.

8   SPRIGGE, SYLVIA. <u>Berenson: A Biography</u>. Boston: Houghton
     Mifflin Co., pp. 142–43, 241, 242.
         Berenson resisted the encouragement of the Steins to praise
     only their favorite artists in his writings.

9   SYPHER, WYLIE. <u>Rococo to Cubism in Art and Literature</u>.
     New York: Random House, pp. 267, 276, 280, 281–82, 295–96,
     304, 310–11.
         Perhaps Stein's ideas on modern art (and writing) are
     cinematic and aid in interpreting the development of twentieth-
     century art.

1   BEATON, CECIL. The Wandering Years: Diaries, 1922-1939.
       Boston: Little, Brown & Co., pp. 281-83.
       Beaton was much impressed with the style and art in Stein's
    apartment on rue Christine.

2   BRIDGMAN, RICHARD. "Melanctha." American Literature 33
       (November):350-59.
       "Melanctha" is "a full-scale reworking of Gertrude Stein's
    first book, Things As They Are, which was written in 1903 and
    published posthumously in a limited edition in 1950. The plot
    has been changed and the central trio reduced by one, but the
    characters and their motivations, the fatalistic philosophy,
    and some phrases remain familiar."

3   BURBANK, REX. Thornton Wilder. New York: Twayne Publishers,
       pp. 82-87, 91, 97.
       In Our Town, Wilder "accomplished what he and Gertrude
    Stein conceived to be the main achievement of the literary
    masterpiece--the use of the materials of human nature to portray
    the eternal and universal residing in the collective 'human mind.'"

4   CORKE, HILARY. "Reflections on a Great Stone Face: The
       Achievement of Gertrude Stein." Kenyon Review 23 (Summer):
       367-89.
       "It is important to emphasize . . . that, although intoler-
    ably conceited, Gertrude Stein was not in any sense a charlatan.
    She never had her tongue in her cheek; she genuinely believed in
    her own uniqueness and incomparable genius; she devoted to the
    prosecution of her 'experiments' the single-mindedness and sense
    of dedication of the greatest of writers and thinkers. She was
    her own first victim."

5   _____. "Reply." Kenyon Review 23 (Fall):696-97.
       Donald Sutherland's defense of Stein for abstractionism
    is ill-founded: "There are certainly abstract or absolute
    elements in literature, just as there are representational
    elements in music. But the one remains concrete, as the other
    remains abstract."

6   FLANNER, JANET. "Letter from Paris." New Yorker 37
       (16 December):106, 108-9.
       Toklas's apartment has now none of the paintings that she
    and Stein enjoyed but now only "faint, empty outlines left by
    the picture frames on the white walls." Toklas herself now is
    an ill old woman.

7   HASSAN, IHAB. Radical Innocence: Studies in the Contemporary
       American Novel. Princeton: Princeton University Press,
       pp. 48-49.

In "Melanctha," Stein used "a kind of radical innocence. It acknowledges a limit; it borders on wisdom without ever entering its tragic realm."

8 HOFFMAN, FREDERICK J. *Gertrude Stein*. Minneapolis: University of Minnesota Press, 48 pp.
   Stein's value to the theory of literature is in carrying "as far as it might go William James's analysis of consciousness. Beyond that, she has stared hard at the prospect of an art objectively hard but autonomously real, using its instruments in strangely new but often startlingly effective ways."

9 MENCKEN, H.L. *Letters of H.L. Mencken*. Edited by Guy J. Forgue. New York: Alfred A. Knopf, pp. 379, 390-91.
   In 1934, Mencken refused to publicize Stein's lecture tour, for he did not admire her work. In 1935, he finally read *Three Lives* and found "some excellent stuff in it," although he did not admire the style.

10 PIVANO, FERNANDA. *La Balena bianca et altri miti*. Verona: A. Mondadori Editore, pp. 175-225.
   Reprint of 1952.7.

*11 _____. "Il Soggiorno romano di Alice B. Toklas." *L'Europa Letteraria* 2 (February):100-105.
   Cited: *American Literature* 34:161.

12 ROSE, Sir FRANCIS. *Saying Life: The Memoirs of Sir Francis Rose*. London: Cassell, passim.
   Rose was highly impressed by Stein and by her collection of paintings--which included many of his own early works.

13 ROSENBLUM, ROBERT. *Cubism and Twentieth-Century Art*. New York: Henry N. Abrams, pp. 38, 64, 96, 109.
   Picasso agreed with Stein that cubism "created" World War I camouflage. His inclusion of Stein's calling-card in a painting encourages the viewer to think of "the two brilliant women who then lived on the Rue de Fleurus."

14 RUSSELL, FRANCIS. *Three Studies in Twentieth Century Obscurity*. Philadelphia: Dufour Editions, pp. 66-122.
   Stein early rejected the real world in favor of childish, egotistical indulgence in juvenile writing. Recognition given her was merely the self-indulgence of a weak age, enmeshed in escapism.

15 SCHORER, MARK. *Sinclair Lewis: An American Life*. New York: McGraw-Hill, pp. 280, 281, 319, 374, 380, 384, 406.
   Lewis resented the praise blindly given to Stein and her followers who fell for her "solemn theology."

16   STEELE, OLIVER L., Jr.   "Gertrude Stein and Ellen Glasgow:
      Memoir of a Meeting."   American Literature 33 (March):76-77.
          Glasgow met Stein in 1935 and recorded that Stein was a
      "wise over-grown child" being laughed at for childish cleverness--
      in short, a charlatan.

17   SUTHERLAND, DONALD.   "Comment."   Kenyon Review 23 (Fall):
      695-96.
          Despite an attack by Hilary Corke and the lessening fashion
      for purely absolutist art, "this does not compromise the eminence
      of [Stein's] accomplishment within her epoch, nor her potential
      fascination for the times when absolutist exaltations are again
      our pleasure."

                              1962

1   BLUNT, ANTHONY, and POOL, PHOEBE.   Picasso: The Formative
      Years--A Study of His Sources.   New York: New York Graphic
      Society, pp. 2, 22-25.
          Stein was accurate in spirit in her commentary on Picasso's
      development.   She contributed to his serenity in the Rose or
      Circus Period.   The Steins were Picasso's first great collectors,
      and Gertrude tried simultaneously in prose some of Picasso's
      artistic techniques.

2   BOAS, GEORGE.   The Heaven of Invention.   Baltimore: Johns
      Hopkins University Press, pp. 37, 81, 82, 235.
          First encounters with such modernist work as Stein's may
      create upset.   Stein is a good example of automatic art, as is
      Jackson Pollack; yet no parody of Stein is so good as Stein.

3   BROWN, DEMING.   Soviet Attitudes Toward American Writing.
      Princeton: Princeton University Press, pp. 89, 96, 101.
          Stein has been influential on Dos Passos (more influential
      than Joyce) and shares a pretended naiveté.

4   BRYHER, [WINIFRED].   The Heart to Artemis: A Writer's Memoirs.
      New York: Harcourt, Brace & World, pp. 152, 201, 210-11, 225,
      271-72, 297.
          Robert McAlmon introduced Bryher to Stein, who did not like
      Bryher's lack of "personal problems" and "intellectual stimulus."
      Now her writing is important, for Stein was a "scientist" of
      writing.

5   CHASE, MARY ELLEN.   "Five Literary Portraits."   Massachusetts
      Review 3 (Spring):513-14.
          Stein visited Chase in England: "Without doubt Gertrude
      Stein was a bit mad in her unfettered manipulations of the Eng-
      lish language, although her early Three Lives proves that she
      could use it quite normally and with superb effectiveness and
      skill."

6   DUPEE, F.W. "Gertrude Stein." Commentary 33 (June):519-23.
     "By the time she died, in 1946, at the age of seventy-two,
Gertrude Stein had become something she wanted still more to be,
historical." Publication of The Autobiography of Alice B. Toklas
made her famous and "remains one of the best memoirs in American
literature."

7   FLANNER, JANET. "Letter from Paris." New Yorker 38
     (29 December):66-68.
     "The long life that Miss Stein and Miss Toklas passed to-
gether in Paris was framed by modern art. [What I Remember] is
like a small canvas filled with representational figures and
their background, still unfaded, sharply drawn, well colored."

8   HERZBERG, MAX, et al. The Reader's Encyclopedia of American
     Literature. New York: Thomas Y. Crowell Co., pp. 1077-79.
     "Miss Stein favored a disconnectiveness that often gave
the effect of inscrutability, if not always of profundity. In
her love of refrain and rhythm she revealed an outlook of the
poet and the child."

9   JOSEPHSON, MATTHEW. Life Among the Surrealists: A Memoir.
     New York: Holt, Rinehart & Winston, pp. 7-9, 11-12, 29, 77,
     and passim.
     Before World War I, Stein lived obscurely in Paris, collect-
ing art and writing work easily ignored by publishers and readers.
Only after the war did Stein achieve fame, especially through
proteges and little magazines. Only after The Autobiography of
Alice B. Toklas (a book often wrong in facts) did Stein achieve
real fame.

10   KESTING, MARIANNE. "Gertrude Stein: Das Experiment des
     Experiments." In Panorama des Zeitgenössichen Theaters: 50
     Literarische Porträts. Munich: R. Piper, pp. 43-49.
     Stein's unrealistic theater pieces (or dramas for reading)
are experiments in what cannot be done (at least easily) in a
theater. Reprint of 1962.11.

11   ____. "Gertrude Steins Dramatische Versuche: Das Experiment
     des Experiments." Neue Deutsche Hefte 88 (July-August):102-9.
     Reprinted: 1962.10.

12   LAWRENCE, D.H. The Collected Letters of D. H. Lawrence.
     Edited by Harry T. Moore. New York: Viking Press, pp. 1075,
     1076.
     In 1927, Lawrence wrote: "Personally I think nothing of
Gertrude Stein. . . ." In 1928 he found Stein amusing, while
Joyce he found stupid.

13   McALMON, ROBERT. McAlmon and the Lost Generation: A Self-
     Portrait. Edited by Robert E. Knoll. Lincoln: University
     of Nebraska Press, pp. 3, 5, 6, 186, 196, and passim.

Publication of The Making of Americans caused trouble between Stein and McAlmon, the latter doubting the business and
common sense of the former.

14   POLLACK, BARBARA. The Collectors: Dr. Claribel and Miss Etta
      Cone. New York: Bobbs-Merrill Co., 320 pp.
         Never trail-blazing critics or daring art collectors,
      Claribel and Etta Cone learned from the four Steins how to use
      their great wealth to build a superb collection of European
      twentieth-century art.

15   TURNBULL, ANDREW. Scott Fitzgerald. New York: Charles
      Scribner's Sons, pp. 149, 151, 153, 189, 253-54.
         Stein early admired Fitzgerald's fiction, crediting him
      with "creating the contemporary world." Fitzgerald cherished
      Stein's praise and resented any hint that she preferred Heming-
      way's talent. On her American tour Stein spent Christmas Eve
      with the Fitzgeralds.

16   WEALES, GERALD. American Drama Since World War II. New York:
      Harcourt, Brace & World, pp. 209-10.
         The drama of Brewsie and Willie, performed off-Broadway in
      1953, was an adaptation in which the dramatists tried to get "the
      correct rhythm" by holding to "the desultory flow of the Stein
      conversation, but to free the individual lines of repeated
      phrases."

                                 1963

1   "ALICE B. TOKLAS AND HER MEMOIR OF GERTRUDE STEIN AND HER
      SALON." Galveston News, 31 March.
         "Likely to prove somewhat disappointing to readers who may
      anticipate getting more out of it than it actually contains is a
      memoir entitled What Is Remembered. . . . For most readers this
      memoir turns out to be not much more than a listing of famous
      names in the international literary and art world of Gertrude
      Stein's time--writers, painters, musicians, sculptors, art con-
      noisseurs, who congregated in her salon in Paris."

2   "ALICE TOKLAS TELLS STORY IN OWN WORDS." Wichita Eagle,
      21 April.
         "Miss Toklas recalls childhood and girlhood in California.
      But it isn't until she meets Miss Stein that life really begins.
      Rich, vital and rewarding it was. Not surprising is the ending--
      the death of Gertrude Stein. Miss Toklas lives on with unfaded
      recollections."

3   ARNAVON, CYRILLE. Histoire littéraire des États-Unis. Paris:
      Librairie Hachette, pp. 323, 326.
         Stein's influence on Anderson's Dark Laughter was unfortu-
      nate, yet she was present at launching Hemingway in Paris in 1923.

                                 168

4   "THE AUTOBIOGRAPHY OF GERTRUDE STEIN." Washington Star,
     31 March.
         "In a way, [What Is Remembered] is a sequel to the cook-
     book. It is not a continuous, and only roughly a chronological,
     story. It is not really a story at all, but rather a collection
     of vividly recaptured moments--and one's admiration increases
     page after page with the discovery that Miss Toklas seldom fails.
     Her tiny measure of quiet delight in each anecdote or picture is
     always present and always piquant."

5   BAKER, CARLOS. Hemingway: The Writer as Artist. 3d ed.
     Princeton: Princeton University Press, pp. 4, 6, 15, 18,
     21-22, and passim.
         When Stein and Hemingway were friends, Stein aided Hemingway
     in giving serious attention to his prose form, and Hemingway
     helped Stein publish her work. His later parody of her style
     and dislike for her influence led to estrangement.

*6   BAKER, ROGER. "Alice B. Toklas." Transatlantic Review,
     no. 13.
         Cited: Sader, Marion. Comprehensive Index to English-
     Language Little Magazines, p. 4540.

7   BARLEY, REX. "Books in the News." Phoenix Republic, 7 April.
         In What Is Remembered, "Miss Toklas has a prodigious memory
     and an extraordinarily staccato and urbane writing style, often
     to a point where she gives the impression that she is jotting
     down a series of notes for a larger, more detailed life story,
     rather than the finished product itself. Many of the stories
     have been told before but Miss Toklas brings a beguiling fresh-
     ness to them, as well as opening the curtain on a number of hith-
     erto unrevealed aspects of her own life, that of Gertrude Stein
     and the brilliant coterie of artists, musicians and writers that
     flocked to 27 rue de Fleurus. . . ."

8   BARO, GENE. "A Memory Is a Memory Is a Memory." New York
     Times Book Review, 14 April, p. 44.
         "Though it is not an analytical or profoundly revelatory
     book, What Is Remembered is an important interpretation of the
     personalities and relationships that centered upon the households
     in the rue de Fleurus, at Bilignin, and in the rue Christine.
     Miss Toklas tells a story well, which is to say sparely."

9   BARRY, JOSEPH. "Miss Toklas on her Own." New Republic 148
     (30 March):21-23.
         "Now, at last, it is possible [with What Is Remembered] to
     explain to the curious what a conversation with Alice Toklas is
     like. . . . And since conversation is the essence of companion-
     ship, and her way with stories the quintessence of Miss Toklas,
     her memoirs tell us all we need to know about that vital aspect
     of her twinship with Gertrude Stein, the most germinal conversa-
     tionalist I have ever known."

10   BERENSON, BERNARD. <u>Sunset and Twilight: From the Diaries of
      1947-1958</u>. Edited by Nicky Mariano. Introduction by Iris
      Origo. New York: Harcourt, Brace & World, pp. 171, 184, 200.
           Berenson could not tolerate Freud, Eliot, Joyce and Gertrude
Stein because he had "anticipated and discarded what in me might
have led to them." Stein once told Berenson that hugging other
women served her "sexually based feelings."

11   BISCHOFF, BARBARA. Review of <u>What Is Remembered</u>. <u>Portland</u>
      (Ore.) <u>Journal</u>, 27 April.
           "This short volume of reminiscences is a real gem in its
pungent and staccato way. . . . Renowned names drop in abundance,
but they are set down, and boiled down, to bare essentials, leaving just the most pertinent details and refreshing essences."

12   BOARDMAN, KATHRYN. Review of <u>What Is Remembered</u>. <u>St. Paul</u>
      <u>Pioneer Press</u>, 10 March.
           "While most readers will want to know what Miss Toklas
remembers about such bigwigs as Hemingway, Fitzgerald, Edith
Sitwell, Paul Robeson, Pablo Picasso and Madame Matisse, there
will be others who will be charmed by her account of her early
years in California. . . . She is witty and sharp and
entertaining."

13   BRADDY, MAMIE H. "The Toklas Memoirs: An Illuminating Book."
      <u>Winston-Salem Journal and Sentinel</u>, 14 April.
           "In 'remembering,' Miss Toklas gives an account [in <u>What</u>
<u>Is Remembered</u>] of her friendship with authors, composers, paint-
ers in name-dropping that includes Picasso, Matisse, Apollinaire,
Bromfield, Eliot, Hemingway. . . . But in addition to graphic
accounts of 'art circles' over a period of years, she introduces
the reader to the warm and more human side of the literary
inseparables."

14   BROWN, LEONARD. "Recalling a Vanished Era." <u>Pasadena Inde-</u>
      <u>pendent Star-News</u>, 14 April, "Scene," p. 10.
           <u>What Is Remembered</u> is "not entirely a mellow reminiscence,
by any means. There are acid and brusque dismissals of unwelcome
people. There are the usual shafts and barbs of salon commentary.
But in the main, Miss Toklas had had a full, odd and evidently
satisfying life. She could have said more, and she lets you know
she remembers a good deal that she isn't saying; propriety and
discretion were a convenient artifice for women of her generation
and class."

15   BROWN, MILTON W. <u>The Story of the Armory Show</u>. Greenwich,
      Conn.: Joseph H. Hirshhorn Foundation, pp. 74, 111, 124.
           Gertrude and Leo Stein collected art and encouraged col-
lection of art by their friends. Reports on the Armory exhibit
likened the obscure art to the obscure prose of Gertrude Stein.

16   BUCHAN, BLISS. "Alice Toklas Now Speaks Own Piece." <u>New</u>
      <u>Orleans Times-Picayune</u>, 7 April.
      "Some modern critics have taken the attitude that Miss
Toklas was Gertrude Stein's drab little slave. If a slave is
still a slave when she glories in her estate, when she would
not change her lot for any conceivable heaven, perhaps Miss
Toklas was in bondage. . . . This book is evidence that she
contributed to the joint menage not only the work of her hands,
but wit, perception, and mental quality of a high order."

17   BUTCHER, FANNY. "Memories Evoked By 'What Is Remembered.'"
      <u>Chicago Tribune Magazine of Books</u>, 24 March, p. 6.
      Toklas's memoir is "a unique volume of reminiscences of the
swirl of people and events which had Gertrude Stein as its vortex
and on the periphery of which were most of artistic Paris from
World War I to the present. . . . Alice Toklas' reminiscences
are fascinating for anyone who wonders about the great creative
days in Europe when eager young Americans migrated to Paris like
lemmings to the sea--many of them to drown."

18   _____. "Revisiting a Literary Fountainhead in Paris."
      <u>Chicago Tribune Magazine of Books</u>, 7 July, p. 6.
      Living without Gertrude Stein and without the art collec-
tion, Toklas, "who never rose from her chair but whose mind
flashed across oceans and continents and among human beings,
made me realize something about old age--that it is only when
the wonder of life goes that old age really begins."

19   CALLAGHAN, MORLEY. <u>That Summer in Paris: Memoirs of Tangled</u>
      <u>Friendships with Hemingway, Fitzgerald, and Some Others</u>. New
      York: Coward-McCann, pp. 50, 114, 129, 139, 184-85.
      Callaghan did not wish to know Stein, for he hated her work
after <u>Three Lives</u>: "As for her deluded coterie, well, I had no
interest in finding one of them who would lead me to her den."

20   CAMBON, GLAUCO. <u>The Inclusive Flame: Studies in American</u>
      <u>Poetry</u>. Bloomington: Indiana University Press, pp. 6, 208.
      Poe is Stein's ancestor in her "furiously wrenching sound
from meaning through objective repetition, as if words were some
kind of fissionable material to be bombarded in a cyclotron. . . ."

21   CAMERON, HATTIE. "'What Is Remembered.'" <u>Montgomery</u>
      <u>Advertiser</u>, 11 August.
      "Many people have written of this far-away land, and the
names of its inhabitants and sojourners are familiar to us all.
Now, however, we are fortunate that Lady Alice has also written
of it. . . . Lady Alice is droll, thereby making her reminiscing
charming. The book is exactly what it says. It is 'What Is
Remembered.' If you like tales about this land across the sea,
get the book and read it. In a hammock would be a fine place."

22   CAMPBELL, COLIN. "Toklas Memoir." <u>Christian Science Monitor</u>,
       4 April, p. 17.
         "This time [in <u>What Is Remembered</u>] Miss Toklas is very much
a member of the cast, and her warm, puckish personality provides
the perfect foil. What she remembers ranges from delightful
bagatelles to cultural profundities, all of it couched in a
prose which has a way of husking an event to its core."

23   CANNELL, KATHLEEN. "A Loving Toklas L'Envoi." <u>Providence
       Journal</u>, 7 April.
         In <u>What Is Remembered</u> "Alice at last speaks for herself.
As one could judge by her two superb cookbooks, Miss Toklas is
a natural born writer, and she has '. . . cooked the material
down to its least possible volume and its highest possible
flavor. . . .' Her beautifully simple statements add up to
extreme sophistication, and delicate wit under which lurks a
robust, faintly astonished humor."

24   _____. "Nightingale Of Perpignan." <u>Christian Science
       Monitor</u>, 4 May.
         ". . . reading aloud is the key to enjoyment of much of
Gertrude Stein's writing. Then the meanings stand out, embel-
lished by jokes, puns and brilliant rhymes, slipped slyly into
pulsating prose."

25   CARROLL, PAUL. "Alice and Gertrude: A Memoir." <u>Chicago
       Daily News</u>, 27 March, p. 46.
         In <u>What Is Remembered</u>, "Miss Toklas is an Alice--passive,
civilized, girlish--wandering through the world behind the Looking Glass which was Gertrude Stein's life, all Humpty Dumpty and
Cheshire Cat. Observations remain on the surface. . . . Do not
expect any confessions of the heart nor vivid, probing experience
of the famous personalities parading through these pages--least
of all, a portrait of Gertrude Stein. None of the style and wit
of Gertrude Stein's autobiography, <u>The Autobiography of Alice B.
Toklas</u>, is even hinted at."

26   CASH, THELMA. "Novel by Alice Toklas Like Memory Catalog."
       <u>Fort Worth Star</u>, 31 March.
         Stein's earlier account of "the unusual friendship reads
like a witty and charming novel, while that of Alice B. Toklas
is similar to a catalog, replete with listings of people and
places but with only the most fragmentary comments about either."

27   "CIRCLING ROUND STEIN." <u>Times</u> (London), 21 November, p. 19.
         <u>What Is Remembered</u> is "a laconic work that is twice the
length its pages indicate, the rest being overtone and implica-
tion. . . . Miss Toklas, out of her intense involvement, observes
with the detached amusement of a Martian. Her sketch of the partnership [with Stein] is a brilliant teaser: imagination can interpret it at will."

28   COMANS, GRACE P.   "People and Events."   Hartford Courant,
      31 March, "Magazine," p. 14.
         In What Is Remembered "Miss Toklas remembers much and that
      sharply. One feels as though one were standing to one side with
      her and observing a fascinating piece of the twentieth century."

29   CROSBY, RALPH W.   "A. Toklas Remembers."   Washington Post,
      31 March.
         "Alice Toklas' What Is Remembered would make a good preface
      for a real book of her remembrances of friendship with Gertrude
      Stein and Gertrude's 'lost generation' assemblage. . . . What Is
      Remembered is filled with too many irrelevant incidents and lit-
      erary bones without flesh. Not what is remembered here, but what
      has been forgotten, might be truly worth a book."

30   DANCE, JIM.   "Living Second Hand."   Detroit Free Press,
      7 April.
         ". . . Gertrude Stein still dominates the story. When she
      is not present, Miss Toklas' experiences in Paris in the early
      1900's read like your Aunt Minnie's trip abroad. But when
      Gertrude takes over, you understand why their circle of friends
      included such diverse talents as Picasso, Hemingway, Alfred North
      Whitehead and the Sitwells."

31   deM., P.   "Miss Toklas Writes with Terse Prose."   Buffalo
      Courier-Express, 30 May.
         What Is Remembered is "really an annotated supplementary
      text. Miss Toklas drops famous names with wild abandon (true,
      all these personages were well known to her), but neither Picasso,
      Matisse, Hemingway, James Joyce, nor any others come alive here.
      The sparse prose, reticent accounts and terse phrases leave much
      to be desired. Miss Toklas left unsaid much that the reader
      would like to have had amplified and analyzed."

32   DURRELL, LAWRENCE, and MILLER, HENRY.   A Private Correspond-
      ence. Edited by George Wickes. New York: E.P. Dutton & Co.,
      pp. 21-22, 28, 76, 81, 128.
         Miller enjoyed Stein's Narration: "Impossible lingo she
      employs, irritating, but clear beneath, very simple, often quite
      profound," Durrell hated Stein's tone--"like a multiplication
      table."

33   EDGERTON, JAY.   "What Is Remembered Isn't Worth It."
      Minneapolis Tribune, 7 April.
         In What Is Remembered "Miss Toklas has material and to
      spare. . . . And yet somehow Miss Toklas, with all this wealth
      of reminiscence, never succeeds in holding your interest. There
      is an unrelieved quality to Miss Toklas' writing, a kind of dull,
      low-pitched monotone, a lack of pace and rhythm that inevitably
      produce[s] a sense of boredom in the reader."

34   "EMERGING FROM SHADOW." Times Literary Supplement,
      5 December, p. 1007.
           "What Is Remembered is not much of a sourcebook for the
      Stein research student seeking dates or table talk or illuminat-
      ing comments on her output. Where it risks achieving permanence
      is, oddly enough, not with the Steinian literature but as a frag-
      ile work of art in its own right."

35   FITZGERALD, ADELINE. "Gertrude Stein In Europe, Chicago."
      Chicago Sun-Times, 24 March.
           "Gertrude Stein was a full-time writer and Alice B. Toklas
      is not, but [What Is Remembered], a fourth the size of Gertrude's,
      has some advantages. It is the first person story of a remarkable
      and wholly unselfish love; it is often objective, and it has a
      dramatic climax Gertrude Stein couldn't have given it--her
      own death."

36   FITZGERALD, F. SCOTT. The Letters of F. Scott Fitzgerald.
      Edited by Andrew Turnbull. New York: Charles Scribner's
      Sons, pp. 122, 166, 169, 174, 182, and passim.
           In June, 1925, Fitzgerald wrote to thank Stein for their
      recent meeting and for her literary encouragement. He later
      wrote that he was fascinated by The Making of Americans and other
      books by her; and in 1934 he entertained her on Christmas Eve.

37   FOOTE, IRVING F. "Toklas Touch Lucid, Witty In Reflection."
      Atlanta Journal and Constitution, 24 March.
           "Very often, in reading Miss Stein's work, one must stop
      and read it out loud in order to be sure what is going on; very
      often, reading [What Is Remembered], one feels impelled to read
      it aloud to innocent bystanders just because she is so lucid and
      so witty. Where Miss Stein is liquid and melodic, Miss Toklas
      is abrupt and percussive. Like the telephone directory, her
      book is most remarkable for its cast of characters. . . ."

38   FURLAND, ALICE NELSON. "Books in Review." Baltimore Sun,
      29 March.
           What Is Remembered is "an autobiography with echoes of,
      and old friends from, Gertrude Stein's The Autobiography of
      Alice B. Toklas and Miss Toklas' own Cookbook. It is as dashing
      and as packed with wit as either of these books, and quite
      different."

39   G., W.B. "Miss Stein's Friend Reaches Into Memory."
      Buffalo Evening News, 14 April.
           What Is Remembered is "an unimpressive miscellany of names
      and places, books and incidents. . . . There is nothing new,
      exciting or revealing about this slender autobiography."

40   GASS, W.H. Review of What Is Remembered. South Atlantic
      Quarterly 62 (Autumn):620.

"Miss Toklas has hidden herself from us, and she has hidden her friend, too. Perhaps one who has lived so long with genius (a little bell told her Gertrude was) has no obligation to report to strangers what feelings animated or what forces shaped that noble Roman frame, or even to relate what took place behind her own dark gypsy skin. It is a difficult question."

41   GILMAN, RICHARD. "The Stage." Commonweal 79 (15 November):
     227.
     Stein's What Happened at the Judson Poets' Theater was "without any question a minor masterpiece, more inventive, more high-spirited and more animate than anything I have seen recently at the higher levels of professionalism."

42   H., A.C. "Toklas' Own Autobiography But Still About the
     Gertrude." Savannah News, 31 March.
     In What Is Remembered "Gertrude Stein is still the dominant character. However, despite the still prevalent personality of Gertrude, Miss Toklas has come off with an account which, to our way of thinking, is anything but an ante-climax. Although years of association and the role of amanuensis necessarily instilled in Alice an identical approach and a similar manner of expression, she achieves a certain flair which goes beyond the affected prose style of her master."

43   HABICH, WILLIAM. "Toklas Memoir." Louisville Courier-Journal,
     7 April.
     In What Is Remembered "there is here a delightful freshness and heady dryness about those times and people due to the unique and slightly giddy manner in which Miss Toklas put it down. . . . It is rich in humor, intelligence and courage."

44   HARDING, WALTER. "Alice B. Toklas Reminisces in Delightful
     Book." Chicago Tribune Magazine of Books, 31 March, p. 1.
     What Is Remembered "is a delightful book. It is copiously illustrated and it presents a witty insight into the Parisian renaissance of American literature. And what is more, it gives us a memorable portrait of two utterly charming individuals-- Alice B. Toklas and Gertrude Stein."

45   HARTLEY, LODWICK. "Sunlight in the Stein's Shadow." Raleigh
     News and Observer, 17 March.
     "In point of fact or in the image itself, [What Is Remembered] adds little or nothing to what we have long had. But it is full of the naive, spicy charm of its author; it provides delicious little surprises in understated anecdotes; and it sometimes achieves vivid and touching accuracy of emotional annotation."

46   HOBBY, DIANA. "The Americans of the Rue de Fleurus."
     Houston Post, 10 March.

"Miss Toklas absorbed Miss Stein's style and writes a con-
densed, gnomic version of it. [In What Is Remembered] she ex-
presses herself without sentimentality or rambling, often with
a biting phrase, sometimes leaving it up to her reader to deci-
pher her reaction to people. . . . Now when there is a Stein
revival underway, Miss Toklas must have great satisfaction in
knowing how well she understood her grand and experimental
companion."

47   HOFFMAN, MICHAEL J. "The Development of Abstractionism in
     the Writing of Gertrude Stein to 1913." Ph.D. dissertation,
     University of Pennsylvania, 285 pp.
          From the early writings of Stein to Tender Buttons Stein's
     work develops increasing abstractionism, along with the use of
     repetition and linguistic patterns that reflect that abstraction-
     ism. Summarized: Dissertation Abstracts International 25:475-76.
     Published: 1965.11.

48   HOLZHAUER, JEAN. "Thinking Back." Commonweal 78 (10 May):
     206-7.
          In What Is Remembered Toklas "has no need to create a pub-
     lic monument to her friend and writes instead from the usual grab-
     bag of lifetime recollections, on the principle that these records
     are important to her. Like Miss Stein, Miss Toklas depends more
     on the effects of an original personality--on style and tone--
     than of content."

49   HOWIE, EDITH. "Story of a Treasured Friendship." Sioux City
     Journal, 16 June.
          What Is Remembered is "a book without detail, somewhat
     reminiscent of travelogues given by European visitors who visit
     ten countries in ten days. If the era of Gertrude Stein inter-
     ests you, by all means read this book. If it doesn't skip it.
     You will not have missed much."

50   "IT DOESN'T ILLUMINATE." Asheville Citizen, 24 March.
          What Is Remembered "resembles a diary, concerned mainly
     with the nervous pilgrimages which Miss Stein made from one
     place to another. It is filled with name-dropping, with anec-
     dotes that sometimes seem pointless, and the minutiae of daily
     life and tourism. There are no revelations of character, no
     significant observations of artistic purpose or literary inspira-
     tion. The book's value lies on the fringes of the footnotes."

51   JONES, FRANK N. "The Real Toklas Memoirs." Baltimore Sun,
     31 March.
          In What Is Remembered "for the first time are numerous
     minor observations from the quiet little lady who sat for 40
     years at the center of a dazzling, and sometimes daffy salon
     frequented by the great names of two generations."

52   KATZ, LEON. "The First Making of The Making of Americans:
      A Study Based on Gertrude Stein's Notebooks and Early Versions
      of Her Novel (1902-1908)." Ph.D. dissertation, Columbia Uni-
      versity, 325 pp.
         Influences on The Making of Americans were personal experi-
      ences that Stein examined psychologically; relationships with
      painters in France; dissatisfaction with earlier, objective
      writing; and interest in "elaborate character typology." Sum-
      marized: Dissertation Abstracts International 27:4255.

53   KIRSCH, ROBERT R. "Alice Toklas' Memoirs Lucid." Los Angeles
      Times, 19 March.
         With What Is Remembered, "the same stress is laid on the
      trivial as on the important. It is written with an uncompromis-
      ing lucidity and compression as though the assertion of her in-
      dividuality is to be found in her ability to dry the materials
      like herbs hanging bunched from a kitchen ceiling. Add water
      and they will expand."

54   LABAN, KATRINE C. "Book Reviews." Woburn (Mass.) Times,
      10 May.
         What Is Remembered does not compete with The Autobiography
      of Alice B. Toklas but "is more a terse condensation of it. Is
      this deliberate or did Stein so completely reveal the real Alice
      that she cannot emerge as a different person in her own book?"

55   LAWRENCE, JOSEPHINE. "Bookmarks." Newark (N.J.) News,
      21 April.
         The simplicity in What Is Remembered is "an effective screen
      that may lull a reader briefly into an acceptance of Miss Toklas
      as a quiet observer on the sidelines of literary life. It's a
      nice role with special advantages for the clever woman who watched
      and listened intelligently and is more than competent to report.
      Trivia is invested with charm and the great and near-great come
      alive as human beings."

56   LeSAGE, LAURENT. "Alice Speaks for Herself." Saturday
      Review 46 (13 April):27.
         In What Is Remembered the pictures are fine and the Stein
      stories are good, but "at least for once and in spite of herself,
      it is the admirable Alice B. Toklas who takes the stage."

57   LEWIS, R.C. Review of What Is Remembered. Book-of-the-Month-
      Club News (April), p. 9.
         "What is remembered by Alice B. Toklas is not so much a
      life story . . . as a series of wonderful scenes. . . . What Is
      Remembered is a wholly endearing memoir."

58   "LITERARY FRIENDS: ALICE TOKLAS TELLS OF LIFE IN PARIS."
      Miami Herald, 24 March.

"Miss Toklas, partner in the most famous literary friendship of our day, [in What Is Remembered] writes like a great
child. She is not immature or undeveloped but the account of
her life with Gertrude Stein has the clarity and precision of
direct vision. The book is a vivid picture of food, flowers,
famous people and Gertrude Stein. . . . It is a most unusual
book. The style alone makes it enjoyable reading, even if you
are too young to have remembered this strange friendship."

59   LITERARY HISTORY OF THE UNITED STATES. Edited by Robert E.
      Spiller, et al. 3d ed. New York: Macmillan Co., pp. 1297,
      1300, 1396.
          Maxwell Geismar finds in Stein's writing that in Paris in-
fluenced so many artists and writers some "curious echoes of
Midwestern talk."

60   MAN RAY. Self Portrait. Boston: Little, Brown & Co.,
      pp. 179-83.
          Man Ray's photographs of Stein first made the world aware
of how the enigmatic woman looked; later he took publicity photographs for her.

61   M'CAFFERY, LAURA. "Alice Toklas Remembers Gertrude Stein's
      World." Fort Wayne News-Sentinel, 23 March.
          What Is Remembered is "a charming recollection done in a
strikingly clear style. It is brief and to the point with none
of the embellishments or explanations which many writers are
prone to give after time has elapsed and memories are recalled.
The photographs are excellent and the index would be an asset
for the knowing reader."

62   MAY, CARL. "Gertrude Spotlight In Toklas Memoir." Nashville
      Tennessean, 31 March.
          "The material [in What Is Remembered] is presented with an
economy of language which is a bit overdone. The reader will
frequently wish for longer descriptions which simply aren't
there. And despite the terseness of style, there is a good deal
of trivial material included which adds nothing to the flow of
the writing."

63   MELLERS, WILFRID. "Autobiographies." New Statesman 66
      (29 November):792-93.
          ". . . the slightly creepy feeling I get from reading What
Is Remembered alongside The Autobiography of Alice B. Toklas
comes from the fact that the books are remarkably alike, yet
distinct. They recount the same incidents, tell the same stories. Oddly enough, however, the version of Miss Toklas, to
whom the events happened, seems neutral, numb, even denatured
compared with Gertrude Stein's vitality and gaiety."

64   MORRIS, MARY B. "A Woman of Great Insight." Roanoke (Va.)
     Times, 19 May.
          Toklas's "pungent comments on the celebrities who contin-
     ually surrounded her show a keen sense of human values and often
     a complete lack of deference. She might be called a 'namedropper,'
     were it not for the fact that she drops unimportant names as
     freely as those well known and never stops to make distinctions
     between the two. She is never impressed by the fact that her
     circle of friends included people of great importance in the
     world of art, letters, wealth and social position. This is the
     natural consequence of living with the incomparable Gertrude and
     she takes it all in her stride."

65   "NEW BOOKS BRIEFLY NOTED." Berkeley Gazette, 23 March.
          "Assuming . . . that you are aware of Miss Stein's role as
     a catalyst of her times, you can obtain further reflections of
     that role in these memoirs [What Is Remembered] of her companion,
     secretary, typist, handy woman and foil. Miss Toklas held a
     unique position in Miss Stein's life."

66   OLIPHANT, DAVE. "Nothing Elegant." Riata, Winter, pp. 51-57.
          Stein "was a poet with a vision, and to enter into her
     vision requires of the reader that he look out from inside her
     creative personality, forsaking meaning in favor of endless gyra-
     tions sometimes grinding out little more than monotonous noise
     or, at other times, music as majestic as Bach's best."

67   PICK, JOHN. "Gertrude Stein Presided, Alice Toklas Listened."
     Milwaukee Journal, 14 April.
          What Is Remembered "is a record of friendships--and some
     quarrelships--a pageant of those who came to their home. . . .
     The portraits are usually incisive, with either a bit of sugar
     or a touch of acid on the pen. . . . There is much mere chit-
     chat, and the chief regret as one closes the book is that Alice
     Toklas did not devote more time and space to the major figures,
     developing their portraits more fully."

68   POWELL, DAWN. "Miss Toklas Without Miss Stein." New York
     Post, 7 April.
          In What Is Remembered "sometimes the Stein-Toklas merger
     seems like a pact between two little girls to stay little girls
     forever, never to engage. Sometimes, in their in[de]fatigible
     collection of celebrities and kicks, the two seem alarmingly
     like any other pair of rich American spinsters on a perpetual
     tour around and above the world. In any case, here is a fasci-
     nating $4 conundrum in a beautiful little book."

69   POWERS, DENNIS. "Alice B. Toklas Recalls Her Life With
     Gertrude Stein." Oakland Tribune, 31 March.
          What Is Remembered "is filled with delightful anecdotes
     and reminiscences, but it is not the book for which I had hoped

179

and waited. As a memoirist, Miss Toklas has the privilege of selection, of course. But with it goes a responsibility, and here she fails me. The book--whose style is heavily influenced by Stein--simply excludes too much."

70　PRIWER, JANE. "All the Empty Years Since." St. Louis Post-Dispatch, 12 May.
　　　"Miss Toklas's dry, ladylike, reticent memoirs cover much of the same ground as her supposed autobiography. The same people appear, frequenters of the Stein salon in Paris. . . . Miss Toklas's style is abbreviated and understated. Unless you have done homework it is not easy to keep all these people, however famous, separate one from another. An inattentive reader could even get Picasso's mistresses confused with Gertrude Stein's poodles!"

71　PRYCE-JONES, ALAN. "Miss Toklas, This Time on Her Own." New York Herald-Tribune Books, 21 April, p. 6.
　　　What Is Remembered is mostly a thin record: "a sorbet rather than an ice. It is also extremely inaccurate. On one illustration alone four out of eight people are mis-named, and the text has not been checked for slips."

72　REVIEW OF WHAT IS REMEMBERED. Charleston News & Courier, 16 June.
　　　"If Alice B. Toklas were not such a notable name herself, I'd say its possessor is the champion name-dropper, for this short book omits few who figured prominently in the arts during the '20s and '30s. . . . Miss Toklas's candid comments and personal observations recreate these rich days with a flair and conciseness that makes the reader reach the last page with disappointment."

73　REVIEW OF WHAT IS REMEMBERED. Charlotte Observer, 24 March.
　　　"It is ludicrous that any one could have daily intimate contact with Ernest Hemingway, James Joyce, Kay Boyle, Jo Davidson and write about it like a school teacher describing a school dance, but Miss Toklas does."

74　REVIEW OF WHAT IS REMEMBERED. Critic 21 (April):81.
　　　Toklas tells too many details of her life with Stein, and too little of Stein's personality.

75　REVIEW OF WHAT IS REMEMBERED. Economist 209 (30 November): 924.
　　　Toklas is generous to her associates but always "no less partisan than her idol."

76　REVIEW OF WHAT IS REMEMBERED. Virginia Quarterly Review 39 (Autumn):cxxxvi.

Stein wrote <u>The Autobiography of Alice B. Toklas</u>; the present volume is "Miss Toklas' own. She is not, alas, the literary equal of her friend, but she adds many snippets and bits of information about the famous salon which might not have been recorded otherwise."

77   S., A.V. "Gertrude Stein's Alter Ego Recalls Trivial Conversation Of The Great." <u>New Haven Register</u>, 16 March.

With <u>What Is Remembered</u>, "although these tidbits of the raconteur may entertain they never shed the slightest light on anything of importance: How did Stein write? And why? Why were she and the author expatriates? And what were the ties that made them inseparable? We must go elsewhere for these answers."

78   "A SALUTE TO GERTRUDE STEIN." <u>Time</u> 81 (22 March):97-98.

"Now, 17 years after Author Stein's death, Alice B. Toklas has at last written her own autobiography with her own hand. Predictably but a little pathetically, [<u>What Is Remembered</u>] reads like Gertrude Stein."

79   STEIN, L.S. "Welcome Footnote To a Definitive Study." <u>Fayetteville</u> (Ark.) <u>Observer</u>, 31 March.

"Alice B. Toklas's prose [in <u>What Is Remembered</u>] bears the strong imprint of Gertrude Stein's personality and style in this book of reminiscences about her life with that literary lady of innovations. Though Miss Toklas's literary style is in punctuation and narrative flow more orthodox, there is about them both a delight in story-telling which results in a compelling 'headlong' quality to their prose."

80   STALEY, THOMAS. "Miss Toklas In Paris, 1907." <u>Tulsa World</u>, 21 April.

<u>What Is Remembered</u> "gives us an excellent picture of the famous writers and painters who peopled the world of Gertrude Stein and Miss Toklas. The book conveys a mood of nostalgia for a more vibrant time; the air is filled with poetry and color."

81   STUART, REECE. "Miss Toklas Was a Lonely But Not Pathetic Figure." <u>Des Moines Register</u>, 7 April.

In <u>What Is Remembered</u>, "there is an arid lack of critical comment on most of [the famous], a prevalence of trivia and a seemingly intentional reduction of literary style to the copybook manner adequate for enumeration of unimportant incident. And one will read on in vain expecting to find somewhere in her memories a reference of real warmth about the companion, an expression of even 'cordial' affection."

82   TAUBMAN, HOWARD. "Theater: Stein Revival." <u>New York Times</u>, 6 March, p. 7.

Yes Is For a Very Young Man does not work out in the theater, although Gertrude Stein certainly had "special intelligence,
sensibility, and an original gift for language."

83   TAYLOR, KATHERINE. "Everywhere That Gertrude Went, Alice Was
      Sure To Go." Greensboro Daily News, 21 April.
      In What Is Remembered, "it is little wonder that [Toklas]
remembers so well people and events that possessed in her eyes
an aura of the extraordinary. Now in her eighties, she writes
of those happy days with grace, clarity and disciplined economy
of words, flavoring the whole with wit as dry as her cooking
sherry."

84   THOMPSON, FRANCIS J. "A Satellite Is a Satellite Is a
      Satellite." Tampa Tribune, 31 March.
      In What Is Remembered, Toklas does not write very admir-
ingly of the great people of the modern age whom she was privi-
leged to know.

85   TINKLE, LON. "Memoirs by Great Or Near-to-Great." Dallas
      Morning News, 31 March.
      In What Is Remembered, "Miss Toklas is brief and laconic
and really unrevelatory. After all, she is now a very old woman
and perhaps memory flags. Her writing has the flavor of a decidedly unique personality, but the book has no style, no disci-
pline, little form."

86   VINES, CARL A., Jr. "Here's catalogue of a life." Augusta
      (Ga.) Chronicle, 14 April.
      "What Is Remembered is a catalogue of events in the life of
one Alice B. Toklas. It comes complete with index and related
photographs . . . [and] it is very dull."

87   WAGNER, MARY. "A Toklas Memoir." Redwood City (Calif.)
      Tribune, 23 March.
      "What Is Remembered is a gentle and perceptive account of
one of the most famous literary friendships of our century . . .
[and] an extraordinary book about a unique era in literary history, an era when individuality was a rewarding quality."

88   WILKINS, MARGARET. "Alice B. Toklas Speaks for Self."
      Norfolk Pilot, 14 April.
      Toklas portrays Stein in What Is Remembered more "gently
than others have" and "adds greatly, in sharp, poignant sketches,
to the picture of an almost legendary group in an almost make-
believe time and place."

89   WILLEFORD, CHARLES. "Remember 'What Is' Is Gossip." Miami
      News, 10 March.
      In What Is Remembered, Toklas "has condensed the essence
of a pertinent period of American letters--wittily, good-naturedly,

and with economy. . . . The prose style is a delight, and some
of Miss Toklas's opinions are equally delightful."

90   WINDHAM, DONALD. Emblems of Conduct. New York: Charles
      Scribner's Sons, pp. 175-76.
         As a youth Windham enjoyed Three Lives, Lectures in America,
and The Autobiography of Alice B. Toklas: "Gertrude Stein was
explaining things to herself; she continually made a joke of her
attempting to offer explanations to others, and her four-square
sentences possessed the density and solidity of objects."

91   WRIGHT, GEORGE T. "Gertrude Stein and Her Ethics of Self-
      Containment." Tennessee Studies in Literature 8 (1963):17-23.
         Stein believed that genius must go counter to public living
and must find "the poise, the balance, that comes with
self-containment."

92   ZASLOVE, BARRY L. "Alice B. Toklas Writes of Stein and Paris
      Life." Baton Rouge Advocate, 24 March.
         What Is Remembered is the story of a friendship believable,
interesting, and satisfactory.

                            1964

1   ARMOUR, RICHARD. American Lit Relit. New York: McGraw-Hill,
      pp. 135-37.
         Stein had two styles of writing--"difficult" and "more
difficult."

2   FIEDLER, LESLIE A. Waiting for the End. New York: Stein &
      Day, pp. 13, 21.
         ". . . the example of [Stein's] war on syntax and coherence
made [Hemingway] a more insidious subverter of common speech than
the readers of Life magazine could ever permit themselves to rec-
ognize even if they were capable of doing so."

3   GILOT, FRANÇOISE, and LAKE, CARLTON. Life With Picasso.
      New York: McGraw-Hill, pp. 68-71, 148.
         Françoise Gilot, impressed with The Autobiography of
Alice B. Toklas, asked Picasso to let her meet Stein. To Stein's
questions Gilot felt herself worse treated than in school. Toklas
unnerved Gilot, who might have offended the woman. Picasso and
Stein quarreled over Stein's alleged ability to continue discov-
ering good artists.

4   HEMINGWAY, ERNEST. A Moveable Feast. New York: Charles
      Scribner's Sons, pp. 9-38.
         Ernest and Hadley Hemingway were welcome in Stein's studio
in Paris, where Stein tried to teach Hemingway to write simply
and directly. But Stein was domineering and prudish about

heterosexual love. She used her garage mechanic's phrase to name
the "lost generation," and yet she was herself dominated by Alice
Toklas.

5   HOFFMAN, FREDERICK J. The Mortal No: Death and the Modern
     Imagination. Princeton: Princeton University Press,
     pp. 358-61.
          "Miss Stein is primarily interested in capturing the quality
     of the 'thing seen,' not only by analyzing but by reproducing the
     rhythm of its being seen." She "had no real subject, but only a
     method. . . ."

6   HUEBSCH, B.W. "From a Publisher's Commonplace Book." Amer-
     ican Scholar 33 (Winter):116, 118.
          Huebsch received his largest manuscript ever in The Making
     of Americans--2428 typed pages--in 1911, and he could not bring
     out the work.

7   JOOST, NICHOLAS. Scofield Thayer and the Dial--An Illustrated
     History. Carbondale: Southern Illinois University Press,
     pp. 167-68, 218.
          Thayer and Pound visited Stein, Pound fell out of a chair,
     and both men were afterward unwelcome at the studio. Stein re-
     sented Thayer's not publishing any of her work in his periodical.

8   McMILLAN, SAMUEL HUBERT, Jr. "Gertrude Stein, the Cubists,
     and the Futurists." Ph.D. dissertation, University of Texas,
     178 pp.
          "The dissertation attempts to show two major parallels
     between Gertrude Stein's work and the painting of the Cubists
     and the Futurists. First, I examine the similarities of their
     work considered as primitive and primitivistic. Second, I show
     that their respective treatments of point of view and perspective
     are analogous." Summarized: Dissertation Abstracts International
     25:2985.

9   MORRELL, Lady OTTOLINE. Memoirs of Lady Ottoline Morrell:
     A Study in Friendship. Edited by Robert Gathorne-Hardy.
     New York: Alfred A. Knopf, p. 166.
          At the Steins' salon, viewing the pictures, Lady Ottoline
     had "one of those interminable evenings where we continually
     wandered round the room, and no one dared to talk, silenced
     perhaps by the clamour that seemed to shout from the walls."

*10 TAKUWA, SHINJI. "The Method of Stein's Three Lives." Eigo
     Eibungaku Ronso 14 (January):127-28.
          Cited: Liston, Maureen R. Gertrude Stein: An Annotated
     Critical Bibliography, p. 102.

11   VAN VECHTEN, CARL. "More Laurels for Our Gertrude." In
     Gotham Book Mart Catalogue: Gertrude Stein. New York:
     Gotham Book Mart, pp. 1-2.

Stein "was always a great writer, a great thinker, a great
conversationalist, and a great woman"; and the Gotham Book Mart
has well encouraged collectors of her writings. Reprinted:
1974.48.

1965

*1 ANDERSON, PETER S. "Gertrude's Stein's Tender Buttons: Two
    Rosaries." Poet and Critic 1 (Winter):32-42.
    Cited: Abstracts of English Studies 9:42.

2   BALMAIN, PIERRE. My Years and Seasons. Garden City, N.Y.:
    Doubleday & Co., pp. 88-90, 113-17.
    Balmain knew Stein and Toklas through his shop and through
pleasant visits with them in rural France. At one showing Stein's
dog attacked another client's dog. Stein's only fashion article
was about Balmain.

3   BERTHOFF, WARNER. The Ferment of Realism: American Litera-
    ture 1884-1919. New York: Free Press, pp. 221, 247-53.
    "Beyond question the forms and the language of contemporary
literature are healthier because Gertrude Stein played her honest
and reasonable games with them. If her example also had the
effect, historically, of endorsing a certain imaginative complacency in the younger writers who put themselves to school
with her--Hemingway for one--their failure to grow out of that
complacency is not, strictly, her fault."

4   CAYTON, ROBERT F. Review of Gertrude Stein's America.
    Library Journal 90 (1 November):4783-84.
    Gertrude Stein's America "is a pleasant sample of Miss
Stein's work, but alas it is only a sample."

5   COPELAND, EDITH. Review of What Is Remembered. Books Abroad
    39 (Winter):92.
    With What Is Remembered, the book's "chief value lies in
the revealing descriptions of the many famous guests who visited
the Paris apartment. . . ."

6   CRANE, HART. The Letters of Hart Crane, 1916-1932. Edited
    by Brom Weber. Berkeley: University of California Press,
    pp. 121-22, 167, 294, 311, 321, 336, 341.
    To Crane, Allen Tate surpassed Stein in cubistic poetry.
He confessed dependence for ideas on Stein and Cummings; yet he
believed that Stein was not a sufficient guide for modern authors.
Crane did enjoy meeting Stein in 1929.

7   DUPEE, F.W. "The King of the Cats" and Other Remarks on
    Writers and Writing. New York: Farrar, Straus & Giroux,
    pp. 69-79.

Immensely purposeful and strong, Stein had behind her public façade of "Steinese" very definite ideas for literature. She
transformed the realist-naturalist tradition into "Jamesian"
study of minds at thought.

8   FEIBLEMAN, JAMES K. "Literary New Orleans Between World Wars."
    Southern Review, n.s. 1 (Summer):712-13.
        Feibleman met Stein in New Orleans and talked with her
    about the thickness of air and about Whitehead. Reprinted:
    1969.8.

9   FORD, FORD MADOX. Letters of Ford Madox Ford. Edited by
    Richard M. Ludwig. Princeton: Princeton University Press,
    pp. 152, 162-63, 179-80, 285.
        Ford would reluctantly let another journal publish The
    Making of Americans; in 1937, he claimed to be writing a history
    of world literature "from Confucius to Gertrude."

10 HART, JAMES D. The Oxford Companion to American Literature,
    4th ed. New York: Oxford University Press, pp. 801-2.
        Stein developed a literature of repetition, the continuing
    present, and freer writing than existed before her time.

11 HOFFMAN, MICHAEL J. The Development of Abstractionism in the
    Writings of Gertrude Stein. Philadelphia: University of
    Pennsylvania Press, 229 pp.
        Publication of 1963.47.

12 _____. "Gertrude Stein in the Psychology Laboratory."
    American Quarterly 17 (Spring):127-32.
        "Gertrude Stein's deterministic theories of personality had,
    if not their beginnings, then certainly a great part of their de-
    velopment in William James' laboratory. Her concepts of conscious-
    ness and the deterministic type, the two pillars of her theory of
    personality, were developed long before she began to publish fic-
    tional constructs of her ideas."

13 _____. "Gertrude Stein's 'Portraits.'" Twentieth Century
    Literature 11 (October):115-22.
        ". . . in reading Gertrude Stein's portraits we must try
    to find ways of talking about them that correspond to the ways
    critics discuss abstract paintings. . . . Gertrude Stein at-
    tempted to make word paintings. Whether she succeeded is another
    matter, but her attempt forces us to re-examine some of our
    approaches toward writings in the English language."

14 "IN BRIEF." New York Times Book Review, 31 October, p. 76.
        In Gertrude's Stein's America, she is "loving and funny
    and often wise. Her reason for living away? She wanted to be
    alone 'with my eyes and my english.'"

15   MacSHANE, FRANK. <u>The Life and Work of Ford Madox Ford</u>.
London: Routledge & Kegan Paul, pp. 152, 155, 157, 158, 160,
and passim.
> Stein tried to save the <u>Transatlantic Review</u> from demise,
but it failed in 1924. Ford, as much as Hemingway, admired <u>The
Making of Americans</u> and published parts of it.

16   OLIVIER, FERNANDE. <u>Picasso and His Friends</u>. Translated by
Jane Miller. New York: Appleton-Century, pp. 138-40.
> At the Steins' salon, Picasso's moodiness was ignored by
the host and hostess: "He had a weakness, common to many great
artists, for admiration and even flattery."

17   ROGERS, W.G. <u>Wise Men Fish Here: The Story of Frances Steloff
and the Gotham Book Mart</u>. New York: Harcourt, Brace & World,
pp. 10, 12, 114, 118, 122, and passim.
> Steloff championed such experimenting moderns as Stein and
stocked Stein in abundance but could not sell every copy of the
volumes of the Plain Edition.

18   SITWELL, EDITH. <u>Taken Care Of</u>. New York: Atheneum,
pp. 17, 87-88, 158-60, 162.
> Sitwell recalled Stein's phrases to capture the characters
of acquaintances; Stein was imperious and good-humored: "She is
the last writer in the world whom any other writer should take as
model; but her work, for the most part, is very valuable because
of its revivifying qualities, and it contains, to my mind, considerable beauty."

19   STERNE, MAURICE. <u>Shadow and Light: The Life, Friends and
Opinions of Maurice Stern</u>. Edited by Charlotte Leon Mayerson.
New York: Harcourt, Brace & World, pp. 48-49, 82-83, 121,
166, and passim.
> Leo Stein was instrumental in choosing the paintings that
Gertrude Stein admired and kept; yet Gertrude was "alive, keen,
and active." Sterne wrote to Stein that the repetition in <u>Three
Lives</u> bothered him, and the friendship ended.

20   STRAUMANN, HEINRICH. <u>American Literature in the Twentieth
Century</u>. 3d ed. New York: Harper & Row, pp. 72, 101, 130,
134-36.
> Stein is among the few authors whose intent is no more
than to use as subject-matter the intellect at work. Few bother
with her content; the style is all. Her influence on the "lost
generation" authors is immense, for she found "the secret of
subtlety through utmost simplicity in the smaller units of
speech."

21   TANNER, TONY. <u>The Reign of Wonder: Naivety and Reality in
American Literature</u>. Cambridge: Cambridge University Press,
pp. 14, 30, 151, 187-204, 241, 256.

The development of the use of vernacular in American literature leads from Twain to Hemingway via Stein. Stein was "the
indispensable provoking theorist" who taught Hemingway, who then
outdistanced the master. Today Stein's historical value over-
shadows her intrinsic interest.

22   THOMSON, VIRGIL. "About 'Four Saints.'" <u>American Record</u>
<u>Guide</u> 31 (February):520–21.
     "Putting to music poetry so musically conceived as Gertrude
Stein's has long been a keen pleasure to me. The spontaneity of
it, its easy flow, and its deep sincerity have always seemed to
me just right for music. Whether my music is just right for it
is not for me to say. But happiness was ours working together,
and a great friendship grew up between us."

23   VAN VECHTEN, CARL. "On Words and Music." <u>American Record</u>
<u>Guide</u> 31 (February):521–22.
     A new performance of <u>Four Saints in Three Acts</u> recaptures
the charm of the original, and lack of feeling for it will fault
an audience: Miss Stein's "words always sound better than they
look, and they sound especially well when projected through the
sensitive medium of Virgil Thomson's music."

1966

1   BARRY, JOSEPH. <u>The People of Paris</u>. New York: Doubleday &
Co., pp. vi, vii, viii, 48, 122, 125, and passim.
     Barry met Picasso while walking with Stein in Paris; later
he visited with Toklas in Paris. Stein never let her American
accent and her habits interfere with her life in Paris, and in
France she kept more of herself than she could have in America.
Stein's heirs misappropriated the paintings that she left to
Toklas, leaving that woman with only her memories.

2   BOTTORFF, WILLIAM K. Review of <u>The Making of Americans</u>.
<u>Library Journal</u> 91 (1 December):5972.
     <u>The Making of Americans</u> is "one of the most peculiar books
ever published: neither novel nor epic, history nor autobiography. There is little dialogue, no conventional sense of narrative. . . . It is a highly individualized, strangely
existentialistic tome of Old Testament proportion and ponder-
ousness--but not a Genesis, a <u>progressus</u>."

3   BRIDGMAN, RICHARD. <u>The Colloquial Style in America</u>. New
York: Oxford University Press, pp. 165–94, and passim.
     Although Stein is not the acclaimed link between Twain and
Hemingway, "she emphasized the underlying structures of colloquial
speech, even as the Cubists isolated and stylized the geometrical
components of the human figure. To accomplish this she worked
out of a tradition congenial to her, the European aesthetic

tradition, particularly as it was represented in the prose of
Gustave Flaubert and Henry James."

4　COBURN, ALVIN LANGDON. Alvin Langdon Coburn, Photographer:
　　An Autobiography. Edited by Helmut and Alison Gernsheim.
　　New York: Frederick A. Praeger, pp. 90, 92.
　　　　"In Paris we visited Gertrude Stein . . . who I think has
　　something to tell us which the world will come to appreciate,
　　which many in the future will value"--a brilliant knowledge of
　　the use of words.

5　FAÿ, BERNARD. Les Précieux. Paris: Librarie Académique
　　Perrin, pp. 137-69.
　　　　Faÿ, Stein and Toklas were friends from 1924 until Stein's
　　death in 1946. Stein tried to get pardon for Faÿ from the French
　　and U.S. authorities after 1944 for his wartime activities. Stein
　　overall had helped Faÿ to love life.

6　GIMPEL, RENÉ. Diary of an Art Dealer. Translated by John
　　Rosenberg. New York: Farrar, Straus & Giroux, p. 430.
　　　　Marie Laurencin agrees that Stein's descriptions of her
　　artist friends in The Autobiography of Alice B. Toklas are un-
　　faithful. Gimpel himself finds that book "deplorable."

7　HEISSENBÜTTEL, HELMUT. Über Literatur. Olten: Walter-Verlag,
　　pp. 11-22.
　　　　Reprint of 1955.7.

8　HOFFMAN, MICHAEL J. "Gertrude Stein and William James."
　　Personalist 47 (Winter):226-33.
　　　　Reprint in part of 1955.7.

9　KNICKERBOCKER, CONRAD. "TV: On Stein." New York Times,
　　19 March.
　　　　"Yes Is For A Very Young Man, one of Gertrude Stein's last
　　works, was given its television premiere last night. . . . The
　　two-act play affirms Miss Stein's stature as one of the larger
　　bores of her time and proves once again that as a playwright,
　　she always was a better self-publicist."

10　LASK, THOMAS. "Repeat Performance." New York Times Book
　　Review, 6 November, p. 68.
　　　　The World Is Round is "made of words of different shapes,
　　sounds. But it seems overlong for its material, and far too
　　abstract. It is not anchored to anything. . . ."

11　LOOS, ANITA. A Girl Like I. New York: Viking Press,
　　pp. 227-30.
　　　　Like all knowledgeable Americans seeing Paris, Loos enjoyed
　　meeting Stein and Toklas. Loos could not like Stein's writings,
　　but her friend Sherwood Anderson did.

12   REVIEW OF <u>GERTRUDE STEIN'S AMERICA</u>. <u>Choice</u> 3 (March):35.
     "A most readable and charming addition to any library, for
its Americana, modern literature, Stein or browsing sections,
this book will help undo some of the literary folklore about
[Stein's] unreadability."

13   RUSS, LAVINIA. Review of <u>The World Is Round</u>. <u>Publishers'</u>
     <u>Weekly</u> 190 (5 September):67.
     With <u>The World Is Round</u>, the work "<u>must</u> be read aloud.
Any reader, young or old, who doesn't hear the cadence of the
words, may be lost before the second page. When it is read out
loud, he will be captured by Gertrude Stein's magic with words
as surely as if that magnificent magician were there to chant
them herself."

14   SHAW, BARNETT. "Encounter with Gertrude Stein, Paris, 1944."
     <u>Texas Quarterly</u> 9 (Autumn):21-23.
     Shaw met and talked with Stein in 1944, in Paris, soon
after the Germans left and before the media rediscovered Stein.

15   STEVENS, WALLACE. <u>Letters of Wallace Stevens</u>. Edited by
     Holly Stevens. New York: Alfred A. Knopf, pp. 267, 290.
     Stevens saw <u>Four Saints in Three Acts</u> in 1934 and wrote
that "if one excludes aesthetic self-consciousness from one's
attitude, the opera immediately becomes a delicate and joyous
work all around."

16   SUTHERLAND, DONALD. "Old Woman River: A Correspondence with
     Katherine Anne Porter." <u>Sewanee Review</u> 74 (Summer):754-67.
     Sutherland tries to explain why Porter so maliciously
attacked Stein in her essays. Perhaps Stein had started the
dislike by not liking Porter's works. Reprinted: 1970.34.

17   SWEET, FREDERICK A. <u>Miss Mary Cassatt: Impressionist from</u>
     <u>Pennsylvania</u>. Norman: University of Oklahoma Press, p. 196.
     Cassatt met Stein in 1908 and immediately loathed the modern
art so loved by Gertrude and Leo Stein.

18   THOMSON, VIRGIL. "A Portrait of Gertrude Stein." <u>New York</u>
     <u>Review of Books</u>, 7 July, pp. 13-16.
     Stein's writing "seemed to come from nowhere and to influ-
ence, at that time, none but reporters and novelists. She herself, considering the painter Cézanne her chief master, believed
that under his silent tutelege a major message had jumped like
an electric arc from painting to poetry. And she also suspected
that its high tension was in process of short-circuiting again,
from her through me, this time to music."

19   _____. <u>Virgil Thomson</u>. New York: Alfred A. Knopf, pp. 46,
     50, 58, 64, 70, and passim.

Stein's "last operas and plays are in the humane tradition of letters, while her monumental abstractions of the late 1920s and early 1930s are so intensely aware of both structure and emotion that they may well be the origin of a kind of painting that came later to be known as 'abstract expressionism.'" Few artists illustrate as well as Stein the quality of "continuous growth."

*20   WYATT, SOPHIA. "Gertrude and the Real Bobolink." <u>Guardian</u> (Manchester), 9 June, p. 8.
    Cited: Liston, Maureen R. <u>Gertrude Stein: An Annotated Critical Bibliography</u>, p. 203.

<u>1967</u>

1   "ALICE AND GERTRUDE." <u>Chicago Tribune</u>, 9 March, p. 20.
    "No one will be seeing either Miss Toklas or Miss Stein any more, but they will be remembered as two vividly alive people who played supporting roles in the life stories of many of the principal authors and artists of their time."

2   "ALICE B. TOKLAS." <u>New York Times</u>, 11 March, p. 28.
    "Like Mrs. Thrale in Johnson's time or Frieda Lawrence in ours, Alice Toklas shone by a light greater figures cast upon her. But like them she was no dead planet."

3   "ALICE TOKLAS, 89, IS DEAD IN PARIS." <u>New York Times</u>,
    8 March, p. 45.
    After living on gifts from friends, Alice B. Toklas has died in Paris. Now Gertrude Stein's art--by Picasso, Gris, and Matisse--will come to U.S. relatives.

4   ALLEN, GAY WILSON. <u>William James: A Biography</u>. New York:
    Viking Press, pp. 305, 373-75, 413, 537, 540.
    James was fortunate to teach Gertrude Stein while she attended Radcliffe and encouraged her to become a philosopher-- or a psychologist. Only <u>Three Lives</u> shows indebtedness to James, "but Gertrude Stein was one of the most sympathetic and grateful students he ever had. . . ."

5   BARNES, CLIVE. "Theater: Gertrude Stein Words at the Judson Church." <u>New York Times</u>, 14 October, p. 12.
    <u>In Circles</u>, a play by Gertrude Stein, opened last night and Barnes "loved it. There was no story, only words dropped in the air like cylinders of tear gas. . . . And, oh yes, it was hilariously funny."

6   BARRY, JOSEPH. "Alice B. Toklas." <u>Village Voice</u>, 16 March,
    p. 8.
    "The little coffin--so like the sad little coffin of children--was lowered next to the older, larger coffin of

Gertrude Stein: Like Abelard and Eloise, who are also buried in
the Père Lachaise cemetery. Gertrude Stein and Alice Toklas are
once again together in the earth of Paris as they were in life."

7   BARRY, NAOMI. "A Memory of Alice B. Toklas." Gourmet 27
     (August):13, 28, 30.
          The world will miss the influence and personality of
     Alice B. Toklas--superb cook when Barry knew her from 1947.

8   deMORINNI, CLARA MORE. "Miss Stein and the Ladies." New
     Republic 157 (11 November):17-19.
          When unexpectedly called on in 1933 to substitute for
     Bernard Faÿ at a Paris luncheon, Stein discussed modern art and
     skillfully handled detractors in her audience.

9   FLANNER, JANET. "Letter from Paris." New Yorker 43
     (25 March):174, 177.
          Toklas is now dead and the artworks owned by Stein are in
     a Paris bank. Only Picasso of the old friends is yet alive.

10   HABERMAN, DONALD. The Plays of Thornton Wilder: A Critical
     Study. Middletown, Conn.: Wesleyan University Press, pp. 7,
     29, 34, 37-38, 41, and passim.
          Wilder's "awakening from the nineteenth century and its
     definition of beauty (Melody) resulted from what Gertrude Stein
     taught him about being an American, in time, in space, and in
     religion."

11   HAHN, EMILY. Romantic Rebels: An Informal History of Bohemi-
     anism in America. Boston: Houghton, Mifflin Co., pp. 147,
     160-66.
          Mabel Dodge's article in Arts and Decoration helped intro-
     duce Stein to America. Later Stein needed her independence from
     early helpers.

12   HARRISON, GILBERT A. "Alice B. Toklas." New Republic 156
     (18 March):24, 37-38.
          Alice B. Toklas has died: "A live Toklas could not cut
     off the past any more than she could a present which reached into
     the everlasting. She would be with Gertrude Stein again. It had
     always been the love 'whose service is perfect freedom.'"

13   HOFFMAN, FREDERICK J. "Gertrude Stein." In Encyclopedia of
     World Literature, III. Edited by Wolfgang Bernard Fleischmann.
     New York: Frederick Ungar Publishing Co., pp. 346-48.
          Stein's "principal role is that of tutor and example, not
     writer. While many of her publications have merit of their own,
     her chief distinction lies in the ways in which she defined new
     attitudes and perspectives in 20th-century literature and art."

14   IZARD, ANNE. Review of The World Is Round. Library Journal
     92 (15 January):330.
          In The World Is Round, "Gertrude Stein's magic makes direct
     communication between a child mind and an adult mind possible.
     Her stream-of-consciousness writing is pure poetry."

15   KOCH, STEPHEN. "Aging Beautifully." Nation 204 (13 March):
     343-45.
          The Making of Americans is "Stein's awareness of others
     rendered as language. This language is designed to have all
     the attributes of consciousness itself. Consciousness is always
     of something and yet it is always something in itself. Stein
     refuses to complicate this dualism. . . ."

16   KOSTELANETZ, RICHARD. Review of The Making of Americans.
     Commonweal 85 (13 January):404-5.
          Erroneous and yet impressive critically, The Making of
     Americans is historically a break with nineteenth-century fic-
     tional conventions beyond almost any others taken at the time
     by any other American.

17   MALONE, KEMP. "Observations on Paris France." Papers on
     Language and Literature 3 (Spring):159-78.
          The style in Paris France seems simple and uncontrived,
     but it is actually complex and crafted: "The whole gives us a
     patchwork of reminiscences, folklore, insight, paradox, and non-
     sense or spoof (one hardly knows which), done in an idiosyncratic
     style commonly though inexactly described as colloquial."

18   "MISS ALICE B. TOKLAS." Times (London), 8 March, p. 14.
          Toklas died in Paris, age 89: "On the typewriter her fin-
     gers became adapted to Gertrude's work. She remained in France
     for most of her life."

19   "MISS ALICE B. TOKLAS." Times (London), 20 March, p. 14.
          The Times obituary should have mentioned Toklas's Cookbook,
     for the Toklas "whose portrait emerges from the unlikely pages
     of a cookery book will be remembered with affection for many a
     year."

20   "NOT MERELY THE MAMA OF DADA." Times (London), 25 November,
     p. 23.
          Writing and Lectures, 1911-1945 (also called Look at Me Now
     and Here I Am) shows that Stein "was from the beginning interested
     in the movement of the mind, the sounds it makes in moving, and
     the time it takes to get from one sound to another. So are mad-
     men interested, who spend their consciousness in repetition and
     dislocation of past experience, and it has to be admitted that
     Stein's attempts to create, from the inside out, a continuous
     present . . . are apt to remind the average reader of his imag-
     inings of the babblings of a lunatic."

21   "OBITUARY NOTES." <u>Publishers' Weekly</u> 191 (20 March):42.
      "Alice B. Toklas, friend and companion of Gertrude Stein,
gourmet cook, and co-proprietress, with Miss Stein, of one of the
literary world's most renowned <u>salons</u>, died in Paris. . . ."

22   OLIVER, EDITH. "Perfect Circles." <u>New Yorker</u> 43
     (18 November):131-33.
      In <u>In Circles</u>, "the spirit is the spirit of Gertrude Stein.
So much that is done Off Broadway nowadays is such portentous
coterie rubbish that even looking for meaning or coherence is
more trouble than it is worth. Miss Stein's quirky lines glitter
with meaning--for everybody. They are, of course, terribly funny,
and the comedy is rooted in wisdom and poetry and pureheartedness.
Non sequitur they may be but never nonsense."

23   "POOTER." <u>Times</u> (London), 25 November, p. 19.
      Sir Francis Rose contends that André Malraux is preventing
just settlement of Stein's estate.

24   POUND, EZRA, and JOYCE, JAMES. <u>Pound/Joyce: The Letters of
Ezra Pound to James Joyce, with Pound's Essays on Joyce</u>.
     Edited by Forrest Read. New York: New Directions, pp. 8,
     157, 211, 232, 255, 256.
      Pound complimented Joyce that even Stein did not "demand a
new style per chapter." Joyce parodied Stein's writing for Pound,
who later doubted the worth of both Joyce and Stein.

25   RAYFORD, JULIAN LEE. "A Little Woman Gabbing." <u>American Book
Collector</u> 18 (September):6-7.
      Reading <u>The Making of Americans</u> raises questions about
Stein's alleged worth: "In spite of its title, the book is not
intuitive enough to encompass America. Gertrude Stein suffered
from logorrhea, and she gloried in it!"

26   REGELSON, ROSALYN. "Was She Mother of Us All?" <u>New York
Times</u>, 5 November, sec. 2, pp. 1, 5.
      "Gertrude Stein is often quoted, and her influence lurks
in the prose of most important American writers, including
Hemingway, Thornton Wilder and Sherwood Anderson. But so far
she has had little direct effect on the theater."

27   SALTER, ELIZABETH. <u>The Last Years of a Rebel: A Memoir of
Edith Sitwell</u>. Boston: Houghton Mifflin Co., pp. iv, 33,
     58, 104, 106-7, and passim.
      Stein introduced Edith Sitwell and Tchelitchew, who remained
friends after Stein dropped the painter. Stein liked Sitwell's
masculine mind, and Sitwell liked Stein's prose experimentation.

28   STEVENSON, ELIZABETH. <u>Babbits and Bohemians: The American
1920's</u>. New York: Macmillan Co., pp. 24, 179.

In Three Lives, Stein "made words follow the very movement of thought itself, hesitant, repetitive, yet supple." The Paris salon was "liberating" to Hemingway and other young men.

29   STEWART, ALLEGRA. Gertrude Stein and the Present. Cambridge: Harvard University Press, 223 pp.
      "This book is focused upon the underlying experience of contemplation and creative dissociation which seems to me to have determined not only Gertrude Stein's metaphysical outlook but also her poetic practices and purposes . . . [for] there is a profound underlying harmony between the search for the 'new word' which inspired, for example, Tender Buttons, and the philosophical views which become explicit in The Geographical History of America. It is a harmony between principle and application that cannot have evolved arbitrarily. It argues a deep experience of some sort, and it is my conviction that this was the psychological experience of deep concentration, self-realization, or 'ingatheredness.'"

30   "TOGETHER AGAIN." Time 89 (17 March):34, 38.
      In Paris, "the artists came and went, but the two women remained inseparable. . . . The relationship between the two women lasted for more than 39 years, until Miss Stein succumbed to cancer in 1946. Last week, 20 years after the loss of her devoted friend, death came in Paris to Alice Boyd Toklas, 89."

31   TYLER, PARKER. The Divine Comedy of Pavel Tchelitchew: A Biography. New York: Fleet Publishing, pp. 31, 63, 156, 381, 308-13, and passim.
      In his painting, Tchelitchew depicts Toklas and Stein as collectors of questionable art. Stein did not choose to keep art by Tchelitchew, and Tchelitchew regretted later his closeness to Stein.

32   VAN VECHTEN, CARL. "The Origin of the Sonnets from the Patagonian." Hartwick Review 3 (Spring):50-56.
      Van Vechten's article on Tender Buttons may have been read or proofread by Donald Evans for the New York Times and subsequently inspired Evans to write his sonnets.

*33   WINSTON, ALEXANDER. "The Delphic Pythoness and How She Came to Be." American Society of Legion of Honor Magazine 38 (1967):9-24.
      Cited: MHRA Bibliography 43:538.

1968

1   BROWN, ASHLEY. "Going on Being." Spectator 221 (6 December): 800-801.

195

On The Making of Americans, "Miss Stein's characters cannot
be distinguished from her voice. In trying to portray their essential being she finally merges them into a kind of collective
unconsciousness."

2   BROWN, FREDERICK. An Impersonation of Angels: A Biography of
    Jean Cocteau. New York: Viking Press, pp. 96, 98, 132, 136,
    141.
        Cocteau heard friends reading from Tender Buttons and was
    influenced by it.

3   BRUGGER, BOB. "Sundays with Miss Stein." New York Times
    Magazine, 15 December, p. 36.
        Regarding Stein's salon in Paris where soldiers visited,
    Brugger enjoyed Sunday visits with Toklas and Stein.

4   CONRAD, DODA. "The Sound and the Fury." Esquire 69 (April):
    188.
        A recent description of Toklas's grave is wrong, and Toklas
    actually is buried in the same vault as Stein.

5   EARNEST, ERNEST. Expatriates and Patriots: American Artists,
    Scholars, and Writers in Europe. Durham: Duke University
    Press, pp. vii, 17, 251, 259, 274.
        Expatriates of the 1920s claimed a guide and forerunner in
    Stein--as well as a defense of Paris as the ultimate home.

6   FRIDAY, BILL. I Love You, Alice B. Toklas. New York:
    Bantam Books, 195 pp.
        The fictional Harold Fine becomes psychologically liberated
    after being fed a Toklas brownie.

7   FRIEDRICH, OTTO. "The Grave of Alice B. Toklas." Esquire 69
    (January):98-103, 121-24.
        Friedrich met Toklas in Paris in 1948 and later visited
    her in the convent years. Toklas's grave is unmarked beside
    Stein's, but "probably soon, a headstone will stand here, with
    the name of Alice B. Toklas chiseled into the stone. But I will
    not have to come back here to see it."

8   GLUECK, GRACE. "Gertrude Stein's Art Collection Is Sought
    for Modern Museum." New York Times, 14 October, p. 55.
        "A group of trustees of the Museum of Modern Art is nego-
    tiating with lawyers for heirs of the Gertrude Stein estate for
    purchase of her collection of paintings. . . . The price is said
    to be between $6 million and $6.5 million."

9   HESS, JOHN L. "Sale of Stein Art Planned by Heirs." New York
    Times, 31 January, p. 38.
        Thirty-eight of Stein's paintings will be sold, now that
    the Toklas claim is void.

10   KELLNER, BRUCE. <u>Carl Van Vechten and the Irreverent Decades</u>.
     Norman: University of Oklahoma Press, pp. 64, 69, 72-75,
     79-80, and passim.
        Stein was known by Van Vechten through Mabel Dodge. Inter-
     ested in "the pioneer and outlaw in all the creative arts," he
     devoted himself to getting her work published and her name pub-
     licized--and remained "her friend, one of the few with whom she
     never quarreled."

11   MELLOW, JAMES R. "The Stein Salon Was the First Museum of
     Modern Art." <u>New York Times Magazine</u>, 1 December, pp. 48-51,
     182, 184-85, 187, 190-91.
        Stein "thought about art, she wrote about it often--some-
     times in profound generalizations and sometimes in maddening
     phrases. But in the end, she was quite willing to put the matter
     simply. . . 'I like to look at it.'"

12   MORNER, KATHLEEN. "O, Fudge, Alice, Where's The Pot?"
     <u>Chicago Sun-Times</u>, 17 December, p. 42.
        Toklas "never concocted a brownie recipe. . . . Not even
     for groovy brownies. The closest she came, and of course her
     recipe is much superior, was in her directions for making hashish
     fudge."

13   "PATIENT MONUMENT." <u>Times Literary Supplement</u>, 8 August,
     p. 845.
        With <u>Look At Me Now and Here I Am</u>, "whatever one may think,
     nowadays, of Gertrude Stein as a creative writer or as an influ-
     ence on other people's writing, there is no doubt at all that she
     could be a first-class literary critic when she chose."

14   PERRINE, LAURENCE. "Frost's 'The Rose Family.'" <u>Explicator</u>
     26 (January):Item 43.
        Frost's poem on roses repeats Stein's famous line and adds
     botanical knowledge to poetic knowledge of roses.

15   PRICE, R.G.G. "Various Reputations." <u>Punch</u> 254 (3 January):
     31.
        <u>Writing and Lectures</u> shows that Stein "remains the great
     example of the modernist fallacy that equated novelty with via-
     bility. Gertrude Stein as a character lives warmly in reminis-
     cences of the 'twenties and she deserves to be honoured for the
     speed with which she recognized and the generosity with which she
     encouraged talent. But when she is talking about herself there
     is a hard, insane assertiveness. Like a madwoman, she scrawls
     and expects the world to see the patterns that she can see."

16   REID, B.L. <u>The Man from New York: John Quinn and His Friends</u>.
     New York: Oxford University Press, p. 105.
        Quinn in Paris mused over Jews who collect art but "did not
     yet foresee that he would soon rival them as a collector of the
     new men."

17   ROGERS, W.G. Ladies Bountiful. New York: Harcourt, Brace &
      World, pp. 14, 17-19, 34, 39-41, and passim.
           Stein used the Cone sisters to aid her artist friends; the
      friendship later cooled, and in America Stein was avoided by Etta
      Cone. At various times Stein was associated with Natalie Barney,
      Nancy Cunard, Lady Ottoline Morrell, Mable Dodge, Jane Heap,
      Margaret Anderson, Sylvia Beach, and Bryher.

18   ROSE, Sir FRANCIS. Gertrude Stein and Painting. Preface by
      Alice B. Toklas. London: Book Collecting & Library Monthly,
      32 pp.
           Stein's quiet life concealed her excitement with new art--
      paintings that pleased her personally. Never a formal critic of
      art, Stein relied on taste to form her collections.

19   SCHORER, MARK. The World We Imagine: Selected Essays.
      New York: Farrar, Straus, & Giroux, pp. 299-382.
           Stein became the matrix to unite, at different times and
      for different purposes, Anderson, Fitzgerald, and Hemingway.

*20   SHULTS, DONALD. "Gertrude Stein and the Problems of Time."
      Kyushu American Literature 11 (1968):59-71.
           Cited: PMLA Annual Bibliography for 1969, p. 152.

21   STEPHENS, ROBERT O. Hemingway's Nonfiction: The Public Voice.
      Chapel Hill: University of North Carolina Press, pp. 5, 6,
      12, 13, 14, and passim.
           After publication of The Autobiography of Alice B. Toklas,
      Hemingway used many occasions in non-fiction to criticize and
      satirize Stein.

22   SULLIVAN, DAN. "Another Delightful Look at 'In Circles.'"
      New York Times, 28 June, p. 36.
           "If you haven't seen it, it can be recommended particularly
      to people with a high capacity for theatrical innovation, but a
      waning tolerance for shock. In Circles is adventurous but polite.
      It wants to be liked."

23   SUTHERLAND, DONALD. "The Conversion of Alice B. Toklas."
      Colorado Quarterly 17 (Autumn):129-41.
           Despite conjecture that Toklas converted from Judaism to
      Catholicism just for possible reassurance of seeing Stein in the
      afterlife, Toklas had had a "Catholic girlhood" and needed causes
      to fill her life after Stein's death. Catholicism was such a
      cause.

24   TUFTE, VIRGINIA. "Gertrude Stein's Prothalamium: A Unique
      Poem in a Classical Mode." Yale University Library Gazette
      43 (July):17-23.
           In Prothalamium, privately printed for the marriage of
      Robert B. Haas, Stein avoids the usual clichés of occasional

poetry: "With admirable deftness and compression, she bends conventional motifs to her own idiom and, working within a tradition, greatly expands the dimensions of her deceptively simple tribute."

25   VAN DYKE, HENRY. Blood of Strawberries. New York: Farrar, Straus & Giroux, pp. 5-7, and passim.
     The fictional narrator remembers developing a fascination with Stein's writings in his youth: "What began as an esoteric joke developed into a serious affair."

26   WAGER, WILLIAM. American Literature: A World View. New York: New York University Press, pp. 196-98.
     Stein's "concentration on her own feelings as they were developing within her and her persistent attempts to get them down on paper in their actual shape, tempo, and texture, as well as her generally unsentimental approach to life, helped open the minds of her contemporaries to possible new formulations of experiences and ideas."

27   WEBB, CONSTANCE. Richard Wright: A Biography. New York: G.P. Putnam's Sons, pp. 93, 96, 243, 245-46, and passim.
     Three Lives excited Wright with authentic Negro speech. In Paris in 1946 Stein befriended Wright; earlier she had included him with her as geniuses. Stein understood Negro fear of whites and--better--whites' fear of Negroes.

28   ZOLOTOW, SAM. "'In Circles' Will Resume." New York Times, 21 June, p. 49.
     In Circles, after 222 performances, will reopen in New York City.

                              1969

1   ANDERSON, ELIZABETH, and KELLEY, GERALD R. Miss Elizabeth. Boston: Little, Brown & Co., pp. 158-64, 167, 169-70.
     In Paris Elizabeth Anderson met Toklas and Stein and found both women friendly. When Sherwood Anderson pretended to be ill, Elizabeth went alone to Stein's party for him.

2   ANDERSON, MARGARET. My Thirty Years' War: The Autobiography. New York: Covici, Friede, pp. 44-45, 49, 248-51, 257.
     Stein says things in her personal way and then repeats them, and her writing would be lessened if repetition were omitted.

3   _____. The Strange Necessity: The Autobiography, Resolutions and Reminiscence to 1969. New York: Horizon Press, pp. 38-39.
     Stein and Toklas met Anderson in 1923 and thought her eccentric and scatter-brained. Anderson offended Stein by not publishing her writings and felt uncomfortable near Stein's egotism.

4   BAKER, CARLOS. Ernest Hemingway: A Life Story. New York:
     Charles Scribner's Sons, pp. 82, 86-87, 91, 100, and passim.
        As fond as Hemingway was of Stein and as needful of her
     help in the early 1920s, he came to resent her claims of literary
     godmothering.

5   CRESPELLE, JEAN-PAUL. Picasso and His Women. Translated by
     Robert Baldick. New York: Coward-McCann, pp. 5, 6, 12, 15,
     50, 53, and passim.
        Picasso and friends mocked Stein behind her back, ridicul-
     ing her vanity and assurance. Leo always had superior taste in
     painting; after the split of brother and sister, Gertrude could
     not choose good art. Picasso and Stein argued over Matisse and
     Gris, but both had sufficient groups of other admirers.

6   CUMMINGS, E.E. Selected Letters of e.e. cummings. Edited by
     F.W. Dupee and George Stade. New York: Harcourt, Brace &
     World, pp. xvi, 132, 168, 176, 267.
        Cummings never met Stein but quoted her in a speech at his
     Harvard graduation. In 1960 he remembered seeing her and trying
     to read The Making of Americans; finally he admired her loyalty
     to anti-Nazi French.

7   DIJKSTRA, BRAM. The Hieroglyphics of a New Speech: Cubism,
     Stieglitz, and the Early Poetry of William Carlos Williams.
     Princeton: Princeton University Press, pp. 12, 13-16, 17,
     28, 51, 109, 139, 194.
        Stieglitz's early publishing of Stein showed his daring in
     art. Stein owed much to Cézanne and the impressionist painters,
     and her cubistic prose influenced William Carlos Williams.

8   FEIBLEMAN, JAMES K. The Way of a Man: An Autobiography.
     New York: Horizon Press, pp. 275-76.
        Reprint of 1965.8.

9   FITCH, NOEL RILEY. "An American Bookshop in Paris: The In-
     fluence of Sylvia Beach's Shakespeare and Company on American
     Literature." Ph.D. dissertation, Washington State University,
     201 pp.
        "Although patrons of the shop included artists from many
     countries, particularly France, England, and the United States,
     this study focuses on the American artists, among whom are . . .
     Gertrude Stein. . . ." Summarized: Dissertation Abstracts In-
     ternational 30A:3005-6.

10   GLASSCO, JOHN. "Memoirs of Montparnasse: At Gertrude
     Stein's." Tamarack Review, no. 50-51 (Second quarter),
     pp. 5-9.
        When Glassco met Stein in Paris, he "had a peculiar sense
     of mingled attraction and repulsion towards her. She awakened
     in me a feeling of instinctive hostility coupled with a grudging
     veneration, as if she were a pagan idol in whom I was unable to
     believe."

11   GLUECK, GRACE. "Modern Museum Gets Stein's Art." <u>New York</u>
      <u>Times</u>, 10 January, p. 39.
          Friends of the Museum of Modern Art have bought for the
      Museum thirty-eight Picassos and nine Grises for between six and
      six and one-half million dollars.

12   HALPERT, STEPHEN, and JOHNS, RICHARD, eds. <u>A Return to Pagany:</u>
      <u>The History, Correspondence, and Selections from a Little Mag-</u>
      <u>azine, 1929-1932</u>. Boston: Beacon Press, pp. 17, 18, 20, 43,
      128, 145, 153, 215, 337.
          Considering Stein an American, not an expatriate, <u>Pagany</u>
      sought contributions from and about her, although her imperious
      nature could dictate publication more strongly than could merit.

13   HUMM. "Gertrude Stein's <u>First Reader</u>." <u>Variety</u>, 24 December.
          "<u>Gertrude Stein's First Reader</u> has been brushed off by sev-
      eral reviewers and looks doomed, but the revue . . . is a bright
      and entertaining show, worthy of a better fate. . . . The show's
      ruthless whimsey becomes a bit cloying toward the end of the sec-
      ond act, and more variation would be welcome, but it's light-
      hearted and likable. . . ."

14   JEBB, JULIAN. "Repeating." <u>New Statesman</u> 77 (24 January):124.
          In <u>The Making of Americans</u>, "Gertrude Stein doesn't seem to
      give a damn that nothing is happening and when absolutely nothing
      is happening for nine hundred and twenty five pages you are not
      having any feeling, any loving, and knowing, any being except
      this very strong feeling of being bored and sometimes angry and
      sometimes mad. And perhaps that is what Gertrude Stein wanted.
      But I doubt it."

15   KAHNWEILER, DANIEL-HENRY. <u>Juan Gris: His Life and Work</u>.
      Rev. ed. Translated by Douglas Cooper. New York: Harry N.
      Abrams, pp. 9, 16, 26, 27, 31, and passim.
          Stein was the second collector to buy a Gris painting. At
      least once she sent him money, although her taste for his work
      occasionally waned.

16   KNOX, GEORGE. "The Great American Novel: Final Chapter."
      <u>American Quarterly</u> 21 (Winter):667-82.
          In <u>The Making of Americans</u>, "Gertrude Stein has captured
      in her unique, if exasperating, way some of the much-discussed
      criteria of The Great American Novel--including the search for
      an American soul-stuff. . . . One can say that structurally its
      apparent formlessness is imitative, utilizing the 'chaos' and
      amorphousness of American life, which critics so often exclaimed
      had to be shaped by the esemplastic imagination of The Great Amer-
      ican Novelist into symmetry and order."

17   MARKS, J. "The New Humor." <u>Esquire</u> 72 (December):329.
          "Both Salvador Dali and Gertrude Stein were promulgators
      of the put-on (Dali's <u>Venus With Drawer</u> or the idea of Stein's

writing somebody else's autobiography), but stoned humor also
found its beginning in surrealism and in Stein's nonobjective
language, like <u>Four Saints in Three Acts</u> or <u>Have They Attacked
Mary, He Giggled</u>. . . ."

18   SULZBERGER, C.L. <u>A Long Row of Candles: Memoirs and Diaries</u>
     <u>(1934-1954)</u>. New York: Macmillan Co., pp. 264-65.
          In 1945 Stein invited Sulzberger to tea and talked about
     World War II. Stein was "a fat, most amiable old woman who lives
     in a strange combination of sloppy comfort and a modern art museum
     with her friend, the cozy, hideous Alice Toklas."

19   UNTERECKER, JOHN. <u>Voyager: A Life of Hart Crane</u>. New York:
     Farrar, Straus, & Giroux, pp. 343-44, 581, 592-93.
          Crane worried about his relationship to the work of Cummings
     and Stein. After meeting Stein, Crane called her "about the most
     impressive personality of all."

20   WICKES, GEORGE. <u>Americans in Paris</u>. New York: Doubleday &
     Co., pp. 1-64, 126, 160-61, and passim.
          In <u>Paris France</u> the elderly Stein produced "a loving tribute
     to the city, the country, and the people." The work explains why
     Stein chose France, where she became legendary.

1970

1   ACTON, HAROLD. <u>More Memoirs of an Aesthete (1939-69)</u>.
     London: Methuen & Co., pp. xiv, 72, 161, 166-69, 171-76, 199,
     219, 254-58.
          Stein introduced Barney to Acton, brought publicity to
     Picasso, and liked some writing by Acton, who often entertained
     Toklas and Stein in Paris.

2   ATKINS, JOHN. "Stein is a Stein is a Stein." <u>Books & Bookmen</u>
     16 (November):15-16.
          In <u>Three Lives</u>, "one finds the structural looseness and
     stylistic casualness that appealed to the young Hemingway like
     a refreshing wine. He took the style, modified and refined it.
     Hats off to Gertrude Stein."

3   BECHTEL, LOUISE SEAMAN. <u>Books in Search of Children: Speeches</u>
     <u>and Essays</u>. Edited by Virginia Haviland. New York: Macmillan
     Co., pp. 46, 85-89, 121.
          Reprint of 1939.1.

4   BLOOM, ELLEN F. "Three Steins: A Very Personal Recital."
     <u>Texas Quarterly</u> 13 (Summer):15-22.
          Bloom met "Cousin Gertrude" in November, 1945, in Paris:
     "I think that her first contact with any member of the family
     after the long war years meant something important to Gertrude
     Stein. She never mentioned her health or any pain she may have

had, but two months later she died, and I have always been grateful for the memory of those relaxed and happy hours I had with her that November in Paris."

5   BRIDGMAN, RICHARD. Gertrude Stein in Pieces. New York: Oxford University Press, 411 pp.
    Stein's literary story must be known "in pieces, because Gertrude Stein saw parts but no whole. . . . In pieces . . . because Gertrude Stein's prose echoed the cacophony of feelings, associations, and memories she distinguished in her mind . . . [and] in pieces, because no term more accurately describes Gertrude Stein's unit of literary expression. . . . Whatever else she may have been, she has proved herself master of the telling phrase, of the memorable and haunting assessment reached when the tide of her persistence carried her to a spontaneous height."

6   BUNNELL, W.A. "Who Wrote the Paris Idyll? The Place and Function of A Moveable Feast in the Writings of Ernest Hemingway." Arizona Quarterly 26 (Winter):334-46.
    Stein is literarily destroyed by Hemingway in A Moveable Feast, ostensibly for being lesbian.

7   BURNES, GERALD. "Why Johnny Can't Write." Southwest Review 55 (Spring):211-12.
    Narration "is the deepest [Stein] ever went into the nature of the audience, as much the concern of intelligent poets as the possibility of narrative verse."

8   CANNELL, KATHLEEN. "Gertrude Stein--'The rhythm is the person.'" Christian Science Monitor, 5 March, p. 15.
    People who expected to meet Stein and find an eccentric charlatan stayed to be charmed by "a friendly American woman, her extraordinary intelligence balanced by benevolence and a sense of humor, who liked detective stories, collegiate football, comic strips, and especially young people."

9   _____. "Saturdays at Gertrude Stein's." Christian Science Monitor, 4 March, p. 15.
    "In the end probably no collector's taste has been more triumphantly vindicated than Gertrude Stein's. Vindicated, not by opinionated, trenchant pronouncements, but by the unseen soft rustle of old-fashioned greenbacks."

10 CASALS, PABLO, and KAHN, ALBERT. Joys and Sorrows: Reflections by Pablo Casals. New York: Simon & Schuster, p. 106.
    When Casals met Stein living with her family in San Francisco, she was not yet famous, just "a sturdy young woman in her twenties with a strong handsome face. She had a brilliant mind and a vivid way of expressing herself."

11   COOPER, DOUGLAS. "Gertrude Stein and Juan Gris." In 1970.33,
     pp. 65-73.
         Stein's writings about Gris may be misinformed, but "what
     mattered most to Juan Gris was her friendship, her admiration
     for his work, their animated artistic discussions, and her stimu-
     lating mind."

12   DAVIS, DOUGLAS. "American in Paris." Newsweek 76
     (14 December):80-81B.
         The Four Americans in Paris exhibit reveals the acuity of
     Stein's appreciation for avant-garde art of her day; seeing her
     family's collected paintings "is like being transplanted back to
     the breathless beginnings of modern art."

*13 DAVIS, ERIC HUNTER. "Gertrude Stein's Return to Narrative."
     Ph.D. dissertation, Harvard University, 226 pp.
         Cited: Liston, Maureen R. Gertrude Stein: An Annotated
     Critical Bibliography, p. 60.

14   GALLUP, DONALD. "Du Coté de Chez Stein." Book Collector 19
     (September):169-84.
         The long development of the Gertrude Stein Collection at
     Yale has built "an inspiration and a potential gold mine for the
     student genuinely interested in literature and the human beings
     who have made it."

15   GASS, WILLIAM H. Fiction and the Figures of Life. New York:
     Alfred A. Knopf, pp. 79-96.
         Reprint of 1958.6.

16   GLASSCO, JOHN. Memoirs of Montparnasse. Introduction by Leon
     Edel. Toronto: Oxford University Press, pp. 30-31, 93-97.
         Reprint of 1969.10.

17   GLUECK, GRACE. "Alcoa Fund Gives $100,000 to Mount Stein
     Exhibition." New York Times, 7 October, p. 38.
         The Museum of Modern Art will use $100,000 from Alcoa for
     the Stein family exhibit, which will later visit other American
     cities.

18   _____. "The Family Knew What It Liked." New York Times,
     13 December, sec. 2, p. 23.
         The Museum of Modern Art exhibit of 225 Stein family pieces
     of art is amazing but excludes 100 other items known but not
     available.

19   _____. "TV: A Program of Readings From Gertrude Stein."
     New York Times, 29 July, p. 79.
         Last night's TV reading of Stein had one problem--being
     too short.

20   GOLSON, LUCILE M. "The Michael Steins of San Francisco: Art
      Patrons and Collectors." In 1970.33, pp. 35-49.
           Gertrude and Leo Stein were only the most public of the
      Stein family of collectors; they must share praise with Michael
      and Sarah Stein.

21   GORDON, IRENE. "A World Beyond the World: The Discovery of
      Leo Stein." In 1970.33, pp. 13-33.
           Unlike Gertrude, Leo Stein could not develop his apprecia-
      tion of modern painting beyond cubism. Yet after he and Gertrude
      separated, her best collecting stopped.

22   GRAMONT, SANCHE de. "Remember Dada: Man Ray at 80." New
      York Times Magazine, 6 September, p. 30.
           Stein's portrait by Man Ray, who thought her an "idiot,"
      actually "makes her look like a pro football linebacker after a
      hard game."

23   HIRSHLAND, ELLEN B. "The Cone Sisters and the Stein Family."
      In 1970.33, pp. 75-86.
           Thanks to the friendship of Stein and the Cones, Etta and
      Claribel Cone trusted Stein's advice to buy modern art, forming
      a superb collection.

24   HUGHES, ROBERT. "Patrons and Roped Climbers." Time 96
      (14 December):76-81.
           Stein's collected art shows that, "in retrospect, the
      sturdy figure of Gertrude Stein looms over the cultural land-
      scape of pre-World I Paris like an old-fashioned radio--squat,
      massive, dark and droning out an endless stream of words. But
      if her words were sometimes tedious, her eye was seldom wrong.
      In fact, no American expatriate was a shrewder judge of Paris'
      radical new art."

25   KATZ, LEON. "Matisse, Picasso and Gertrude Stein." In
      1970.33, pp. 51-63.
           Stein and Matisse quarreled because of the painter's obses-
      sive incivility to his friends, driving Gertrude to become a
      devotee of Picasso and his kind of art.

26   KESTING, MARIANNE. Entdeckung und Destruktion: Zur
      Strukturumwandlung der Künste. Munich: Wilhelm Fink Verlag,
      pp. 286-87.
           In Stein's operas are no dramas but rather manipulations
      of words and sentences, characters and roles. Stein creates
      exercises in meditation based on rhythmic repetition, and her
      interest is indeed in musical effects.

27   KRAMER, HILTON. "In the Heydey of the Paris Avant Garde."
      New York Times, 27 December, sec. 2, p. 25.
           The exhibit Four Americans in Paris is "a beautiful show,
      beautifully installed."

28 _____. "Paris Era Recalled in Stein Collections." New York
Times, 18 December, p. 50.
"One of the legendary chapters in the history of modern
art--the pioneer collecting efforts of the American writer
Gertrude Stein, her brothers Leo and Michael Stein, and her
sister-in-law Sarah Stein . . . during their expatriate years
in Paris--has now been commemorated in a stunning exhibition at
the Museum of Modern Art."

*29 LANATI, BARBARA M. "Gertrude Stein ovvero avanguardia e
sonsumo?" Sigma 27 (1970):74-105.
Cited: PMLA Bibliography for 1971, p. 159.

30 LASK, THOMAS. "Gertrude Stein amidst Her Talented Friends."
New York Times, 21 December, p. 71.
The television portrait of Stein, "When This You See,
Remember Me," would have pleased Stein, a hound for publicity.
Yet the tribute may have been too favorable to Stein, whom not
all liked.

31 MELLOW, JAMES R. "Exhibition Preview: Four Americans in
Paris." Art in America 58 (November):84-91.
Four Americans in Paris reveals that Stein luckily bought
paintings that she personally responded to and liked.

32 _____. "Gertrude Stein on Picasso." New York Times Book
Review, 20 December, pp. 4, 21.
Stein's essay on Picasso, while "not the most informative
work on the painter in the English language, is easily the most
ingratiating: warm, discursive, full of vivid anecdotes, charming insights and what can only be called breathtaking
generalizations. . . ."

33 MUSEUM OF MODERN ART. Four Americans in Paris. Introduction
by Margaret Potter. New York: Museum of Modern Art, 175 pp.

34 PORTER, KATHERINE ANNE. The Collected Essays and Occasional
Writings of Katherine Anne Porter. New York: Delacorte
Press, pp. 251-70.
Reprint of 1927.13; 1928.18; 1947.33; 1966.16.

35 PURDY, STROTHER B. "Gertrude Stein at Marienbad." PMLA 85
(October):1096-1105.
"In 1934, Gertrude Stein wrote 'the cinema has never read
my work'; I think we can now say that it has." In Last Year in
Marienbad Stein's influence is shown in repetition that "pre-
sents a powerful synthesis of life and art."

36 REVIEW OF SELECTED OPERAS AND PLAYS. Publishers' Weekly 197
(29 June):104.

Stein's dramas have achieved no popularity beyond her fans. Perhaps the current collection may demonstrate that Stein foreshadows Beckett, Pinter, and Ionesco.

37 ROBERTSON, BRYAN. "When the gifted young men were 23." *Times* (London), 30 December, p. 30.
Seeing the exhibit Four Americans in Paris reveals "the real love of painting and authoritative understanding with which the extraordinary Stein family built up their collections, invigorated by the way in which Gertrude saw herself, with characteristic lack of modesty, as a fellow artist."

38 ROSS, ISHBEL. *The Expatriates*. New York: Thomas Y. Crowell Co., pp. 5, 155, 164, 176, 221-26, and passim.
Stein formed her salon before expatriation became common in the 1920s, and yet only her association with the 1920s expatriates gave her fame.

39 SITWELL, EDITH. *Selected Letters*. Edited by John Lehmann and Derek Parker. London: Macmillan Co., pp. 31, 35.
Late in 1924, Sitwell took tea with Stein in Paris; Stein described Picasso's youth to Sitwell.

40 STEWART, LAWRENCE D. "Hemingway and the Autobiographies of Alice B. Toklas." In *Fitzgerald/Hemingway Annual 1970*, pp. 117-23.
The Autobiography of Alice B. Toklas and *What Is Remembered* reveal that Hemingway resented Stein's "popular" style--close to his own--and the frightening person of Toklas.

41 STOCK, NOEL. *The Life of Ezra Pound*. New York: Pantheon Books, pp. 253, 311.
Pound in the early 1920s saw Stein "a few times but they did not get on together." To Pound, Hemingway claimed that Stein's good advice often accompanied much rubbish.

42 THOMAS, FRANKLIN RICHARD. "The Literary Admirers of Alfred Stieglitz, Photographer." Ph.D. dissertation, Indiana University, 171 pp.
Stieglitz, "the most influential practitioner of the art of traditional photography in his time, had a profound impact upon the aesthetics, the styles, and the Weltanschauungs [sic] of four of his literary friends and admirers: Gertrude Stein, William Carlos Williams, Hart Crane, and Sherwood Anderson." Summarized: *Dissertation Abstracts International* 31:2404A.

43 WEINSTEIN, NORMAN. *Gertrude Stein and the Literature of the Modern Consciousness*. New York: Frederick Ungar Publishing Co., 150 pp.
Instead of considering Stein as an isolated experimenter with words and patterns, it is helpful to consider her in the

entire spectrum of twentieth-century experimentation--including
such approaches as "speech pathology, psycholinguistics, structural linguistics, and linguistic anthropology. . . ."

1971

1   ABELMAN, LESTER. "A Stein Is a Stein Is a Stein. . . ."
    New York Daily News, 7 February.
         The Museum of Modern Art Exhibit Four Americans in Paris
    "richly serves a double purpose. It not only evokes a particu-
    larly significant moment in the development of 20th Century art
    but also illuminates the personalities of the Steins."

2   ALLOWAY, LAWRENCE. "Art." Nation 212 (11 January):61-62.
         Four Americans in Paris is a "dual-purpose exhibition, and
    satisfying on both levels: it is an excellent group of early
    School of Paris paintings and a documentary of the taste of the
    Stein family."

3   ASHBERRY, JOHN. "G.M.P." Art News 69 (February):44-47, 73.
         "Surrounded as [Stein] was by brilliant minds in her chosen
    place of exile, Gertrude Stein was peculiarly alone. It would
    have been difficult to find an audience anywhere in the world at
    that time for such highly experimental writings, but especially"
    in conservative Paris, leaving Stein free and pushed into pur-
    suing her art interests.

4   BARNES, CLIVE. "New York Notebook." Times (London),
    6 February, p. 20.
         Stein had the uncanny ability to foresee what art would
    come to matter, and her collection demonstrates the crossroads
    at which she stood in Paris early in the twentieth century.

5   BAUR, JOHN I.H. Joseph Stella. New York: Praeger
    Publishers, pp. 29-30.
         Stella recorded his first impressions of the Stein studio:
    "The lady of the house was an immense woman carcass austerely
    dressed in black. Enthroned on a sofa in the middle of the room
    where the pictures were hanging, with the forceful solemnity of
    a priestess or sibylla, she was examining pitilessly all new-
    comers, assuming a high and distant pose."

6   BENSE, MAX. "Was erzählt Gertrude Stein?" In Die Realität
    der Literatur: Autoren und Ihre Texte. Cologne: Kiepenheuer
    & Witsch, pp. 45-69.
         Stein's concern was the possibilities of speech, creating
    a new idea of grammar and syntax and leaving behind her technical
    reality as such.

7 BORGES, JORGE LUIS, and TORRES, ESTHER ZAMBORAIN de. <u>An Introduction to American Literature</u>. Translated and edited by L. Clark Keating and Robert O. Evans. Lexington: University of Kentucky Press, pp. 55-56.

Gertrude Stein was more important an influence than a writer; yet, in applying modern art theories to words, she enriched literature.

8 BURNS, GERALD. "An Anthology. . . ." <u>Southwest Review</u> 56 (Winter):102.

<u>Selected Operas and Plays</u> might encourage production of Stein's dramas: "A Stein play is first of all good talk, and an acting group that plows through this will have practiced most of the sounds you hear on a stage."

9 BUTLER, JOSEPH T. "The American Way with Art." <u>Connoisseur</u> 178 (October):134-35.

Four Americans in Paris is a "major exhibition of important early 20th century paintings."

10 CHURCHILL, ALLEN. <u>The Literary Decade</u>. Englewood Cliffs, N.J.: Prentice-Hall, pp. 21, 67, 80, 84, 144, and passim.

Stein, Pound, and Eliot were the beckoning expatriates appealing to literati in the post-war generation. In later years, Stein was among the few never to move back to the U.S.A.

11 COFFELT, BETH. "The Incredible Stein Influence." <u>San Francisco Examiner and Chronicle</u>, 14 August, "Sunday Living," pp. 14-15, 17-18.

The life of Stein is the important thing to remember—along with the fact that she "was a monumentally great woman and a writer that for many can be compared in this country only to Walt Whitman."

12 COHN, RUBY. <u>Dialogue in American Drama</u>. Bloomington: Indiana University Press, pp. 201-7, 211, 218, 219.

"Gertrude Stein's drama is a reaction against the whole dramatic tradition. In order to plunge the reader-spectator into the immediate <u>thereness</u> of her continuous present, Stein stripped her plays of plot, character, event, theme, subject, and meaningful dialogue. Instead, she gives us disjunctive and rhythmic dialogue, often spoken by undesignated voices."

13 CONSTABLE, ROSALIND. "Gertrude and Leo and Alice and Michael and Sarah." <u>Book World</u>, 31 January, pp. 1, 3.

<u>Four Americans in Paris</u> is wonderfully revealing of the Steins and their art acquisitions. In Gertrude Stein on Picasso, Stein is "crystal clear, sparkling with intelligence and understanding of Picasso's personality, and with concern lest that personality traduce the artist."

14   COOPER, DOUGLAS. "Gertrude Stein and Juan Gris." Apollo,
      n.s. 93 (January):28-35.
         Although it cannot be found in the meeting of Stein and
      Gris, Stein liked Gris, possibly because of her belief that
      Spanish painters best handled Cubism. Gris's dealer became
      upset when Stein lent money to the artist, a disagreement ensu-
      ing that estranged the friendship to 1924.

15   COX, JAMES M. "Autobiography and America." Virginia Quarterly
      Review 47 (Spring):276-77.
         Stein--"as American, as man-woman, as new Buddha--seems to
      me to be both the fact and the mystery at the end of American
      autobiography."

16   DAY, DOUGLAS. "Gertrude Stein." In Notable American Women,
      1607-1950, III. Edited by Edward T. James. Cambridge:
      Harvard University Press, pp. 355-59.
         With Stein, "extremists of one sort see her as a charlatan;
      those of another sort, as a strange amalgam of Wise Child and
      Great Mother. More likely, Gertrude Stein was a very intelli-
      gent and very lucky woman, who was fortunate enough to step pre-
      cisely into the center of the cultural life of her century, and
      clever enough to make herself indispensable to those at the
      center."

17   DETONI-DUJMIĆ, DUNJA. "Knjiẑerni Marionetizam Gertrude
      Stein" [Puppet plays of Gertrude Stein]. Kolo 8 (1971):
      838-42.
         In Hungarian. Stein's puppet theatre; seen but not
      translated.

18   FARNHAM, EMILY. Charles Demuth: Behind a Laughing Mask.
      Norman: University of Oklahoma Press, pp. 7, 25, 60, 67,
      73, and passim.
         Because Demuth enjoyed literature as much as art, he
      cherished Stein's friendship. Although Stein influenced Demuth,
      the details are conjectural--naiveté, simplicity, unintelligibil-
      ity, originality, whimsy, and humor.

19   FENDELMAN, EARL BARRY. "Toward a Third Voice: Autobiograph-
      ical Form in Thoreau, Stein, Adams, and Mailer." Ph.D. dis-
      sertation, Yale University, 255 pp.
         "The process of self-portraiture is a central drama in the
      personal narrative of Thoreau, Stein, Adams, and Mailer. The
      act of reflection itself, more than a past record of accomplish-
      ments, forms the nucleus of what they have to tell about them-
      selves. As a result, these autobiographies appear to operate
      in at least two frames at the same time, one historical and the
      other imaginative." Summarized: Dissertation Abstracts Inter-
      national 32A:6972.

20 FRACKMAN, NOEL. "The Stein Family and the Era of Avant-Garde
    Collecting." Arts Magazine 45 (February):41-43.
        Seeing Four Americans in Paris shows by contrast how diffi-
    cult is art collecting today and how the Steins remained friends
    with their artists.

21 GERVASI, FRANK. "The Liberation of Gertrude Stein."
    Saturday Review 54 (21 August):13-14, 57.
        Eric Sevareid organized a group of reporters to liberate
    Stein in wartime France; Gervasi had a delightful luncheon and
    talk about the war effort and writing when he met the two women.
    More than other famous people, Toklas and Stein were "genuine
    human beings, loving and lovable, and endowed with the gift of
    friendship."

22 GOLDMAN, ARNOLD. "Gertrude Stein." In The Penguin Guide to
    American Literature. Edited by Malcolm Bradbury, Eric Mottram,
    and Jean Franco. New York: McGraw-Hill Book Co., pp. 239-40.
        With Stein, the important "departure in her stylistic ex-
    perimentation was her attempt to develop a 'cubist' literature,
    a prose independent of meaningful associations, relying merely
    on sound-orchestration. Why she felt that 'meaning' had to be
    abandoned to create a multi-dimensional art remains something of
    a mystery. . . ."

23 HAMILTON, GEORGE HEARD. "Art: Pre-Columbian to Pinstripe."
    Saturday Review 53 (28 November):41.
        Gertrude Stein on Picasso shows "the spell Picasso exerted
    on those who first saw and understood his work."

24 [HOFFMAN, FREDERICK J.] "Gertrude Stein." In Encyclopaedia
    Judaica. 15. Jerusalem: Encyclopaedia Judaica, pp. 351-52.
        "Gertrude Stein was an experimenter with words, playing
    with them both for their sound and rhythm and for their subcon-
    scious associations. At first she had to pay for the publica-
    tion of her work. Yet she could also write lucidly and engagingly,
    and her reputation grew. Even at its height, attitudes toward
    her swung between adulation and scorn. . . ."

25 KAHNWEILER, DANIEL-HENRY, and CREMIEUX, FRANCIS. My Galleries
    and Painters. Translated by Helen Weaver. Introduction by
    John Russell. New York: Viking Press, pp. 11, 81, 134.
        Toklas has "reverently preserved" Stein's art collection.

26 KENNER, HUGH. The Pound Era. Berkeley: University of
    California Press, pp. 41, 385.
        Stein had "a mystique of the word," encouraged by the
    neglect of her words in her lifetime. She wrote hermetic words
    to be understood, someday somewhere.

27   _____. "The Seemingly Wise." New Republic 164 (16 January):
        25-26, 30.
            Publication of Gertrude Stein on Picasso collects Stein's
        sometimes wise and sometimes childish words on the artist, along
        with illustrations and reproduction: "If you buy the book,
        you'll have bought a chunk of history, as mute and in its way
        as authentic as a fossil."

28   KNAPIK, HAROLD. Haute Cuisine Without Help. New York:
        Liveright, pp. x-xi, xviii-xix.
            Knapik knew Toklas intimately in Paris, shared her kitchen,
        and disliked Toklas's overuse of herbs.

29   LOERCHER, DIANA. "Gertrude Stein in the Beginning."
        Christian Science Monitor, 7 October, p. 6.
            Stein's earliest writings recall Jane Austen, Henry James,
        and the liturgy.

30   McBRIDE, MARY. Review of Fernhurst, Q.E.D. and Other Early
        Writings. Library Journal 96 (August):2548.
            The characters in Stein's earliest fiction never become
        living beings, but the works will be of value in the history of
        the novel and of American popular and literary culture in deal-
        ing with the "singular" person.

31   MARSHALL, ARTHUR. "Boots Boots." New Statesman 82 (23 July):
        118.
            In Paris France, "every now and then a strictly minimal
        American talent breaks surface and hoodwinks the public."

32   MAYFIELD, SARA. Exiles from Paradise: Zelda and Scott
        Fitzgerald. New York: Delacorte Press, pp. 93, 103, 106-07,
        and passim.
            Hemingway introduced Fitzgerald to Stein and her art col-
        lection. Fitzgerald did not understand her paintings but liked
        the woman and courted her praise. Zelda in 1934 was disapprov-
        ing of Stein.

33   MAYHALL, JANE. "On Things As They Are." In Rediscoveries.
        Edited by David Madden. New York: Crown Publishers,
        pp. 197-208.
            Q.E.D. (or Things As They Are) "may be Stein's most daring
        book. If only in terms of subject, it is outspoken, coherent,
        ultramodern. To a large measure, it outdistances what is now
        considered bold."

34   MAYHEW, ALICE. "Critics' Choices for Christmas." Commonweal
        95 (3 December):233.
            Paris France "is for Stein addicts, but then the book-
        buying public is potentially full of Stein addicts. IF they
        only knew it."

35 MELLOW, JAMES R. "A Crucial Stop in Paris." <u>New York Times</u>,
    3 January, sec. II, p. 19.
        Seeing Four Americans in Paris is "an odd, sentimental
    journey, a final glimpse into a past in which art and life were
    marvelously intermingled--the extraordinary lives of the four
    Steins with their enthusiasms, their quarrels, their vivid per-
    sonal ambitions and the equally extraordinary art they chose to
    live with."

36 MEYEROWITZ, PATRICIA. "Lesbianism Never?" <u>New York Review
    of Books</u>, 7 October, p. 41.
        Stein's physical condition at death revealed that she could
    not have been lesbian: "Simply stated, Alice and Gertrude made
    a home for themselves with an emotional attachment as the bond
    that kept them together. But lesbianism--never. . . ."

37 MIZENER, ARTHUR. <u>The Saddest Story: A Biography of Ford
    Madox Ford</u>. New York: World Publishing Co., 234, 329, 334,
    336, and passim.
        Hemingway's first move on the <u>Transatlantic Review</u> was "to
    insist the <u>Transatlantic</u> print Gertrude Stein"; Ford dedicated
    <u>A Mirror to France</u> to Stein.

38 "MUSEUM OF MODERN ART EXHIBITION: THE FAMOUS STEINS."
    <u>Pantheon</u> 29 (May):256.
        The exhibit Four Americans in Paris is "the season's most
    successful show," for "the Steins and their friends established
    close relationships with gifted men they admired." Even Picasso
    profited from the Steins' aid and acknowledgment.

39 PRIDEAUX, TOM. "Four Patron Saints in One Great Act." <u>Life</u>
    70 (23 April):56-62, 65.
        Four Americans in Paris includes Stein's collection and
    "nearly 200 other pictures, sculptures, drawings and prints. . . .
    Even the Steins themselves never saw, all at once, such a collec-
    tion as this."

40 RATCLIFF, CARTER. "New York Letter." <u>Art International</u> 15
    (March):50, 56.
        Four Americans in Paris would clear up several points
    about modernism in Europe and about the difficulty of forming
    art collections. Yet Gertrude Stein herself "had little taste,
    only a commitment to modernism."

41 REVIEW OF <u>FERNHURST, Q.E.D. AND OTHER EARLY WRITINGS</u>.
    <u>Publishers' Weekly</u> 199 (19 April):45.
        Such early Stein work is "of note only because it really
    is apprentice work and shows the rather stilted and self-
    conscious beginnings of the later artist. It also carries the
    leitmotifs that were to develop and strengthen in her work as
    the years went by."

42   REVIEW OF <u>FERNHURST, Q.E.D. AND OTHER EARLY WRITINGS</u>. <u>Kirkus</u>
      <u>Reviews</u> 39 (15 May):573.
          "This volume of early writings does much to bridge the
      distance [Stein] herself, by style and sheer advance of outlook,
      helped to enforce, and invites a kind of sympathy she would never
      again permit."

43   REVIEW OF <u>GERTRUDE STEIN ON PICASSO</u>. <u>Choice</u> 8 (June):541-42.
          "How delicious to discover a truly fresh contribution
      amidst the torrent of books that have been pouring forth. . . .
      While the other works <u>use</u> the Stein material, this book <u>presents</u>
      it, and every page is a pure delight."

44   REXROTH, KENNETH. <u>American Poetry in the Twentieth Century</u>.
      New York: Herder & Herder, pp. 61, 72, 75, 79, 82, 89, 103.
          Perhaps Stein influenced <u>The Waste Land</u> in "dissociated
      verbs and nouns, adjectives, and adverbs," and her <u>Tender Buttons</u>
      influenced cubist poetry. Stein "belongs with the American an-
      thropologists and philologists who have made the most radical
      studies of language. . . ."

45   ROE, NANCY ELLEN. "Gertrude Stein: Rhetoric and the 'Modern
      Composition.'" Ph.D. dissertation, University of Michican,
      184 pp.
          "Writers have usually tried to make words follow upon one
      another in a deliberative order, according to what can be called
      'Aristotelian grammar,' to the end of informing and persuading
      audiences by logical means. But Stein has purposes and methods
      for writing that differ both from those of the Aristotelian and
      the 'new' or neo-Aristotelian schools of rhetoric." Summarized:
      <u>Dissertation Abstracts International</u> 32A:6450.

46   ROSE, Sir FRANCIS. "Gertrude Stein: still leading, her eye
      for art, her gift of word." <u>Vogue</u> 157 (1 January):88-89,
      133, 135.
          Stein and Toklas were "un-Lesbian women who made their
      lives by protecting one another. There were never the sordid
      squabbles and jealousies that surround Lesbians: There was
      complete peace as the two women went about their daily duties
      for many, many years."

47   ROSENBERG, HAROLD. "The Art World." <u>New Yorker</u> 46
      (30 January):71-75.
          Four Americans in Paris as an exhibit proves that of the
      Steins in Paris, Gertrude did not "absorb culture" or "copy it"
      but made culture as "she saw the new."

48   SQUIRES, RADCLIFFE. <u>Allen Tate: A Literary Biography</u>.
      New York: Pegasus, pp. 86-87.

Hemingway once took Tate to Stein's apartment, Hemingway being afraid to go alone. Stein praised Emerson's love of abstraction and Henry James's abstract construction. All led to Gertrude Stein: "Tate did not really take to Miss Stein."

49   STARKE, CATHERINE JUANITA. Black Portraiture in American Fiction: Stock Characters, Archetypes, and Individuals. New York: Basic Books, pp. 183-86, 211, 212.
     "Melanctha" is "a complex portrait of a Negro in transition from cultural determinism to individualistic self-assertion."

50   TATE, ALLEN. "Miss Toklas' American Cake." Prose, no. 3 (Fall), pp. 137-61.
     Tate met Toklas and Stein in Paris in 1928, when he marveled at her speed in writing poetry. In 1929, he and Hemingway were at 27 rue de Fleurus to hear Stein discuss American literature and her eminent place in it.

51   THIGPEN, JANET. "A Manual for Teaching Counselor Trainees Existential Concepts through an Exploration of the Life and Writings of Gertrude Stein." Ph.D. dissertation, East Texas State University, 367 pp.
     "Gertrude Stein was not an existential writer by professed design. She was, however, very individualistic and intensely committed to her beliefs and her work, and one can find in her life-style and her creative work a manifestation of values that are existential." Summarized: Dissertation Abstracts International 33A:838.

52   THOMSON, VIRGIL. "Lesbianism Never?" New York Review of Books, 7 October, p. 41.
     Stein and Toklas were not merely sentimental spinsters but were fully emotional women.

53   TOMKINS, CALVIN. Living Well Is the Best Revenge. New York: Viking Press, pp. 29, 37.
     Gerald Murphy found Stein and Toklas "phenomenal together," recharging witnesses to their presence.

54   VON NOTE, ROY NELSON. Review of Gertrude Stein on Picasso. Library Journal 96 (15 February):623.
     Stein's "early discovery and lionization of Picasso is legendary, and in these writings her warm personal fondness for him is obvious throughout."

55   WATTS, EMILY STIPES. Ernest Hemingway and the Arts. Urbana: University of Illinois Press, pp. 4-5, 17, 19, 20, 31, 40, and passim.
     ". . . Hemingway spent many happy and profitable hours at Miss Stein's, surrounded by the paintings of Picasso, Gris, and other contemporaries."

56   WEAVER, MIKE. William Carlos Williams: The American Back-
      ground. New York: Cambridge University Press, pp. 33, 51,
      154, 155, 214.
            "The Gnostic ladder . . . is surrounded by a female figure,
      and the guardians to the Gateway to Eternal Wisdom are Gertrude
      Stein and Alice B. Toklas."

57   "WONDROUS WORDSMITH." MD 15 (April):201-8.
            With Stein, "however obscure and capricious her work,
      agreement is general that she set her mark on twentieth century
      writing. Her achievement was a series of highly original liter-
      ary effects: the mating of language, rhythm and character, a
      freshness of insight and the creation of a new literary time
      sense."

58   YOUNG, MAHONRI SHARP. "Springtime in Paris." Apollo, n.s.
      93 (February):135-40.
            Four Americans in Paris reveals the "immense service [the
      Steins] rendered--not so much to Matisse and Picasso--as to the
      innumerable visitors who came to know the work of those artists
      at the Saturday night gatherings in both the Stein households."

                              1972

1   APOLLINAIRE, GUILLAUME. Apollinaire on Art: Essays and
      Reviews, 1902-1918. Translated by Susan Suleiman. Edited by
      Leroy C. Breuning. New York: Viking Press, pp. xviii, 29.
            In 1907, Vallotton "is exhibiting six paintings, among
      which is a portrait of Mlle. Stein, that American lady who with
      her brother and a group of her relatives constitutes the most
      unexpected patronage of the arts in our time."

2   BOWLES, PAUL. Without Stopping: An Autobiography. New York:
      G.P. Putnam's Sons, pp. 104, 106, 107, 108, 111, and passim.
            Stein and Toklas disliked Bowles's first name, his German
      wife, his "dirtiness," his laziness, his poems, and his taste in
      food.

3   BUCKMAN, PETER. "Summer Uplift." New Statesman 84 (4 August):
      169.
            Fernhurst "is an extraordinary exercise in devotional pub-
      lishing," and Stein's early work is peculiarly bloodless and
      moralistic.

4   BURNETT, AVIS. Gertrude Stein. New York: Atheneum, 187 pp.
      Biography for juveniles.

5   BUTCHER, FANNY. Many Lives, One Love. New York: Harper &
      Row, pp. 57, 78, 210, 267, 306, and passim.

Butcher early read <u>Three Lives</u> and knew "experimentation, as well as great talent." Knowing cubists and surrealists encouraged Stein to duplicate in prose their techniques. Butcher met Stein in France and then delighted in Stein's 1934 tour of the U.S.A.

6   COPLEY, FRANK O. "Aristotle to Gertrude Stein: The Arts of Poetry." <u>Mosaic</u> 5 (Summer):85-102.
       Among definitions of poetry one finds Stein's differentiation of prose and poetry according to method and manner.

7   "DOUBLE, DOUBLE, TOIL AND TROUBLE." <u>Serif</u> 9 (Summer):44.
       One copy of <u>Yes Is for a Very Young Man</u> exhibits peculiarities in presswork.

8   FENDELMAN, EARL. "Gertrude Stein Among the Cubists." <u>Journal of Modern Literature</u> 2 (November):481-90.
       Early in this century, Stein collected Cubist paintings that for her "expressed a new theory about aesthetic perception, one which demanded that the artist, the object, and the audience be drawn together in a unified reality that would remain incomplete if it lacked any one of its components. . . ."

9   FISHER, EDWARD. "Lost Generations, Then and Now." <u>Connecticut Review</u> 6 (October):13-17.
       Hemingway denied Stein's contention about a lost generation but used the idea for <u>The Sun Also Rises</u>. Perhaps Stein early recognized the symptoms of Hemingway's self-destruction.

10   FRASER, ROBERT S. Review of <u>Sherwood Anderson/Gertrude Stein</u>. <u>Library Journal</u> 97 (1 December):3911-12.
       The revelations in Anderson's and Stein's letters are few and the data are scanty.

11   FROST, ROBERT. <u>Family Letters of Robert and Elinor Frost</u>. Edited by Arnold Grade. Foreword by Lesley Frost. Albany: State University of New York Press, p. 162.
       "I suppose Gertrude Stein has come in confluently to encourage the imitators. . . . A little of her is fun, but goes a long way."

12   GREENWALD, ARTHUR. "Gertrude Stein Seriously." <u>Yale Daily News Magazine</u> 94 (12 December):6-7.
       Because Yale University ignores Stein, only outsiders make use of the University's fabulous Stein collection.

13   HEMINGWAY, ERNEST. <u>The Nick Adams Stories</u>. Preface by Philip Young. New York: Charles Scribner's Sons, p. 239..
       Nick Adams foresees himself as an author for whom Stein would "know if he ever got things right."

14   HOUSEMAN, JOHN. Run-Through: A Memoir. New York: Simon &
      Schuster, pp. 96-97, 99-127.
         Houseman helped Thomson stage Four Saints in Three Acts,
      having sought and received much aid in understanding the text
      being sung.

15   HUGHES, ALLEN. "Lenox' 'Mother of Us All' Lacks Nothing but
      Seats for the Crowd." New York Times, 3 July, p. 7.
         "Gertrude Stein's witty and moving text comes through with
      perfect clarity in Mr. Thomson's idiomatic setting of the plain
      but poetic American English. . . ."

16   KAWIN, BRUCE F. Telling It Again and Again: Repetition in
      Literature and Film. Ithaca: Cornell University Press,
      pp. 6, 50, 88, 94-95, 108-10, and passim.
         Stein asserted that she did not write repetitiously; but,
      like Beckett later, Stein attacked time and language with "repe-
      tition in the continuous present." Stein felt that she succeeded
      in her task of creating "writing which in itself is."

17   LIPCHITZ, JACQUES, and ARNASON, H.H. My Life in Sculpture.
      New York: Viking Press, pp. 23, 63.
         Lipchitz liked Stein's personality, salon, and paintings.
      His statue of her as a fat Buddha pleased her. By 1938, Stein
      had reduced to resemble more a rabbi.

18   LONGSTREET, STEPHEN. We All Went To Paris: Americans in the
      City of Light, 1776-1971. New York: Macmillan Co., pp. 242-56.
         Original in lifestyle and writing, Stein is admired by loy-
      alists and in academic circles, but she contributed little to
      taste in art or to French culture.

19   MANLEY, SEON, and BELCHER, SUSAN. O, Those Extraordinary
      Women! Philadelphia: Chilton Book Co., pp. 237, 247-51, 288,
      296, 298-99, 301.
         Never publicly honored, Stein was "a wild American maverick
      and, though born in Pennsylvania, a California Colossus, an
      Edwardian barbarian" who added to Europe the literary experimen-
      tation coming from America.

20   MAYNARD, REID. "Abstractionism in Gertrude Stein's Three
      Lives." Ball State University Forum 13 (Winter):68-71.
         "To be sure, a conventional, time-tested type of plot is
      not necessarily a requisite for some stories--not for stories
      that have strong substitute elements. But the only significant
      substitute element in Three Lives is a purely stylistic one. A
      texture provided by imagery would be a redeeming element, but
      imagery is minimal. In short, Stein's stories are almost devoid
      of both backbone and flesh--of solid structure and texture."

21   MEADES, JONATHAN. Review of Fernhurst. Books and Bookmen
      18 (December):109-10.
         "The three pieces published in this volume, although they
      are apprentice works, give a good indication of what a fine
      writer [Stein] was; they further indicate a route for aspiring
      novelists to tread--they are constructed, occasionally convoluted
      and, for the most part, determinedly impressive."

22   MELLOW, JAMES R. "The Door Is Still Open to Gertrude Stein's
      Summer Salon." New York Times, 7 May, sec. X, pp. 1, 10, 120.
         "For those who wish to visit the temporary locale of a
      great literary figure in an extremely pleasant part of France
      where the food is excellent, or for those who merely want to
      drive and eat their way through French countryside in a leisurely
      manner, the territory is excellent."

23   MOERS, ELLEN. "Women's Literature: Profession and Tradition."
      Columbia Forum, n.s. 1 (Fall):27-30.
         Stein is in the tradition of women authors of the nine-
      teenth century.

24   NICHOL, bp. "Some Beginning Writings on Gertrude Stein's
      Theories of Personality." Open Letter, 2d ser. 2 (Summer):
      41-48.
         Because The Making of Americans is "a major work by a major
      and very neglected writer," it must be studied to understand
      Stein's "theories of personality of interaction & individual
      perceptual systems."

25   NORMAN, CHARLES. The Magic-Maker: E.E. Cummings.
      Indianapolis: Bobbs-Merrill Co., pp. 38, 45, 46, 48, 116,
      117, 133, 156, 226, 278.
         Cummings may have learned Futurist art from Tender Buttons,
      but he did not read Stein's work comfortably: "She's a symbol--
      she's an excellent symbol, like a pillar of Portland cement. You
      can't budge her. Philistines bump into her and get bruised."

26   PETERSEN, CLARENCE. "Paperbacks." Book World 6 (28 May):9.
         Selected Operas and Plays is "a splendid sampling of Miss
      Stein's work arranged chronologically and covering her entire
      career, with its many changes of style, form, and content."

27   REVIEW OF EVERYBODY'S AUTOBIOGRAPHY. Choice 8 (February):
      1587-88.
         "Since it covers the period of the Spanish war, it also
      provides the center section between the witty Toklas and one of
      her major works, the humane Wars I Have Seen (1945). The style
      is her 'plain' style, bordering on the chatty."

28   REVIEW OF FERNHURST. Choice 9 (March):62.
         Fernhurst is "fascinating for enthusiasts, but specialist
      material; of limited value to undergraduate libraries."

29   REVIEW OF IDA. <u>Choice</u> 8 (February):588.
"Thirty years [out of print] and a decade before Holden
Caulfield [in <u>The Catcher in the Rye</u>], this pioneering search-
for-identity novel avoids the current introspection by objectifying: almost everyone in the novel has a twin."

30   REVIEW OF <u>A PRIMER FOR THE GRADUAL UNDERSTANDING OF GERTRUDE
STEIN</u>. <u>Choice</u> 9 (July):648.
"Twenty-five years in the planning, this elegant gathering
is a minor masterwork. . . ."

31   REVIEW OF <u>SELECTED WRITINGS OF GERTRUDE STEIN</u>. <u>Publishers'
Weekly</u> 201 (27 March):80.
". . . a splendid sampling, but it's not the whole corpus,
nor should it be considered more than an introduction to one of
the most enigmatic and exasperating and talented American writers."

32   ROSENBERG, HAROLD. <u>The De-Definition of Art: Action Art to
Pop to Earthworks</u>. New York: Horizon Press, pp. 74, 167, 177.
Unlike most Americans searching for culture in Paris, Stein
sought "not to absorb culture or to copy it but to make culture."
Leo Stein saw tradition; Gertrude Stein saw "the new." Her thrust
was to diagnose European culture as becoming world culture, with
Parisians as hosts but not sole creators.

33   SECOR, CYNTHIA. "Alice and Gertrude." In <u>Female Studies VI:
Closer to the Ground</u>. Edited by Nancy Hoffman. 2d ed. Old
Westbury, N.Y.: Feminist Press, pp. 150-51.
<u>The Autobiography of Alice B. Toklas</u> is good as the work of
an important woman and as a domestically happy woman.

34   SHAPIRO, HARRIET. "<u>Four Saints in Three Acts</u>: An Interview."
<u>Intellectual Digest</u> 3 (October):22-26.
Thomson and Stein worked well together after Stein conceived
the libretto for <u>Four Saints in Three Acts</u>. Thomson's close control assured artistic fidelity in the production.

35   STEWART, LAWRENCE W. "Gertrude Stein and the Vital Dead."
In <u>Mystery & Detection Annual</u>. Beverly Hills: Donald Adams,
pp. 102-23.
Stein often wrote of death and the "process" of death, and
in <u>Blood on the Dining Room Floor</u> she wrote her version of a detective story.

36   SUTHERLAND, DONALD. "Alice and Gertrude and Others."
<u>Prairie Schooner</u> 45 (Winter):284-99.
Sutherland recalls visiting Toklas in Paris in the 1960s;
and he had a last letter from her in 1967. Their conversations
had amplified the Stein-Toklas stories and comforted Toklas in
her poor and sad last years.

37 ZANIELLO, THOMAS ANTHONY. "The Moment of Perception in Nineteenth and Twentieth Century Literature." Ph.D. dissertation,
Stanford University, 236 pp.
    The moment of perception is illustrated in Stein's use of
"continuous present." Summarized: <u>Dissertation Abstracts</u>
<u>International</u> 33A:4377.

<u>1973</u>

1 BAKER, WILLIAM D. "Lighting Birthday Candles for Gertrude
Stein." <u>Widening Circle</u> 1 (Fall):1-2.
    To celebrate Stein's centennial in a special issue: "this
is not the place for definitive studies or decisive new theories. . . . This is the time to remember, to admire, to light
some birthday candles for this remarkable woman, and to let impressions of Gertrude Stein flow, moving into the space inside,
coaxing them to ooze down the arm."

2 BARRY, JOSEPH. "<u>Paris France</u> Reviewed." <u>Widening Circle</u> 1
(Fall):3-5.
    <u>Paris France</u> was published the day the Germans took Paris
in 1940: "There is still no better. It holds up as well as the
city. As Gertrude's conversations, some of whose sentences never
end."

3 "BEST AND BRIGHTEST." <u>Book World</u>, 9 December, p. 2.
    The letters in <u>Staying on Alone</u> "form a composite portrait
of a woman of wit, intelligence and genuine character growing old
in loneliness and sometimes in pain but without self-pity."

4 BLOMME, GAYLE CAMPBELL BARNES. "Gertrude Stein's Concepts of
the Self and Her Literary Characters." Ph.D. dissertation,
University of Michigan, 232 pp.
    "Because the written work, in its themes and its verbal
patterns, can parallel the movements and stillnesses of twentieth-
century man, embodying the spatial and temporal essentials to
which he has been reduced, Gertrude Stein found it more than
metaphysically true to suggest that the literary work itself is
a human being." Summarized: <u>Dissertation Abstracts International</u>
34A:1892.

5 BRIDGMAN, RICHARD. "Auld Lang Stein." <u>Book World</u>,
16 December, pp. 2-3.
    <u>Staying on Alone</u> shows that Alice Toklas "never yielded to
the curses of old age. She wasn't a bore, or a nuisance, and she
didn't complain. Rather, her letters indicate, she remained suc-
cinct in communication, independent in her ideas and always
loving."

6   CASERIO, ROBERT LAWRENCE, Jr. "Plot, Story and the Novel:
     Problematic Aspects of English and American Narrative, From
     Dickens to Gertrude Stein." Ph.D. dissertation, Yale Univer-
     sity, 418 pp.
          In contrast to earlier authors, Stein believes and demon-
     strates that both plot and story are "antiquated narrative con-
     ventions." Summarized: <u>Dissertation Abstracts International</u>
     34A:2613-14.

7   CASH, E.A. Review of <u>Sherwood Anderson/Gertrude Stein</u>. <u>Best</u>
     <u>Sellers</u> 32 (15 March):564-65.
          "What results [from the authors' letters] is a perspective
     on the two literary figures which, because of its honesty, inti-
     macy, humor, and sometimes passion, no secondary criticism could
     hope to give."

8   CONE, EDWARD T. "The Miss Etta Cone, the Steins, and M'sieu
     Matisse." <u>American Scholar</u> 42 (Summer):441-60.
          Etta Cone sided with Leo Stein against Gertrude Stein and
     felt supplanted by Toklas. In France in 1933 Miss Cone did not
     associate with Stein and Toklas and did not see Stein in the
     thirties when Stein toured America.

9   COPELAND, CAROLYN FAUNCE. "Narrative Techniques in the Works
     of Gertrude Stein." Ph.D. dissertation, University of Iowa,
     219 pp.
          To study Stein's techniques, the use of the narrator is
     major because Stein changes her narrator to fit her style of
     experimenting. Summarized: <u>Dissertation Abstracts International</u>
     34A:5960-61. Published: 1975.4.

10   COWLEY, MALCOLM. <u>A Second Flowering: Works and Days of the</u>
     <u>Lost Generation</u>. New York: Viking Press, pp. 50, 52, 54, 56,
     62, and passim.
          Hemingway learned from Stein "a colloquial--in appearance--
     American style, full of repeated words, prepositional phrases,
     and present participles, the style in which he wrote his early
     published stories"--along with the ability to write of self, of
     the inner world.

11   ELIAS, ROBERT H. <u>"Entangling Alliances with None": An Essay</u>
     <u>on the Individual in the American Twenties</u>. New York:
     W.W. Norton & Co., pp. 194-95.
          Stein labored to achieve individuation of character in her
     writing, separating her creations from time and content. She
     paralleled Eliot in finding use for the continual present.

12   FABRÉ, MICHEL. <u>The Unfinished Quest of Richard Wright</u>.
     Translated by Isabel Barzun. New York: William Morrow & Co.,
     pp. xvi, 111, 141, 166, 192, and passim.
          Wright reviewed <u>Wars I Have Seen</u> and Stein in gratitude in-
     vited him to visit in Paris, where she helped the younger author
     to adjust to European living.

13 FITZ, L.T. "Gertrude Stein and Picasso: The Language of
    Surfaces." American Literature 45 (May):228-37.
       In Picasso, "Stein seems to be saying that . . . other
    painters used an avant-garde technique to express, however
    obliquely, something that could be expressed by any technique--
    namely, the natural world as they and everyone else thought they
    saw it. But Picasso used his unusual technique not to enhance an
    old vision of reality but to delineate a new one."

14 FOLEY, JACK. "Idem the same: a Letter to Ed Peters about
    Gertrude Stein." Open Letter, 1973, pp. 74-85.
       ". . . Tender Buttons is like a landscape into which we
    have walked for the first time. We know that the landscape has
    boundaries, that it ends, yet we are so delighted by the newness
    of its aspects--and by the capacity for discovery which that new-
    ness awakens in us--that we lose our sense of limitations."

15 FRIEDLING, SHEILA. "Problems of Perception in the Modern
    Novel: The Representation of Consciousness in Works of Henry
    James, Gertrude Stein, and William Faulkner." Ph.D. disserta-
    tion, University of Wisconsin, 694 pp.
       ". . . I discuss Three Lives to illustrate how Stein's
    representations of pure time and the durational self reflect the
    ideas of William James and Henri Bergson about time, self and
    language, especially the problematic relationship of language to
    the representation of 'asymbolic' experience or the transitive
    aspects of the stream of thought." Summarized: Dissertation
    Abstracts International 34A:3391.

16 GALLUP, DONALD. "Introducing Gertrude Stein." Widening
    Circle 1 (Fall):6-10.
       Introducing Stein for an address in Paris in 1945, Gallup
    found his task formidable but his reward--Stein's friendship and
    growing trust--quite worthwhile.

17 GARVIN, HARRY R. "The Human Mind & Tender Buttons." Widening
    Circle 1 (Fall):11-13.
       "I think all critical interpretations of Tender Buttons
    . . . should be based at least initially on the critic's feeling
    in his own consciousness while actually reading each portrait."

18 GASS, WILLIAM H. "Gertrude Stein, Geographer, I." New York
    Review of Books, 3 May, pp. 5-8.
       "The Geographical History of America is a culminating work,
    though not the outcome of [Stein's] meditations. . . . The book
    is the stylized presentation of the process of meditation itself,
    with many critical asides. In the manner of her earliest piece,
    Q.E.D., it demonstrates far more than it proves, and although it
    is in no sense a volume of philosophy (Gertrude Stein never
    'argues' anything), it is, philosophically, the most important
    of her texts." Reprinted: 1978.16.

19   _____ . "Gertrude Stein, Geographer, II." New York Review of
        Books, 17 May, pp. 25-29.
            Setting out to render life, Stein "realized that language
        itself is a complete analogue of experience because it, too, is
        made of a large but finite number of relatively fixed terms which
        are then allowed to occur in a limited number of clearly speci-
        fied relations, so that it is not the appearance of a word that
        matters but the manner of its reappearance. . . ." Reprinted:
        1978.16.

20   GEORGE, JONATHAN C. "Stein's 'A Box.'" Explicator 31
        (February):Item 42.
            "In her extraordinary prose poem, 'A Box,' Miss Gertrude
        Stein has created a cubist still life in words, using what we
        might call a 'pseudo-deductive' order which is her unique blend
        of Kantian idealism and William James' theory of consciousness."

21   GREENFELD, HOWARD. Gertrude Stein: A Biography. New York:
        Crown Books, 151 pp.
            "Her name was Gertrude Stein, and she was one of the most
        original and compelling figures in the world of art and litera-
        ture for almost half a century. Though her position in that
        world was a complex and somewhat mysterious one, she became a
        reigning empress within it."

22   GRUMBACH, DORIS. "Fine Print." New Republic 169 (8 December):
        32.
            Staying on Alone reveals Toklas's desolation and loneliness
        after Stein's death: "There are those persons who live in the
        shadow of the lives of the rich or the talented or the famous,
        who seem to be little more than efficient satellites to Stars,
        whose lives are full of quiet, unassuming devotion and service.
        Alice B. Toklas was such a woman."

23   HAAS, ROBERT BARTLETT. "A Bolt of Energy, or Why I Still
        Read Gertrude Stein." Widening Circle 1 (Fall):14-17.
            Haas wrote to Stein when he was quite young, met her in
        California in 1935, and hoped to publish her finally unpublished
        writings.

24   HARRISON, GILBERT. "A Remembrance." Widening Circle 1 (Fall):
        18-19.
            Harrison met Stein in California in 1934 and later visited
        the woman in France.

25   KIRSTEIN, LINCOLN. Elie Nadelman. New York: Eakins Press,
        pp. 19, 177, 183, 184, 190-91, and passim.
            Stein admired Nadelman's maleness and his originality and
        in return was one of the few friends of this sculptor.

26   LORD, JAMES. "Where the Pictures Were: A Memoir." <u>Prose</u>,
      no. 7 (Fall), pp. 133-87.
          Picasso arranged for Lord to meet Stein and Toklas, and the
      meeting pleased all three. Stein talked before and below her
      tableau of paintings. Lord disagreed with Stein's ideas about
      post-war soldiers. Later he visited Toklas and kept up with the
      disposal of the art collection.

27   McCAFFERY, STEVE. "Apropriopriapus: Prefatory Notes on Stein
      & the Language Hygene [<u>sic</u>] Programme." <u>White Pelican</u> 3
      (Autumn):50-60.
          "stein's body was a page of lethal vedic hymn. . . ."

28   McCAFFREY, JOHN. "'Any of Mine Without Music to Help Them':
      The Operas and Plays of Gertrude Stein." <u>Yale / Theatre</u> 4
      (Summer):27-39.
          "The existing music [scores] for the Stein plays and operas
      have sought out many directions in dealing with seemingly dense
      verbiage. Most of them have overcome apparent odds. There are
      still avenues yet to be tried with others of her plays." New
      scores can be composed, and plays can be performed without music.

29   MEYEROWITZ, PATRICIA. "Say Yes to Everything." <u>Widening
      Circle</u> 1 (Fall):20-22.
          Stein's writing is "an exploration of writing as it was
      being written. And this is how she is different from almost all
      other creative writers that there have ever been as far as I know
      it. This is what makes her one of the very few who spend their
      lives exploring as deeply as they can the very heart of what it
      is they are doing."

*30   NAZZARO, LINDA. "'A Piece of Coffee': A Stylistic Descrip-
      tion of the Work of Gertrude Stein." <u>English Review</u> 1 (1973):
      50-54.
          Cited: <u>PMLA Bibliography</u> for 1973, p. 175.

31   NICHOL, bp. "Some Beginning Writings on Gertrude Stein's
      Theories of Personality." <u>White Pelican</u> 3 (Autumn):15-23.
          Stein presented in her work aspects of personal development.

32   PERKINS, WILLIAM A. "Gertrude Stein: What Is the Question?"
      <u>Virginia Woolf Quarterly</u> 1 (Spring):85-89.
          <u>Geography and Plays</u> and <u>Lucy Church Amiably</u> reveal Stein's
      drive to private, hermetic language--despite her thirst for fame.

33   POLLARD, ARTHUR. <u>Webster's New World Companion to English and
      American Literature</u>. New York: World Publishing Co.,
      pp. 639-40.
          Stein "tried to cultivate a style akin to abstraction as
      she admired it in the painters' work, developing an approach she
      had begun at Radcliffe of experimenting with spontaneous, auto-
      matic writing."

34   REVIEW OF <u>A BOOK CONCLUDING WITH AS A WIFE HAS A COW</u>. <u>Choice</u>
      10 (October):1198.
           Long out of print and almost never discussed, here is a
      book "worthwhile for study; charming for all."

35   REVIEW OF <u>HOW TO WRITE</u>. <u>Choice</u> 10 (October):1199.
           Newly available is this "most hermetic of Stein's self-
      exegetical works."

36   REVIEW OF <u>MATISSE PICASSO AND GERTRUDE STEIN</u>. <u>Choice</u> 9
      (February):1593.
           These pieces "are Stein's verbal equivalent of the Rorschach
      method--her apologists and her enemies disagree not only about
      the value of these stories in the Stein canon, but also, bluntly,
      about their subject matter."

37   REVIEW OF <u>SHERWOOD ANDERSON/GERTRUDE STEIN</u>. <u>Virginia Quarterly
      Review</u> 49 (Spring):lxxvi.
           "There are no great literary revelations in these letters,
      but there is an added view of the subjects."

38   REVIEW OF <u>SHERWOOD ANDERSON/GERTRUDE STEIN</u>. <u>Choice</u> 10 (May):
      452.
           "Not likely to become a legendary correspondence, it is
      still an illuminating one, of multiple appeal and use, a book
      for all libraries."

39   REVIEW OF <u>STAYING ON ALONE</u>. <u>Kirkus Reviews</u> 41 (1 October):
      1148.
           Toklas's letters may present an unfortunately tedious por-
      trait of Stein's companion.

40   REVIEW OF <u>STAYING ON ALONE</u>. <u>Publishers' Weekly</u> 204
      (22 October):110.
           Toklas's letters qualify for "that overused superlative,
      'major literary event. . . .' Miss Toklas emerges as a much
      more interesting person in her own right than is commonly
      supposed. . . ."

41   ROGERS, W.G. <u>Gertrude Stein Is Gertrude Stein Is Gertrude
      Stein</u>. New York: Thomas Y. Crowell Co., 237 pp.
           Stein "was laughed at madly and wildly praised. She was
      cheered for revitalizing English and reviled for abusing it. Her
      writing was supposedly incomprehensible yet it was generally com-
      prehended. . . . She was a dreamer and a visionary yet she
      acquired a fortune. She was unknown one day and a celebrity
      the day after. She came back to the starting line and was the
      first over the finish line."

42   _____. "I Remember Gertrude." <u>Widening Circle</u> 1 (Fall):
      23-24, 30.

"I first knew Gertrude when I was not yet of voting age, when I had written only some bumbling verses . . . when I had never heard of Gertrude Stein. So I first met the woman, friendly, helpful, genial, putting herself out at great pains to be of service. I last saw her in Bilignin just before the outbreak of World War II."

43   ROSE, Sir FRANCIS. "A Gift of Roses." Widening Circle 1 (Fall):25-27.
     Rose met Stein in Paris in the late 1920s and enjoyed seeing his paintings that she had collected. Later visits cemented the friendship.

44   SOLOKOFF, ALICE HUNT. Hadley: The First Mrs. Hemingway. New York: Dodd, Mead & Co., pp. 41, 50, 61, 70, 79, 91.
     Mrs. Hemingway did not get to enjoy Stein, as Toklas usually took over female-female conversations. Stein's discovery that Hemingway feared fatherhood amused her but later she attended the christening of Hemingway's first child. Later, Hadley lived alone near the Stein apartment.

45   SPRIGGE, ELIZABETH. "To Begin with Beginning." Widening Circle 1 (Fall):28-30.
     Being involved in a production of one of Stein's plays led to Toklas's inviting Sprigge to write a life of Stein.

46   STEWART, ALLEGRA. "Flat Land as Explanation." Widening Circle 1 (Fall):31-33, 22.
     "A shrewd and for the most part objective observer of national character, Gertrude Stein was well aware that it is not only the flatness of American land that is important in the twentieth century." She appreciated the "flattening" effect of awareness of technology.

47   SUTTON, WALTER. American Free Verse: The Modern Revolution in Poetry. New York: New Directions, pp. 43, 144, 180, 197, 203.
     Stein's encouragement of modernist art in general and her prose experiments place her in the body of influences on free verse.

48   SUTTON, WILLIAM A. "All Life Is Important." Widening Circle 1 (Fall):36-37.
     Sutton met Stein in 1946 and can believe that she will "be studied as one who grasped in literature and language the full idea of experimentation, carrying on the ideas of the nineteenth century (and others of centuries before). When she wrote, she remembered that William James had insisted that nothing is proved."

49 SWARTZ, SHIRLEY. "Between Autobiographies: Gertrude Stein
    and the Problem of Audience." White Pelican 3 (Autumn):40-47.
        The reaction to The Autobiography of Alice B. Toklas caused
    Stein to write Everybody's Autobiography, in which "the narration
    of events and of Stein's musings on audiences and identity have
    the same ontological status. . . ."

50 TAYLOR, F. SCOTT. "By Design." White Pelican 3 (Autumn):
    34-37.
        "The first modern thing to cross the Atlantic was Gertrude
    Stein. By design."

51 WALKER, CHERYL LAWSON. "The Women's Tradition in American
    Poetry." Ph.D. dissertation, Brandeis University, 323 pp.
        Stein remains outside the homogenous tradition of poetry
    by women, along with Marianne Moore and Amy Lowell. Summarized:
    Dissertation Abstracts International 34A:4294-95.

52 WATSON, SHEILA. "Gertrude Stein: The Style is the Machine."
    White Pelican 3 (Autumn):6-14.
        Wyndham Lewis criticized Stein's mindless, unintellectual
    writing.

53 WILSON, ELLEN. They Named Me Gertrude Stein. New York:
    Farrar, Straus & Giroux, 134 pp.
        From overweight adolescent girl to world-famous author and
    personality, Stein always found life interesting. Toklas contrib-
    uted the love and stability necessary to Stein's literary
    creativity.

54 ZIEGLER, MARY PRADT. Review of Staying on Alone. Library
    Journal 98 (15 November):3379.
        "The memory of Stein is pervasive--in the letters dealing
    with the posthumous publication and criticism of Stein's work
    and the affectionate notes to friends. . . ."

1974

1   ARMATAGE, ELIZABETH KAY. "The Mother of Us All: The Woman in
    the Writings of Gertrude Stein." Ph.D. dissertation, Univer-
    sity of Toronto.
        "This dissertation argues that although shifts in her atti-
    tude toward women occurred regularly throughout [Stein's] writing
    career, the nature of women and relationships between men and
    women--at times presented in a specifically political context--
    were continuing and predominant in the writings of Gertrude
    Stein." Summarized: Dissertation Abstracts International 38A:
    6116.

2   BEER, PATRICIA. "At the Court of Queen Gertrude." <u>Times</u>
     <u>Literary Supplement</u>, 8 November, p. 1252.
          <u>Reflections on the Atomic Bomb</u> and <u>How Writing Is Written</u>--
     Stein's last uncollected writings--reveal that "nobody could dis-
     pute Gertrude Stein's perceptiveness. At a time when most people
     were content with prose and poetry as they were inherited from
     the nineteenth century, she saw that changes had to be made, and
     her theories for bringing about the necessary changes had stature,
     nobility even. It is her practice that so often betrays her."
     In <u>Staying on Alone</u> Toklas has dropped the reality of living with
     Stein in favor of good memories.

3   BOWERING, GEORGE. "That was Ida said Miss Stein." <u>Open</u>
     <u>Letter</u> 8 (1974):37-47.
          With <u>Ida</u>, "there is no final real identity at the end of
     the rainbow, & the end of the rainbow anyway continues receding
     over yonder hills the self walks toward. No resolution, no solu-
     tion, the story of Ida is not over till the <u>reader</u> dies."

4   CANNELL, KATHLEEN. "Alice Alone: A Voice Not an Echo."
     <u>Christian Science Monitor</u>, 23 January, sec. F, p. 5.
          Cannell, who long knew Stein and Toklas in Paris, found
     Toklas's letters in <u>Staying on Alone</u> revelatory of art and lit-
     erature and Toklas's existence from 1946 to 1966.

5   CARGAS, HARRY JAMES. Review of <u>Gertrude Stein's America</u>.
     <u>Catholic Library World</u> 46 (September):86.
          "It would fare better reprinted for the [U.S.A.] bicenten-
     nial in 1976. No great contribution to understanding here."

6   COOPER, DAVID D. "Gertrude Stein's 'Magnificent Asparagus':
     Horizontal Vision and Unmeaning in 'Tender Buttons.'" <u>Modern</u>
     <u>Fiction Studies</u> 20 (Autumn):337-49.
          <u>Tender Buttons</u> is "surely chaotic. But, oddly enough, it
     is the point. <u>Chaos is the point</u>. Strange as it may seem, the
     horizontal visionary <u>begins</u> with the assumption that there is
     order in the world, whereas the self-expressionist and vertical
     visionary proceed from the rock-bottom premise that, no, the
     world begins with chaos."

7   DICK, KAY. "Alice in lonelyland." <u>Spectator</u> 232 (13 April):
     453-54.
          <u>Staying on Alone</u> will as letters be of some use to histori-
     ans and biographers. The letters "let out pitiful echoes of
     regret and loss, not only for Gertrude's positive life, but for
     those thirty-eight years of Alice's reduced individuality."

8   FAŸ, BERNARD. <u>De la prison de ce monde</u>. [Paris]: Librairie
     Plon, p. 95.
          While imprisoned for World War II activities in France,
     Faÿ enjoyed thinking of his friendship with Stein.

9   GEDDES, VIRGIL. "Leo and Gertrude Stein." Lost Generation
      Journal 2 (Winter):16-17.
          "Gertrude Stein spent most of her life in the kindergarten
      of life learning the alphabet. Once she mastered that, her self-
      glorified self raised her ego to the nth degree and she straight
      forward became, in her own mind, a genius."

*10   GIACOMELLI, ELOAH F. "Gertrude Stein." O Estado de São Paulo,
      Supplemento Literário 15 (September):1.
          Cited: PMLA Bibliography (1974):189.

11   GINSBERG, ALLEN. Allen Verbatim: Lectures on Poetry, Poli-
      tics, and Consciousness. Edited by Gordon All. New York:
      McGraw-Hill Book Co., pp. 32, 145, 157-59.
          Kerouac did not learn nonrevision from Stein, but their
      literary visions are similar. The Making of Americans is "a
      thousand pages of insane consciousness babble. . . . One of the
      great prose masterpieces of the century. . . . [Stein] was
      interested in modalities of consciousness, and she was interested
      in art as articulation of different modalities of consciousness,
      and she was interested in prose composition as a form of medita-
      tion, like yoga."

12   GOLD, ARTHUR, and FIZDALE, ROBERT. "How Famous People Cook."
      Vogue 163 (February):132-33.
          In Staying on Alone, "the letters, so womanly and wise,
      written by Miss Toklas between the ages of sixty-nine and eighty-
      nine, are a charming and poignant record of the last twenty years
      of her life. As she herself was apt to say about books she ad-
      mired, they 'hold the attention.'"

13   HAYNES, MURIEL. "After Gertrude." Ms 2 (March):32.
          Staying on Alone reveals that Toklas's talent, unlike
      Stein's, was for "loving friendship": "She knew, or met, it
      seems, everybody, and the names that crowd her letters in witty
      sketches and sometimes ascerbic appraisal, are part of the his-
      tory of music, painting, and literature in the 20th century."

14   HINDUS, MILTON. "Ethnicity and Sexuality in Gertrude Stein."
      Midstream 20 (January):69-76.
          Remembering that Stein was both Jewish and lesbian aids in
      understanding the private meanings of her published works.

15   HORTON, ROD W., and EDWARDS, HERBERT W. Backgrounds of Amer-
      ican Literary Thought. 3d ed. Englewood Cliffs, N.J.:
      Prentice-Hall Co., pp. 329, 363.
          "The great forerunner of the Freudian movement in American
      literature is Gertrude Stein," for before 1900 she was experiment-
      ing with the psychology of writing.

16 HOWITT, WAYNE ANDREW. "Reading as a Creative Effort: A Study Utilizing Gertrude Stein's Tender Buttons." Ph.D. dissertation, State University of New York at Buffalo, 158 pp.
"It is believed that a reader adds meaning to a piece of writing in as fundamental a way as the author. The result is a creative partnership in which the author supplies the materials which the reader uses to assemble meaning. Such a conception of criticism is shown to complement the psychoanalytic and structural approaches." Summarized: Dissertation Abstracts International 35A:4479.

17 JEFFERSON, MARGO. "Passionate Friend." Newsweek 83 (7 January):67.
Staying on Alone reveals of Stein and Toklas that "in the lexicon of literary affairs--D.H. and Frieda Lawrence, Zelda and Scott Fitzgerald, Leonard and Virginia Woolf--theirs is one of the few marked both by passion and unceasing friendship."

18 JOHNSON, MANLY. "Stein Arose." Lost Generation Journal 2 (Winter):3-7.
Whatever Stein wrote, her subject was always writing itself: "That attracts us today because of our sense that we know too much of what is happening and have seen too much of the world much photographed. Her writing releases us from the tyranny of data. It offers us, instead, the incandescence of the creative process in which we can participate."

*19 KANAZEKI, HISAO. "Gertrude Stein and the Atomic Bomb." Rising Generation 120 (1974):418-19.
Cited: American Literary Scholarship for 1974, p. 455.

20 KIRK, H.L. Pablo Casals: A Biography. New York: Rinehart & Winston, pp. 164, 195.
Casals heard of Gertrude Stein from her older relatives as a bored medical student and "an adequate pianist." Later he visited Leo and Gertrude Stein in Paris and remembered Gertrude "always reading in the same chair."

21 KLAICH, DOLORES. Woman + Woman: Attitudes Towards Lesbianism. New York: Simon & Schuster, pp. 80, 167, 170, 180-81, 202-14, 215, 230-31.
Stein and Toklas kept their lesbianism private, unlike the flamboyant lesbians of Paris. Only after Toklas's death did open discussion of the women's relationship occur. The reticence of Stein toward open sexuality contributes to the obscurity of her writing, often making her "erotic love poetry . . . a mixture of fun and her famous juggling of words. It is also sometimes just plain coy and silly."

22 KNAPIK, HAROLD L. "With Alice B. Toklas." Gourmet, March, pp. 35-36, 90, 92-93.

Knapik knew Toklas in Paris after 1948 and in 1953 went
with her to Spain: "For one who values conversation, being with
Alice was a luxury."

*23   KONO, YOTARO. Gertrude Stein No Kozo. Sagamihara, Japan:
       Taiyosha, 316 pp.
       Cited: MHRA Bibliography for 1974, p. 839.

24   LAMBERT, GILBERT. "A Life after Death." Books & Bookmen 19
      (April):12-13.
           Staying on Alone reveals Toklas as "one of the great liter-
      ary wives of the period, a combination of housekeeper, cook,
      typist, critic, social secretary and gossipmonger."

25   LOWENKRON, DAVID. "The Linguistic World of Melanctha." Lost
      Generation Journal 2 (Winter):8-11.
           In "Melanctha," Stein uses ambiguous pronominal references,
      repetitions, missing transitions, and concrete and abstract sym-
      bols; yet "it is Gertrude Stein's voice that runs through the
      inky world of Melanctha Herbert."

26   MELLOW, JAMES R. Charmed Circle: Gertrude Stein & Company.
      New York: Praeger Publishers, 528 pp.
           "Out of curiosity, plain affection, and an extremely shrewd
      understanding of how to conduct a career in the modern world,
      Gertrude cultivated the young in every generation. At the be-
      ginning of the century, she promoted the vanguard artists of
      Paris; in the twenties, she took on young writers, journalists,
      publicists, and the editors of the little magazines . . . ; in
      the thirties, she sought out a new crop of admirers by lecturing
      college and prep-school students during a much-publicized Amer-
      ican tour; in the forties, she adopted, wholesale, the American
      GIs of World War II--thus providing herself with a perennial
      audience. It was a splendid strategy."

27   _____. "Gertrude Stein Rediscovers America." Columbia Forum
      3 (Winter):20-29.
           Always excited on her American tour, Stein was a phenomenon
      for the press more than an author with ideas.

28   PEAVY, LINDA. "A Look at Stein's Straight-Forward Writing."
      Lost Generation Journal 2 (Winter):34-35.
           The simpler narration in the Redfern section of The Making
      of Americans may have created "a masterpiece in its own right."

29   POWELL, LAWRENCE CLARK. "A Valentine to Gertrude Stein."
      Westways 66 (February):18-22, 68.
           California has honored Stein--"our Oakland girl who made
      good"--with collections and exhibits of her works.

30   RATHER, LOIS. <u>Gertrude Stein and California</u>. Oakland, Cal.:
      Rather Press, 106 pp.
         Stein and Toklas were children in California and returned
      on Stein's American lecture tour.

31   REVIEW OF <u>REFLECTIONS ON THE ATOMIC BOMB</u>. <u>Choice</u> 11 (April):
      262.
         Stein's work on the bomb is part of a new collection of
      hitherto uncollected writings from 1913 through 1946 that repre-
      sent her periods, styles, and genres.

32   REVIEW OF <u>STAYING ON ALONE</u>. <u>Choice</u> 11 (March):95.
         ". . . Toklas reveals in these letters great intelligence
      and ready wit. She also gives a fascinating glimpse into the
      literary and artistic life of post-war Paris. . . ."

33   REVIEW OF <u>STAYING ON ALONE</u>. <u>Booklist</u> 70 (15 February):628-29.
         "In reflecting on Parisian life with Gertrude Stein and in
      the years alone Toklas reveals herself a competent and devoted
      companion."

34   ROBINSON, ELEANOR. "Gertrude Stein, Cubist Teacher." <u>Lost
      Generation Journal</u> 2 (Winter):12-15.
         "Gertrude Stein understood the cubist's desire to work as
      nature works, to create rather than represent the works of nature
      or man."

35   SCHMITZ, NEIL. "Because and Become." <u>Partisan Review</u> 41
      (Summer):283-89.
         As revealed in <u>The Geographical History of America</u>,
      Gertrude Stein through language "did find, after all, an identity
      that preserved her from the disenchantment and isolation of her
      American compatriots in Europe."

36   _____. "Gertrude Stein as Post-Modernist: The Rhetoric of
      <u>Tender Buttons</u>." <u>Journal of Modern Literature</u> 3 (July):
      1203-18.
         Important to post-modern authors as Stein may be, after
      <u>Tender Buttons</u> "she ceased to ask the technical questions about
      story and character so desperately current in modern writing."
      Yet Barthelme and Brautigan, among others, learned from her.

37   SECREST, MERYLE. <u>Between Me and Life: A Biography of Romaine
      Brooks</u>. New York: Doubleday & Co., pp. 216, 314, 325, 327-
      28, and passim.
         Never one of Stein's salon group, Brooks was "on excellent
      terms with that lady and her companion, Alice B. Toklas." The
      acquaintance was through Natalie Barney.

38   SHAW, SHARON. "Gertrude Stein and Henry James: The Differ-
      ence Between Accidence and Coincidence." <u>Pembroke Magazine</u>
      5 (1974):95-101.

Stein and James in different ways are "bracketing experience in order to better understand it." James succeeds where
Stein fails--in remembering to "reassimilate the bracketed or
realized experience into the whole."

39   SHERE, CHARLES. "Stein--The Oakland Years." Oakland Tribune,
      27 January, sec. EN, pp. 27, 29.
          "The Young Gertrude Stein spent her formative years here,
      from first grade through high school, and it can fairly be said
      that the personality which stamps her writing was determined by
      her childhood."

40   SIMON, LINDA, ed. Gertrude Stein: A Composite Portrait.
      New York: Avon Books, 192 pp.
          Reprint of various introductions to Stein's works and
      1965.16; 1936.27; 1965.2; 1924.1; 1964.4; 1963.60; 1951.9;
      1965.18; 1970.1; 1966.18; 1961.12; 1970.15; 1947.34.

41   SOLOMON, ALBERT J. Review of Staying on Alone. Best Sellers
      33 (15 March):546.
          ". . . only a pencil sketch of Alice, roughly drawn (and
      mostly by the reader)."

42   STEINER, WENDY LOIS. "Gertrude Stein's Portrait Form."
      Ph.D. dissertation, Yale University, 259 pp.
          Study of Stein's portraits in literary form reveals the
      development of the writer's criteria for literature and her
      application of those criteria to a genre. Summarized: Disserta-
      tion Abstracts International 36A:331-32. Published: 1978.34.

43   STELOFF, FRANCES. "The Making of an American Visit: Gertrude
      Stein." Confrontation 8 (Spring):9-17.
          Steloff made sure to meet Stein on her lecture tour, for
      the Gotham Book Mart had stocked her works for years. Reprinted:
      1975.29.

44   SUTHERLAND, DONALD. "The Pleasures of Gertrude Stein." New
      York Review of Books, 30 May, pp. 28-30.
          Reflections on the Atomic Bomb and How Writing is Written
      are welcome collections of Stein materials, illustrating her mind
      joining the object in narration.

45   _____. "A Wicked Alice in Wonderland." Denver Quarterly 9
      (Spring):80-83.
          Staying on Alone is "a volume of letters so lively and so
      good they may well rank . . . with those of Madame de Sévigné.
      I think they do, and that there is even something of the Sévigné
      manner in them, the affection, the spiritedness, and even a
      courtliness."

46   THOMSON, VIRGIL. "Wickedly Wonderful Widow." <u>New York Review</u>
      <u>of Books</u>, 7 March, pp. 12-15.
          "No bouquet of letters by Alice Toklas could fail the reader;
      she was such a vivid character, vivid and voluble. So voluble in-
      deed that after thirty-eight years with Gertrude Stein, for Toklas
      a time of relative reticence, during the next twenty she fulfilled
      herself in words, both spoken words and epistolary [as in <u>Staying</u>
      <u>on Alone</u>], to a degree hardly less than Stein herself had done."

47   THURMAN, JUDITH. "A Rose Is a Rose Is a Rose Is a Rose:
      Gertrude Stein." <u>Ms</u> 2 (February):54-57, 93-95.
          Toklas's love released Stein to freedom to write creatively
      and fully. The women were neutral to sexual and world politics
      but examples of female success.

48   VAN VECHTEN, CARL. "More Laurels for Our Gertrude."
      <u>Confrontation</u> 8 (Spring):18-19.
          Reprint of 1964.11.

49   WHITE, WILLIAM. Review of <u>How Writing Is Written</u>. <u>Library</u>
      <u>Journal</u> 99 (1 May):1305.
          "The later essays . . . are more conventional and easier
      to decipher; many readers will find several of the first ones
      meaningless or impossible to understand. Stein is too important
      and influential to dismiss, so major libraries must have this
      volume."

50   _____. Review of <u>Reflections on the Atomic Bomb</u>. <u>Library</u>
      <u>Journal</u> 99 (1 April):1039.
          "Some readers will find most of these newly found writings
      gibberish; to others they will be absolutely indispensable, espe-
      cially for an understanding of one of the most important influ-
      ences on American literature and art in this century."

51   WICKES, GEORGE. "Who Really Wrote <u>The Autobiography of Alice</u>
      <u>B. Toklas</u>?" <u>Lost Generation Journal</u> 2 (Winter):38, 37.
          Toklas "was gracious enough to be amused at [Wickes']
      proposal that she write the autobiography of Gertrude Stein,
      but she never took it seriously." Yet in <u>What Is Remembered</u>
      Toklas did just what Wickes had suggested.

52   WILSON, ROBERT A. <u>Gertrude Stein: A Bibliography</u>. New York:
      Phoenix Bookshop, 227 pp.
          Primary bibliography.

53   WINANT, FRAN, and ULMSCHNEIDER, LORETTA. "Gertrude Stein."
      In <u>Women Remembered: A Collection of Biographies</u>. Edited by
      Nancy Myron and Charlotte Bunch. Baltimore: Diana Press,
      pp. 71-75.
          Stein's will left Toklas in a degrading position, dependent
      on lawyers and Stein's relatives for the income that Stein

intended for Toklas. Stein arranged this will to avoid the scandal of directly leaving her estate to Toklas.

54　WOOD, DELORES. "Fine Recipes of Alice Toklas Are for Imaginative Cook." Lost Generation Journal 2 (Winter):31.
　　　"A few hours with The Alice B. Toklas Cookbook will intrigue most readers who whet appetites on exotic foods and off beat history. Reading should not be fattening."

55　WOOD, TOM. "The Rose Was Not a Shrinking Violet." Lost Generation Journal 2 (Winter):18-21.
　　　"If we use Miss Stein as a model, no author should be embarrassed to publish his own works, to praise them in public or private, or to button-hole anyone who might help the cause of advancing the fame-hungry writer."

56　WYNDHAM, FRANCIS. "H. de Dactyl." New Statesman 87 (1 March):298-300.
　　　The letters in Staying on Alone, "apart from their intrinsic interest to admirers of the extraordinary Miss Stein, . . . are altogether admirable in themselves: gallant, honest, articulate and extremely amusing."

57　WYSOR, BETTIE. The Lesbian Myth. New York: Random House, pp. 250-52.
　　　Fernhurst and Q.E.D., published after Stein's death, are among the early works that "represent the beginning of her life-long probing of human emotional psychology."

58　ZINNES, HARRIET. "Lively Syndicate of Modernism." Nation 218 (18 May):631-32, 634.
　　　"The letters of Staying on Alone are lively. They are not only gossipy but reveal a woman whose intelligence and knowledge of art and literature, whose charm on her own account, wooed the old friends of Stein to her door and brought new friends to her." In Reflections on the Atomic Bomb, there is "a good place to begin to get a quick feeling for Stein," despite Stein's conservative politics.

1975

1　ALKON, PAUL K. "Visual Rhetoric in The Autobiography of Alice B. Toklas." Critical Inquiry 1 (June):849-81.
　　　In The Autobiography of Alice B. Toklas, "there is no mere anecdote, no merely photographic naturalism. Surface reality is transformed, not transcribed. . . . And the book is indeed composed of different pieces of different pictures which finally do prevent us from trying only to imagine what the models really looked like or said, and which force us to concentrate instead on those truths communicated by the images before us."

2   BONEY, ELAINE E. Review of <u>How to Write</u>. <u>Virginia Woolf</u>
    <u>Quarterly</u> 2 (Winter-Spring):156.
        Despite Stein's short-circuiting style, in <u>How to Write</u> one
finds humor and delightful sounds.

3   _____. Review of <u>The Making of Americans</u>. <u>Virginia Woolf</u>
    <u>Quarterly</u> 2 (Winter-Spring):156-58.
        "Although the difficulty of style and material insure that
this work will never be a best-seller, its inquiry into the nature
of human character reveals insights which are rewarding for the
serious reader and assure this work a permanent place in American
literature."

4   COPELAND, CAROLYN FAUNCE. <u>Language & Time & Gertrude Stein</u>.
    Iowa City: University of Iowa Press, 182 pp.
        Publication of 1973.9.

5   FENDELMAN, EARL. "Happy Birthday, Gertrude Stein."
    <u>American Quarterly</u> 27 (March):99-107.
        The many publications in Stein's centennial have "been a
happy birthday for Gertrude Stein. Little by little the great
adventure she undertook when she chose art as a life as well as
an occupation is beginning to emerge from under the bunting where
it has been hidden. We are beginning to see that the only real
story of Gertrude Stein is that of her lifelong endeavor to see
things clearly. . . ."

6   FIFER, ELIZABETH. "Put the Language in the Waist: Stein's
    Critique of Women in <u>Geography and Plays</u>." <u>University of</u>
    <u>Michigan Papers in Women's Studies</u> 2 (September):96-102.
        In some of her plays Stein "draws an unusually clear and
representational outline of her feminist critique. Her map of
romantic love, social interaction, aggression versus dependency-
submission, education and models, marriage, narcissism and identity, is composed entirely of conversations overheard."

7   FORD, HUGH. <u>Published in Paris: American and British Writers,</u>
    <u>Printers, and Publishers in Paris, 1920-1930</u>. Foreword by
    Janet Flanner. New York: Macmillan Co., pp. 10, 28, 55-56,
    60, 73, and passim.
        The Plain Edition was to ease Stein's publication problems.
Stein sold a Picasso painting to pay for her project but found
out the difficulties of self-publishing. After the success of
her <u>Autobiography</u>, she had few problems finding publishers.

8   FREILING, KENNETH. "The Becoming of Gertrude Stein's <u>The</u>
    <u>Making of Americans</u>." In <u>The Twenties: Fiction, Poetry,</u>
    <u>Drama</u>. Edited by Warren French. DeLand, Fla.: Everett/
    Edwards, pp. 157-70.
        <u>The Making of Americans</u> fits into the 1920s, for in it,
"Stein faced the impending wasteland of her chosen subject

material and the void of any audience, then attempted aestheti-
cally to transcend the dreary, banal history of immigrant families in America by developing a processual style increasingly
concerned with the form of the writer's consciousness and with
the medium's gradual rarefication into a non-representational
rhythmic 'becoming.'"

9   GOLDSTONE, RICHARD H. Thornton Wilder: An Intimate Portrait.
    New York: Saturday Review Press, E.P. Dutton & Co., pp. 102,
    103, 104-5, 108, and passim.
        Stein was less influence than catalyst on Wilder, having
    demonstrated story without plot and action. She sought to voice
    life's ritual and formed Wilder's determination to write drama.

10 GOULD, JEAN. Amy: The World of Amy Lowell and the Imagist
    Movement. New York: Dodd, Mead & Co., pp. 6-7, 134, 135,
    164, 191-96, 219, 240, 304.
        Perhaps Lowell and Stein were influenced astrologically by
    the nearness of their births. They were alike in looks, sexual
    preferences, and ego; had they met, they would not have gotten
    on well: "But both, in their separate ways, contributed to the
    freedom of modern American literature, and, by the lives they
    led, to the liberation of women, lesbian or otherwise, the world
    over."

11 HOBHOUSE, JANET. Everybody Who Was Anybody: A Biography of
    Gertrude Stein. New York: G.P. Putnam's Sons, 244 pp.
        Stein became a legend by the time of her death. Her home
    was a landmark in Paris. She was a fascinating personality and
    a quite serious writer.

12 KELLNER, BRUCE. "Ellen Glasgow and Gertrude Stein." Ellen
    Glasgow Newsletter 2 (1975):13-16.
        Glasgow and Stein met twice, expressed friendship, and
    probably never read or understood each other's works.

13 KENNER, HUGH. A Homemade World: The American Modernist
    Writers. New York: Alfred A. Knopf, pp. 18, 43, 45, 121-22,
    127, 134, 144.
        Stein was "the most programmatic of expatriates and the
    most stubborn," especially about her confessed obsession with
    the United States.

14 KOSTELANETZ, RICHARD. "Gertrude Stein: The New Literature."
    Hollins Critic 12 (June):1-15.
        "Though her work as a whole is uneven and repetitious, no
    other twentieth-century American author has had as much influence
    as Stein; and none influenced his or her successors in as many
    ways." Her influence continues through her own works and those
    of her pupils in writing.

15   LEWIS, R.W.B. Edith Wharton: A Biography. New York:
      Harper & Row, p. 400.
          "Neither Gertrude Stein nor her brother nor her companion
      ever came to know Edith Wharton, or to be a member of the inter-
      national assortment of poets and novelists, painters, playwrights,
      and socialites that flowed through 53 rue de Varenne. The two
      rich human and artistic Paris worlds of these two expatriate
      American writers astonishingly failed to overlap. . . ."

16   LODGE, DAVID. "Metaphor and Metonymy in Modern Fiction."
      Critical Inquiry 17 (Spring):83-86.
          Tender Buttons and The Making of Americans are modernist
      documents that render elusive "existence." Stein's repetition,
      itself modernist, influenced Hemingway's desire to be both modern-
      ist and realist.

17   McCONNELL, FRANK D. "Uncle Tom & the Avant-Garde." Massachu-
      setts Review 16 (Autumn):741-43.
          In "Melanctha," Stein may have discovered rhythms of prose
      and thought, but she is racist toward Negroes.

18   McMILLAN, DOUGALD. transition: The History of a Literary Era,
      1927-1938. New York: George Braziller, pp. 16, 18, 39, 45,
      48, and passim.
          "Unquestionably Miss Stein shared with Jolas and the other
      writers of transition fundamental assumptions which separate them
      from most of their contemporaries. Her association with the mag-
      azine, however, was based on a wide variety of personal and his-
      torical considerations which have suggested a closer theoretical
      relationship than actually existed."

19   PADGETTE, PAUL. "Sculpture Became Her Language." Lost Gener-
      ation Journal 3 (Fall);20-23.
          Annette Rosenshine, childhood friend of Alice B. Toklas,
      met Stein in Paris in 1907 and corresponded with her thereafter.

20   RULE, JANE. Lesbian Images. New York: Doubleday & Co.,
      pp. 62-73, 87, 154, 155.
          Q.E.D. is "probably the only book about lesbian relation-
      ship which confronts its characters with the raw war between
      desire and morality and reveals the psychological geometry of
      the human heart without false romanticizing or easy judgment."

21   SCHOONOVER, DAVID EUGENE. "The Long Way Home: American Lit-
      erary Expatriates in Paris, 1919-1929." Ph.D. dissertation,
      Princeton University, 310 pp.
          "Chapter One demonstrates how Gertrude Stein's long resi-
      dence in Paris and her early interest in modern art and major
      artists allowed her to bridge expatriate generations as well as
      artistic and literary circles, so that by 1919 she had become an
      arbiter of practice and taste through her salon. . . ." Summa-
      rized: Dissertation Abstracts International 37A:1556.

22   SMOLLER, SANFORD J. Adrift Among Geniuses: Robert McAlmon--
      Writer and Publisher of the Twenties. University Park:
      Pennsylvania State University Press, pp. 1, 6, 39-40, 49,
      72, and passim.
            McAlmon met Stein in 1923 and resisted becoming one of her
      disciples. Troubles over publication of The Making of Americans
      caused bitterness, never totally healed.

23   SOMERS, PAUL, Jr. "Sherwood Anderson Introduces His Friend
      Ernest Hemingway." Lost Generation Journal 3 (Fall):24-26.
            Anderson arranged for Hemingway to meet Stein, Lewis
      Galantière, and Joyce in Paris.

24   SORRELL, WALTER. Three Women: Lives of Sex and Genius.
      Indianapolis: Bobbs-Merrill Co., pp. 71-128.
            Stein "became a focal point for some of the great minds and
      artistic rebels of her time." Perhaps there is some meaning be-
      hind the protective armor Stein built around herself--some mean-
      ing to the aggressiveness and the magic ability to touch others'
      lives.

25   SPACKS, PATRICIA MEYER. The Female Imagination. New York:
      Alfred A. Knopf, pp. 282-83, 284, 285.
            Stein eschewed passion in her writing in favor of craft,
      dominating the world instead of reproducing it: ". . . she pre-
      serves her freedom by severing herself from most aspects of
      'normal' feminine experience."

26   SPENCER, BENJAMIN T. "Gertrude Stein: Non-Expatriate." In
      Literature and Ideas in America: Essays in Memory of Harry
      Hayden Clark. Edited by Robert Falk. Athens: Ohio Univer-
      sity Press, pp. 204-27.
            Stein avoided "a modish immersion in the expatriate temper
      during her decades abroad. Incisively and persistently probing
      the phenomena of American history and experience, she fashioned
      an organically national literary style and aesthetics the perva-
      sive influence of which on her country's literature is a matter
      of record."

27   SPRINGER, MARY DOYLE. Forms of the Modern Novella. Chicago:
      University of Chicago Press, pp. 102, 117-25.
            Stein is one of the modern masters of "the cumulative
      effect." "Melanctha" is a study of degeneration in a character
      who cannot understand the constraints imposed on her.

28   STEINER, WENDY. "The Steinian Portrait." Yale University
      Library Gazette 50 (July):30-40.
            Stein's early portraits were typologizing and repetitive.
      Next came portraits that presented subjects as data. Third were
      portraits in which subjects came to imitate objects.

29   STELOFF, FRANCES. "In Touch with Genius: Gertrude Stein."
     Journal of Modern Literature 4 (April):795-99.
          Reprint of 1974.43.

30   WALKER, JAYNE LEE. "Gertrude Stein and Her Objects: From
     'Melanctha' to Tender Buttons." Ph.D. dissertation, Univer-
     sity of California, 277 pp.
          "By approaching Stein's text in the context of painting,
     this study attempts to clarify the aesthetic and epistemological
     premises underlying Stein's new techniques of representation, in
     order to achieve a better understanding of the texts themselves."
     Summarized: Dissertation Abstracts International 37A:4340-41.

31   WASSERSTROM, WILLIAM. "The Sursymamericubealism of Gertrude
     Stein." Twentieth Century Literature 21 (February):90-106.
          Stein added her voice to current ideas of modernism, making
     herself a "phenomenal figure in any history of modernist thought:
     "A thaumaturge of wondrous invention, she concentrated on, im-
     mersed herself in and served as midwife to that exuberant force
     enclosed inside the private parts of speech."

32   WATSON, SHEILA. "Gertrude Stein: The Style is the Machine."
     Open Letter 3d ser. 1 (1975):167-78.
          Stein "has a robust intelligence, but when she lapses into
     the role and mental habits of childhood or into the illiterations
     of a Malanctha or Anna she gives to the life to which she condes-
     cends her own mechanical bias and destroys its reality."

33   WOOD, CARL. "Continuity of Romantic Irony: Stein's Homage to
     Laforgue in Three Lives." Comparative Literature Studies 12
     (June):147-58.
          In Three Lives, Stein demonstrates Laforgue's idea of the
     writer and the dilemma of modern life.

34   ZDERAD, JOSEF. "Dear Gertrude Dear: A Letter to Miss Gertrude
     Stein." Ohio Review 16 (Spring):32-34.
          "Thank you dear dear Gertrude dear Gertrude and forgive me
     please for being so slow so late so very late to see you and to
     tell you."

1976

*1   BACHMANN, JAKOB. "Ideal einer Generation: Gertrude Stein,
     'Paris Frankreich.'" Neue Zürcher Zeitung, 10-11 January,
     p. 48.
          Cited: MHRA Bibliography for 1976, p. 784.

2   BAKER, WILLIAM. "Stein Put Down Hecklers after University
     Lecture." Lost Generation Journal 4 (Winter):24, 30-31.
          Stein had no troubles with her hecklers at Oxford and
     Cambridge.

3   BERGMANN, HARRIET FRIEDMAN. "Gertrude Stein: Identity, Event and Time." Ph.D. dissertation, State University of New York at Albany, 129 pp.

       Stein's "meditations on the philosophical abstractions identity, time and event produced work in the three modes in which she wrote: the straightforward essay, the philosophical meditation, and the fully creative work." Summarized: <u>Dissertation Abstracts International</u> 37A:6482.

4   BRADY, RUTH H. "Stein's 'A Long Dress.'" <u>Explicator</u> 34 (February):Item 47.

       The images in Stein's "A Long Dress" are of "a long A-line dress made of an iridescent fabric which hangs in folds and makes a swishing sound."

5   CARTER, DAVID. "Grammar Takes a Trip." <u>Times Literary Supplement</u>, 12 March, p. 284.

       "In <u>How to Write</u> Stein attempts to show us what she believes language can be and do. Instead of being used to produce an effect, here language is made to explore itself, something which only writing (which is communication) can do."

6   COOLEY, THOMAS. <u>Educated Lives: The Rise of Modern Autobiography in America</u>. Columbus: Ohio State University Press, pp. x, 55, 69, 126, 139, 143, and passim.

       In the story of her own life and her reputation, Stein found "the perfect story of 'existing.'" Her autobiographies are less narrative and documentary than "narratives of existing"--"a state of continuous motion or mental vibration in which the consciousness passionately appropriates the objects of its detached contemplation."

7   COUSER, G. THOMAS. "Of Time and Identity: Walt Whitman and Gertrude Stein as Autobiographers." <u>Texas Studies in Language and Literature</u> 17 (Winter):787-804.

       ". . . two of our most eccentric writers and autobiographers--Walt Whitman and Gertrude Stein--seem to share many intriguing similarities. Deeply patriotic, both were committed to egalitarian principles in life and to the exploration of the commonplace in art." Both cared for soldiers and experimented in autobiography: "For both, autobiography ultimately became an attempt to write everybody's autobiography."

8   DeKOVEN, MARIANNE. "Explaining Gertrude Stein: A Criticism for Experimental Style." Ph.D. dissertation, Stanford University, 300 pp.

       "To the extent that Stein liberates and renews literary language but does not trivialize it by abandoning meaning, her work represents a viable option for avant-garde writing." Summarized: <u>Dissertation Abstracts International</u> 37A:6474-75.

9   DUBNICK, RANDA KAY. "Gertrude Stein and Cubism: A Structural
     Analysis of Obscurity." Ph.D. dissertation, University of
     Colorado, 211 pp.
          "Stein's previous unintelligibility is due to consciously
     exaggerated syntax and minimized vocabulary in [one] style, and
     to consciously extended vocabulary and truncated syntax in the
     second. Stein's analogies linking her work to cubism, then, are
     not inappropriate applications of artistic theories to litera-
     ture, but rather illuminate basic linguistic structures, concerns
     appropriately explored in literature." Summarized: Dissertation
     Abstracts International 37A:5103-04.

10   _____. "Two Types of Obscurity in the Writings of Gertrude
     Stein." Emporia State Research Studies 24 (Winter):5-27.
          Stein differentiated prose and poetry, claiming that her
     style in The Making of Americans was prose and that in Tender
     Buttons poetry. Perhaps her differentiation reflects some "dual-
     istic distinction" of "structuralist thought."

11   EDGINGTON, K. ANN. "Abstraction as a Concept in the Criticism
     of Gertrude Stein and Wassily Kandinsky." Ph.D. dissertation,
     American University, 72 pp.
          ". . . I consider the concept of abstraction to be of value
     to the study of literature and painting, but I have not found
     that the works of Stein and Kandinsky demand a nontraditional
     critical approach." Summarized: Dissertation Abstracts Inter-
     national 37A:1540.

12   FARBER, LAWREN. "Fading: A Way. Gertrude Stein's Sources
     for Three Lives." Journal of Modern Literature 5 (September):
     463-80.
          Possible echoes of German names taken literally, saints'
     and martyrs' lives, and biblical allusions may help explicate
     Stein's concealed purposes in Three Lives.

13   GRAHAM, JUDITH. "Gertrude Stein's Early Prose, 1905-1913."
     Thesis, University of Hawaii, 102 pp.
          "The present work proposes a way to read Gertrude Stein and
     focuses on her early prose. I suggest that 'sound' is the key to
     her writing and that her prose is clear and meaningful if one
     listens."

14   GREENBERG, ARNIE. Goddy: A Play. Montreal: Vanier Press,
     85 pp.
          "Goddy is a two act play involving some of the people who
     moved within the 'charmed circle' of Gertrude Stein. The play
     takes place in the carpenters loft of Ernest Hemingway in Paris
     in 1924. It centres around the party that the Hemingways had to
     celebrate the christening of their son John, known as Bumby
     (called Goddy by Gertrude Stein)."

15   GREY, M. CAMERON. "Miss Toklas Alone." Virginia Quarterly
     Review 52 (Autumn):687-96.
          Grey met and enjoyed Toklas in Paris in 1949 but stood her
     up for an appointment and was not forgiven.

16   HOFFMAN, MICHAEL J. Gertrude Stein. Boston: Twayne Pub-
     lishers, 159 pp.
          Concentration on Stein's writings from 1902 to 1913 reveals
     the complexity of her experiments in writing. Her abstract style
     took several stages to develop from realistic fiction to cubistic
     portraiture.

17   KATZ, JONATHAN. Gay American History: Lesbians and Gay Men
     in the U.S.A. New York: Thomas Y. Crowell Co., pp. 13, 60,
     447-48, 513, and passim.
          Even sophisticated literary historians have hesitated to
     portray accurately the lesbian love of Stein and Toklas.

18   KORNFELD, LAWRENCE. "From a Director's Notebook: How the
     Curtain Did Come--Conflict and Change." Performing Arts
     Journal 1 (Spring):33-39.
          Kornfeld directed since 1957 some six plays by Stein:
     "What happened in these productions was what happened to the
     people who did them; the words and music were not what happened:
     what happened was that the people who acted and sang and danced
     were the action, the music and the dancing."

*19 LALLI, B. TEDESCHINI, ed. Gertrude Stein: L'Esperimento
     dello scrivere. Naples: Liguori.
          Cited and described: American Literary Scholarship for
     1976, pp. 449-50.

20   McMENIMAN, LINDA JEANNE. "Design and Experiment in The Making
     of Americans by Gertrude Stein." Ph.D. dissertation: Uni-
     versity of Pennsylvania, 257 pp.
          In her great novel Stein seeks "to change the world view
     of her countrymen and women. She wishes to awaken people to the
     vivid present, and to help them transcend their lives of self-
     aggrandizement, accumulation and power." Summarized: Disserta-
     tion Abstracts International 37A:2185-86.

21   MOERS, ELLEN. Literary Women. Garden City, N.Y.: Doubleday
     & Co., pp. xix, 43, 64-66, 67, 84, and passim.
          Knowledge of Stein's works can help one re-evaluate past
     works by other women: "As to Gertrude Stein's peculiar style in
     prose, of course her experiments with syntax, repetition, word
     order, and the rest grew essentially from her philosophical views
     of the nature of language. But anyone who thinks no one else
     ever wrote as Stein did, and especially, no woman, simply does
     not have all of women's literature in mind."

22 ROTHER, JAMES. "Gertrude Stein and the Translation Experience." Essays in Literature 3 (Spring):105-18.

To Stein, "literature, if it was to have any relevance at all in the twentieth century, would have to re-educate its readers to experience writing very much like a native element; as, indeed, a universal language caught perenially in the act of objectifying its own wonder-suffused consciousness."

23 SAYRE, HENRY MARSHALL. "A World Unsuspected: Gertrude Stein, William Carlos Williams, and the Rise of American Modernism." Ph.D. dissertation, University of Washington, 296 pp.

Stein tried to adapt hermetic cubism to writing, causing her to use repetition, verbals, mental portraits, and abstract language. Summarized: Dissertation Abstracts International 37A:2879.

24 SHIRER, WILLIAM. 20th Century Journey: A Memoir of a Life and the Times. New York: Simon & Schuster, pp. 12, 106, 229, 240, 271, and passim.

Shirer visited Stein three times in Paris and was impressed with her ego and ambition. Unfortunately, he sensed her lack of power to communicate.

25 THAU, ANNETTE. "Max Jacob's Letters to Gertrude Stein: A Critical Study." Folio, no. 9 (October), pp. 47-54.

Jacob and Stein were friendly and exchanged letters but did not interest each other as writers.

26 WAGNER, LINDA W. "Sherwood, Stein, the Sentence, and Grape Sugar and Oranges." In Sherwood Anderson: Dimensions of His Literary Art--A Collection of Critical Essays. Edited by David D. Anderson. East Lansing: Michigan State University Press, pp. 75-89.

Anderson stressed Stein's basic Americanism and praised her emphasis on the tactile and sensual.

*27 WHITE, WILLIAM. "Gertrude Stein on Detective Stories." Presenting Moonshine 3 (1976):3-6.

Cited: MHRA Bibliography for 1976, p. 785.

28 WICKES, GEORGE. The Amazon of Letters: The Life and Loves of Natalie Barney. New York: G.P. Putnam's Sons, pp. 9, 10, 109, 110, and passim.

Stein and Barney were not close, perhaps because the salons competed in Paris and perhaps because of Barney's notorious lesbian activity. But Stein "evidently found Natalie worth listening to. And Natalie in turn paid rare tribute to Gertrude's [esthetic] judgment."

<u>1977</u>

1   ADAMS, TIMOTHY DOW. "The Mock-Autobiography of Alice B.
     Toklas." <u>American Notes & Queries</u> 16 (September):10-12.
         By blurring fiction and non-fiction in <u>The Autobiography</u>
     <u>of Alice B. Toklas</u>, Stein has created "a new genre . . . the
     mock-autobiography--which has come to be one of the most preva-
     lent and important forms of literature used by contemporary writ-
     ers in America in the 1970's."

2   ALLAN, TONY. <u>Americans in Paris</u>. Chicago: Contemporary
     Books, pp. 11, 34, 35, 63-72, and passim.
         Stein and Barney--both lesbian--formed salons in Paris and
     earned great places in literary history.

3   "AMERICAN WRITERS: WHO'S UP, WHO'S DOWN?" <u>Esquire</u> 88
     (August):77, 78.
         To Kay Boyle, Stein and Anderson took American writing "out
     of the dust and cobwebs of the English tradition." To Malcolm
     Cowley, Pound and Stein are often unreadable.

*4   ARMATAGE, KAY. "Gertrude Stein and the Nineteenth Century
     Women's Movement." <u>Room of One's Own</u> 3 (1977):28-36.
         Cited: <u>American Humanities Index</u> (Spring 1980), p. 89.

5   BLASING, MUTLU KONUK. <u>The Art of Life: Studies in American</u>
     <u>Autobiographical Literature</u>. Austin: University of Texas
     Press, pp. 34, 129, 157-58.
         <u>The Autobiography of Alice B. Toklas</u> has Stein as a charac-
     ter, "still the creative force of the work, for her work becomes
     a compositional center."

6   BLAU, ELEANOR. "50 Nonstop Hours of Gertrude Stein." <u>New</u>
     <u>York Times</u>, 30 December, sec. C, p. 3.
         The fourth annual continuous reading of <u>The Making of Amer-</u>
     <u>icans</u> will take place in New York City--a marathon event.

7   BRINNAN, JOHN MALCOLM. "Gertrude Stein." In <u>Collier's Ency-</u>
     <u>clopedia, 21</u>. New York: Macmillan Educational Corporation,
     pp. 517-18.
         "Gertrude Stein's place in literary history is likely to
     be established by the influence of her personality and aesthetic
     philosophy as much as by her writings. Although she was an in-
     novator in the uses of language, her works tend to show the ana-
     lytical bias of the scientist more than the expressive power of
     the novelist or poet."

8   _____. "Gertrude Stein." In <u>The Encyclopedia Americana</u>
     <u>International Edition</u>. Vol. 22. New York: Americana Corpor-
     ation, pp. 673-74.

Stein's career was "unique and remains controversial. Though her writing progressed through several phases, her most distinctive contribution in such works as Tender Buttons (1914) and Geography and Plays (1922) suggests that she is related to literature in much the same way that Constantin Brancusi and Piet Mondrian are to painting."

9   CERF, BENNETT. At Random: The Reminiscences of Bennett Cerf. New York: Random House, pp. 97, 101-8, 148.
Cerf met Stein in Paris in April of 1934 and was impressed with her business sense. He invited her to America to publicize Portraits and Prayers and she proved to be a great "publicity hound."

10   FERGUSON, SUZANNE. Review of Dear Sammy. Resources for American Literary Study 7 (Autumn):213-16.
Dear Sammy is among the "flood of trivia" resulting from recent interest in Stein.

11   FLEISSNER, ROBERT F. "Roots: The Germinal Soil of Frost's Rose Family." Research Studies 45 (September):168-70.
Stein, Austin Dobson, and Robert Burns are ancestors of Frost's content in his poem "The Rose Family."

12   _____. "Stein's Four Roses." Journal of Modern Literature 6 (April):325-28.
Concerning the line "Rose is a rose is a rose is a rose": ". . . the line incorporates four basic meanings. These are, briefly, (1) the impressionistic, (2) the technical, (3) the meaning of the rose itself, and (4) the anagogical."

13   HAHN, EMILY. Mabel: A Biography of Mabel Dodge Luhan. Boston: Houghton, Mifflin Co., pp. 46, 47, 48-49, 54, and passim.
Mabel Dodge liked Stein and invited her to visit the Villa Curonia--subject of an early Stein composition. The friendship ended when Stein became sexually attracted to Dodge, offending Alice.

14   HOOPES, JAMES. Van Wyck Brooks: In Search of American Culture. Amherst: University of Massachusetts Press, pp. 221, 224, 234.
Brooks was disappointed in intellectuals who defended the esthetics of Stein and later adopted unesthetic leftist causes; he believed that Stein had abandoned roots in realism for gibberish.

15   JELINEK, ESTELLE C. "The Tradition of Women's Autobiographies." Ph.D. dissertation, State University of New York at Buffalo, 272 pp.

In The Autobiography of Alice B. Toklas, despite Stein's
"anecdotal style and nonchronological narrative," critics have
found much to praise among women's autobiographies. Summarized:
Dissertation Abstracts International 38A:5479-80.

16   KAZIN, ALFRED. "Hemingway the Painter." New Republic 176
     (19 March):24-26.
       Hemingway learned from Stein herself and from her art col-
     lection much about writing. He learned that painting was a method
     and craft.

17   KELLNER, BRUCE. "Baby Woojuns in Iowa." Books at Iowa 26
     (1977):3-18.
       Publication of Van Vechten's complete obituary for Stein
     confirms his relationship with the woman and aids understanding
     of his role in her publishing career.

18   LANATI, BARBARA. L'Avanguardia americana: Tre esperimenti--
     Faulkner, Stein, W.C. Williams. Turin: Giulio Einaudi,
     pp. 61-118.
       Stein--priestess of the word--in the name of cerebration
     cultivated sensual faculties. She destroyed form and syntax as
     received.

19   LARSEN, ERLING. "I Know, Pablo, I Know." Carleton Miscellany
     16 (Fall-Winter):159-81.
       Recent publications emphasizing Toklas's writings put new
     light on her part of the Stein legend.

20   LODGE, DAVID. The Modes of Modern Writing: Metaphor,
     Metonymy, and the Typology of Modern Language. Ithaca:
     Cornell University Press, pp. ix, 45-46, 144-55, 156-58, 264.
       Stein's writing "oscillated violently between the metonymic
     and metaphoric poles, pushing out in each direction to points
     where she began to exhibit symptoms . . . aphasia." Stein is
     more interesting as theorist of writing than writer of literature.

21   MELLOW, JAMES R. "Gertrude Stein Among the Dadaists." Arts
     Magazine 51 (May):124-26.
       Stein's word-portraits influenced the new school of Dadaists
     in Paris before World War I.

22   PADGETTE, PAUL. "Gertrude Stein's Letters." San Francisco
     Examiner & Chronicle, 31 July, "World," p. 46.
       Dear Sammy is "a memoir that is gentle, loving, and inti-
     mate. Only one who was there could have written it."

23   PASQUIER, MARIE-CLAIRE. "Le Théâtre comme paysage: Gertrude
     Stein et le théâtre américain d'aujourd'hui." Cahiers de la
     Compagnie Madelaine Renaud-Jean Louis Barrault 94 (1977):
     100-06.

Not interested in drama as representation, Stein in her plays influenced the avant-garde contemporary theatre.

24   PHILLIPS, KATHY JANETTE. "Self-Conscious Narration in the Works of Henry James, Marcel Proust, Gertrude Stein, and Alain Robbe-Grillet." Ph.D. dissertation, Brown University, 185 pp.
       "Stein and Robbe-Grillet imbed running commentary on their own techniques in such 'manuals' for art as Tender Buttons and Dans le labyrinthe." Summarized: Dissertation Abstracts International 38A:7314-15.

25   ROSE, MARILYN GADDIS. "Gertrude Stein and Cubist Narrative." Modern Fiction Studies 22 (Winter):543-55.
       Analysis of "The Good Anna," Lucy Church Amiably, and Ida shows that Stein makes narrative into "a form of research." Being a cubist artist, Stein "can force us to analyze the elements of narration by abstraction and rearrangement."

26   SAUNDERS, JUDITH P. "Gertrude Stein's Paris France and American Literary Tradition." South Dakota Review 15 (Spring): 7-17.
       "Stein's Paris France is itself an imaginative construct; it is a created fiction, a spiritual rather than a literal place, where apparent contradictions are the source of wholeness."

27   SAYRE, HENRY M. "Imaging the Mind: Juan Gris and Gertrude Stein." Southern Humanities Review 11 (Spring):204-15.
       In 1926 Stein illustrated A Book Concluding with As A Wife Has A Cow. A Love Story with four Gris lithographs; her text was influenced by the illustrations, not otherwise, as one might expect.

28   SIMON, LINDA. The Biography of Alice B. Toklas. New York: Doubleday & Co., 324 pp.
       After loving and serving Stein from 1907 into 1946, Toklas "desperately wanted the dead not to be dead . . . and she lived alone with Gertrude's memory. Never a pleasant or comfortable personality, Toklas after Stein's death devoted herself to publication of Stein's unpublished works and her own memoirs and cookbooks and to protecting her memories of Stein: "For twenty-one years, she wanted only reunion. She lies beside Gertrude."

29   STEINER, WENDY. "Gertrude Stein in Manuscript." Yale University Library Gazette 51 (January):156-63.
       Stein in her early writings tended to copy in words the illustrations on the covers of her notebooks. The reader, not having seen the illustrations seen by Stein, has reason to feel misused.

30   STIMPSON, CATHERINE R. "The Mind, The Body, and Gertrude Stein." Critical Inquiry 3 (Spring):489-506.

Stein was a Jew who did not emphasize her Jewishness, a rich woman of high education, and a puritannical woman who adopted a happy lesbian love.

31   TOWNSEND, JANIS BARBARA LUBAWSKY. "The Singing Self: Philosophy, Autobiography and Style in Gertrude Stein's Lyrical Mallorcan Works." Ph.D. dissertation, Wayne State University, 153 pp.
"Gertrude Stein's lyrical writings of 1915-1916 done on Mallorca have a facility and integrity which demand their serious study. These works illustrate Stein's thinking about the operation of consciousness, her adoption of the lyrical mode, and autobiographical features which make these works more accessible than those done at other times." Summarized: Dissertation Abstracts International 38A:6731-32.

32   WATTS, EMILY STIPES. The Poetry of American Women from 1632 to 1945. Austin: University of Texas Press, pp. 3, 6, 135, 142, 165-68, and passim.
Stein's writing denies the wasteland metaphor of modern literature, combines adult and children's perspective, influenced younger women poets, innovated philosophically, and continually rebegan.

33   WILSON, EDMUND. Letters on Literature and Politics, 1912-1972. Edited by Elena Wilson. New York: Farrar, Straus & Giroux, pp. 104-5, 112, 133, 149-50, and passim.
Wilson enjoyed Geography and Plays, although he considered Stein farthest from conventional literature. He enjoyed seeing Four Saints in Three Acts, visited Stein and Toklas in 1935, and told her of the death of Fitzgerald.

1978

1   ADAMS, TIMOTHY DOW. "Autobiographical Boundaries: The Contemporary American Mock-Autobiography." Ph.D. dissertation, Emory University, 227 pp.
The Autobiography of Alice B. Toklas is a mock-autobiography because it parodies "the usual conventions of the autobiographical genre." Further, Stein substitutes a "non-heroic figure for the famous person we expect at the center of personal narrative." Summarized: Dissertation Abstracts International 40A:255.

2   _____. "Obscuring the Muse: The Mock-Autobiographies of Ronald Sukenick." Critique 20 (1978):27-52.
The Autobiography of Alice B. Toklas is the prototype for all recent mock-autobiography such as the ones by Sukenick.

3   ARDAT, AHMAD KHALIL. "A Linguistic Analysis of the Prose Styles of Ernest Hemingway, Sherwood Anderson, and Gertrude Stein." Ph.D. dissertation, Miami University, 221 pp.

Use of "generative transformational grammar, clause-to-sentence synopsis, and generative rhetoric" to analyze fifty sentences from Three Lives reveals how the work resembles and differs from In Our Time and Winesburg, Ohio. Summarized: Dissertation Abstracts International 39A:4915-16.

4   BANTA, MARTHA. Failure & Success in America: A Literary
     Debate. Princeton: Princeton University Press, pp. 4, 6,
     101, 118, 130, and passim.
        Stein chooses the role of "saint" in her meditative writing,
which is eye-oriented, in contrast to the ear-oriented works by
Hemingway. Stein liked to write of families, not individuals.

5   BASSOFF, BRUCE. "Gertrude Stein's 'Composition as Explana-
     tion.'" Twentieth Century Literature 24 (Spring):76-80.
        Composition as Explanation is "a kind of premonitory con-
densation of some of the salient principles of semiotic analysis
from Walter Benjamin to Claude Levi-Strauss."

6   BERG, A. SCOTT. Max Perkins: Editor of Genius. New York:
     E.P. Dutton, pp. 88-89, 98-99, 113, 217-18, 283-84, 393, 419.
        Perkins admired The Making of Americans but doubted the
patience of any readers who encountered it. He regretted the
satire in The Autobiography of Alice B. Toklas and Hemingway's
comments in Green Hills of Africa.

7   BERZON, JUDITH R. Neither Black Nor White: The Mulatto Char-
     acter in American Fiction. New York: New York University
     Press, pp. 14, 63-64.
        In Three Lives, "as Stein presents her, Melanctha displays
the seemingly irrational, moody conduct that has been viewed as
a function of the racial disharmony of the mulatto."

8   BLOOM, LYNN Z. "Gertrude Is Alice Is Everybody: Innovation
     and Point of View in Gertrude Stein's Autobiographies."
     Twentieth Century Literature 24 (Spring):81-93.
        Because of its fireworks quality, The Autobiography of
Alice B. Toklas "can be set off only once. Its innovative strat-
egy and form and variations on point of view exhibit the unique-
ness, innovativeness, and memorability of its creator. It leaves
a dazzling afterglow against the more somber sky of conventional
autobiographies."

9   BURNS, EDWARD. "Gertrude Stein: Selected Criticism."
     Twentieth Century Literature 24 (Spring):127-34.
        Primary and secondary bibliography.

10   BUSH, CLIVE. "Toward the Outside: The Quest for Discontinu-
     ity in Gertrude Stein's The Making of Americans." Twentieth
     Century Literature 24 (Spring):27-56.

"The process of The Making of Americans is the rejection of inheritance, an externalized autobiography. Gay, Jewish, trained as an experimental psychologist and a pragmatist, [Stein] wanted to recover the freedom of creative consciousness, to be an artist not a teacher, nor only a collector. . . ."

11 CORNWELL, ETHEL F. "Gertrude Stein: The Forerunner of Nathalie Sarraute." International Fiction Review 5 (July): 91-95.
  Stein and Sarraute force words into communicating feelings "which occur on a preverbal level." Both women "approach their work as scientists rather than artists. And, significantly, the end result, in both cases, has been a tendency toward generalized, abstracted types, and a technique which demands a great deal of the reader."

12 COMMINS, DOROTHY. What Is an Editor? Saxe Commins at Work. Chicago: University of Chicago Press, pp. 9, 27-33.
  At Random House, Commins edited Four Saints in Three Acts, although "no book of [Stein's] could be edited." Later he read the manuscript of Wars I Have Seen "with a sense of outrage he could not restrain," stating in his report that reading Stein "is an experience similar to taking the drop-by-drop water torture" and despising Stein's apparent tolerance for Nazis and Nazi-sympathizers.

13 CURTIS, JEAN-LOUIS. "Une Pionnière des lettres. La Quinzaine Littéraire 282 (1-15 July):4.
  Publication in France of Ida, Everybody's Autobiography and Picasso shows Stein as a formidable person and unique individual, among the great ones of her generation, a powerful creator of literature.

14 DAVY, KATE. "Richard Foreman's Ontological-Hysteric Theatre: The Influence of Gertrude Stein." Twentieth Century Literature 24 (Spring):108-26.
  "While the influences on Foreman as playwright, director, and scenographer are numerous and diverse, he maintains that Gertrude's Stein's theoretical writings are the primary influence on his writing method, technique, or style."

15 FRAZER, WINIFRED L. "Two Revolutionaries: Gertrude Stein and Emma Goldman." STTH 1 (Winter):70-78.
  "Whereas Gertrude Stein went abroad to escape the Philistines, Emma Goldman resolved to bring enlightenment to them at home."

16 GASS, WILLIAM H. The World Within the Word. New York: Alfred A. Knopf, pp. 63-123.
  Reprint of 1973.18; 1973.19.

*17   GRAFE, FRIEDA. "Zwei Jahre aus Meinem Leben mit Gertrude
       Stein." Republik, no. 18-26 (30 April), pp. 134-463.
       Cited: Catalogue of the University of Munich.

18   HADAS, PAMELA. "Spreading the Difference: One Way to Read
       Gertrude Stein's Tender Buttons." Twentieth Century Litera-
       ture 24 (Spring):57-75.
            The story implicit behind Tender Buttons is "of how one
       lives with perceptions of change and differences of all sorts,
       from the unreliable meanings of language to those psychological
       differences between men and women, past and future, brothers and
       sisters, and signs of life among them."

19   HALL, DONALD. "Gertrude Stein and Her Fords." Ford Times 71
       (June):48-51.
            Stein "looked like an old car herself. Not the kind parked
       with other, rusted junk at the side of a barn, windows smashed
       and wheels gone. Gertrude Stein was a vintage hulk, blocky and
       durable, possibly slow to start but capable of long journeys at
       low mileage."

20   HOFFELD, LAURA. "Gertrude Stein's Unmentionables." Lion and
       the Unicorn 2 (Spring):48-55.
            The World Is Round "speaks, like a fairy tale, to our deep-
       est emotions. In fact it is a story about emotions, about human
       feelings and the tears we find in the nature of things."

21   JAWORSKI, PHILLIPE. "Gertrude Stein et la modernité." La
       Quinzaine Littérarire 292 (16-31 December):8.
            Publication in France of The Geographical History of Amer-
       ica, Lectures in America, and Luna-Park [sic] illustrate Stein's
       interests and abilities with strength, precision, daring, spare-
       ness, and humor.

22   KATZ, LEON. "Weininger and The Making of Americans." Twenti-
       eth Century Literature 24 (Spring):8-26.
            Stein read Otto Weininger's Sex and Character and was
       "prodded toward emulating Weininger's systematization of psy-
       chology" in The Making of Americans.

*23   KRETZOI, CHARLOTTE. "Gertrude Stein's Attempt at 'The Great
       American Novel.'" Studies in English and American 4 (1978):
       7-34.
            Cited: PMLA Bibliography (1979):234.

24   LANDON, RICHARD BROOKS. "Extremes of Parataxis: Nonrational-
       ism in the Writing of Gertrude Stein and Thomas Berger." Ph.D.
       dissertation, University of Texas, 306 pp.
            "Using a reader-centered approach explained as that of a
       'playing reader,' this study analyzes the distinguishing para-
       tactic nonrationalism in the works of Gertrude Stein and Thomas

Berger. Both writers employ techniques that are characteristically paratactic, combining elements in the literary text in ways that defy expected relationships. . . ." Summarized: Dissertation Abstracts International 39A:2275.

*25   NISHIO, IWAO. "Cézanne, Stein to Hemingway." Eigo Seinen 124 (1978):447-48.
        Cited: PMLA Bibliography (1978):208.

26   PADGETTE, PAUL. Review of Dear Sammy. Lost Generation Journal 5 (Winter):23.
       Stein's and Toklas's letters to Samuel Steward are witty, absorbing, and full of important information.

27   RAAB, LAWRENCE. "Remarks as Literature: The Autobiography of Alice B. Toklas by Gertrude Stein." Michigan Quarterly Review 17 (Fall):480-93.
       "The surface of the Autobiography is clear but complicated, and the clarity is in the complication. Just as any object or landscape could be the subject of a painting, any remark could also be the material for the sentence that could become literature. . . . While the stories entertain, the sounds of [Stein's] sentences sink into our minds."

28   RAABERG, GLORIA GWEN. "Toward a Theory of Literary Collage: Literary Experimentalism and Its Relation to Modern Art in the Work of Pound, Stein, and Williams." Ph.D. dissertation, University of California--Irvine, 275 pp.
       Stein tried to imitate cubism in literary art: "Her experiments took her from an interest in narrative structure to an interest in language as the basic structural element. Applying the principles of the new Cubist sign system to literature, she maintained that the language of the poem is not concerned with the relation between the sign and an external referent but the internal structural relations of the signs within the work." Summarized: Dissertation Abstracts International 39A:2932-33.

*29   SCHLAEGER, JÜRGEN. Grenzen der Moderne: Gertrude Steins Prosa. Constance: Constance-Univ.-Verlag, 49 pp.
        Cited: PMLA Bibliography (1979):234.

30   SCHMITZ, NEIL. "Portrait, Patriarchy, Mythos: The Revenge of Gertrude Stein." Salmagundi 40 (Winter):69-91.
       Mocking the autobiographical form, Stein in The Autobiography of Alice B. Toklas could "begin from the inside an ironic demystification of traditional narrative, restate the problem of the external and the internal in discourse through her final and surprising use of the Crusoe myth, and send rippling back over Alice's simplicities a confusion. Revenge is not, therefore, too strong a word to use in characterizing her formal strategies in the Autobiography."

31   SCHWARTZ, STANLEY. "The Autobiography as Generic 'Continuous
     Present': <u>Paris France</u> and <u>Wars I Have Seen</u>." <u>English Stud-
     ies in Canada</u> 4 (Summer):224-37.
          Because Stein's autobiographies are "singularly autotelic"
     and atemporal, they relate to the works of Proust and Pound:
     "Stein has given the autotelic attributes of much twentieth-
     century literature an authenticity in autobiography."

32   SECOR, CYNTHIA. "<u>Ida</u>, A Great American Novel." <u>Twentieth
     Century Literature</u> 24 (Spring):96-107.
          <u>Ida</u> shows Stein's reflections on her "marriage" to Toklas,
     an event at once restrictive and liberating.

33   STEELE, JOY COGDELL. "Time and American Autobiography: Four
     Twentieth-Century Writers." Ph.D. dissertation, University of
     Iowa, 288 pp.
          "In <u>The Autobiography of Alice B. Toklas</u> Stein returns to
     a more normal narrative style, yet the participles and repeated
     beginnings--of her early experiments--retard the narrative. . . .
     After the public identity she created caused her to question her
     true nature, the constant themes of <u>Everybody's Autobiography</u>
     become identity and time." Summarized: <u>Dissertation Abstracts
     International</u> 39A:3559.

34   STEINER, WENDY. <u>Exact Resemblance to Exact Resemblance: The
     Literary Portraiture of Gertrude Stein</u>. New Haven: Yale Uni-
     versity Press, 225 pp.
          Publication of 1974.42.

35   WANK, MARTIN. "Gertrude Stein and Alain Robbe-Grillet:
     Toward a New Literature." <u>Intellect</u> 106 (June):500-505.
          Stein dismantled the direct meaning of literary expression
     and by her deconstructionism influenced Robbe-Grillet.

<u>1979</u>

1   BANTA, MARTHA. "James and Stein on 'Being American.'"
     <u>French-American Review</u> 3 (Fall):63-84.
          "Two of the most famous expatriates from America to Europe
     are Henry James and Gertrude Stein." Living in France gave James
     and Stein personal and esthetic freedom and important modernist
     perspectives, France representing an edge on which to test the
     newness of America.

2   BEATON, CECIL. <u>Self Portrait with Friends: The Selected
     Diaries of Cecil Beaton, 1926-1974</u>. Edited by Richard Buckle.
     London: Weidenfeld & Nicolson, pp. 2, 42-43, 71-72, 164-65,
     377.
          In 1935, Beaton visited Stein's new apartment and was sur-
     prised at the impressive and impeccable artworks. In 1944, Stein
     and Toklas showed the effects of hiding from Germans in rural
     France.

3   BRESLIN, JAMES E. "Gertrude Stein and the Problems of Auto-
      biography." Georgia Review 33 (Winter):901-13.
          In The Autobiography of Alice B. Toklas, "by renouncing a
      simple center and a continuous design, by exploring the formal
      dilemmas of the genre, Gertrude Stein at once accepted, denied,
      and created autobiography." Reprinted: 1980.7.

4   CAMFIELD, WILLIAM A. Francis Picabia: His Art, Life and
      Times. Princeton: Princeton University Press, pp. 57, 63,
      243-55, 246, 250, 251, and passim.
          Picabia met Stein in 1913 and liked her. After some trou-
      bles, they remained friends until Stein's death.

5   CARSON, SYDNEY SYLVIA ROSENBAUM. "Indefiteness in the Novel--
      Jane Austen, Virginia Woolf, Gertrude Stein." Ph.D. disserta-
      tion, University of California, 234 pp.
          "In all three novelists, especially in Virginia Woolf and
      Gertrude Stein, events have the appearance of being randomly
      chosen and are not hierarchically arranged into big and little.
      All three minimize, if not ignore, the physical aspects of
      reality. . . ." Summarized: Dissertation Abstracts Inter-
      national 40A:4011.

6   CHALON, JEAN. Portrait of a Seductress: The World of
      Natalie Clifford Barney. Translated by Carol Barko. New
      York: Crown Publishers, pp. 144, 160, 163-64, 170, 180, 181.
          Stein and Barney shared sexual natures, salon-keeping, and
      friendly walks about Paris; but Barney envied Stein her famous
      friends.

7   COUSER, G. THOMAS. American Autobiography: The Prophetic
      Mode. Amherst: University of Massachusetts Press, pp. 148-63.
          "Although The Autobiography lacks a truly prophetic impulse,
      [Stein] makes prophetic gestures in it; in fact, she poses as a
      prophet of modern art. . . . Everybody's Autobiography . . .
      nicely epitomizes her desire to write collective or inclusive
      autobiography in the prophetic mode. . . . Wars I Have Seen . . .
      enabled and encouraged her to assume a fairly traditional stance
      as a prophet."

8   DANIEL, ALIX DuPOY. "The Stimulating Life with Gertrude &
      Co." Lost Generation Journal 6 (Summer):16-18.
          Daniel knew Stein in Paris and enjoyed her dealings with
      other writers: "There were many other writers either living or
      visiting in Paris at that time. . . . But it was Ford Madox Ford
      and Gertrude Stein who enriched and highlighted Paris for me and
      gave me an inkling of what immortality was like."

*9   FIFER, ELIZABETH. "Is Flesh Advisable: The Interior Theater
      of Gertrude Stein." Signs 4 (1979):472-83.
          Cited: PMLA Bibliography (1979):234.

10   GIBBS, ANNA. "Helene Cious and Gertrude Stein: New Direc-
     tions in Feminist Criticism." Meanjin 38 (1979):281-93.
         Cious and Stein are alike in de-emphasizing plot and using
     discontinuous time, in exploring strictures upon language, and
     in understanding feminine literary consciousness.

*11 HELL, VICTOR. "Gertrude Stein et l'esthetique du xxee siècle."
     In Arts de l'association internationale de littérature comparée.
     Edited by Milan V. Dimić and Jean Ferraté. Stuttgart: Bieber
     Verlag, pp. 427-31.
         Cited: PMLA Bibliography 1 (1980):261.

12   LEVIN, GAIL. "Wassily Kandinski and the American Literary
     Avant-Garde." Criticism 21 (Fall):347-55.
         Stein is among the few avant-garde writers who actually
     met Kandinsky, in 1906-7; but she was not favorable to his art.
     Perhaps her phobia of German things motivated her dislike.

13   LISTON, MAUREEN. Gertrude Stein: An Annotated Critical
     Bibliography. Kent: Kent State University Press, 230 pp.
         "Although this checklist is selective rather than complete,
     I have attempted to present the different critical approaches to
     Stein's work, the literary influences she had, and other artists'
     responses to her. These views tend to be repetitious and I have
     chosen to exclude numerous articles and books in order to produce
     a research tool both practical and usable for critic and student."

14   MAJOR, CLARENCE. "Three Lives and Gertrude Stein." par
     rapport 2 (1979):53-66.
         "Through repetition and dislocation, Gertrude Stein man-
     aged, by creating Three Lives, to give everyday American English
     a new life. Each word in the book commands attention. It care-
     fully opened the way for a new consciousness of literary art."

15   MICHA, RENA. "Traduire Gertrude Stein." Critique 35 (May):
     492-93.
         Translating Stein into French is as complicated as explain-
     ing a painting.

16   MINC, JANET BARNETT. "An Interdisciplinary Study of the
     Early Works of Gertrude Stein in the Context of Cubism,
     1904-1913." Ph.D. dissertation, State University of New
     York at Binghamton, 251 pp.
         "It is concluded that while any relationship between
     Stein's writings and the work of the Cubist painters must remain
     on a metaphorical level, an interdisciplinary study of Stein's
     work in the context of Cubism can provide fruitful insights into
     these early works. While they utilized different mediums, both
     Stein and the Cubists became increasingly convinced of the obli-
     gation of art to reflect the subjective mind as well as the ex-
     ternal world." Summarized: Dissertation Abstracts International
     40A:2666.

17   MURRAY, VALORY. "An Analysis of the Plays and Operas of Gertrude Stein." Ph.D. dissertation, Kent State University, 234 pp.
     "My study suggests that the dramatic quality of Stein's plays is a function of her unique ways of manipulating language and experience rather than of traditional forms of conflict between or within individual characters. Characters' voices are less important than Stein's speaking behind and through them." Summarized: <u>Dissertation Abstracts International</u> 40A:2064–65.

18   NEUMAN, S.C. <u>Gertrude Stein: Autobiography and the Problem of Narration</u>. Victoria, B.C.: Department of English, University of Victoria, 88 pp.
     "Stein's autobiographies, though differing in method from Montaigne's, are like his in being singularly autotelic. They transcend history to become art-constructs through the creative exemplification of an atemporal theory of literature."

19   PERLOFF, MARJORIE. "Poetry As Word–System: The Art of Gertrude Stein." <u>American Poetry Review</u> 8 (September–October): 33–43.
     "To read a text like <u>Tender Buttons</u> can be exasperating and boring if one expects to find actual descriptions of the objects denoted by the titles . . . But Stein's are by no means Imagist poems. Rather, the author offers us certain threads which take us into her verbal labyrinth, threads that never quite lead us out on the other side. . . ."

20   SAYRE, HENRY M. "Distancing 'The Rose' from <u>Roses</u>." <u>William Carlos Williams Newsletter</u> 5 (Spring):18–20.
     Williams may have seen Stein's painting <u>Roses</u> by Gris and been influenced by it.

21   SKINNER, B.F. <u>The Shaping of a Behaviorist: Part Two of an Autobiography</u>. New York: Alfred A. Knopf, pp. 134–36.
     Stein liked Skinner's article on her "automatic" writing, but she claimed to put into her art more work than automatism.

22   WALDROP, KEITH. "Gertrude Stein's Tears." <u>Novel</u> 12 (Spring): 236–43.
     "Believing that "ordinary life (what [Stein] calls 'human nature') is an endless, hopeless repetition, at once product and producer of politics, religion, propaganda, and war" and that "it is controlled by age, sickness, and death," Stein escaped by her use of language into a "realm of pure play--she calls it 'the human mind.'"

*23   WALKER, JAYNE L. "Exercises in Disorder: Duncan's Imitations of Gertrude Stein." In <u>Robert Duncan: Scales of the Marvelous</u>. Edited by Robert J. Berthoff and Ian W. Reid. New York: New Directions.
     Cited: <u>PMLA Bibliography</u> 1 (1979):209.

24   WILDER, THORNTON. <u>American Characteristics and Other Essays</u>.
     Edited by Donald Gallup. Foreword by Isabel Wilder. New York:
     Harper & Row, pp. 183-222.
         Reprint of introductions to various Stein works.

                              1980

1   ADAMS, TIMOTHY DOW. "'She Will Be Me When This You See':
     Gertrude Stein's Mock-Autobiography of Alice B. Toklas."
     <u>Publications of the Arkansas Philological Association</u> 6 (1980):
     1-18.
         Publication in part of 1978.1.

2   ARDAT, AHMAD K. "The Prose Style of Selected Works of Ernest
     Hemingway, Sherwood Anderson, and Gertrude Stein." <u>Style</u> 14
     (Winter):1-21.
         "Of the three authors studied in this paper, Stein is most
     often different. She writes longer sentences and shorter clauses,
     and uses prenominal adjectives and medial branching modification
     differently. In general, she writes a style that attempts to cap-
     ture the complexity of the mind through an apparent simplicity of
     syntax."

3   BATT, NOËLLE. "Gertrude Stein ou la composition faite sens:
     <u>An Exercise in Analysis</u>." <u>Delta</u>, no. 10 (May), pp. 61-88.
         Stein's "An Exercise in Analysis" shows formal organization.

4   BELL, MILLICENT. "'Melanctha' and Metonymy." <u>Delta</u>, no. 10
     (May), pp. 19-31.
         In "Melanctha" Stein incrementally phrases her dialogue
     and narration, showing finally the "irreconcilable disparity
     between individuals."

5   BLAKE, HARRY. "Biddle-Making Gertrude Stein." <u>Delta</u>, no. 10
     (May), pp. 121-28.
         One follows Stein to call for a new novel for a new age--
     a "Biddle."

6   BLAKE, NANCY. "Here and Now with Gertrude Stein." <u>Delta</u>,
     no. 10 (May), pp. 3-8.
         "If writing is doing, the only way to be reading Gertrude
     Stein is to continue thinking and writing. That is the only way
     to avoid school and to live modernly, here and now."

7   BRESLIN, JAMES E. "Gertrude Stein and the Problems of Auto-
     biography." In <u>Women's Autobiography: Essays in Criticism</u>.
     Edited by Estelle C. Jelinek. Bloomington: Indiana Univer-
     sity Press, pp. 149-62.
         Reprint of 1979.3.

8   CARROLL, PAT. "Re-creating Stein in Paris." <u>Horizon</u> 23
     (November):38-41.
         Carroll admired Stein's toughness and brilliance--qualities
     recaptured in her performance <u>Gertrude Stein Is Gertrude Stein Is</u>
     <u>Gertrude Stein</u>.

9   CORDESSE, GÉRARD. "Sur les falaises de Stein: La lecture-
     limite." <u>Delta</u>, no. 10 (May), pp. 89-101.
         Stein was torn between the desire to be admired and the
     fear of being ridiculed. Hence, she became a writer with nerve
     and daring.

10   DUNBAR, JEAN CATHERINE. "Words in a Line: Process as Novel-
     istic Concept and Technique." Ph.D. dissertation, University
     of Virginia, 329 pp.
         ". . . the fullest discussion of fiction's dual nature is
     offered by Gertrude Stein and demonstrated in her fiction.
     Stein's apparently obscure fiction actually explores clearly
     the strongest explanation of this split in fiction, namely its
     dependence on language." Summarized: <u>Dissertation Abstracts</u>
     <u>International</u> 41A:1574-75.

11   FIFER, ELIZABETH. "Guardians and Witnesses: Narrative Tech-
     niques in Gertrude Stein's <u>Useful Knowledge</u>." <u>Journal of</u>
     <u>Narrative Technique</u> 10 (Spring):115-27.
         "In <u>Useful Knowledge</u>, the language itself functions both as
     primary vehicle and disguise, simultaneously concealing and re-
     vealing her purposes. It is as if [Stein's] extreme need to
     speak the unspeakable forced its way into a new channel--a way
     to both say and unsay at once."

12   GRIMAL, CLAUDE. "La Musique de Gertrude Stein." <u>Delta</u>,
     no. 10 (May), pp. 33-41.
         Stein is a superb librettist, whatever her knowledge of or
     taste in music.

13   HOFFMAN, MICHAEL J. "Gertrude Stein." In <u>Academic American</u>
     <u>Encyclopedia, 18</u>. Princeton: Areté Publishing Co., p. 247.
         "Stein abandoned conventional narrative and meaning to
     experiment with linguistic rhythms and impressions."

14   HUNKER, M. BETH STERNER. "Gertrude Stein: Rationale and
     Content for an Introduction to the Aesthetics of Modernism."
     Ph.D. dissertation, Ohio State University, 373 pp.
         "For students, Stein's work is a broad experience in Modern-
     ism. Her writing is a revelation of the possibilities of liter-
     ary freedom which often encourages creative 'discovery' in the
     student's own writing. Her unconventional realization of con-
     ventional genre forms encourages acceptance of what is inventive
     and unconventional in art."

15   MARCET, JEAN. "'Ring a Ring o': Le cercle enchanté de
     Gertrude Stein." Delta, no. 10 (May), pp. 11-18.
          Stein's rose represents a general, not a particular, trait:
     the orbicular dynamism of writing, for the writing turns and re-
     turns on itself.

16   MARTIN, JACKY. "Gertrude Stein et la théâtralité du langage."
     Delta, no. 10 (May), pp. 103-18.
          One reads "An Exercise in Analysis" freshly, without "trans-
     lating for direct meaning."

17   MELLOW, J.R. "At Gertrude Stein's in Paris." Horizon 23
     (November):32-36.
          Alice Toklas's recipes confirm the memories of guests who
     delighted in dinners at Stein's studio.

18   NIN, ANAÏS. The Diary: 1966-1974. Edited by Gunther
     Stuhlmann. New York: Harcourt Brace Jovanovich, p. 172.
          "I only met Gertrude Stein once, and I didn't like her
     personally because she insisted on dominating everyone she was
     with."

19   PASQUIER, MARIE-CLAIRE. "Gertrude Stein: Un théâtre 'Post-
     Moderne'?" Delta, no. 10 (May), pp. 43-58.
          Perhaps in her strange drama Stein was already beyond
     modernism in literature.

20   RYAN, BETSY ALINE. "Gertrude Stein's Theatre of the Absolute."
     Ph.D. dissertation, University of Illinois, Chicago, 320 pp.
          "This critical study establishes the playwriting aesthetic
     of Gertrude Stein as a serious attempt to deal with the twentieth
     century, and reveals the techniques whereby she realized that
     aesthetic in her seventy-seven plays." Summarized: Dissertation
     Abstracts International 41A:2359.

21   WISER, WILLIAM. Disappearances. New York: Atheneum,
     pp. 119-23, and passim.
          Stein and Toklas are background figures in Paris, where--
     the protagonist of this novel recalls--he pursued a real Blue-
     beard case . . . and grew up.

                              1981

1   BRINNAN, JOHN MALCOLM. T.S. Eliot & Truman Capote & Others.
     New York: Delacorte Press, Seymour Lawrence, passim.
          Knowing Toklas through research for his biography of Stein,
     Brinnan found her the eternal widow, living in her past with
     Gertrude Stein and waiting for afterdeath.

2   HEMINGWAY, ERNEST. <u>Selected Letters: 1917-1961</u>. Edited by
     Carlos Baker. New York: Charles Scribner's Sons, pp. 45, 60,
     62-63, 72, 74, and passim.
          After enjoying Stein's friendship and encouragement,
     Hemingway could no longer tolerate Toklas's dominance over
     Stein and Toklas's dislike of the Stein-Hemingway friendship:
     "G.S. and I were good friends when she died and we always would
     have been good friends if it had not been for Alice Toklas."

3   LANDON, BROOKS. "'Not Solve It But Be In It': Gertrude
     Stein's Detective Stories and the Mystery of Creativity."
     <u>American Literature</u> 53 (November):487-98.
          Stein liked detective stories as a parallel to the discovery
     process that she expected to be applied to her own writings.
     <u>Blood on the Dining Room Floor</u> is her exemplum of solving a
     problem in rhetoric.

4   WALLACE, IRVING, et al. <u>The Intimate Sex Lives of Famous
     People</u>. New York: Delacourt Press, pp. 141, 164, 169-72, 521.
          Stein wrote more of her homosexuality with Toklas as the
     women grew older--and bolder.

Index

Mauk, J.F., 1946.30
Maule, Harry E., 1953.6
Maurois, André, 1945.27
Mayerson, Charlotte, 1965.19
Mayerson, Leon, 1965.19
Mayfield, Sara, 1971.32
Mayhall, Jane, 1971.33
Mayhew, Alice, 1971.34
Maynard, Reid, 1972.20
Maxwell, Elsa, 1941.17
Meades, Jonathan, 1972.21
"Melanctha," 1929.6; 1937.4, 24;
    1945.49; 1950.2; 1960.3;
    1961.2, 7; 1971.49; 1974.25;
    1975.17, 27; 1978.7; 1980.4
Mellow, James, 1955.12; 1968.11;
    1970.31-32; 1971.35; 1972.22;
    1974.26-27; 1977.21; 1980.17
Mellquist, Jerome, 1940.17-18
Mencken, H.L., 1914.23-24;
    1923.16-17; 1927.9;
    1937.26; 1961.9
Meyer, Agnes E., 1953.7
Meyerowitz, Patricia, 1971.36;
    1973.29
Micha, Rena, 1979.15
Michaud, Régis, 1928.15
Michelson, Herb, 1957.11
Mill, Antonio Sabate, 1945.28
Miller, Bertha Mahoney, 1959.2
Miller, Henry, 1956.9; 1963.32
Miller, Jane, 1965.16
Miller, Rosalind S., 1949.13
Millett, Fred F., 1940.19;
    1957.12
Milliet, Antoine, 1945.29
Milton, John, 1923.8
Minc, Janet Barnett, 1979.16
Miró, Joan, 1948.10
Mirror, 1935.9
A Mirror to France (Ford),
    1971.37
"Miss Furr and Miss Skeene,"
    1923.7; 1924.7
Mitchell, Joseph, 1934.104
Mizener, Arthur, 1971.37
Mlle. Stein (Appollinaire),
    1972.1
Moers, Ellen, 1972.23; 1976.21
Moffett, India, 1934.105
Mondrian, Piet, 1977.8

Mongan, Agnes, 1939.19
Montaigne, Michel, 1979.18
Moore, A.C., 1939.20
Moore, Edward, 1934.106-7
Moore, Harry T., 1962.12
Moore, Marianne, 1926.10;
    1936.19; 1973.51
Morley, Christopher, 1934.64
Morner, Kathleen, 1968.12
Morrell, Lady Ottoline, 1964.9;
    1968.17
Morris, George L.K., 1939.21
Morris, Lloyd, 1929.8; 1947.30;
    1951.17
Morris, Mary B., 1963.64
Mother Goose, 1945.35
The Mother of Us All, 1947.18,
    21-22, 32, 39, 41-42, 44-45;
    1972.15
Mottram, Eric, 1971.22
A Moveable Feast (Hemingway),
    1970.6
Mrs. Reynolds, 1943.1; 1944.3;
    1952.5, 11-12, 14-15; 1954.8
Muller, Herbert J., 1937.27
Munson, Gorham B., 1923.19;
    1929.9
Murdoch, Walter, 1940.20
Murphy, Gerald, 1971.53
Murray, J. Middleton, 1930.6
Murray, Marian, 1934.108
Murray, Valory, 1979.17
Mydans, Carl, 1944.8
Myron, Nancy, 1974.53

Nadelman, Elie, 1948.18; 1973.25
Narration, 1935.7-8; 1936.1, 5,
    7, 10, 18, 21-22; 1963.32;
    1970.7
Nash, Ogden, 1934.109
Nathan, George Jean, 1934.110;
    1935.41
Nazzaro, Linda, 1973.30
Neihardt, John G., 1928.17
Nelson, John Herbert, 1934.111
Neuman, S.C., 1979.18
Neville, Helen, 1958.9
New York Times, 1967.32
Nichol, bp., 1972.24; 1973.31
Nin, Anaïs, 1980.18
Nishio, Iwao, 1978.25

Index

Sigaux, Gilbert, 1946.46
Sillen, Samuel, 1937.31
Simon, Abbott, 1934.134
Simon, Jean, 1949.17
Simon, Linda, 1974.40; 1977.28
Simon, Robert A., 1947.39
Simons, L.S., 1963.79
Sinclair, Upton, 1935.36
Sitwell, Edith, 1923.28;
    1925.7; 1926.14; 1934.135;
    1948.25; 1951.5; 1963.12,
    30; 1965.18; 1967.27; 1970.39
Sitwell, Osbert, 1948.25
Skinner, B.F., 1934.6, 136, 153;
    1979.21
Skinner, Richard Dana, 1934.137
Slocombe, George, 1936.26
Sloper, L.A., 1928.26; 1947.40
Smith, A.E., 1959.20
Smith, Cecil, 1947.41-42
Smith, Harrison, 1946.47
Smith, T. Henry, 1959.21
Smoller, Sanford J., 1975.22
Soby, James Thrall, 1947.43;
    1957.15; 1958.15
Solokoff, Alice Hunt, 1973.44
Solomon, Albert J., 1974.41
Somers, Paul, Jr., 1975.23
Sorrell, Walter, 1975.24
Soskin, William, 1934.138-39
Spacks, Patricia Meyer, 1975.25
Spencer, Benjamin T., 1975.26
Spencer, Theodore, 1934.140
Spiller, Robert E., 1955.18;
    1963.59
Sprigge, Elizabeth, 1955.19;
    1957.16; 1973.45
Sprigge, Sylvia, 1960.8
Springer, Mary Doyle, 1975.27
Squires, James Radcliffe,
    1946.48; 1971.48
Stade, George, 1969.6
Staley, Thomas, 1963.80
Stanton, Jessie, 1939.32
Stanzas in Meditation, 1956.3;
    1957.1, 4, 10, 14; 1958.17
Starke, Catherine Juanita,
    1971.49
Staying on Alone, 1973.3, 5, 22,
    39-40, 54; 1974.2, 4, 7, 12,
    17, 24, 32-33, 41, 45-46,
    56, 58

Stearns, Harold E., 1935.49;
    1940.25
Steele, Ellen, 1939.32
Steele, Joy Cogdell, 1978.33
Steele, Oliver L., Jr., 1961.16
Steell, Willis, 1926.15
Steffens, Lincoln, 1931.14;
    1935.36; 1938.9
Stein, Leo, 1937.14; 1947.45;
    1948.17-18; 1950.14; 1951.3;
    1953.7; 1960.5; 1963.15;
    1965.19; 1969.5; 1970.23, 28;
    1971.13; 1972.32; 1973.8;
    1974.9, 20
Stein, Michael, 1970.23, 28;
    1971.13
Stein, Sarah, 1970.23, 28;
    1971.13
Steiner, Wendy Lois, 1974.42;
    1975.28; 1977.29; 1978.34
Stella, Joseph, 1971.5
Steloff, Frances, 1965.17;
    1974.43; 1975.29
Stephens, Robert O., 1968.21
Sternberg, Sadie Hope, 1925.8
Sterne, Maurice, 1965.19
Stevens, George, 1934.141
Stevens, Holly, 1966.15
Stevens, Wallace, 1966.15
Stevenson, Elizabeth, 1967.128
Stewart, Allegra, 1957.17;
    1967.29; 1973.46
Stewart, Lawrence D., 1970.40
Stewart, Lawrence W., 1972.35
Stieglitz, Alfred, 1937.13;
    1969.7; 1970.42
Stieglitz, Alfred, III., 1947.46
Stimpson, Catharine R., 1977.30
Stock, Noel, 1970.41
Storm, John, 1934.145
Story, 1937.11; 1939.6
Stout, Rex, 1954.21
Straumann, Heinrich, 1965.20
Strauss, Harold, 1935.50
Strunsky, Robert, 1934.146
Stuart, Reece, 1963.81
Stuhlmann, Gunther, 1980.18
Sugrue, Thomas, 1948.26
Sukenick, Ronald, 1978.1
Suleiman, Susan, 1972.1
Sullivan, Dan, 1968.22

279